The Demands of Citizenship

THE DEMANDS OF CITIZENSHIP

Edited by

Catriona McKinnon
Iain Hampsher-Monk

CONTINUUM
London and New York

Continuum
Wellington House, 125 Strand, London WC2R 0BB
370 Lexington Avenue, New York, NY 10017-6503

First published 2000

British Library Cataloguing-in-Publication Data
A catalogue record for this book is available from the British Library.
ISBN   0-8264-4771-6   (hardback)
       0-8264-4772-4   (paperback)

Library of Congress Cataloging-in-Publication Data
The demands of citizenship/edited by Catriona McKinnon, Iain Hampsher-Monk.
      p.cm.
   Includes bibliographical references and index.
   ISBN 0-8264-4771-6 (HB) – ISBN 0-8264-4772-4 (PB)
   1. Citizenship. I. McKinnon, Catriona. II. Hampsher-Monk, Iain, 1946–

   JF801 .D38 2000
   323.6–dc21

                                                                    00-027624

Typeset by BookEns Ltd, Royston, Herts.
Printed and bound in Great Britain by Biddles Ltd, Guildford and King's Lynn

Contents

CONTENTS

PART THREE   Identity

PART FOUR   Patriotism

Notes on Contributors

Rainer Bauböck is Assistant Professor at the Institute for Advanced Studies, Vienna, and Senior Lecturer at the Universities of Vienna and Innsbruck. His research interests are in normative political theory and in comparative research on citizenship, migration, ethnic conflict and nationalism. Recent books include *Blurred Boundaries: Migration, Ethnicity, Citizenship* (co-edited, Ashgate, 1998), *The Challenge of Diversity: Integration and Pluralism in Societies of Immigration* (co-edited, Avebury, 1996) and *Transnational Citizenship: Membership and Rights in International Migration* (Edward Elgar, 1994).

Margaret Canovan is Professor of Political Thought at Keele University. Her publications include *Nationhood and Political Theory* (1996), *Hannah Arendt: A Reinterpretation of her Political Thought* (1992), and books and articles on many other aspects of political thought.

Erik Eriksen is Professor at ARENA, University of Oslo, Norway. He has written many books and articles on politics and deliberative democracy. Recent publications include *The Rationality of the Welfare State* (with Jørn Loftager, 1996), *Communicative Action and Deliberative Democracy* (with Jarle Weigård, 1999, in Norwegian) and *Democracy in the European Union: Integration through Deliberation?* (edited with John Fossum, Routledge, 2000).

Iain Hampsher-Monk is Professor of Political Theory and Head of the Department of Politics at the University of Exeter. He is (with Janet Coleman) founder and editor of the journal *History of Political Thought*. He is the author of *A History of Modern Political Thought* (Blackwell, 1992), and most recently he has co-edited and contributed to *History of Concepts: Comparative Perspectives* (Amsterdam University Press, 1998).

Michael Ignatieff is Professor of International Relations at LSE. He is a well-known writer, broadcaster and producer working on political and historical topics. Among his books are *The Warrior's Honour* (Chatto and Windus, 1998) and *The Needs of Strangers* (Vintage, 1984). *Blood and Belonging* (Vintage, 1994) won Canada's top literary award and was the basis of an acclaimed television series. His authorized biography *Isaiah Berlin* was published by Metropolitan Books in 1998, and *Virtual War* by Chatto and Windus in 2000.

Duncan Ivison teaches in the School of Philosophy at the University of Sydney. He is author of *The Self at Liberty* (Cornell University Press, 1997) and co-editor of the forthcoming *Political Theory and the Rights of Indigenous Peoples* (Cambridge University Press).

Bill Jordan is Professor of Social Policy at Huddersfield University, Reader in Social Studies at Exeter University and Visiting Professor at the Max Planck Institute for the Study of Societies, Cologne. He was a practising social worker from 1965 to 1985. He has recently been European Professor of Social Policy at the Universities of Bratislava and Budapest, and is the author of twenty books on political thought, social theory and social work, including *A Theory of Poverty and Social Exclusion* (Polity, 1996) and *The New Politics of Welfare* (Sage, 1998).

Catriona McKinnon is Lecturer in Political Theory at the University of Exeter. She has published papers on the role of self-respect in liberal justification, and on neo-Kantian constructivist approaches to justificatory values. She is co-editing a book on toleration and is writing a monograph in defence of political constructivism. She is an associate editor of *Imprints: A Journal of Analytical Socialism*.

Alan Patten is Assistant Professor of Political Science at McGill University and author of *Hegel's Idea of Freedom* (Oxford University Press, 1999). His current work examines issues relating to cultural recognition, cultural protection, and self-determination from a liberal perspective.

Mark Philp is Lecturer in the Department of Politics at the University of Oxford and a Fellow of Oriel College. Publications include Godwin's *Political Justice* (Duckworth, 1996), *Paine* (Oxford University Press, 1989) and a range of papers on political theory and the history of political thought. He is currently working on a book on political conduct and misconduct.

Judith Squires is Lecturer in Political Theory at the University of Bristol. She is author of *Gender in Political Theory* (Polity Press, 1999) and has edited several collections, including *Feminisms* (Oxford University Press, 1997), *Space and Place: Theories of Identity and Location* (Lawrence and Wishart, 1995), *Cultural Remix: Theories of Politics and the Popular* (Lawrence and Wishart, 1993) and *Principled Positions: Postmodernism and the Rediscovery of Value* (Lawrence & Wishart, 1993). She was editor of the journal *New Formations* from 1990 to 1997.

James Tully is Professor and Chair of Political Science, University of Victoria, British Columbia, and Adjunct Professor of Philosophy, McGill University, Montreal, Quebec. He works in the area of contemporary political philosophy and its history. His recent works include *An Approach to Political Philosophy: Locke in Contexts* (Cambridge University Press, 1993), *Strange Multiplicity: Institutionalism in an Age of Diversity* (Cambridge University Press, 1995), deriving from the first Seely Lectures, and 'To Think and Act Differently' in *Foucault contra Habermas*, edited by Samantha Ashenden and David Owen (Sage, 1999).

Philippe Van Parijs is Professor of Economic and Social Ethics at the Université Catholique de Louvain. He has also held visiting positions at the Belgian National Science Foundation, the Universites of California (Berkeley), Wisconsin (Madison), Québec (Montréal), the European University Institute (Florence), the Federal University of Rio de Janeiro, the Chinese Academy of Social Sciences, All Souls College Oxford and Yale University. His books include *Evolutionary Explanation in the Social Sciences* (Rowman & Littlefield, 1981), *Qu'est-ce qu'une société juste?* (Seuil, 1991), *Arguing for Basic Income* (edited, Verso, 1992), *Marxism Recycled* (Cambridge University Press, 1993) and *Real Freedom for All* (Oxford University Press, 1995).

Maurizio Viroli is Professor of Political Theory at the University of Princeton, and lives and works partly in the United States and partly in Italy. Among his recent works in English are *From Politics to Reason of State* (Cambridge University Press, 1992), *Machiavelli* (Oxford University Press, 1998) and *For Love of Country* (Oxford University Press, 1995).

Jarle Weigård is Associate Professor in the Department of Political Science, University of Tromsø, Norway. He has published several articles in the field of political theory and has most recently written – with Erik Eriksen – a book on the social and political theory of Jürgen Habermas.

Stuart White is Tutorial Fellow in Politics at Jesus College, Oxford. He is interested in distributive justice and economic citizenship, and is currently working to complete a manuscript on this topic entitled *The Civic Minimum: An Essay on the Rights and Obligations of Economic Citizenship*.

Acknowledgements

The essays in this volume derive from a number of sources. The majority were presented at a seminar series entitled The Social and Political Resources of Market Societies run in the Politics Department of the University of Exeter 1995–7 by Dario Castiglione, Alan Patten and Iain Hampsher-Monk with a pump-priming grant from the University Research Committee, whose support we would like to acknowledge here. Several other chapters (those by Ignatieff, Van Parijs, Tully and Viroli) were delivered in Siena in September 1998 at a conference supported partly by the European Science Foundation via its network Republicanism: A Shared European Heritage, and partly by the Banco di Monti dei Pascchi, and the Comune di Siena. We should like to acknowledge the support of all these bodies, and the work of Martin van Gelderen (Sussex), who organized the conference, and of the other members of the steering committee of the ESF Network: (Quentin Skinner (Cambridge) (chair), Hans Bödeker (Göttingen), Ivo Comparato (Perugia) and Catherine Larrère (Bordeaux). Two further chapters (those of Squires and McKinnon) were especially commissioned for the volume. We would like to thank Caroline Wintersgill at Continuum, and Gail Prosser for her work in helping us to prepare the manuscript.

Catriona McKinnon
Iain Hampsher-Monk

Introduction

CATRIONA MCKINNON AND IAIN HAMPSHER-MONK

Citizenship comprises the qualities and conditions – and also the ideals – in and through which individuals who share membership of a political community can act as political equals. Since the seventeenth century, much thought – which subsequently came to be called 'liberal' – has increasingly focused on the rights or other legal attributes of individuals conceived of as free, equal and capable of independent economic and political action. But, as many in the republican tradition have noted, the increasing *ascription* of rights to individuals in the name of citizenship fails to register the importance of sustaining certain sorts of conditions and community which make meaningful, or in some cases even possible, the exercise of these rights. At the heart of these lies the sustainability of a political community with the will and power to protect those rights. More broadly, equal economic conditions, shared ethical expectations, ethnic or religious identity, modes of communication, patterns of activity and other social properties have all been identified as needing to be fostered and sustained for the rights of citizenship to be sustainable. Hence the concern, reflected in the title of this collection,[1] not so much with what can be *ascribed* to citizens, but with what might have to be *demanded* of them in the name of protecting their liberty, and the stability and sustainability of their polity.

An authentically political concern with the duties demanded of citizens must derive from the conditions required for successful, enduring political self-rule, defined not in the austere and often militaristic terms of classical republicanism, but rather in terms of ideas within the broad understanding of liberal democracy. This polarity is often presented as one between republicanism and liberalism, particularly in the United States.[2] The point at issue is misconceived, however, if it is seen as a debate between a republicanism which represents the political individual as wholly subordinate to the state and a liberalism which refuses to acknowledge that the claims of individualism must be tested against their likely social and political consequences. Liberalism cannot sustain the kind of individual it praises

1

unless it can show that it can sustain the polity in which he or she is to live, nor can republicanism sustain its claims to liberty unless it can provide space for the individual to flourish. The question of the demands of citizenship nevertheless swivels the focus from considering citizenship as an accretion of individual rights or liberties to considering the configuration of these liberties, not as possessing some independent authority deriving from the character of the pre-political individual, but as ultimately determined by the needs of a free state. Recent analytical and historical writing by both liberals and republicans has started to show this recognition. It has also been reflected in various debates about the possibility and desirability of universalistic accounts of citizenship which impose formally uniform demands on all, as opposed to particularistic accounts which make these demands a function of substantive and differing commitments and loyalties. After two decades of strident individualism, and oft-expressed claims that the liberal democratic state is doomed to collapse under the divergent threats of localization and globalization, and in the midst of a theoretical debate about the possible and desirable limits of individual autonomy between 'communitarians' and liberals, political theorists are recognizing the importance of considering the demands of citizenship.

Our contributors straddle a wide range of genres of political writing, from the linguistically analytical through the technicalities of economic modelling to the broader reaches of sociologically informed political history to the history of political thought. This again is timely. Political theory embraces many disciplinary approaches and it is important to realize that they tackle similar problems. After a period in which the historical study of political thought in particular seemed to be separated from its contemporary practice, there seems to be a genuine desire on the part of its exponents to reassert the contemporary significance of historical theories and discourses.[3]

Civil Society and Economic Justice

From being identified with the very existence of the incorporated citizen body,[4] civil society has come to be understood as designating an arena of non-governmental institutions and associations which are nevertheless supportive of civic well-being and the sense of purpose, agency and freedom of citizens. Measuring the demands citizenship makes upon this sphere involves considering how political culture, engendered by extra-political factors, can affect the viability of our political institutions. Clearly this is a reciprocal relationship, and much depends on what our polity requires of our citizens.

Erik Eriksen and Jarle Weigård open this collection by mapping the implications for civic unity of two different models of citizenship. One is associated with Rousseau: citizens participate in a public debate to discover what is good for society as a whole. The other is inspired by liberal, utilitarian and economic thinking: the polity is a mode of processing the private choices of self-interested individuals. Here the citizen role becomes one of client, user or customer, and justice is in danger of being replaced by efficiency as the measure of good government.

Neither the economic nor the Rousseauian model of citizenship addresses feminist worries about the extent to which the concept of citizenship is gendered. Judith Squires reviews the growing feminist literature on this question and focuses on new ways of conceiving of social and political citizenship which avoid what is perceived to be the mythical universality of both liberal and civic republican approaches to citizenship, while drawing on their insights about the need for truly democratic participation in the political sphere. Squires argues that these emerging feminist accounts of citizenship eschew civil society as the primary site of citizenship activity. But this emphasis on the political sphere as it is tied to the state requires justification: why not conceive of citizenship as participation in a broader, non-state-based, perhaps international, arena? Squires shows that there is more work to be done by feminist thinkers attempting to move citizenship beyond the liberal/republican dichotomy.

Civil society is a realm in which economic activity produces inequalities of wealth, and early modern republican reflections on citizenship notoriously stressed the threat posed to it by inequality. Famously, Rousseau claimed that 'in respect of riches, no citizen shall ever be wealthy enough to buy another, and none poor enough to be forced to sell himself'.[5]

Liberal theorists, by contrast, claimed to be able to distinguish civic rights – now often linked to negative liberty – from welfare rights, as they came to be known, and claimed that the state should concern itself only with the former.[6] Interestingly, within the earlier natural rights tradition, which is often identified with liberal politics, we also find arguments for a strong degree of at least initial citizen equality.[7] Whereas republican arguments for equality stressed the threat that the rich would be able to influence the votes of the poor, and so undermine the independence required of those charged with upholding liberty, liberals' arguments characteristically derive not from consequentialist considerations about the impact of inequality on political liberty but from the obligation of political society not to deprive individuals of access to resources that would have been available to them in its absence.

These two major conceptions of citizenship have therefore had rather different concerns with inequality, yet a convergence can be seen. Classical republicans, recognizing that the proper exercise of civic responsibilities required judgemental, and therefore economic, independence, denied citizenship to all who did not possess this. Welfare liberalism sought at a minimum to meet the material and social needs of all, and in some versions to ameliorate the greater disparities of wealth simply in pursuit of a degree of equality. Welfare liberalism might therefore be seen as supplying, for all, those material conditions of independence and autonomy of judgement which classical republicans identified as necessary for the essentially privileged exercise of citizenship. In a famous restatement by T.H. Marshall outlining the growth of modern liberal citizenship, welfare rights were linked to earlier republican rights as the final phase of a three-stage development in the dimensions of citizenship, adding welfare to civil and political rights.[8] However, sustaining a collective political commitment on the part of the well-off to such policies in the context of a market society can be difficult.

Bill Jordan highlights a tension between the requirements of egalitarian distributive justice and the conditions of civic unity. Jordan argues that distributive justice is best understood not in terms of reciprocity, but rather in terms of 'gainful exchange'. A global framework of gainful exchange generates obligations which are not always defeated by the existence of able-bodied people not willing to take unpleasant work for low wages. Such people should not be viewed as free-riding on our efforts, but rather as entering into a gainful exchange with us which enables us to prosper. At the same time, a sense of mutual responsibility is required for civic unity. The challenge is to find a mechanism of redistribution which acknowledges gainful exchange without undermining civic unity. Jordan suggests that unconditional basic income should be assessed according to its consequences in these two respects.

Accepting the claim that economic equality – understood as the eradication of material disadvantage due to brute bad luck – is necessary for successful citizenship, Stuart White outlines the 'egalitarian earnings subsidy scheme' (ESS) as a way of compensating for these disadvantages. By drawing attention to how the public classification of citizens into categories according to their talents required for ESS militates against mutual equality of civic esteem and respect, White highlights a tension in egalitarian civic thinking, and suggests that an alternative 'childhood privilege tax' might ameliorate this tension.

Turning away from the particular concern with equality, Rainer Bauböck explores various understandings of civil society, how the institutions it contains interact, and the roles for individuals within these institutions. He argues that an appreciation of the complexity of civil society, and the heterogeneous demands it makes of citizens, should prompt us to lower our expectations of citizenship.

Citizen Dispositions

Even when material conditions and the culture and institutions of civil society make citizenship possible, the difficult question of how to motivate people to act as citizens remains. Traditional justifications have been monist in seeking to provide a single, universal explanation of civic commitment. Duncan Ivison argues that more particularistic modes of political justification, which acknowledge the differences between people, offer the best hope of a *modus vivendi* between citizens, wherein political principles are supported by a multiplicity of publicly accessible reasons. Ivison argues that principles reflecting pluralism in this way will generate reasons for diverse and differing people to act as citizens by supporting these principles.

Catriona McKinnon takes up the theme of motivating citizenship with an exploration of John Rawls's account of civility. Arguing that the 'skills of civility' are necessary for engaging in public reason so as to participate in political discourse as a good citizen, she traces connections between the skills of civility and the search for self-respect in associational life. Given the fundamental importance of self-respect to a flourishing life, she argues that the assumption that people have the skills of civility necessary for public reason is not an implausibly universalistic dogma, and that it is a mistake to think that accounts of good citizenship invoking these skills demand that a person deny or ignore his or her most deeply held convictions. Rawls's conception of good citizenship can, in this way, withstand scrutiny as an ideal.

A severe blow to the notion of active citizenship was struck in the early 1950s by the 'competing elite' theorists of democracy, who drew on empirical evidence of civic political apathy to characterize democracy as a system of alternative elites.[9] Furthermore, subsequent rational choice modelling suggested that it was difficult to account for political participation on rational choice grounds. Since then, normative theorists with a 'strong' conception of citizenship have had to confront the criticism that their demands for participation are unrealistic. Analysing the participation needed for liberal citizenship as both horizontal and vertical, Mark Philp criticizes both *modus vivendi* and Rawlsian accounts of citizenship on the grounds that they do not explain the motivation for vertical participation in particular. He offers an alternative account of the threshold of participation necessary for the maintenance of a liberal democratic polity. On this account, not all citizens need participate vertically when institutional pluralism ensures that groups have an interest in defending the rights of citizens with vertical participation, and in which transparency ensures deference to the norm of public reason. Arguing for the possibility – indeed, legitimacy – of less than universal vertical participation defuses the problem of motivation in an account of citizenship: if not all citizens need to be motivated to participate for a stable and just polity, then we need not search for reasons fit to convince every citizen that they ought to participate in that dimension.

Identities

Even on an account like Philp's, whereby we need only identify a low threshold of participation, there may still be problems of motivating this level of participation in the absence of a shared identity. Although participation functions to protect something of value to the participants, some accounts of citizenship hold that in the absence of a shared identity, participants may lack either sufficient shared values, or a strong enough commitment to the polity to act to sustain that protection. Since at least the nineteenth century 'the nation' has been identified as the bearer of that shared identity, and the coincidence of citizenship (as a constitutional status) and nationality (as a historico-cultural identity) became the pervasive political model.[10]

Two centuries of nationalism have made political theorists distinctly nervous about its invocation. If nationalism fails as an attempt to foster a shared identity on liberal and republican perspectives, must we give up on the idea that people can be motivated to good citizenship? In the absence of ways to cultivate a shared identity compatible with liberal and republican commitments to equality, must we put equality first and citizenship second?

James Tully's analysis of current theories of dialogical politics suggests that the opposition between citizenship and equality is a false dichotomy. He claims that republican principles can be construed, through this politics, so as to be sensitive to the demands for a 'politics of recognition' by many cultural minorities. If a shared national or cultural identity is not necessary for sustaining a polity structured around the rule of law and self-rule by a free people, then calls for patriotism towards more than the principles protecting the rule of law and self-rule are not necessary for good citizenship. On Tully's view, republican principles make nationalism superfluous by grounding the sensitivity to difference necessary for motivating citizenship in an ineradicably diverse world. Can liberal principles perform the same function?

Alan Patten argues the liberal case for the possibility of avoiding the cultivation of shared national identities while acknowledging difference. He claims that a liberal theory of citizenship should include a principle of equal recognition, making liberal justifications and principles sensitive to the differences between the identities of citizens. This principle must be reflected in the public sphere in which political boundaries are drawn, school curricula are decided and the language of public discourse is set. Equal recognition demanding sensitivity to different identities in the public sphere is implied by the liberal commitment to treating persons with equal concern and respect, and need not fragment a liberal society in such a way as to undermine the shared commitment of citizens to the values and principles which unify that society. On this view, a commitment to liberal equality does not imply the denial of difference, and nor does it ignore the particular loyalties without which good citizenship cannot be expected.

Acknowledging the need for recognition as a catalyst for effective citizenship on both a republican and a liberal perspective, what policy implications can we draw? Taking the fact of pluralism as the problematizing aspect of citizenship in Europe, Philippe Van Parijs describes the history of Belgian responses to Belgium's own cultural and linguistic pluralism in order to assess the suitability of any of these responses as a blueprint for policy on citizenship in Europe. He rejects the policy of 'generalized unilingualism' (enforcement of the dominant language), common among early state-builders, as inappropriate for a Belgium and a Europe already, as it were, 'Babelized'. This leaves a variety of options: 'generalized bilingualism' in both soft (enforced official recognition of second language) and hard (enforced teaching of second language) versions; non-territorial separation in which groups are represented and administered linguistically but not territorially; and territorial separation, in which groups are represented territorially from areas which correspond to linguistic differences. Although within a Belgian context the attempt to 'fix' such boundaries has created opportunistic relocation, this might be less likely within a culturally and linguistically discrete Europe. Attempts to equalize across such boundaries through social policy will prove politically difficult if political representation cannot also be structured across national lines.

Patriotism

Some thinkers argue that the rejection of nationalism is too quick. Attempts to generate a common political identity motivating good citizenship by asserting a principle of recognition justified by the value of equal concern and respect are unnecessary, it is argued, once it is recognized that the form of nationalism being rejected is a straw man. A more nuanced, classical form of nationalism is possible, and is known as patriotism. The three final chapters explore aspects of this seductive approach to citizenship.

Michael Ignatieff charts the history of the nation-building project from Versailles through Yalta and into the present with the collapse of the Berlin Wall and the Soviet Empire. An unforeseen consequence of this third moment of nation-building has been, he argues, the ascendance of nationality and ethnicity as the only grounds fit to mobilize people to citizenship. The nationalism of post-Cold War Europe is far from realizing the ideal of a *patria* necessary for the patriotism which many in the republican tradition invoke as the real alternative to liberal freedom. Europe's republicanism supported exclusions which expressed doubts about the possibility of a universalistic and homogeneous citizenry. In contemporary Europe, marked by pluralism and difference, the republican project of inculcating patriotism without encouraging nationalism may be asking too much: asking citizens simply to trust one another may be a more realistic aspiration sufficient to sustain a functioning and approximately just society or federation.

In the face of Ignatieff's worries about how patriotism can bleed into nationalism, Maurizio Viroli argues that prior to the emergence of post-Herderian ethnic nationalism, patriotism – the love of one's *patria* – was understood entirely in political terms, with no ethnic element, and yet, as such, was capable of generating huge commitment on the part of citizens. Viroli makes an eloquent plea for the rehabilitation of a pure, pre-modern patriotism, reviving traditions of republican thinking disinfested of ethnic oppositions and national loyalties.

In the last chapter, Margaret Canovan challenges a range of 'post-national' alternatives to 'blood and soil' nationalism. Against 'constitutional' patriotism she argues that the democratic values and common political culture serving as the object of this patriotism are not, in fact, shared by putative patriots who lack a shared nationality: state and nation cannot be uncoupled. Against 'rooted republican' patriotism she argues that the critical love of one's polity is not, in the end, sufficiently distinguished from blood and soil nationalism.

If, as Ignatieff argues, patriotism carries the risk of being used in the rhetoric of nationalist fervour and ethnic hatred, and if, as Canovan argues, patriotism cannot be conceptually decoupled from nationalism, then republicans are perhaps best advised to turn to approaches like Tully's in their search for ways to motivate good citizenship which are sensitive to difference and yet have universal scope.

Notes

1. Felicitously coined by Mark Philp.
2. For a discussion of the controversy and references to the literature, see the comprehensive review by Alan Gibson (forthcoming) 'Ancients, Moderns and Americans: the Republicanism–Liberalism Debate Revisited', *History of Political Thought.*
3. See J. Dunn (ed.) (1993) *Democracy: The Unfinished Journey, 508 BC–1993 AD*, Oxford: Oxford University Press, and J. Tully (1993) *An Approach to Political Theory: Locke in Contexts*, Cambridge, esp. ch. 10, although this dissents from our presentation of the republican/liberal dichotomy above.
4. Most notably by John Locke (1967 [1690]) *Second Treatise* §89, ed. Peter Laslett.
5. Jean-Jacques Rousseau (1973) *The Social Contract*, book II, Chapter 11, trans. and with an introduction by G.D.H. Cole, London: Dent, p. 225. See also Machiavelli, *Discorsi* I, 3, 4; James Harrington (1977) *Oceania*, in *The Political Works*, ed. J.G.A. Pocock, Cambridge: Cambridge University Press, pp. 161, 231ff.
6. For a balanced statement of the modern liberal view and the issues, see Norman Barry (1990) 'Markets, Citizenship and the Welfare State: Some Critical Reflections', in Raymond Plant and Norman Barry (eds) *Citizenship and Rights in Thatcher's Britain: Two Views*, London: *Institute for Economic Affairs.*
7. For example, William Ogilvie (1781) *An Essay on the Right of Property in Land*; John Thelwall, *The Rights of Nature against the Usurpations of Establishments*; Thomas Paine (1795) *Agrarian Justice*; Henry George (1879) *Progress and Poverty*; and more recently Hillel Steiner (1994) *An Essay on Rights*, Oxford: Blackwell.

8. T.H. Marshall (1950) *Citizenship and Social Class*, Cambridge: Cambridge University Press.

9. See Quentin Skinner (1973) 'Empirical Theorists of Democracy and their Critics', *Political Theory*, I, 287–306 and I.W. Hampsher-Monk (1980) 'Classical and Empirical Theories of Democracy: the Missing Historical Dimension?', *British Journal of Political Science*, 10, 241–51.

10. Pervasive only in terms of world politico-cultural dominance. Such a coincidence was rare, even in Europe, where it has been claimed that Portugal and Iceland provide the only two examples of perfect nation-state identity.

PART ONE

*Civil Society and Economic
Justice*

CHAPTER ONE

The End of Citizenship? New Roles Challenging the Political Order [1]

ERIK ERIKSEN AND JARLE WEIGÅRD

(Translated from Norwegian by Sandra Halvarson in co-operation with the authors)

Introduction

The growth of the public sector in modern society has led to the emergence of new relationships between citizens and the public authorities. The territorially defined concept of citizenship links the legitimacy of the state to the protection of citizens' general political and legal rights. We have, however, witnessed a development in the direction of different types of rights. This has resulted in a challenge to the traditional basis for government legitimacy and diminished the significance of citizenship itself. In many respects citizens have acquired the role of *clients*, i.e. recipients dependent on benefits provided by the welfare state. They are more frequently defined as *users* of public institutions' services, and they are also to an increasing extent involved in *customer relationships* vis-à-vis public institutions, more or less as they are in relation to private-sector producers in the market. Furthermore, attitudes towards the public sector seem to be changing as well. It is no longer only the more libertarian parties that use market terminology when discussing central and local government. For two decades now, such vocabulary has been characteristic of the general political debate and everyday speech. This is due to new reform strategies employed in the public sector – that is, New Public Management, based on techniques taken from private-sector management theory. These reforms were effectively stimulated by the Reagan administration in the United States and the Thatcher government in Britain, and are now part of the *global* terminology of good management.[2]

New Public Management has given rise to new forms of management such as management by objectives, deregulation, decentralized budgeting, contracting out, internal competition, and a new personnel policy based on an *incentive model*. One common feature of all these reforms is the disconnection of what the public sector provides – what it produces – from the realm of political action. In addition, these reforms are based on the premise that the price of and demand for public goods are best determined if the citizens are given the freedom to choose. Finally, 'production' is conducted by hived-off result units. The rise in productivity comes about by means of increasingly sophisticated information processing and organizing technologies, and by allowing political leaders more room for manoeuvring.[3]

In the light of these developments, the question of whether the old model of government legitimacy and citizenship status still provides meaningful explanatory categories is becoming increasingly topical. Is it now obvious that those who claimed that politics may be sufficiently accounted for by models taken from the market economy were right? In other words, has the economic view of democracy become an adequate expression of the relationship between public authorities and society? Social scientists have for some time made use of market analogies in the study of political behaviour. At the same time, some would also claim that citizens are demonstrating an increasing orientation towards individual benefit, or egoism. For example, Albert O. Hirschman refers to a transition during the 1970s and 1980s from involvement to exchange.[4] It is the desire for higher income and more welfare that motivates the citizens in their political activity. Thus, citizen status may be reduced to customer status, implying the substitution of taxes for customer goods, and the substitution of regulation for loyalty, as the ruling principles of political activity.

In the following, we shall argue against this assumption on the basis that the issue of legitimacy may not be resolved quite so easily. At the same time, it is obvious that the new roles represent responses to new challenges facing public authorities in their contact with citizens. First we shall give a brief presentation of the 'classical' view of citizenship and on that basis proceed to a critique of the economic view of politics. In the next section, we shall discuss the emergence of new roles that people assume vis-à-vis the authorities, on the basis of Norwegian and other Scandinavian experience. In conclusion, we shall consider the consequences of these roles both functionally and with respect to legitimacy.

The Citizen Role

In German, the concept of '*Bürger*' (like its Scandinavian equivalent '*borger*') contains an interesting duality which, in languages like French and English, is signified by two separate concepts, i.e. '*citoyen*'/'*citizen*' and '*bourgeois*'.[5] The origins of the *citizen* concept may be traced as far back as to the ancient Greek city-states, where being a 'citizen' entailed membership in a specific political community from which non-citizens were excluded. The modern idea that citizenship involves individual legal rights which are guaranteed by the state, and which can even be applied against the state, would have seemed quite alien to the ancient Greeks. The only right attached to citizenship for the Greeks was the right to participate in the public life of the state, which was more in the line of a duty and a responsibility to look after the interests of the community – an *obligation* (though one assumed with pride).[6] The only form of individual reward to be had from this kind of public involvement was honour and respect, and such values may not be transferred into the private sphere for 'consumption'. They were meaningful only in the same public sphere, among the same citizens, from which they emerged. Thus, Greek citizenship was of an irreducibly collective nature.

The concept of the *bourgeois* has its roots in Europe in the late Middle Ages, as new means of production and new societal forms and needs sprang up within protected city walls. Medieval cities were in many ways enclaves, separate from the surrounding feudal society. In the cities, individual freedom was generally greater and class barriers fewer than in the surrounding agricultural society. Thus, conditions were more in line with the functional demands of nascent capitalism. Rights protecting property owners from arbitrary state intervention into private affairs were an important pre-requisite for the prospering of commercial life. At the same time, protection of personal integrity and private property could also be granted legitimacy on the basis of humanist ideals. The functional and normative arguments underlying such a conception of rights underpinned the institutionalization of what Hegel refers to as *Die bürgerliche Gesellschaft* (the civil society) – that is, economic life as it developed under capitalism.[7]

These two different conceptions of the citizen may be said to be united in the modern concept of citizenship. As T.H. Marshall has pointed out, citizenship is constituted first of all by *civil* rights, which protect the citizen from the state.[8] The individual may exercise these rights in order to prevent state misuse of power, and one of the primary constituents of the legitimacy of modern states is in fact the protection of such rights. This is the principle of the *Rechtsstaat*, which is achieved when and to the extent there is equality before the law. Such a system requires the abolition of the structure of feudal society, with its special rights and obligations derived from the individual's status and group affiliation.[9] Second, citizenship involves *political* rights, which allow for participation in the governing of society. This is the principle of the *democratic* state, which may be said to have been achieved when all adult citizens have gained the same access to effective political influence. Third, Marshall also includes *social* rights in a concept of citizenship, i.e. rights which ensure a material safety net. These constitute the *welfare state* principle, which is considered realized to the extent that members of a society have the same social security in terms of health, life and welfare. Today's citizenship concept can thus be understood as a collection of rights linked to the individual, based on the fundamental principles of liberty, universalism, equality and legality.

Georg Jellinek has pointed out that various types of rights differ in nature.[10] Civil rights may be said to have a typically liberal, *negative* status ('*status negativus*') in that they guarantee freedom *from* state intervention in the private sphere. Social rights, on the other hand, have *positive* status ('*status positivus*'), as they grant members of a society access *to* certain goods through the state's reallocating interventions in civil society in general and in the market economy in particular. Finally, political rights have an *active* status ('*status activus*'), as they provide citizens with participatory rights.

These distinctions, according to Habermas, result in a special position for the active, political rights.[11] They constitute the nucleus of citizenship. Only such rights may be used to increase autonomy in that they equip the citizen with the 'self-referential competence' that enables him or her to affect matters which will influence his or her role in society. Civil and social rights, on the other hand, do not actually extend beyond the private dimension, in that their contribution is to secure the individual's position as a private actor. It is, however, fair to say that such rights secure the legal and material basis necessary for the realization of political rights and are thus justified. But in principle, these may also coexist with paternalistic and authoritarian political conditions in society. Only political rights of participation are of an irreducibly collective nature, as they involve the citizens in processes of opinion and will formation above and beyond their own private reality.

On a political level, citizenship rights imply an opportunity to take part in deciding how society is to be governed. But, on the other hand, they also imply an obligation to subject oneself to government.[12] Ideally, this is expressed through the formation of what Rousseau called *la volonté générale*.[13] This is an expression of those interests that the citizens share, which in Rousseau's opinion, notably, are not the sum of or a compromise between their private interests. The general will is understood as the various special interests, united, or merged at a higher level, which gives them an impersonal and impartial nature. The general will is thus an expression of the interests of the individuals as citizens, and thus of the *collective interest* of a society.

A collective interest need not immediately coincide with each individual's personal interests. Ideally, however, it should be such that each individual can rationally see that the collective interest represents the best solution from the point of view of those who *do not have* a personal interest in the matter. In other words, the collective interest of a society must be an expression of the principle that like shall be treated like, and unlike treated unlike – that is, in accordance with a general principle of justice. This is required in order for 'the common will', as expressed in collective decisions, to appear legitimate and thus rationally binding also for those who may have conflicting personal interests in any given matter. However, determining what is in the interest of the society at large, or what is to be considered the most reasonable and just solution, may only be done in a free deliberative process preceding decision-making, in which all interests and points of view may be presented, scrutinized and criticized. The preferences have to be laundered,[14] and the legitimacy of decisions tested in an open public debate. Thus ultimately it is the validity of the arguments that determines what constitutes a rational, collective will in a political context, and we can only know what the people will when everybody is heard.

The people exist only in a public sphere.[15] It is only when private individuals come together as a group that the will of the people may be formed. Thus, citizenship refers to a free political public sphere, which is the requisite means for testing the legitimacy of a governing body. The authority granted to public institutions to make binding decisions on behalf of the collective originates in the communicative relationship inherent in citizenship, as the citizens exercise their right to form a collective will. This is also the basis for present-day forms of government, though, among other things, the differentiation in the structure of responsibilities has made the process and means of establishing legitimacy more indirect and insecure. There are, for example, clear indications that 'the general' is being increasingly challenged by 'the particular'.

In the early stages of the modern constitutional state it was more obvious than today that issues on the public agenda involved the common problems of society. In other words, government business at that stage more clearly revolved around issues which affected society *collectively*, rather than issues whose consequences were felt only by certain groups or individuals. Such matters included, for example, the institutionalization of a legal system, a security system for peace and order, laying the groundwork for financial institutions and economic activity, and building infrastructure in general. All of these are very clearly public goods – that is, goods whose individual utility is difficult to delimit once they are provided. During this period in history, the responsibility of government was, in other words, to guarantee the stabilizing conditions for society. At that time, however, governments were far less interested in intervening, and able to intervene, actively in society than they are today. The individual was in direct contact with government authorities in far fewer situations than is the case in more recent times.

An Alternative Conception of Politics: The Economic Approach

The previous section presented an understanding of the 'nature' of politics based on citizenship as a form of participation in a genuine state community, founded on certain basic assumptions of a clearly normative nature. There is, however, another important approach to the study of politics which we may refer to as the economic approach, as it imports models from the economic sciences and applies them to political phenomena.[16] Briefly, this approach claims that politics may be understood as a parallel to economics, and that the political decision-making process is economic in both objectives and form.[17] Its objectives are perceived as economic because it is primarily economic issues that are on the political agenda. In this sense, politics appears as a supplement to the market, for example through realizing public goods which would not be provided if left to private interests, or by attempting to correct the imbalances in the distribution of income which result from the free operation of market forces. The form is considered economic because, like economics, politics builds on decentralized private decisions made by the individual voter. Voting becomes the most important, virtually the *only*, political action the citizens perform. Just like the consumer in his or her role as a market actor, voters are believed to choose between political alternatives on the basis of highly private and specific personal interests.

In spite of the fact that there are certain striking similarities between competition in the market and modern political competition, an economic approach still does not represent an adequate framework for understanding the phenomenon of politics. This contention may be grounded in an empirical, a logical-analytic as well as in a normative way. From an empirical point of view, the economic model cannot reasonably be claimed to give a complete explanation of what political life is actually like. Such a conclusion has both intuitive and scientific validity. Research using this approach in the study of election results has shown that it is *not* possible to demonstrate that self-interest is a very significant factor for people's voting behaviour.[18] Furthermore, political activity is also closely linked to a medium which distinguishes it clearly from the economy, i.e. *public debate*, which systematically focuses attention in a collective direction. In other words, public debate is necessarily about what is good for society – the common good. It is only by arguing on the basis of the public interest that one is able to persuade others to share one's point of view. An argument referring to private wants or interests carries little weight.

In the market sphere, on the other hand, things are different. Under our economic system, it is generally accepted that actors put their own interests before the common good through basic institutions such as the market and the private right to own and use property. Politics may therefore be interpreted as a parallel to the economy only if voting behaviour is considered analogous to market behaviour in isolation – that is, if one does not take into consideration that voting behaviour is related to public debate. The franchise becomes effective only when citizens' various motives, interests, needs and desires are integrated through public debate. It is only under such conditions that a vote is qualified.[19]

From a logical-analytic perspective, our rejection of the economic view of politics implies that it is also impossible to *imagine* that politics would be able to function according to the principles that that model requires. As mentioned earlier, an economic interpretation is, among other things, based on the idea that politics functions as a supplement to the market and that political measures may be taken to intervene in the event of market failure.

But this presupposes that politics follows a type of logic that is different from the market. Along with Rawls, we may say that although the market is oriented towards *efficiency*, the main objective of politics is *justice*.[20] A market economy may be understood as the mutual adaptation of independent actors to external forces in an equilibrium system. Politics, on the other hand, is based on actors' joint efforts to work out reasonable interpretations of reality and to drum up support for programmes of action. As such, the market is an expression of a form of *instrumental logic*, while politics is an expression of a *communicative logic*. Nevertheless, there are also mechanisms in the political sphere which serve to relieve communication from its co-ordinative functions, such as the principles of legality and majority vote. These principles function in specific contexts to exempt actors from the need to justify their actions. Even so, there is a fundamental difference between the two systems in that political solutions involve a balanced co-ordination of the views of several actors, whereas market solutions are based on the principle that each individual actor acts on his or her own behalf and in isolation.

The economy and the political system are thus in many respects, if not completely, structured according to different types of functional logic and standards of rationality. Furthermore, social institutions that are dependent on general acceptance and *trust* are built on foundations of collective interpretations of reality. And these foundations are maintained not least through processes of political opinion formation. Without such institutions (e.g. the contract and statute law) to serve as a framework, strategic interaction in the market could not last. If politics were based on private, egoistic preferences, as the economic model of politics requires, not only would it be impossible for the state to function as a necessary supplement to the market by producing and allocating goods on a basis *other than self-interest*, but the very ground under the institutions supporting the market itself would crumble.

This leads to a rejection of the economic view of democracy also on logical-analytic grounds. In general, it cannot provide a satisfactory explanation of how a qualified and broad acceptance of political decisions comes about. It is not sufficient to interpret such decisions as the sum total of, or the average of, the individual actors' preferences.[21] Such a tack is inadequate because it implies that the result is contingent or arbitrary: it could always just as well have been another. Decisions that are reached in such a fashion are open to criticism from every direction, even though they are derived from voting procedures which are correct enough, technically speaking. In itself, a majority decision merely represents the will of the many, not the will of the people. In order for decisions to achieve sufficient authority, there must be recourse to their *substantive* rationality. In other words, there must be the possibility, if necessary, of demonstrating through open argumentation that the decisions are generally *good* or legitimate solutions to the problem being considered. Public opinion, as expressed through formal elections and technical decision-making procedures, requires further legitimation, which implies that it must be in accordance with, or based on, acceptable grounds. Thus, politics involves efforts at both interpretation and co-operation: it is therefore necessary to agree, first, on a relevant interpretation of the situation (what really is the case), and second, on what to do about it. The particular rationale of politics is, in many respects, a matter of being able to present options as sensible and reasonable – that is, as actions that everyone must agree to, all things considered.

Finally, an economic interpretation of politics may also be criticized on normative grounds. Politics built on the unmediated private and selfish preferences of the people would be dominated by the *aggregating* rather than the *integrating* aspects of politics, which would undermine legitimacy in the long run. If political leaders only adapt to what voters already believe, they will not be perceived as leaders, but as followers. If a representative democracy is to function, it requires a reciprocal relationship between voters and politicians. Politicians must listen to what the voters want, and at the same time suggest solutions and muster support for their proposals. It may not be assumed that good political options are pre-existent in the form of voter 'preferences', and that the politicians' job is merely to take note of those preferences.[22] In most cases, such alternatives – as well as the support for them – are themselves the result of a political process.

Another aspect of the problem is that politics is anchored in the principle of justice. The principle of justice is most clearly expressed ideologically in the liberal traditions of constitutional law and the social democratic welfare state tradition, respectively. The latter is linked to the more extensive aim of rectifying existing discrepancies, and thus creating a fairer social distribution. It is difficult to see how the social objective, which is a primary part of politics and public activity as we know it today, can be promoted through policies dominated by the same fundamental self-interest which has, through the operation of the market, created the very same discrepancies that the political decisions are meant to remedy. For that reason, it is necessary that politics, through the role of active citizens, is grounded in a public sphere where it is the convincing power of the better argument that ultimately determines the outcome.

In spite of the fact that the economic view of politics seems to be untenable on the basis of several matters of principle, it has nonetheless become the dominant model for Western, particularly American, political thought in the post-Second World War era. Several factors may have contributed to such a development. First, there is the decline of important areas of the public sphere which several theoreticians claim to have demonstrated.[23] Second, the formation of political parties and interest groups and the changing role of the mass media have led to a more instrumentalized politics, which is also an aspect of the relegation of the public sphere. Political parties have become more concerned with maximixing the number of votes won than with discussing the question of what constitutes a good and just society, or how such a society may be realized. Interest organizations are designed to further the interests of a narrowly defined group of members, and to employ the means of extra-legal influence, which in turn reduces the significance of the primary political rights of the citizens. The mass media have, some contend, become just as much a channel for propaganda and for mindless and manipulative sensationalism as for investigative journalism and critical debate. Finally, citizens, through the construction of the welfare state, have been granted new rights which emphasize the administrative aspect of the public sector and debilitate the genuine role of the citizen.

The Emergence of New Roles: Clients, Users and Customers

By the rise of the welfare state, the state became an instrument of social improvement, as a parallel and supplement to what could be achieved through the market system. By establishing a number of social, medical and educational services, the public sector assumed responsibility for providing benefits in areas where the market did not, or where some individuals were unable to avail themselves of what the market had to offer. However, in spite of the fact that such social services were given a universal design, they still resulted in a division among citizens: between those who actually benefited from the government-provided services and those who did not. The majority of these services were directed at groups that had a real need for help, so that it was the sick, the elderly, the poor and the unemployed who received government assistance. These groups consequently assumed a new relation-ship with the state in addition to their position as citizens: they became *clients* of the welfare state. These people's rights as clients could be exercised in a relatively automatic way (by being defined into a group on the basis of a set of objective criteria). This marks a contrast to the case of citizens' political rights, which only guarantee the right to try to influence public policy. However, even though clients enjoyed certain rights, their role also implied a disempowered position at the same time. First of all, being labelled a welfare client entailed a certain *stigmatization* of the individual: these people were considered part of the consuming rather than of the 'contributing' part of society – hence the problem of dependency. Second, groups of welfare clients had little opportunity to change their own situation; they were largely subject to decisions made by various professionals and government bureaucrats – hence the problem of paternalism.

An additional aspect of the development of the social citizenship role is that *local governments* became an increasingly important administrative tier. The welfare *state* was often, in practice, the welfare commune (i.e. the municipality).[24] In this development several factors were important. First of all, it was often the local councils that were the most innovative in introducing services which later gained status as nationally guaranteed rights, e.g. retirement pensions. Second, it was often the local or regional councils which were given executive authority in welfare matters. This is the case for schools and day-care institutions, health and social services, and care for the elderly. Today it is usually the state that has direct authority for legislating nationally standardized benefits, such as pension payments, while local governments are left to deal with areas in which the provision of services takes place through real-life contact with the clients.

As the range of services and benefits provided by the welfare state was gradually extended to an increasing number of different areas, many saw the paternalism involved in the provision of services as increasingly problematic. This is true for areas such as schools, day-care facilities, health services and services for the elderly. Today such services are an integrated part of 'everybody's' normal life, which in itself legitimates their use. Those who receive them thus avoid the stigma which is otherwise easily attached to benefits awarded to those with a 'particular need'. Consequently, they have less reason to accept the subordinate status of 'client'. Furthermore, the idea that the substance of such services should be determined, in detail, by public authorities without participation of those most affected does not conform to current views of democracy. Management of services may also represent a workload problem for government authorities, particularly for local-level political bodies whose members are part-time politicians.

The solution to these difficulties has to some extent been to move away from a perception of those who make use of public services as passive *recipients* of benefits to a view of these individuals as active *users* of them. This implies, among other things, that the various groups are allowed to be involved in the process of determining the services, within a given framework and guidelines. This has been most prevalent in the education sector, where, as a result of the radical student movement in the late 1960s and early 1970s, there has been a growth in the establishment of committees and boards with student representatives – and, at the elementary level, parent representatives too. This user-democratic tendency has coincided with a trend towards industrial democracy, whereby in many countries employees in public institutions have also been given a voice in matters concerning their workplace. The result of these tendencies has been, primarily, a diminishing of the old-school authority associated with the positions of school headmaster/principal, or professors at the universities, but also a certain degree of increased institutional self-government at the expense of higher political and administrative authorities. Even though user representation currently seems to be less common and less formalized in the governing bodies of health and social service institutions than in educational institutions, there nevertheless seems to be a *change of mentality* taking place in these institutions as well. Administrative authorities, institutional management and employees seem, to a larger degree, to *perceive* the individuals in question more as users than as clients, and are thus to a greater extent addressing their expressed desires. The user role is in many respects an expression of a new component in the relationship between the people and the authorities, and it is based on the principle that affected parties should have a say. This in many ways implies a broadening of democracy, though, as we shall see later, a user democracy may not be immediately equated with a citizens' democracy.

The involvement of the public sector has also extended to areas other than those which may reasonably be called welfare policy areas. In contrast to welfare policy, these areas are not ones in which citizens enjoy a legal right as a result of the social component of citizenship. But they are services which the authorities – for various reasons – still consider it their responsibility to provide, and they are usually delivered in exchange for cash payment. As these programmes are not usually financed through the treasury, they are also often hived off from the regular public institutions and government budgets and organized in separate companies. For the most part these organizations provide technical, infrastructure-related services, though they may also be found in, for example, the cultural sector. Some of the organizations are run by the state government, and some also have quite a long history: for example, national communications institutions such as the postal service, the railway system, the telecommunications service and the aviation services. However, the majority of these institutions are run by local governments, and they were for the most part built up during the period of local government expansion after the Second World War. Examples of local government organizations of this type include transportation services, power plants, waterworks, sanitation services of various types, land development, and cultural amenities such as cinemas, theatres and museums. Such services may be subsidized to varying degrees; they may operate on a break-even basis; or they may generate a net profit for their government owners. Since people pay in return for a specific service, their use of these services places them in a relationship vis-à-vis the government which is at least somewhat analogous to a market relationship. However, this customer-like relationship is not always perceived as real. For example, one may be required to pay a given fee for sanitation and water services simply by virtue of one's place of residence. Such fees may not be considered significantly different from ordinary property taxes by most people. One is likely to experience more of a customer-like status when purchasing a ticket for a film, or when buying a piece of property from the local government, or even when connecting to the local telephone service.

On the whole, public organizations have produced these services under monopoly conditions, which means that the markets for these services have not been open for competition. But in Scandinavia there has been a clear trend toward market liberalization in recent years. This overall trend has taken various forms in different areas. For the postal and telecommunication services, for example, there has been a certain degree of private access to the market. Through changes in communications legislation, the authorities have also aimed to introduce a greater degree of competition between private, semi-private and public corporations in bus services. In the area of electricity distribution, new legislation in Norway has opened the way for competition between a large number of mostly publicly owned power companies.

An additional tendency towards privatization has been witnessed within a number of municipalities. These local councils have opted to allow private companies to compete for contracts to provide various services, such as sanitation. Thus private companies provide services on behalf of the local government, a procedure known as contracting out. And finally, liberalization has also been seen in instances where local councils have chosen to demerge certain parts of the public service organization and establish separate companies, or quasi-companies with more or less autonomous status vis-à-vis the municipality's administrative and political bodies.

The boundary between public and private economic activity may consequently seem unclear and under pressure. And it is not always intrinsic features of the public services themselves which call for public-sector organization. For that reason, it is logical to ask whether the management of resources is as efficient as it could be. One of the most highly noticeable consequences has been the attempt to replace management using detailed regulatory frameworks with management by objectives.[25] By such overall guidelines, subordinate units are given greater freedom to choose the means by which to reach the specified ends.

According to this ideology, the public sector ends up in the role of a *commodity-producing firm*, and the citizens wind up as customers to be satisfied by having their demands met in the market for public services. This model is particularly relevant at the local government level, and it may be that many people primarily perceive the local government in precisely this way. Many have been puzzled over the fact that voter turnout is much lower for local elections than for national, parliamentary elections. This low turnout is particularly surprising in light of studies which show that people are generally most concerned with, and most satisfied with, activities that are the responsibility of local government.[26] Part of the explanation may lie in the fact that most people are involved with the local government primarily in its capacity as producer of services and less so in its capacity as political entity: in other words, they see the local council more from a consumer perspective than from the perspective of political co-determination.[27]

The client, user and customer roles all seem to represent a challenge to the classical role of the citizen. We are witnessing an increasing number of contexts in which attempts are made to structure people's interaction with government authorities in accordance with logics which spring out of each of these roles. If these attempts succeed, what will the consequences be? Will such a development constitute the undermining of the citizen role?

The Client Role: A System of Rights

Suppose that an increasing number of people receive welfare benefits from the state (or from the local governments), and that such benefits become available in an increasing range of areas. This may be achieved by passing more legislation guaranteeing rights to specific types of benefits. If this line of action was taken to the extreme, the result would be a public sector running on autopilot. If we imagine a point at which this system of rights is 'complete', then both politics and, consequently, the political rights of the citizen will have lost all significance. The only thing that would remain would be management of existing systems and programmes, which would be carried out by various professions and the welfare bureaucracy. The people would assume the role of taxpayers, on the one hand, and consumers of public services on the other. Such a scenario may be accounted for in terms of a functionalist system.[28]

The problems inherent in this scenario appear quite soon. First of all, there are the practical limitations of a fiscal nature. There are often big problems financing today's programmes and services, and hardly room for introducing a lot of new ones. The most important objections, however, are of a more principled nature. These objections are related to the fact that the citizens, in such a situation, are reduced to being passive recipients of services provided by the public sector and prevented from being actively involved in the construction of this sector. Thus this model represents a clear loss of political *autonomy*. People lose the opportunity to participate publicly, on the basis of their status as citizens, to affect matters that impinge on their own lives. Their interests vis-à-vis the government would have to be entirely private in nature. Fora that allow for the deliberation and formation of public opinion and channels for the transformation of such opinion into political programmes and practical results will become insignificant. The legitimation of programmes of social reallocation, which is necessary for the welfare state and is an important component of the political process, will thus be undermined. The clear tendencies towards a *private-oriented* public opinion, which have been observed in most democratic countries, and which, among other things, are expressed through demands for lower taxes, will most probably spread, particularly to those groups of the population who believe that they pay more into the system than they receive in return. Opposition may grow so strong that it may destroy the foundations of the system of rights and the collective consciousness underlying the extended client role.

It is nevertheless clear that, in our society, the role of client has a justified (though limited) position. In some areas it is necessary to guarantee the rights of the individual in order to compensate for the often arbitrary misfortune and suffering of individuals and groups. Welfare rights are necessary for realizing full citizenship. An important aspect of such rights is that even though political decisions form the basis for their existence, other principles of co-ordination are significant as well. First, it is clear that a welfare programme, because it is established as a *right*, is in a way exempted from the ongoing political process. Only amending legislation, not ordinary political or administrative decisions, can legally withdraw a given right from an individual. Welfare clients who believe that they have been deprived of their rights do not need to travel the long and uncertain road of the political process – that is, to try to win a majority for their point of view. A number of *politically independent* institutions, such as appeals boards, ombudsman's offices and, ultimately, the courts, are available in order to ensure that the individual's right to public welfare services is preserved. In a way, it may be claimed that this is also an expression of the fact that the concern for absolute democracy must yield to the concerns of the rule of law.[29] This issue is particularly topical in connection with local and regional governments' administration of national legislation. For example, is lack of financial resources sufficient justification for failure to provide the benefits guaranteed by legislation in the social and health sectors? If it is, it may always be claimed that local decision-makers could and should have had different priorities.

Second, we see that client rights are dissociated from politics through a kind of market mechanism that regulates the supply of welfare benefits. The authorities try to adapt their supply to changes in the demand – that is, they try to adjust input to match the level of the clients' claims.[30] One of the aims of introducing management by objectives in the public sector is to make the service-providing system more flexible and able to tune into and respond to needs as they are expressed locally. Instead of the traditional governing by rules, which channels efforts and input in accordance with programmes set at superior levels in the political system, the new approach aims at governance from *below*. In other words, it is the 'real' needs of the clients that are to determine the allocation of resources. There are advantages and disadvantages associated with both the desire for and the possibility of the realization of such a management principle. On the one hand, it is obvious that the objective of welfare policy must be to allocate funds to where the need is greatest. On the other hand, it is equally clear that balancing the various needs observed, at least at a higher level, can only be done on a political basis.[31]

The User Role: Privatized Democracy

The concept of management by objectives is often linked to a *user perspective* and a *public service perspective* on government. The main task of public bodies is to produce services, and to produce the services that the users *want*. One of the problems here is how to pick up the relevant signals from the users. Within the market economic system this is fairly easy, as this type of system has the money medium to serve as a quick and efficient reflector of changes in demand. A similar medium is not usually present with the production of public services.[32] Possible remedies to the problem may be to carry out user surveys to record people's views on public services or to have user representation on the bodies governing service-producing institutions.[33]

Such measures are important ways in which the influence of the individual on public administration can be increased. For that reason, they are duly entitled to a place in any system of government which, in general, is in need of more input from below. It is also clear that much of the day-to-day interaction between public providers and users has a genuinely communicative basis, at least when justifications are exchanged. Nevertheless, from a broader perspective, this represents a form of limited government. In particular, it is clear that, strictly speaking, such a system only allows for the expression of *special interests*. It is those individuals or groups who are 'particularly affected' by a certain decision who are allowed to express their views, and who are granted the opportunity to put forward their own demands, without at the same time being forced to see their needs relative to those of other contending groups. Thus these interests retain a private nature: they are not subject to the same legitimation demands as ordinary political expressions. They may therefore express only a limited, not a general, validity.

When the time comes to balance various interests and needs, and rank priorities relative to each other, we are unable to base our decisions on user signals alone. The fact that a particular welfare benefit or service is demanded by more people is not necessarily an unambiguous indication that this service should be given top priority from a general point of view. The political and professional decision-makers at high levels, whose job it is to consider the interests of the *whole*, must be able to consider the quantity of the demand relative to the quality of the demand. In other words, this question involves asking how fundamental a need is for those affected, relative to how many are affected. Furthermore, such decision-makers are responsible for looking after the interests of weaker groups who find it difficult to make their voices heard. All these normative considerations, which cut to the heart of the welfare state, are difficult to incorporate, or account for, within a broad user-based perspective. Such a perspective is primarily useful within limited contexts, in which questions more often imply the application of an efficiency standard than a standard of justice. In other words, it is most applicable in contexts where decisions concern making effective use of available resources according to well-defined criteria, rather than determining priorities among contending needs.

The Customer Role: Market Management of Public Services

There is also a growing tendency towards describing the relationship between the government and the people in terms of a customer relationship. This is particularly noticeable, as mentioned, at the local level, where the contact between the authorities and 'the public' is most direct. This perspective has been accompanied by a desire for the public sector to adapt *internally* to the standards operative in the private sector. For example, a company group model for local government organization has been launched and partially implemented in several districts. In this model the head administrator plays the part of managing director and the various sectors are subsidiary companies.[34]

We may say that a customer-type relationship exists when the recipient must pay for access to a service. As mentioned earlier, there are many examples of this type of relationship in the public sector. The issue at stake is whether it is possible to conceive of the relationship between government and the people in *general* in such terms, and if so, whether this is a desirable development. In order to consider the question, it is necessary to distinguish between three areas of public responsibility. The first area of responsibility includes tasks related to administration of the civil and political components of citizenship – that is, execution of *political authority* in a strict sense. Another area of responsibility includes administration of the social aspects of citizenship, or welfare *service provision*. The third area is composed of those activities which may not be immediately linked to any specific aspect of citizenship rights, and includes, in practice, production of *collective goods* and public *commercial activity*.

As for the first area, it represents the basic domain of public-sector activity. This area includes activities which are difficult to privatize or commercialize. The government cannot leave ultimate control over the core legal, political and power institutions to others without at the same time dissolving itself. It may delegate the job of legal and political governance of certain tasks to private organizations or other levels of administration, but the *ultimate* control must still remain in the hands of the central government. And if the activities of the executive government, the parliament and the public administration were commercialized in the sense that private interests were forced to pay every time a decision was made, the result would be the transformation of these institutions into a caricature of what they were meant to be. Such a caricature already exists in many societies and is referred to as *corruption*. These activities are typical examples of collective tasks in a society, and they therefore must be financed through public spending.

The third area includes several tasks which have some features in common with the tasks included in the first category. Indeed, though they cannot be said to represent anything like constitutive state responsibilities, they do share certain characteristics to the extent that they may all be considered natural areas of government activity. These members of the category may also be referred to as *public goods*, as they benefit everyone once they are realized.[35] As a result, these goods cannot be commercialized, as private business enterprises will usually not invest in their realization. Examples of such activities include various infrastructure measures and projects aimed at achieving cleaner air or water, etc. A slightly different category is that of *natural monopolies*. In these cases, investors may cover their expenses through customer payment, but mostly the level of investment required is so high that it is very difficult for several businesses to construct parallel systems to provide competing services. Examples here include power and telephone lines, water and sewer systems, filtering plants, and railway and trolley lines. In the case of natural monopolies, it is not immediately obvious that it is the state that should be responsible for building and operating the services. But it has traditionally been considered more secure and appropriate that the monopoly be public rather than private. However, drawing the line between those tasks which, for practical reasons, must be carried out by the state and those for which it may be possible to permit private initiative is not easy. This becomes clear from a comparative perspective, whether one compares cross-nationally, or over time. In the United States today, for example, there are examples of privately operated, commercially financed fire brigades. Similarly, the 'nightwatchman state' is often used as a label for the period in the development of the state in which government responsibilities were at an absolute minimum. Today, with our much expanded public sector, we are witnessing the paradox that security services are a booming industry: private companies are paid to protect private property much as the publicly employed nightwatchman did in the nineteenth century. An example of the opposite development might be the operation of lighthouses, which are often mentioned as the type of service that would be impossible to operate commercially. Even so, there was a period during the eighteenth century when some lighthouses in Norway were privately financed through a system of fees charged to passing ships.

But the third category also includes a number of activities which could, in principle, be left to the market, but which for various reasons are still carried out by the public sector. An example might be local government regulation, development and sale of land. It is possible to argue for a much freer sale and use of real estate, but governments in Norway and other countries have taken it upon themselves not only to regulate land use and development, but also to develop real estate for use. In return, local governments charge directly for this service through a number of fees. This arrangement seems to represent an unproblematic solution, in terms of both practice and principle. To take another example, in most countries the operation of cinemas is left to the free operation of market forces. But in Norway, cinemas are run by the local government authorities, on cultural policy grounds. On the other hand, local governments may choose to allow, or not to allow, private companies to compete for contracts to provide various other services such as sanitation, snow removal, or laundry and cleaning in public institutions. With the exception of due considerations of the situation of affected employees, it is difficult to imagine any objections in principle in any case. A local government's decision to provide these kinds of services itself or to pay a private company to do so should be based on a pragmatic evaluation of what is most efficient. There is no point in a local government body producing such services if private agents can do it equally well at a lower price.[36] For local government sanitation employees fighting to keep their jobs, there is no more valid criterion to refer to than that their public services are *competitive* with the private alternatives.

The normative problems that arise are primarily related to the areas of responsibility included in the second category – that is, those pertaining to individual social rights, or welfare benefits. Within this category there has been an obvious rise in commercialization. This tendency most often takes the form of introducing or increasing user charges,[37] especially in the area of health and social services. Similar arrangements may also be conceivable in the education sector in the form of school tuition fees (although so far they have not been introduced in the public education system in Scandinavia). A dilemma arises in considering charging for such services because, on the one hand, *in practical terms* it is perfectly feasible to introduce a commercial element (and indeed, it may often seem *necessary* on financial grounds). On the other hand, it seems that doing so could change the nature of these services in a fundamental way. Quite simply, the issue represents a collision of the inclusionary principles of citizens' rights and the exclusionary principles of the market. Citizens' rights are characterized by their universality: such rights are guaranteed to all who meet certain objective criteria. The market, on the other hand, is built on the (from a normative angle) arbitrary criterion that only a person with purchasing power may have access to a good. The modern public sector is built on a basic recognition that the market economy produces social dysfunctions which necessitate a corrective mechanism. The welfare state model holds that the most fundamental conditions for the life and well-being of an individual must be ensured by society, and not left to chance, merit or charity.[38]

It seems, then, that only in areas which are not fundamentally related to citizenship rights may commercial forms of trade be introduced relatively painlessly. This implies that the citizen role can be redefined as a customer role only at the expense of considerable loss of legitimacy. The customer role can be found suitable only for publicly produced goods which from an *allocational* point of view could just as well have been produced by the market. This also implies that for *some* publicly produced goods for which payment is received, it is impossible to argue in principle against privatization in one form or another.

However, privatization may take many forms.[39] One of the most common involves separating certain tasks from the ordinary administrative organization and deregulating the bodies responsible for them by turning them into smaller, more or less autonomous companies, or quasi-corporate organizations which are still publicly owned. In most cases the objective is to make the organizations more efficient and adaptable by allowing for simpler decision-making routines, etc. This is often achieved, but local government experience suggests that very often, little remains of the government's opportunity to exercise *political* control in such companies.[40] The principles of private law sanctioned in business legislation are often in conflict with the governing principles of public law which must be followed by political and administrative organizations. But if the political-administrative ability to govern these tasks disappears, perhaps the justification for government ownership involvement also disappears. If the ability to meet commercial demands is allowed to dominate an area, then a private-sector company may, in many cases, be better able to do the job than a publicly owned one.

Conclusion

There is a clear and increasing tendency today towards evaluating actions taken by public bodies according to criteria which originally were meant for private actions in the market. Efficiency is in the process of becoming the primary measure of quality in this sector too, while other considerations are being displaced. If such considerations are allowed to dominate public-sector activity, then the government is reduced to just another commodity-producing firm, which may just as well be run privately. At risk is thus our understanding of the distinction between public- and private-sector activities as one of kind – that is, our belief that certain things may be traded in the market without that being detrimental to citizenship, while other things are inherently matters of public concern. However, it is also possible that efficiency considerations will not be allowed to dominate, and that they may be reconciled with traditional public-sector values such as equality, accountability and control. In addition, the 'difference in kind' between public and private may not (as we have seen) coincide with the division between what *actually* are private- and public-sector responsibilities. It may be that certain tasks are carried out in the public sector for reasons that are little related to matters of principle, and more due to arbitrary reasons.

Citizenship has changed over time, and its significance has also varied in different historical periods.[41] Many scholars have interpreted increasing privatization and political ambivalence in modern states as a result of consumer- and utility-oriented morals. In other words, citizens seem to show a somewhat passive orientation towards rights rather than actively participating in society.[42] The new roles that individuals are given may also contribute to this development, as they structurally relieve people from the necessity to consider their own needs and demands relative to others'. This may be particularly critical in times when a society is facing collective problems. In times of recession, for example, when redundancies and restructuring are necessary, or in times of crisis, accident or disaster, an ability to act collectively is imperative. A shared understanding of the situation must be established, as must a co-operative motivation for action. Such requisites may come about only by activation of the genuine citizen role. It is only in this capacity that there exists a forum in which, in principle, everyone's interests may be heard. It is only in such a forum that decisions may be made with the authority sufficient to regulate special interests. Citizenship status is based on the idea that all members of a society function in two capacities: as private actors and as public actors. As public actors they function in political contexts constituted on an understanding-oriented perspective. It is this consensus-seeking deliberation which serves as the basis for legitimating government decisions.

It does not follow from the above that it is possible to settle all questions concerning the public agenda through a revitalization of political discourse in the classical sense. The political agenda is too big for that; it is too heterogeneous and complex, and there are too many differentiated roles and legal rights for good arguments alone to suffice as a means of settling differences. For that reason, it is important to have realistic expectations as regards the contribution of the citizen role and the open debate to the political process. But as one aspect of an extra-parliamentary and non-institutionalized public sphere, which may serve to test the legitimacy of political decisions, it is irreplaceable.

Notes

1. This is a revised version of an article published in Norwegian in *Norsk Statsvitenskapelig Tidsskrift* 9 (1993), and in the book *Kommunikativ ledelse* by Erik O. Eriksen (1999), Bergen: Fagbokforlaget.
2. At least according to the slogan TINA: 'There is no alternative.'
3. See, for example, P. Self (1993) *Government by the Market?*, London: Macmillan; C. Hood (1991) 'A Public Management for All Seasons?', *Public Administration* 69, 3–19; C. Hood and M. Jackson (1991) *Administrative Argument*, Aldershot: Dartmouth; C. Pollitt (1993) *Managerialism and the Public Services: The Anglo-American Experiment*, Oxford: Blackwell; J.P. Olsen and B.G. Peters (1996) *Lessons from Experience: Experiential Learning in Administrative Reforms in Eight Democracies*, Oslo: Scandinavian University Press.
4. A.O. Hirschman (1982) *Shifting Involvements: Private Interest and Public Action*, Oxford: Martin Robertson.
5. Cf. K. Marx (1844/1963) 'On the Jewish Question', in T.B. Bottomore (ed.) *Early Writings*, London: C.A. Watts; M. Walzer (1989) 'Citizenship', in T. Ball, J. Fazz and R.L. Hanson (eds) *Political Innovation and Conceptual Change*, Cambridge: Cambridge University Press; L. Nauta (1992) 'Changing Conceptions of Citizenship', *Praxis International* 12, 20–34.
6. H. Arendt (1958) *The Human Condition*, Chicago: University of Chicago Press; G.H. Sabine (1937) *A History of Political Theory*, London: Harrap.
7. G.W.F. Hegel (1821/1967) *Philosophy of Right*, Oxford: Oxford University Press.

8. T.H. Marshall (1965) *Class, Citizenship and Social Development*, New York: Anchor Books.
9. G.H. Sabine (1952) 'The Two Democratic Traditions', *Philosophical Review*, 61, 451–74.
10. G. Jellinek (1911/1919) *Allgemeine Staatslehre*, Berlin: O. Häring.
11. J. Habermas (1996) *Between Facts and Norms*, Cambridge, MA: MIT Press.
12. Aristotle (1962) *The Politics*, London: Penguin.
13. J.J. Rousseau (1762/1988) *The Social Contract*, New York: Prometheus Books.
14. R.E. Goodin (1986) 'Laundering Preferences', in J. Elster and Aa. Hylland (eds) *Foundations of Social Choice Theory*, Cambridge: Cambridge University Press/Oslo: Universitetsforlaget.
15. C. Schmitt (1923/1988) *The Crisis of Parliamentary Democracy*, Cambridge, MA: MIT Press, p. 16.
16. J.A. Schumpeter (1942) *Capitalism, Socialism, and Democracy*, New York: Harper & Row; A. Downs (1957) *An Economic Theory of Democracy*, New York: Harper & Row; W.H. Riker (1982) *Liberalism against Populism*, San Francisco: Freeman.
17. Cf. J. Elster (1986) 'The Market and the Forum: Three Varieties of Political Theory', in Elster and Hylland (eds) *Foundations of Social Choice Theory*.
18. L. Lewin (1991) *Self-Interest and Public Interest in Western Politics*, Oxford: Oxford University Press; cf. D.P. Green and I. Shapiro (1994) *Pathologies of Rational Choice Theory*, New Haven, CT: Yale University Press.
19. Cf. J. Rawls (1971) *A Theory of Justice*, Oxford: Oxford University Press, pp. 356ff.; Habermas, *Between Facts and Norms*, pp. 178ff.
20. Rawls, *A Theory of Justice*, p. 360.
21. D. Miller (1993) 'Deliberative Democracy and Social Choice', in D. Held (ed.) *Prospects for Democracy*, Cambridge: Polity.
22. J.G. March and J.P. Olsen (1989) *Rediscovering Institutions*, New York: Free Press.
23. M. Weber (1922/1978) *Economy and Society*, Berkeley: University of California Press; Schmitt, *The Crisis of Parliamentary Democracy*; Schumpeter, *Capitalism, Socialism, and Democracy*; J. Habermas (1989) *The Structural Transformation of the Public Sphere*, Cambridge: Polity.
24. In the Norwegian case, at least (T. Grønlie (1988) 'Velferdskommunen', in R. Aamot (ed.) *Fra lekmenn til profesjonelle kommuner*, Oslo: Kommuneforlaget).
25. Cf. P.F. Drücker (1976) 'What Results Should You Expect? A User's Guide to MBO', *Public Administration Review* 36, 12–20.
26. T. Hansen (1989) 'Mot en ny kommuneinndeling?', *Plan & Arbeid* 4, 18–23.
27. T. Fevolden and R. Sørensen (eds) (1989) *Kommunal organisering*, Oslo: Tano.
28. J. Habermas (1987) *The Theory of Communicative Action*, vol. 2, Boston: Beacon Press, p. 320.
29. E. Smith (1992) 'For fellesskapets beste?', *Nytt Norsk Tidsskrift* 9, 99–117.
30. H. Baldersheim and K. Ståhlberg (eds) (1994) *Towards the Self-Regulating Municipality*, Aldershot: Dartmouth.
31. E.O. Eriksen (1996) 'Justification of Needs in the Welfare State', in E.O. Eriksen and J. Loftager (eds) *The Rationality of the Welfare State*, Oslo: Scandinavian University Press.
32. With the exception, of course, of those public services that are sold in a commercial market in competition with other producers.

33. Cf. I. Culpitt (1992) *Welfare and Citizenship: Beyond the Crisis of the Welfare State*, London: Sage, pp. 139ff.
34. H. Baldersheim (1986) *Men har dei noko val? Styrings- og leiingsprosessar i storbykommunane*, Oslo: Universitetsforlaget.
35. M. Olson (1965) *The Logic of Collective Action*, Cambridge, MA: Harvard University Press.
36. However, this is not to say that the authorities may as well surrender all control over a particular service.
37. A percentage of the total cost charged to the user for a given service.
38. Cf. R. Dworkin (1981) 'What Is Equality?', parts 1 and 2, *Philosophy and Public Affairs* 10, 185–246/283–345; R. Plant (1993) 'Free Lunches Don't Nourish: Reflections on Entitlements and Citizenship', in G. Drover and P. Kerans (eds) *New Approaches to Welfare Theory*, Aldershot: Edward Elgar.
39. K. Ascher (1987) *The Politics of Privatisation: Contracting Out Public Services*, London: Macmillan.
40. Weigård, J. (1993) *Kommunal selskapsorganisering: om bruk av fristilte organisasjonsformer i kommunesektoren*, Tromsø: NORUT Samfunnsforskning.
41. Nauta, 'Changing Conceptions of Citizenship'; W. Kymlicka and W. Norman (1994) 'Return of the Citizen: A Survey of Recent Work on Citizenship Theory', *Ethics* 104, 352–81.
42. R. Bell (1976) *The Cultural Contradictions of Capitalism*, New York: Basic Books; R. Bellah, R. Madsen, W.M. Sullivan, A. Swidler and S.M. Tipton (1986) *Habits of the Heart*, Berkeley: University of California Press; R. Bellah, R. Madsen, W.M. Sullivan, A. Swidler and S.M. Tipton (1991) *The Good Society*, New York: Alfred Knopf; M.J. Sandel (1996) *Democracy's Discontent: America in Search of a Public Philosophy*, Cambridge, MA: Belknap Press.

CHAPTER TWO

The State in (and of) Feminist Visions of Political Citizenship*

JUDITH SQUIRES

Introduction

The relationship between feminist theory and citizenship theory has changed quite profoundly in recent years. Not only is there a renewed interest among feminists in theorizing citizenship explicitly, there is also a notable, if cautious, trend towards explorations of (post)-liberal forms of citizenship models. I take both these moves to be broadly positive, but want to suggest that there is a potential weakness in this emergent literature, which arises from a failure to fully engage with the concept of 'the state'.

It has been suggested that there is a growing readiness within Western feminism 'both in theory and in practice, to participate in the politics of the liberal democratic state'.[1] This willingness to engage theoretically with the liberal democratic state occurs simultaneously with the rise in explicit engagement with the concept of political citizenship. Rian Voet notes that the general neglect of citizenship by feminists has recently been replaced by a growing and noteworthy literature on feminism and citizenship.[2] Kate Nash also suggests that there is significant a trend to 're-think the liberal state'.[3] There has, as yet, been no sustained analysis of the relationship between these two trends, or detailed consideration of what theory of the state, if any, underpins the new feminist theories of citizenship. This would, I suggest, be a fruitful line of enquiry.

One of the most noted developments in recent feminist theorizing has been the problematization of 'woman' as a category. The early feminist confidence about taking 'woman' as a stable category of analyses has been lost, challenged by the diverse voices of post-structuralism and multiculturalism. One important implication of this challenge to the unity of the category of 'woman' is that attempts to consider what a woman-friendly citizenship might entail are hedged around with anxieties about essentialism. In this context, there is an emerging consensus that the central project in relation to citizenship is to articulate an inclusive citizenship that avoids the twin pitfalls of false impartiality and restrictive essentialism.

Nash depicts Iris Young, Anne Phillips and Chantal Mouffe as all engaged in the project of developing alternatives to the abstract individualism and false impartiality of liberalism – alternatives that will enable us to take the differences between the sexes into account without at the same time essentializing sexual difference. Nash also emphasizes the extent to which both Young and Phillips, though not Mouffe, take the institutions of representative democracy as their focus, offering a more state-centric conception of politics than might have been foreseen in the wake of the early second-wave feminist determination to develop a more extensive definition of the political.[4] My concern here is not to criticize this renewed focus on the state, but to question why the state invoked takes such a unitary form. Indeed, I would suggest, contra Nash, that there is, as yet, no sustained attempt to 're-think the liberal state'. There is a clear commitment to exploring new forms of representative democracy among feminist political theorists and to exploring new forms of welfare state policies among feminist social theorists, but neither literature offers an explicit theory of the state. My suggestion is that this reduces the efficacy and conceptual clarity of the conceptions of citizenship offered. Were these theorists to adopt a notion of the state as 'a by-product of political struggles', their conception of citizenship would, I suggest, be less rigid and more pertinent.

My suggestion is that surprisingly few of the recent feminist theorists of citizenship have actively worked with a complex concept of the state as process rather than institution. Many have adopted the insights of the post-structuralist account of gendered identification – indeed, this may well be what is propelling them to explore the possibilities of engagement with the formal institutions of the state – but most seem to operate with an unhelpfully unified conception of the state, generating a surprisingly narrow conception of the possible forms of state–individual relations, and tying their conception of citizenship to the state at a time when this link is itself widely challenged.

Social and Political Citizenship

There is a clear bifurcation within recent feminist and citizenship literature between those who are working with a concept of 'social citizenship' and those working with a concept of 'political citizenship'. Social theorists depict citizenship as a legal status in a manner that echoes Marshall's conception of citizenship.[5] Political theorists, on the other hand, depict it as political participation, leading them to focus on democracy and involvement in decision-making. The social aspects of citizenship have been the focus of an extensive feminist literature.[6] The dominant concern has been that women have been denied full citizenship status. The response to this perceived exclusion has generated diverse proposals, ranging from the idea that women campaign for greater inclusion via entry into the labour market, to, in direct contrast, the idea that women's position as carers should be revalued. Some social theorists have endorsed both options. Notably, Ruth Lister demands both the entry of women into the public labour market and that their presence in the private sphere of caring be acknowledged.[7] The feminist debate about social citizenship is, it appears, well established.

The feminist literature on the political aspects of citizenship is much less clearly developed. Indeed, located within a political rather than social theory tradition, Rian Voet claims that 'feminists on the whole have not taken the issue of citizenship seriously enough and should pay more explicit attention to it'.[8] For those familiar with the extensive social theory literature on citizenship, this claim would appear odd. Anne Phillips confronts the apparent paradox directly when she notes that feminist considerations of citizenship have tended to concentrate on the social, almost to the exclusion of considering 'the kind of politics that citizenship implies'.[9] The feminist rejection of the narrow focus on the political has led, Phillips suggests, to the political aspects of citizenship being somewhat underdeveloped – hence Voet's claims that 'Until recently, feminism was not a topic considered by citizenship theorists, nor was citizenship a topic considered by feminist theorists.'[10] Voet concurs with Phillips on the explanation for this, suggesting that the reason lies in the fact that most feminists have explicitly aimed to reject precisely what citizenship theory seemed to embody: a focus on the formal membership of a state.

Early second-wave feminists, adopting a radical feminist approach, sought to find explanations for women's oppression in structural accounts of patriarchy. These accounts transcended particular states in historical and geographical scope. If the state was theorized, it was as a patriarchal state – an institutional manifestation of structurally determined power relations. More recent post-structuralist forms of feminist theorizing, which reject the universal accounts of patriarchy offered in these radical feminist analyses, also find citizenship 'too universal a narrative to be appropriate for specific groups of women'.[11] And yet there is now a growing literature on feminism and political citizenship, which indicates that something has changed regarding feminist conceptualization of either the state or the individual, or the relations between them.

Mainstream Citizenship Models

The liberal model of citizenship, conceived as a set of rights enjoyed equally by every member of the society in question, embodies the ideal of justice as impartiality. In his later writings, Rawls offers a version of this conception of citizenship, with public political status taking precedence over private personal identities in the sense that the pursuit of the latter can take place only within the boundaries set by the former. This is a cerebral citizenship comprising subscription to a certain set of principles of justice that potentially all can accept, whatever their personal identity. While people's personal identities may be deeply entrenched or 'encumbered', as citizens they 'claim the right to view their persons as independent from and as not identified with any particular conception of the good, or scheme of private ends'.[12] Citizenship is here formal, rights based, individualistic and transcendent of particularity.

Where the liberal conception of citizenship is overtly based upon the fact of pluralism, the civic republican one more directly presumes the common traditions and heritage of a culturally homogeneous society. It aspires to a substantive rather than a formal conception of citizenship, jettisoning the liberal attempt to distinguish the right from the good. In contrast to the liberal conception of citizenship, which communitarians feel subordinates fraternity to the pursuit of liberty and therefore stresses rights at the expense of a due recognition of responsibilities, the communitarian vision of citizenship stresses the importance of balancing liberty with fraternity, rights with responsibilities. Citizenship here is collective, responsibility based, communal and embedded in particular traditions.

There are those who attempt to adopt elements of each of these perspectives. Some critics have argued that enabling individuals via access to state structures, in the form of new democratic mechanisms, and empowering individuals via constitutional frameworks, is vital but does not in itself require an 'affirmation of what it means to live as part of a community'.[13] Others suggest that although formal civil and political rights inscribe the liberal conception of citizenship, more substantive social and economic rights would actually help realize the civic-republican conception of citizenship by creating the conditions for full social and political participation.[14]

Developing this insight, there is a significant literature that argues that to concentrate citizenship debates too closely on the state is to overlook the fact that the community for membership of which people struggle is not only the state but also civil society. Arguments that the acquisition of full citizenship requires the ability to act in both political and social life lead some to contemplate civil society and demands for social inclusion.[15] But the shift to including the demand for substantive rather than simply formal inclusion in citizenship debates has been a double-edged sword for many minority groups. Whereas radical democrats make appeal to civic republicanism, stressing the importance of political participation and substantive social and economic inclusion,[16] more conservative forms of contemporary communitarianism adopt similar discourses of social exclusion to focus instead upon social obligation and the importance of cultural assimilation.[17] In the face of these assimilatory tendencies within republican citizenship discourses, many ethnic groups have found the liberal citizenship discourse rather more appealing.

And yet, it has become increasingly clear that to contemplate citizenship from the standpoint of particular group identities is to confront the presumed universality of traditional citizenship rhetorics. The very factors that propel such a wide range of theorists to make appeal to 'citizenship' as a common status which might provide a framework for a just and peaceful coexistence also seem to expose citizenship as an impossible and even oppressive discourse. The simultaneous desirability and impossibility of the neutral state and universal citizenship becomes the increasingly pronounced paradox that haunts these debates.

Feminist Alternatives

In the light of the insight that the claimed universality of citizenship discourses has in reality been a form of partiality, many feminists have responded by rejecting the formal, universalist, conception of citizenship altogether and advocating its antithesis in the form of a maternalist citizenship, replacing the individual politics of self-interest with a more compassionate and altruistic ethic. Maternalist visions of citizenship are specifically conceived so as to counter the impoverished vision offered by the individualist, rights-based, conceptions of citizenship proposed by liberal theorists. As Elshtain, widely held to be one of the key advocates of this position, states, 'no substantive sense of civic virtue, no vision of political community that might serve as the groundwork of a life in common, is possible within a political life dominated by a self-interested, predatory, individualism'.[18] In direct contrast to the ideal of formal, universalist and statist conception of citizenship (which in reality justifies a conflictual and instrumental practice), this maternalist vision is informal, particularist and communitarian. It stands in direct opposition to the liberal conception: 'for the maternalist, such a notion is at best morally empty and at worst morally subversive since it rests on a distinctly masculine conception of the person as an independent, self-interested, economic being.'[19]

The maternalist version of citizenship, which proposes the specific feminine values of the private sphere as the basis for a new model of citizenship, is usually attributed to Ruddick and Elshtain.[20] It is, in effect, a version of the communitarian vision which prioritizes community as the basis for politics, a community which shares not only a spirit of benevolence and certain shared final ends but also a common vocabulary of discourse.[21] Here the community is conceived of as a community of women, and the good is conceived of as a feminized good. Maternalist citizenship works to reject the dominant terms in the dichotomous pairings generated by liberal political theory and to revalorize the subordinate pairings as the basis for a reconceived citizenship. It is founded on the values of the private sphere, on emotional rather than rational relations, on the recognition of difference rather than the aspiration to equality and an ethic of caring rather than justice. Maternal thinking, Elshtain claims, requires paying a special sort of attention to the concrete specificity of each child; it turns on a special kind of knowledge of this child, this situation, without the notion of seizure, appropriation, control or judgement by impersonal standards. What maternal thinking could lead to ... is a wider diffusion of what attentive love to all children is about and how it might become a wider social imperative.[22]

Maternalist citizenship is largely held to manifest the same strengths and weaknesses as the communitarian, responsibility-based vision. Its strengths, vis-à-vis the liberal conception, are that it encompasses more than the reductive notion of individualist, rights-based contractual citizenship and offers a vision of a substantive good which might mobilize a sense of loyalty, belonging and caring in members of a community. Its weakness is that its vision of community is often nostalgic and cohesive, actually working to exclude all who do not conform to its particular conception of the good.

Pursuing this line of critique, Young claims that the 'striving for mutual identification and shared understanding among those who seek to foster a radical and progressive politics, can and has led to denying or suppressing differences within political groups or movements'.[23] To demand such cohesion, she argues, is to deny the possibility of a fully inclusive citizenship. It is also to appeal to an implicitly essentializing notion of identity and to reify authentic voice.

In the face of the practical dissolution of the women's movement and the notion of cohesive community which had underpinned its operation, and with the development of theoretical perspectives informed by genealogical assertions of the importance of celebrating diversity, both feminist practice and feminist theory have moved away from the search for unity, and have frequently reinvoked the procedural mechanisms of formal, rights-based citizenship as a means of negotiating the pluralism of multiple differences.

Such approaches to citizenship debates allow the liberal conception of citizenship to be evaluated with greater precision and renegotiated with greater confidence than was previously the case. Rather than presenting the liberal (formal, universal and statist) conception of citizenship as a single coherent entity, to be accepted or rejected as a whole, the project now gets characterized as an unmasking of the instability within liberal thought, followed by a radical reconfiguration of its various constituent parts.

For example, James argues that

> it is a mistake to see the oppositions around which liberal theory is organised as lined up like two rows of dominoes, each male term facing its inferior female counterpart with implacable hostility. The relations within and between pairs are ... much more diverse.[24]

This perception is characteristic of the recent trend towards the deconstruction of false dichotomies. This deconstructionist project undermines the clear-cut distinction between mainstream and feminist positions and destabilizes the political opposition between oppressive and liberatory discourses. As James states, there is 'more continuity between liberal and feminist conceptions of citizenship than is generally appreciated'.[25] Similarly, Nash argues that the relation between liberalism and feminism is ambivalent rather than simply unhappy.[26] And Phillips argues that the 'preoccupation with liberal democracy as a totalizing system we must be either "for" or "against" proves relatively unhelpful, for it attributes to liberal democracy a greater theoretical fixity than is confirmed by its subsequent history'.[27]

It is important, Phillips tells us, to understand the extent to which liberal democratic citizenship has already evolved, under the pressure of labour and social democratic parties and also of feminism, in ways that have altered the boundary of the public and changed the character of citizenship. Given this, it is unhelpful to assume that it is not capable of further modification in order to deal with the differential treatment of women.[28] On a more abstract plane, Nash also claims that feminists have been able to use liberalism in distinctively feminist ways because of the equivocality of the category of woman in liberal political thought.[29] Liberalism, she suggests, offers invaluable resources for feminism – precisely because of its ambivalence about the nature and role of women.

Feminist critiques of liberal conceptions of citizenship should not, then, be interpreted as necessarily requiring the rejection of liberal citizenship, but rather as a call for further democratization within the framework of liberal democracy itself. As Phillips says, 'A richer and more equal democracy may still be possible within the broad framework liberal democracy implies.'[30] Or, as Nash says, 'the feminist project – which aims for equal rights for women – must be part of a wider project, that of radical democracy – which is concerned with equal rights for all, including men'.[31]

Among those calling for the further democratization of citizenship there is disagreement as to whether the civic republican tradition has useful insights to offer or not. Dietz argues that it does, Mouffe and Young argue that it does not. Dietz's position is that the civic republican tradition prioritizes democratic participation in its stress on collective action and the transformation of individual interests and identities into shared ideals through democratic engagement.[32] Mouffe, on the other hand, equates civic republicanism not so much with active political participation as with a communitarian 'insistence on a substantive notion of the common good and shared moral values'.[33] In other words, for Mouffe, civic republicanism implies not political participation but social obligation. She therefore differentiates her own position from both of these: citizenship, she tells us, 'is not just one identity among others, as it is in Liberalism, nor is it the dominant identity that overrides all others, as it is in Civic Republicanism'.[34] Similarly, Young finds both the liberal and the civic republican traditions equally guilty of projecting 'an ideal of universal citizenship'.[35] She too warns against simply replacing an impoverished conception of liberal citizenship with a civic republican conception that provides the notion of the general will. The civic republican tradition may stand in 'critical tension' with individualistic contract theory, but both share a common commitment to universalism. And this commitment necessarily entails the exclusion of all groups that threaten to explode the unity of the polity.[36]

The significant point about the reconsideration of liberalism and civic republicanism (whatever the particular perspective adopted) is that the debate between these theorists is one that has moved away from the earlier maternalist agenda, which adopted an extensive conception of the political and which accordingly extended the citizenship debate into personal, social and political arenas. In contrast, these debates about democratic participation (whether liberal, civic republican or group-differentiated) return us to a specifically political conception of citizenship and a bounded and procedural conception of the political.

In other words, an important feature of this move to displace the oppositional relation between liberalism and maternalism is the focus then placed on democratic participation in an expressly political sphere. Dietz, for example, argues that 'democratic citizenship is a practice unlike any other; it has a distinctive set of relations, virtues, and principles all its own'.[37] Mouffe also argues for the assertion of a distinctly political realm and the reassertion of political liberalism as a valuable framework for realizing the ideals of freedom and autonomy.[38] The absence of a political frontier, Mouffe states, 'far from being a sign of political maturity, is the symptom of a void that can endanger democracy'.[39] And Phillips notes that, in contrast to that vision of citizenship that stresses social responsibilities, she finds citizenship 'most useful and meaningful when it is considered as a primarily *political* term'.[40]

This turn towards theorizing a distinctly political citizenship is shared even by theorists who disagree on the precise form that the political should take. As Phillips has pointed out, despite their differences, Dietz and Young both adopt a conception of citizenship that is primarily political. Both understand politics to be 'a very particular kind of relationship' and 'arrive at the absolute centrality of politics'.[41] This, Phillips argues, marks a distinct shift within the terms of debate about gender and citizenship, which in previous decades tended to use the claim that 'the personal is political' to sidestep the political and instead 'concentrate on transforming and democratizing the economic and social spheres'.[42] In contrast, this recent feminist move to affirm a specifically political citizenship works to rearticulate the significance of the boundary around a public political sphere.

This renewed defence of the expressly political clearly marks a reaction against the earlier feminist focus on questions largely thought to stand outside politics, and directly engages with the terms of democratic participation. Given this feminist affirmation of a distinct boundary to the political, it is important to note that although the concern about the individualism and formalism of liberal conceptions of citizenship remain, concerns about its statism and universalism have become muted.

The rejection of universalism within mainstream traditions of political thought, and the celebration of particularity, represents such a significant strand within recent feminist theory that a substantial sea-change in theoretical mood is marked when Phillips ponders, 'When people query the universalizing pretension of previous traditions, do they thereby limit their radical potential and blunt the edge of any critical attack?'[43] Phillips's sense is that they do; that 'ditching all the abstract universals and putting concrete difference in their place' is not progress.[44] The truly important project is to build unity without denying social difference. The pursuit of this project will require that feminists avoid overstating the opposition between these two: 'presenting the orthodoxy as more straightforwardly abstract and universal than is in fact the case'.[45]

The point, then, which captures perfectly the mood for going beyond dichotomous thinking, is that the feminists who challenge the universalism of traditional citizenship theory are at 'their most persuasive, not in counterposing the particular to the general, the sexually specific to the universal, but in emphasizing the interplay between the two'.[46] Or, in the words of Lister, 'rejecting the "false universalism" of traditional citizenship theory does not mean abandoning citizenship as a universalist goal. Instead we can aspire to a universalism that stands in creative tension to diversity and difference.'[47] Neither Phillips nor Lister underestimates the extent of the challenge posed in negotiating such a differentiated universalism as the basis for a feminist formulation of citizenship, but both see the tension as a creative one.

In this 'new language of citizenship', politics is not dissolved into everything else; a relation is political only if it takes place in a public arena, and becomes increasingly associated with the formal institutions of the state. As David Miller suggests, if one defines politics as presupposing pluralism, entailing deliberation, leading to decision-making and requiring legitimate authority, 'it is no surprise that the chief arena of politics, in the modern world, should be the state'.[48] This rather orthodox conception of the political, which explicitly refuses to accept the challenge posed by the statement 'the personal is political',[49] is, rather surprisingly, one that these recent theorists of feminist citizenship appear to endorse. The irony here is that whereas the refusal to understand citizenship in terms of a procedural notion of politics alone was characteristic of early second-wave feminism, it is now the establishment Commission on Citizenship (in the UK) and not feminist theorists, which argues that 'The participation of citizens in their society is both a measure and a source of that society's success; democracy and involvement are not, and should not be, reducible to the narrowly political, but concern the very business of life.'[50] The recent wave of feminist writing on both social and political citizenship appears to assume that citizenship is, after all, to be understood in terms of one's relation to the state. In short, recent feminist theories of citizenship appear to have drawn the boundaries of citizenship inwards, offering visions of political citizenship that are less extensively concerned with civil society and more directly concerned with the institutions of the state than before.

Feminist Theories of the State

There was, in the 1970s and early 1980s, a small literature on feminist theories of the state. Since then, very little attention has been paid within the feminist theoretical literature to the state as a category. One result of this diminished focus on the state is that when feminist theorists return to theorizing a form of citizenship that entails a modified engagement with certain features of the liberal model, they do so with an unhelpfully unified and static notion of the state. Other, more heterogeneous models of the state have been articulated within feminist writings. These could, I suggest, be drawn upon in the attempt to articulate a feminist vision of differentiated citizenship.

A number of distinct feminist theories of the state have developed.[51] Liberal feminist analyses of the state accept the dominant liberal conception of the state as the embodiment of the priority of the right over the good, producing a neutral state that acts only to ensure the maximum equal freedom of all. Liberal feminists perceive the contemporary state to be only contingently distorted by the prejudices and interests of men. They seek to hold liberalism to account for its own professed ideals and aspire to be 'in' rather than 'against' the state in order to realize this ambition. In contrast, both Marxist and radical feminists offered a fundamental critique of this model. The Marxist–feminist analysis offers a vision of the state as a capitalist state, acting in the long-term interests of capital, 'preserving the dominant class relations and assisting the accumulation of capital'.[52] Radical feminist analysis offers a patriarchal conception of the state as the institutional embodiment of male interests, 'a state that maintains or actively supports the oppression of women'.[53] Both offer structural analyses of the state as the embodiment of dominant groups. Both view the state as a negative force, to be criticized and challenged. Each form of analysis endorses a form of political activity that is primarily located outside the formal institutions of the state. They are 'against' the state. A fourth distinct feminist approach to the state emerges with the growth of the social-democratic welfare state. Here the state is argued to have taken over from individual men in the task of supporting women who cannot support themselves. This shift in dependency marks a general improvement in women's condition in that it has given women 'new resources of mobilization, protest and political influence'.[54] This literature, predominantly Scandinavian, represents the beginning of a return to a more benign approach to the state. But the influence of this approach was limited by the general decline in interest in theorizing the state at all within the feminist literature – at least within Western developed countries.

The debate between these competing conceptions of the state was largely played out by the early 1980s, resulting in a subsequent undertheorization of the state.[55] Indeed, it was argued by Judith Allen in the 1990s that the failure to develop a distinct theory of 'the state' represented a positive feminist insight, in that the concept of the 'the state' is simply 'too aggregative, too unitary, and too unspecific to be of much use in addressing the disaggregated, diverse and specific (or local) sites that must be of most pressing concern to feminists'.[56] When it does re-emerge as the object of analysis, it is as a much more fluid and inchoate entity than previously envisaged.

Drawing on the work of Foucault, Watson develops the insight that the state might best be viewed not as an institution (whether oppressive or benign), but as a form of social relations. From this more post-structuralist perspective, the state is understood as 'a by-product of political struggles'.[57] This conception of the state is necessarily complex, lacking the unifying narrative of unitary function attributed to it in other accounts. This recognition that the state is not a unity implies, according to Watson, the existence of 'a series of arenas which constitute that state both discursively and through shifting interlocking connections and practice'.[58] Moreover, the relation between the state and 'interests' is reconceptualized. Whereas Marxist and radical feminists assumed that the state acted on behalf of the interests of capital or men, and whereas liberal feminists assumed that the state arbitrated between the interests of plural individuals, or collectivities, this approach explores the extent to which the state is an 'arena in which capital's or men's interests are actively constructed rather than given'.[59] And, given that the state is not unified, the manner in which these interests are constructed will not be unitary either.

Watson notes that

> We have come a long way from the simple formulation of the state as acting primarily in the interests of capital, or as an institution which must be either smashed or which will wither away with the inevitable advance of socialism.[60]

But, in the light of the survey of recent developments within feminist theories of citizenship, it would appear that the path travelled has served to return us rather closer to a liberal starting-point, with its benign conception of the state as a unified and neutral arbiter, than Watson might have hoped. The measures proposed to realize a fully inclusive democratic polity within the recent feminist citizenship literature do rely heavily on the state – on particular forms of state legislation, funding and institutional arrangements. These visions of differentiated citizenship are, if anything, much more actively dependent on the state than the conventional liberal models that they criticize.

I have suggested that recent feminist visions of citizenship have made increased appeal to the state, but that the conception of the state itself has been left largely untheorized. I am, in the process, suggesting that a more explicit theorization of the state along the lines of the model offered by Watson would be a positive development. But let me conclude by signalling another potential concern about this return to a statist conception of citizenship.

Transnational Citizenship

The recent move to theorize an explicitly and distinctly political form of citizenship offers invaluable resources for considering issues of political participation and representation. But it can also work to refocus citizenship debates back on the state. The political focus illuminates questions regarding the criteria of inclusion within the nation-state, but does little to address the continuing issue of exclusion from the nation-state.

As Uma Narayan notes, the term 'citizenship' has been used in struggles by marginalized groups to secure greater participation with the nation-state, but has also *simultaneously functioned* to justify the exclusion of other members of the national community.[61] Feminist usages of the term have, she notes, often replicated the tendency to focus on strategies of inclusion rather than issues of exclusion by failing to consider the plight of those who still do not have citizenship status. In other words, by relying too heavily on citizenship discourses as the sources of respect, rights and resources, feminists perpetuate the nation-state as the locus of power.

The concern with the territoriality of citizenship debates and the fate of non-citizens is particularly urgent for feminists not only because immigrant women and their dependent children are particularly vulnerable if denied rights to welfare and medical care, but also because the acquisition and denial of citizenship status remains a gender-differentiated process. Narayan notes that in the context of the United States, women often automatically lose their citizenship rights when they marry foreign nationals and cannot confer their nationality on their children or spouse, yet the same does not apply to men.[62]

Feminists need to consider issues of territoriality in their reflections on citizenship. To focus only on relations within the state is to exclude from consideration all those who are excluded from it: it is to privilege the terms of inclusion of a particular group of women at the expense of the structural exclusion of others. It is because of these concerns that Nira Yuval-Davis advocates a 'multi-layered' conception of citizenship – a vision of citizenship that is analytically separated from the 'nation-state'.

Yuval-Davis adopts Marshall's vision of citizenship as a starting-point because he focuses on citizenship as full membership of 'the community', and this community can be, and increasingly needs to be, distinguished from the state. She proposes that such a citizenship would entail full membership in a series of communities: 'local, ethnic, national, state, cross- or trans-state and supra-state'.[63] Recent technological, economic and political developments have made the need for such a multi-layered conception of citizenship increasingly important, especially, she argues, when viewed in a 'non-westocentric' way.[64] In short, Yuval-Davis wants to challenge the association of citizenship with 'nation-states', which 'constructs an image in which the globe is divided into different territories, each of which belongs to a nation, which ideally has its own state'.[65]

Also working more closely within the international relations tradition, Jan Jindy Pettman is equally sensitive to the difficulty posed by the state to feminists attempting to theorize citizenship. She notes that one way of understanding citizenship is to define it as a person's relationship with their state, and continues: 'But the state has always been an ambiguous and difficult issue in feminist politics.'[66] Specifically, she notes that notwithstanding the recognition that state-consolidation projects frequently reinforce masculine power, feminists 'continue to address all kinds of claims towards the state, and articulate these claims in terms of women's formal citizenship and social rights'.[67] Moreover, the feminist ambivalence regarding the state is complicated further by the changing form of the state itself. In this context Pettman challenges us to reflect on what we might make of citizenship when we shift our focus beyond state boundaries: 'can we only imagine citizenship tied to a state, or a collection of states?'[68] Although feminist international relations scholars have not as yet offered fully developed answers to this question, they are posing the question. Recent writings by feminist political theorists on citizenship seem to indicate not only that they imagine citizenship tied to a state, but that the link is perceived to be increasingly significant.

The disjuncture between this literature and the international relations literature on citizenship regarding this issue of the relation between the state and citizenship appears striking. There is certainly a difference of emphasis; the political theory literature is cautious about invoking the concept of the state, but appears to return implicitly to a fairly orthodox appeal to the state as the central arbiter of citizenship status. The feminist international relations literature, in contrast, is often explicit in its denial of the necessary link between citizenship and the state.

In this context it is worth reflecting on the claim that one of the most urgent problems of a 'new politics of inclusion' is to 'rethink the design of democratic institutions for including citizens on a local, regional, national and European basis'.[69] To facilitate participation in an age of globalization and migration, a whole new set of participatory social and political institutions may be needed.[70] Any such proposals for differentiated powers on communal, provincial, state and supra- and international levels entail a critique not only of traditional conceptions of the existing state-system, but also of the traditional treatment of citizenship. And yet most of the models for political citizenship surveyed above have not only a strong state, but also a strongly parochial bias at odds with 'transnational citizenship'.[71] In other words, not only may recent feminist theories of citizenship have drawn the boundaries of citizenship more tightly than before by offering visions of political citizenship that are less extensively concerned with civil society and more directly concerned with the institutions of the state, but they may be doing so at a time when the need to theorize transnational citizenship is ever more evident. The ambition of recent feminist theorists of citizenship has been to offer a more fully inclusive citizenship model than previously existed. But this goal becomes increasingly complex as the tight correlation between state and citizenship itself becomes a subject of contestation.

Conclusion

It may be unfair to assume that these feminist theorists of political citizenship are suggesting a statist conception of citizenship and a unified conception of the state. But there is little in their writing to positively refute this assumption. Not only is the more extensive conception of the political, which might include the interactions of civil society and the private sphere, specifically ruled as non-pertinent, there is also little attempt to consider citizenship beyond the boundaries of the state. Both the internal and the external boundaries of political citizenship are clearly prescribed.

Notes

* Some of the sections in this chapter appeared in an earlier form in Chapter 7 of Judith Squires, *Gender and Political Theory* (Polity, 1999).

1. Vicky Randall (1998) 'Gender and Power: Women Engage the State', in Vicky Randall and Georgina Waylen (eds) *Gender, Politics and the State*, London: Routledge, p. 188.
2. Rian Voet (1998) *Feminism and Citizenship*, London: Sage.
3. Kate Nash (1998) 'Beyond Liberalism? Feminist Theories of Democracy', in Randall and Waylen (eds) *Gender, Politics and the State*, p. 45.
4. *Ibid.*, pp. 45–6.
5. Ruth Lister (1997) *Citizenship: Feminist Perspectives*, Basingstoke: Macmillan; Sylvia Walby (1997) *Gender Transformations*, London: Routledge.
6. Ruth Lister (1990) *The Exclusive Society: Citizenship and the Poor*, London: Child Poverty Action Group; Lister, *Citizenship*; Diemut Bubeck (1995) *Care, Gender and Justice*, Oxford: Clarendon; Caroline Glendinning (1990) 'Dependency and Interdependency: The Incomes of Informal Carers and the Impact of Social Security', *Journal of Social Policy* 19 (4), 167–97; Barbara Nelson (1984) 'Women's Poverty and Women's Citizenship: Some Political Consequences of Economic Marginality', *Signs* 10 (2), 209–31.
7. Lister, *The Exclusive Society*, p. 464.
8. Voet, *Feminism and Citizenship*, p. 2.
9. Anne Phillips (1993) *Democracy and Difference*, Cambridge: Polity Press, p. 79.
10. Voet, *Feminism and Citizenship*, p. 5.
11. *Ibid.*, p. 6.
12. John Rawls (1985) 'Justice as Fairness: Political not Metaphysical', *Philosophy and Public Affairs* 14, 223–51, p. 241.
13. Geoff Mulgan (1991) 'Citizens and Responsibilities', in G. Andrews (ed.) *Citizenship*, London: Lawrence & Wishart, p. 38.

14. Lister, *Citizenship*.
15. Nira Yuval-Davis (1997) *Gender and Nation*, London: Sage.
16. Lister, *The Exclusive Society*.
17. Amitai Etzioni (1997) *The New Golden Rule: Community and Morality in a Democratic Society*, London: Profile Books.
18. Jean Bethke Elshtain (1982) 'Feminist Discourse and Its Discontents: Language, Power and Meanings', *Signs* 3 (7), 603–21, p. 617.
19. Mary Dietz (1998) 'Context Is All: Feminism and Theories of Citizenship', in Anne Phillips (ed.) *Feminism and Politics*, Oxford: Oxford University Press.
20. Sara Ruddick (1983) 'Maternal Thinking', in J. Treblicot (ed.) *Mothering: Essays in Feminist Theory*, Totowa, NJ: Rowman and Allanheld; Sara Ruddick (1989) *Maternal Thinking: Towards a Politics of Peace*, Boston: Beacon Press; Jean Bethke Elshtain (1981) *Public Man, Private Woman: Women in Social and Political Thought*, Oxford: Martin Robertson.
21. Michael Sandel (1996) *Democracy's Discontent: America in Search of a Public Philosophy*, Cambridge, MA: Harvard University Press.
22. Jean Bethke Elshtain (1998) 'Antigone's Daughters', in Phillips (ed.) *Feminism and Politics*, p. 375.
23. Iris Marion Young (1990) *Justice and the Politics of Difference*, Princeton, NJ: Princeton University Press, p. 72.
24. Susan James (1992) 'The Good Enough Citizen: Citizenship and Independence', in Gisela Bock and Susan James (eds) *Beyond Equality and Difference: Citizenship, Feminist Politics and Female Subjectivity*, London: Routledge, p. 49.
25. *Ibid.*, p. 49.
26. Kate Nash (1998) *Universal Difference: Feminism and the Liberal Undecidability of 'Women'*, Basingstoke: Macmillan.
27. Phillips, *Democracy and Difference*, p. 105.
28. *Ibid.*, p. 109.
29. Nash, *Universal Difference*, p. 140.
30. Phillips, *Democracy and Difference*, p. 114.
31. Nash, *Universal Difference*, p. 146.
32. Dietz, 'Context Is All'.
33. Chantal Mouffe (1992) 'Feminism, Citizenship and Radical Democratic Politics', in J. Butler and J.W. Scott (eds) *Feminists Theorize the Political*, New York and London: Routledge, p. 378.
34. *Ibid.*
35. Iris Marion Young (1998) 'Polity and Group Difference: A Critique of the Ideal of Universal Citizenship', in Phillips (ed.) *Feminism and Politics*, p. 401.
36. *Ibid.*, pp. 404–5.
37. Dietz, 'Context Is All', p. 390.
38. Chantal Mouffe (1993) *The Return of the Political*, London: Verso, p. 7.
39. *Ibid.*, p. 5.
40. Anne Phillips (1991) 'Citizenship and Feminist Politics', in Geoff Andrews (ed.) *Citizenship*, London: Lawrence & Wishart, p. 77.
41. Phillips, *Democracy and Difference*, p. 84.
42. *Ibid.*, p. 85.
43. *Ibid.*, p. 58.
44. *Ibid.*, p. 65.

45. *Ibid.*, p. 70.
46. *Ibid.*, p. 70.
47. Lister, *Citizenship*, p. 66.
48. David Miller (1991) 'Politics', in David Miller, Janet Coleman, William Connolly and Alan Ryan (eds) *Blackwell Encyclopedia of Political Thought*, Oxford: Blackwell, pp. 390–1.
49. *Ibid.*
50. HMSO (1990) *Encouraging Citizenship: Report of the Commission on Citizenship*, London: HMSO, p. 42.
51. Sophie Watson (1990) 'The State of Play', in Sophie Watson (ed.) *Playing the State*, London: Verso, pp. 6–8; Georgina Waylen (1998) 'Gender, Feminism and the State: an Overview', in Randall and Waylen (eds) *Gender, Politics and the State*, London and New York: Routledge, pp. 1–18.
52. Watson, 'The State of Play', p. 6.
53. Drude Dahlerup (1987) 'Confusing Concepts – Confusing Reality: A Theoretical Discussion of the Patriarchal State', in Anne Showstack-Sassoon (ed.) *Women and the State*, London: Hutchinson, p. 103.
54. *Ibid.*, p. 121
55. Waylen, 'Gender, Feminism and the State', p. 3.
56. Judith Allen (1990) 'Does Feminism Need a Theory of the State?', in Watson (ed.) *Playing the State*, p. 22.
57. Rosemary Pringle and Sophie Watson (1992) 'Women's Interests and the Post-structuralist State', in Michele Barrett and Anne Phillips (eds) *Destabilizing Theory*, Cambridge: Polity, p. 67.
58. Watson, 'The State of Play', p. 7.
59. *Ibid.*, p. 8.
60. *Ibid.*, p. 5.
61. Uma Narayan (1997) 'Towards a Feminist Vision of Citizenship: Rethinking the Implications of Dignity, Political Participation, and Nationality', in Mary Lyndon Shanley and Uma Narayan (eds) *Reconstructing Political Theory: Feminist Perspectives*, Cambridge: Polity, p. 49.
62. *Ibid.*, p. 62.
63. Nira Yuval-Davis (1999) 'The Multi-layered Citizen: Citizenship in the Age of "Glocalization"', *International Feminist Journal of Politics* 1 (1), 119–38, p. 122.
64. *Ibid.*
65. *Ibid.*, p. 125.
66. Jan Jindy Pettman (1999) 'Globalisation and the Gendered Politics of Citizenship', in Nira Yuval-Davis and Pnina Werbner (eds) *Women, Citizenship and Difference*, London: Zed Books, p. 207.
67. *Ibid.*, p. 208.
68. *Ibid.*, p. 216.
69. Colin Crouch and Klaus Eder (1996) Introduction to European Forum Seminar: Social and Political Citizenship in a World of Migration, 22–4 February.
70. Veit Bader (2000 forthcoming) 'Institutions, Culture and Identity of Trans-national Citizenship', in C. Crouch and K. Eder (eds) *Social and Political Citizenship in a World of Migration*, Oxford: Oxford University Press.
71. *Ibid.*, p. 6.

CHAPTER THREE

*Justice and Reciprocity**

BILL JORDAN

Many arguments about social justice rest on the notion of reciprocity between members of a system of co-operation.[1] In particular, most arguments for redistributions among members are derived from appeals to the contributions that they make to such a system, and especially their work contributions. In classical socialist analyses, members' entitlements are related to the social value of their labour contributions, and those who do not qualify directly in this way are included on the basis of either past contributions or valid excuses for non-contribution. Social democratic institutions (such as social insurance) reflect much of the same kind of thinking.

If arguments from reciprocity collapse, so does the case for redistributive justice, it seems. This explains a number of features of the debate on justice in recent years. For instance, one of the strongest arguments against unconditional basic income as a means of achieving redistributive justice is that it violates the reciprocity principle by allowing some individuals to free-ride on the productive efforts of others. Conversely, socialists and social democrats are increasingly convinced by the case – originally made by conservatives[2] – for making benefits and services *more* conditional.[3] In a world of unemployment and insecurity, those seen as potential free-riders are required to demonstrate their deservingness by recognizable eagerness to do unpleasant work for low wages, or by manifest incapacity to do anything. In this escalating process, it seems only a matter of time before the relevant benefits are renamed 'Desperately Seeking Employment Allowance' and 'Total Incapability Supplement'.

In this chapter, I hope to show that under present-day economic conditions the reciprocity principle is a polite fiction that is derived directly from the equally fictitious notion of the economy as a unitary system of co-operation. If we substitute the more practical and credible notion of gainful exchange for reciprocity, and if we recognize that 'systems of co-operation' are nothing more than temporary clusters of such exchanges, then the idea of justice based on reciprocity largely collapses.

In order to rescue any arguments for redistributive justice, it is necessary to make a different analysis of co-operation, in which work contributions take a lesser role. This in turn provokes a new line of enquiry into institutional instruments for social justice.

Distributive Justice in a Global Economic Environment

Any liberal democratic theory of justice requires as its units sovereign individuals with sufficient moral autonomy to make important decisions about their life-projects and commitments.[4] Without this capacity to determine their own good, and contribute to collective decisions about the common good, the theory becomes paternalistic and anti-democratic. Yet – as is often argued by market-minded theorists – it is difficult to see how such individuals can be extricated from an interactional environment of private property and gainful exchange. Collective arrangements over justice (political institutions) must be broadly consistent with free markets, free trade, and so on; hence democratic politics must be reconciled with global capitalism.

And this is the real nub of the problem of distributional justice in today's economic context. Any realistic account of what we each owe to all others must include the idea that exchanges of all kinds take place across political boundaries, and that opportunities for advantageous trade or reallocation of resources will pay little heed to issues of political membership. Conversely, redistribution cannot expect to enjoy majority political support if it violates the freedom to move across borders.

Let us begin with a (not-too-counterfactual) situation. Imagine a city (say Plymouth) in which all the owners of productive resources suddenly decide that it is more profitable for them to relocate their factories and workshops in a city elsewhere (say Shanghai). Under the various contractual arrangements with their employees, they therefore terminate all employment in Plymouth, leaving their workers with various amounts of compensation, from a week's wages to a sizeable sum of redundancy money. The workers in turn are left with the decision of whether to seek some other (service) employment in Plymouth, or to travel elsewhere in search of work and pay similar to that they previously enjoyed.

Meanwhile a group of people in a third city (say Manila) decide to set sail for Plymouth in search of a better life than they are able to enjoy there. Taking full advantage of the information available on the Internet, they systematically use each loophole in the immigration law to enter that city, and gain employment (or other means of subsistence) on terms that native Plymothians would regard as more unfavourable than they would be willing to accept (for instance, as domestic servants, or as wives to very unattractive men). This double whammie leaves a considerable proportion of the population of Plymouth facing destitution.

So far this story is supposed to illustrate a set of exchanges which are not only legal within present rules but also fair within any possible liberal democratic rules of justice. The capitalists would be under no further obligation to their workers, so long as there was a more profitable production site somewhere else in the world; the Manilans would be under no prohibition arising from a supposed injustice to their labour-market competitors in Plymouth. What's more, under most economic assumptions, overall welfare would have been increased (in global terms), since the wages enjoyed by a larger number of employees in Shanghai would raise their incomes by more than the loss in income to Plymouth workers, and the welfare gain made by the Manila immigrants would be greater than the loss incurred by their Plymouth counterparts.

But if all these transactions are consistent with liberal democratic rules of fairness, how are we to understand the obligations of distributive justice that members of a system of co-operation owe each other? Such obligations are supposed to indicate good reasons for favouring particular individuals over others whose circumstances may be superficially similar. For example, the rules governing social assistance require me to pay taxes to relieve the income deficits of eligible British claimants, even though I earned my salary for the past five months by working in Slovakia, where almost everyone is poorer than the most hard-pressed in Britain. Simple reciprocity would seem to require me to try to find ways to compensate those who toiled for low wages under communism in Bratislava, but instead the rules of the British tax-benefit system insist that I show solidarity with claimants back home.

The point is that present-day exchanges make it painfully clear that gainful interactions under contract do not constitute a 'system of co-operation' in the sense claimed by theories of social justice.[5] Rather, there are many clusters of transactions, linked through institutions that are increasingly transnational. Last year, as a stakeholder in a pension fund, most of my (postponed) income probably came from Seoul; as a worker, I was paid my salary in Vienna; as a patient, I received health care in Bremen; as a consumer, I shopped in Stuttgart and holidayed in Florence; and as an employer, I received the assistance of a researcher from Rio de Janeiro. The relevant units of co-operation are finance houses, firms, universities and health insurance plans that group together as 'members' diverse individuals from many countries. There is no reason, arising directly from our interactions within these 'systems of co-operation', for favouring any particular individuals or groups above any others in issues of redistribution. And for the past five years of my life as an itinerant professor, any 'reciprocity' that can be located in any of these transactions has pointed away from British welfare claimants, and towards foreigners, as potential beneficiaries of redistributive justice.

The pessimistic conclusion to be drawn from this is that any claims from principles of reciprocity have been greatly weakened by globalization; hence, if social justice rests on reciprocity, social justice itself has been weakened. Empirically this is obviously true, especially in the United Kingdom. Tax resistance has grown, and compassion for the poor, homeless, sick and troubled has diminished. And social and economic theorists increasingly insist that this is inevitable, since increased mobility of productive factors constantly puts further limits on redistribution. Every attempt to breach these limits is punished by flights of capital and the best-qualified people, lower productivity and loss of competitiveness, hence falling national income and total welfare.[6]

Another approach to this problem, however, is to recognize that the work-based reciprocity principle has never played an important role in any theory of justice other than the socialist (and hence hopelessly anachronistic) one. This becomes rather obvious when we trace theories of justice, citizenship and democracy to their Greek origins. Justice was about relations between citizens, a status from which most of those who offered work contributions to employers (and all who offered them to husbands, fathers or owners) were automatically debarred.[7]

If any contributions counted for justice, citizenship and democratic rule, they were contributions to public goods. Justice required citizens to fight for their political association in wars against rival polities, and to take part in the process of government. The just distribution of burdens and benefits addressed issues of responsibility for warlike activity abroad and peaceful collective decision-making at home. Economic activity merely financed these.

Of course, it is true to say that (since the nineteenth century at least) the whole project of distributive justice was strongly linked with the socialist notion of value as derived from labour-power, and hence of labour contributions as the stuff of social equity. But there are two very obvious things to say about this: first, that it is totally discredited as a basis for political institutions; and second, that it was always supposed to constitute a transitional stage towards the higher Marxian society in which distributional issues were quite unrelated to work contributions. Under communism, it would be need that could determine people's shares of the social product, not work.

Let us return to the earlier example of the three cities. If British capitalists owe nothing more to their former workers once they have discharged their contractual obligations, and legal immigrant workers have as good a claim to employment as indigenous ones, what possible considerations could privilege the claims of impoverished Plymothians over much poorer peasants in China, or destitute street-people in the Philippines? Why do we need an institutional system (the welfare state) to enforce our obligations to maintain their living standards and keep out many other willing workers who would flock to Britain for the sake of even lower wages?

The Case for Conditional Welfare States and Social Citizenship

To be a consistent free-market liberal individualist, I would argue, requires the answer that nothing justifies such institutions, and that no one deserves their claims to be so privileged. If gainful exchanges are the true source of welfare in human interactions, and if only welfare-enhancing institutions should gain political support, then the optimal institutional system is a global market in which nothing blocks or distorts the free movement of *all* the factors of production. Welfare states are systematic distortions favouring particular distributional coalitions, and acting as brakes on the optimal allocation of resources and the maximization of global welfare.[8] We should all be pleased that free markets can raise living standards far faster in China and Indonesia than they could be raised in Europe under current restrictive systems of social regulation. Gains there will more than compensate losses in Europe. If the world is our unit of account, distributional justice is best served by the collapse of all national systems of social protection (including immigration restrictions).

Anyone willing to argue this position deserves respect for the coherence and consistency of their analysis. However, it would be rather easy to pick holes in it, starting from the problem of collective action. In such a world, institutional arrangements would be ordered in such a way as to *prevent* all forms of collective action that constituted restraints on free exchanges between individuals. In such an order, most forms of co-operation would be banned, since co-operation is, virtually by definition, a restraint of competition.[9] Reversing the liberal individualist's 'problem of collective action' (how can free individuals ever choose to act together when they could gain more immediate pay-offs from competing?), the question would be how groups could be prevented from forming to protect themselves and each other by forswearing competition.

In no known society has there been an absence of this kind of collective action.[10] Indeed, human flourishing has only been possible, since the time of our earliest ancestors, because individuals protected each other in groups, rather than competing for scarce resources. Early capitalism spawned corporations and guilds to protect merchants and skilled workers. Cartels and trade unions put collective interests above individual short-term gain. And welfare states were possible because organized capital agreed to restrain competition with organized labour for the sake of faster growth in national income. Mutual protection through rules against rivalrous individual action is the first principle of all human associations.

Seen in this light, it becomes clear that the essential feature of co-operation (especially in a market context) is not the *contribution* of members, but the *restraint of competition*. A trade union can afford to dispense with the dues of unemployed members, rather than have them act as blackleg labour in a strike, or drive down wages as part of a non-union 'lump'. Political parties would rather that their members were passive than that they broke away to form a new party. Professional associations would rather tolerate the incompetent or ethically dubious than allow unlicensed practice. A polity can stand ten years of economic inefficiency caused by tardiness in institutional modernization better than it can sustain six months of civil war.

If the reciprocity principle means anything in the present-day context, it is nothing more than the principle that each member of a collective unit will favour the claims of other members over those of non-members. In other words, it is a kind of pledge not to compete on certain issues much more than it is an exchange of services. Exchanges are individualistically motivated, impersonal and global; co-operation is parochial, partial and collective. Members join together to bind each other to restraint and solidarity, and then seek gainful deals with non-members.

Under these circumstances, the best claim that one has on the resources of another is a claim arising from membership of an association whose rules forbid certain forms of rivalry (in consumption or production). One's standard of living ultimately depends on solidarity in upholding such rules, whether in a professional association or university or polity. If the first admitted non-graduates and the second required staff to compete annually for their contracts, insisting that students did the first two years of their courses through distance learning, I would be in trouble.

The rewards for restrained competition are substantial. Until recently, non-productive academics in Britain were paid the same as those whose output threatened whole rain forests. All enjoyed absolute security of employment, however abysmal their teaching methods and primitive their communication skills. In accepting government-sponsored competition between universities in the Thatcher years, the profession opened the door to competition between individuals and universities, with all its other costs. Now everyone's teaching is assessed, and all must produce articles and books; everyone's workrate is greatly intensified, everyone's insecurity is increased, and only a few are better paid (though more are called professor).

Whatever faint resentment I may have felt about sharing equally with lazy colleagues, I recognize now that I was much better off then (except in so far as I have been able to escape abroad, or exploit the system by selling portions of myself to various competing institutions just before the Research Assessment Exercise). But it is too late for British academics to remedy these losses: the logic of collective action, once decisively in their favour, now precludes those forms of co-operation.

All this implies that it is well worth most people's while to pay a portion of their salaries to those who might otherwise be tempted to jeopardize their security and status. It is to the *inaction* of our associates that we owe a large part of our welfare. Just as civil indifference, not heroic virtue, is the source of everyday security, so the lack of competitive action, not the spirit of enterprise, is the origin of our ordinary comfort.

Indeed, in most forms of association this is exactly what we do. Despite the growth of individual contracts, personal pensions and private health and welfare plans, in Britain most of us are still employed by large organizations, contribute to even larger superannuation schemes, and support the National Health Service. We rely on decision-makers in these organizations to manipulate aggregates and averages in such a way as to maximize collective benefit. If our employers cannot sustain a steady rise in salaries for all core staff, we hope that they will identify the most infirm and unproductive, and arrange for them to be paid not to come to work. We trust that pension funds will collaborate with this process, and doctors will collude in it. All over Northern Europe, huge numbers of over-50-year-olds are classified as 'disabled' in this way, and pensioned off before their time. Esping-Andersen classifies a whole category of welfare states (the dominant type in Europe) as seeking to reconcile justice with efficiency through 'labour-time reduction' – through excluding older workers and married women from the labour market by various tax and benefit inducements.[11] German prosperity has hitherto been founded on this strategy.

It seems, therefore, that restrained competition has always been an important element in distributive justice within a system of co-operation, and that with globalization of market exchange and resource allocation it has become the dominant element in those large employing institutions and national welfare states that continue to try to protect the living standards of their workers. As Robert Solow has pointed out, the efficiency wages paid to 'insiders' in the labour market can be protected only as long as 'outsiders' (and especially the unemployed) believe that it is worth their while to wait for better jobs, rather than to offer their services for a much lower reward.[12] In this sense, unemployment benefit is clearly a way of restraining competition that appeals strongly to traditional trade unions, and to all who uphold the kinds of protective measures (such as minimum wages and guaranteed conditions) defended in the Maastricht Treaty.

But in countries where economic individualism and market-minded Utopianism have taken deeper root – notably the United States, United Kingdom and New Zealand, as well as several South American states – restrained competition has been largely abandoned in favour of the principle of gainful exchange. As Polanyi demonstrated in *The Great Transformation*,[13] free-market Utopianism abhors any system of protection for human associations and insists on global accounting for welfare measurement; hence it requires the unemployed to compete for work, even if this substantially reduces the wages of those in employment, and devastates the communities and social institutions built around their systems of co-operation. Hence in the 1980s, even when these states embraced the international version of capitalism through privatization and deregulation, market-oriented politicians and political theorists could not openly abandon the notions of national interest and social justice in favour of global maximization. Instead they sought principles to reconcile free trade and the new international division of labour with falling wages and rising insecurity among their domestic constituencies.[14]

Among these, the principle of reciprocity has emerged most strongly, to justify the denial of benefits and services to those unwilling to accept new levels of pay and impermanence, danger and exploitation at work. Those who receive benefits and services from the state are required to show reciprocal meekness, and even masochistic enthusiasm, in the face of these conditions. Hence workfare schemes, compulsory retraining and an overall increase in conditionality of benefits have received strong endorsement, first from conservative and later from labourist politicians.[15] Reciprocity requires *more* competition, *more* activity and *more* compulsion, whatever the social costs.

Understandably, poor and excluded people have not complied passively with these new developments. Denied the protection of state systems, they have taken collective resistance action in the form of crime, begging, prostitution, hustling, dealing and various other kinds of 'informal economic activity', especially working while claiming benefits.[16] As these activities have increased, so governments have been drawn into retaliatory measures, and the social costs of enforcement have soared.[17] Already the state of California spends considerably more on penal corrections than on higher education; at current rates of growth of criminal justice expenditure, by the middle of the twenty-first century every person will be either a prisoner or a prison guard.[18] This will solve the problem of social justice at a stroke, in a neatly reciprocal way.

The notion of reciprocity between members of a system of co-operation is based on a powerful intuition about justice, but it is a one-sided one. It recognizes the reciprocal element in such relations, but links this to work activity in a highly competitive, unprotected labour market. It ignores the other face of co-operation – restraint of competition among members – with costly consequences.

Hard Choices for Welfare States in a Global Economy

Most forms of association have rules reflecting both these principles. Members are required to make contributions (of money, work or both) for the sake of collective benefits that are co-operatively produced or consumed (or both). But they are also obliged not to act in ways that damage the interests of their fellow members, even when these would enhance their individual interests. These rules serve to exclude non-members, and to mobilize members for successful competition with these outsiders. Mutuality and restraints on rivalry are closely linked in the cultures of every association, from professional organizations to friendly societies.

The benefits that accrue from these associations can therefore be seen partly as rewards for reciprocity among members, and partly as pay-offs for restraint. However, they are seldom experienced in this way. Rules against competition (advertising by professionals, strike-breaking or undercutting wages by union members) come in the form of strict prohibitions, rather than dividends or shares. Restraints on rivalry are implicit features of the culture, and seldom recognized as contributing directly to the collective goods or individual gains created by co-operation.

In the heyday of welfare states, something like this combination seemed to hold good. National prosperity was linked to a 'truce' between labour and capital, and various institutions for negotiating shares of a growing national cake. Members of the organizations that were represented at such 'peak' negotiations were required to reflect this truce in their actions, in return for the gains this gave them. Welfare benefits in the age of full employment were unproblematically linked with work performance, at least in the formal sense of willingness to take available jobs. There was always a covert task for welfare services in managing a residue of those who did not fit comfortably into the world of employment: regulating the poor and unruly, caring for the disabled, controlling the deviant, and supporting the frail and dependent.[19]

If globalization has shattered this happy fit between reciprocity and restraint (never *that* happy, actually; there was a high price in terms of enforced conformity and dullness), how might the two be reconciled again without compulsory exclusion (continental European model) or compulsory working poverty (British–American model)? Could any institutional system reclaim some elements of reciprocity and demonstrate the direct link between restraint and mutual benefit in a way that was consistent with justice?

At this point it may be useful to summarize the main problems of reciprocity and restraint that face governments.

Reciprocity

1   With globalization it is increasingly difficult to bind individual capitalists, or capital collectively, into reciprocal 'social contracts' with organized labour, guaranteed by nation-states. This is true even in countries with strong corporatist traditions, such as Sweden and Germany.[20]

2   Appeals to the 'reciprocal rights and duties of citizens' are less and less binding when a large proportion of residents/workers do not have the status of citizens.[21]

3   For many who are outside the formal labour market, or in low-paid, impermanent or part-time employment, positive inducements for participation are very small. Hence costly coercion is needed to require them to take such work.[22]

Restraint

1   With the new international division of labour, the most destructive competitive forces are located beyond national boundaries and hence are not susceptible to national regulation; these are especially found in competition from labour power in newly industrializing countries.[23]

2   Such competition increasingly erodes the salaries and security of previously protected employees, even 'insiders' such as skilled workers, professionals and managers. The previous restraints on women (who occupied roles of 'secondary earners' in segmented labour markets) are breaking down.[24]

3   Those who lack incentives to participate in formal labour markets have strong inducements to carry out 'informal economic activity', including casual cash work. This contributes to the competition which drives down wages and erodes protection at the lower end of the labour market ('hypercasualization').[25]

From this summary it is clear that the neat reciprocity of post-Second World War welfare states is now impossible, and the restraints based on corporatist institutions are largely ineffective. The best that can be hoped for is to encourage forms of participation (inside or outside the formal labour market) which embody *some kind* of reciprocity between members (thus promoting the sense of mutual responsibility, and creating an overall environment in which considerations of social justice have *some* relevance); and to foster *some kind* of restraint which minimizes the *internal* pressure on living standards and basic security, yet is consistent with social inclusion and participation.

To return to our initial puzzle, how might such arrangements look in the scenario set out in the first section?

It is now widely acknowledged that morality and the sense of community are necessary conditions for justice in social interactions. Without some sense of mutual responsibility among members of an association, who value their shared resources, public facilities and common quality of life, considerations of justice scarcely arise; this much, at least, of the communitarian critique of liberalism penetrated into the political orthodoxies of the 1990s.[26] Hence one aim of social policy in Plymouth would be to create institutions that promoted the sense of involvement in and obligation towards the common good, in which all residents (citizens and immigrants) had a stake.

There is little agreement around the elements in an institutional system that fosters such a civic culture. In particular, it is difficult to determine how to move from a situation in which people respond in terms of economic individualism, privatism, social division, exclusion and resistance to one of community. In the present context, authoritarian approaches (zero tolerance, conditionality, punishment) are seen by many as preconditions for greater mutual responsibility.[27] Alternatively, a few argue that such coercion can

60

only escalate, given the lack of positive inducements for a growing minority to take formal employment or keep the rules of tax–benefit systems.[28] Rather than initiate a cycle of rising enforcement costs and punitive measures, policy should seek ways in which the spontaneous reciprocities of informal and voluntary associations might be encouraged, and informal economic activity legalized and channelled into productive forms, thus contributing to the quality of life of disadvantaged communities, and the better integration of whole societies.[29]

In the former view, *reciprocity* must be sought through requiring all to demonstrate their willingness to be bound by compulsory conditions attached to citizenship, and expressed through obedience to rules enforced by state officials. In the latter, existing reciprocities are recognized, and new ones fostered, among associations and communities that arise through everyday interactions. Membership in the first instance is obligatory and requires the performance of public work duties; in the second it is supposed to arise spontaneously, and to be steered towards activities consistent with the common good.

As far as *restraint* is concerned, since the main sources of competition that threaten living standards and security lie outside the purview of the nation-state, any regulation must focus on potential damage to these (and to overall quality of life) through the unrestrained actions of internal competitors (individuals or groups). The fundamental question here is this: how can the actions of 'outsiders' be prevented from damaging the interests of 'insiders' (those with secure jobs which pay efficiency wages and salaries)?

Until recently, certain restraints worked reasonably well. Despite three decades of feminism, empirical evidence shows that until recently women have restrained their labour-market competition with men, and that this restraint appears to operate through domestic processes of modified patriarchy. Although most women were labour-market outsiders, their stake in the job assets of their partners (who were mostly insiders) ensured that they were unlikely to want to compete away the advantages (incremental salaries, pension rights, perks and occupational welfare) enjoyed by men.[30] But progressively, as more men's job assets succumb to competition from abroad, women are drawn into greater labour-market activity, including striving for the increments and fringe benefits that go with insider status. Thus they constitute a threat to the very assets that they seek, since it was the restraint of such competitive pressures that has hitherto protected male insiders' substantial advantages.

In relation to those with no security and little earning power, their threat comes from their willingness to do undeclared cash work, or other informal, casual jobs that undermine the insider status, wages and conditions of those remaining regular employees at this end of the market.[31] Present regulations attempt to restrain this form of competition either through minimum wages and conditions, or through the conditions that exclude the unemployed and sick from any active labour market participation, other than that undertaken in special, supervised, official 'workfare' schemes. The United Kingdom's present Labour government aims to tighten these restrictive regulations by its minimum wages and 'welfare to work' measures.[32]

All this implies that limited forms of reciprocity and restraint can still be accomplished through official, authoritative interventions, but that the long-term costs associated with these are already high and likely to go on rising. In the United Kingdom, in the years between 1979 and the present, increased spending on criminal enforcement alone cancelled out the savings in all social services expenditure so laboriously achieved by the Thatcher and Major reforms – hence neither public expenditure nor overall taxation was significantly reduced.[33] What institutional changes might contribute to the alternative approach?

Restraint without Coercion

If one aim of policy in a liberal democracy is to minimize coercion (and hence enforcement costs), then people must be given good reasons to refrain from competitive actions that damage others – positive inducements and reasoned arguments, as well as negative sanctions. Reciprocity demands participation, involvement, activity and inclusion, if not in the formal labour market, then at least in socially useful work of some kind. Restraint demands that this should not undermine the remaining institutional protections that uphold the living standards of insiders.

I have argued that globalization is beneficial to the world economy mainly in so far as the recruitment of new industrial workers in the poor, rural economies of China, Indonesia, etc. increases labour, productivity, efficiency and output. This implies that an increasing proportion of employment in First World countries will take the form of producing goods and services for local markets (i.e. forms of social reproduction of these societies). This in turn means that issues of justice over the division of labour will focus on roles and responsibilities,[34] much as it has always done in households. Questions about how to divide up and reward formal and informal, paid and unpaid activities will predominate as employment in the internationally competitive sector, producing for world markets, continues to shrink. Indeed, the aim of policy will be to reduce competitive pressures in this sector by providing some security for those participating in work for social reproduction in the 'domestic' economy.

What we seem here to be seeking is some mechanism to subsidize various kinds of socially useful activities for environmental and communal conservation, political renewal, neighbourhood regeneration and marginal economic activity, consistent with reciprocity between groups of outsiders, or within associations including outsiders, that absorbs the energies of such people, and their need (and duty) to contribute to a democratic community as members, without undermining the prosperity of those who are centrally involved in the internationally competitive sector of the economy. In this way, potentially damaging competitive activity will be restrained, yet a valid and valuable contribution to the common good will have been secured.[35] The main stumbling-block to such an institutional system is, it seems, the problem of justifying to the participants the fact that they are being excluded from the (more rewarding) sector of the economy.

This problem has arisen before. After the Second World War, women, who had made a major contribution to the wartime economy and the national war effort, were largely excluded from the labour market – to avoid the competitive pressures that had led to unemployment and falling wages after the First World War. This was achieved through rhetoric about women's 'place' in the home, their contribution to the maintenance of the 'stock' and 'culture' of British civilization, and their status as 'partners' within the household economy.[36] It was reinforced by inducements in the tax system, and allowances for them as 'dependants' in the benefits system. Married women were not *forbidden* to enter the world of paid work, or required to demonstrate willingness or competence as housewives or mothers. They were excluded by persuasion, by inducements and by compensation. Reciprocity was confined to the domestic sphere; restraint was ideological and institutional.

In so far as these issues are still relevant in the present situation (because the restraints that acted on women as joint partner stakeholders in men's job assets are breaking down), it is clear that such arguments and arrangements will not do.[37] For the sake of justice in relations between men and women, the minimum conditions for any settlement that implied restrained competition would be:

(a) an acknowledgement of equal citizenship, and equal and independent status in the tax and benefit system;
(b) equal status in the household, with tax and benefit inducements for men to share unpaid domestic responsibilities and tasks;
(c) a level playing field (in terms of taxation rates) when women do enter the labour market;
(d) some form of income, corresponding with existing unpaid duties, but allowing these to be shared (or childcare and domestic assistance to be purchased);
(e) equal access to training and retraining.

In other words, what would be at stake in such a settlement would not be confining women to the home with minimal compensation, but recognizing unpaid work as an essential aspect of the common good, and offering income to *men or women* willing to forgo labour market opportunities in order to do it – income the receipt of which would in no way jeopardize their present or future rights to more extensive or intensive labour-market activity. This could be seen either as sharing the benefits of insiders' assets so as to protect these,[38] or as compensation for restrained competition, or a combination of both.

It is difficult to see what form such income might take, except that of an unconditional basic income paid to individual men and women irrespective of their household status.[39] Only this system would allow them to form households, co-operate and share unpaid duties in ways consistent with the principles listed.

The case of very insecurely employed people, and those outside the labour market altogether, is far more difficult. Supposing that they – simply by virtue of being men and women – were to receive the basic income under the principles already outlined. Would this constitute a fair form of restraint which also sufficiently encouraged reciprocal participation in non-market activities?

The obvious answer is that – taken in isolation from other measures – it would not. On the contrary, basic income would encourage such people to take all sorts of bits and pieces of work, at rather low rates of pay, because they would no longer face the unemployment and poverty traps that characterize the present system. In this sense it might accelerate the existing hypercasualization and drive down wages even faster. It might also create conditions in which employers could more readily liquidate insiders' job assets and farm out more work to self-employed consultants and home-based outworkers. In other words, it could increase competitive pressures in the labour market and accelerate the very tendencies which threaten pay and security.[40]

It is ironic that this reverses the long-standing criticism of the basic income principle that it allows free-riding. Intuitively, reciprocity appears to demand a test of willingness to work or train as a condition for receiving any kind of benefit, supplied from taxes on the income of those who contribute labour to a system of co-operation.[41] This has long been seen as the knock-down argument against unconditional benefits.[42]

From the point of view of justice in a global economy, however, the difficulty of basic income on the foregoing analysis is not so much that it encourages too much free-riding, but that it promotes labour-market participation too strongly. If the aim of policy is to restrain competition so as to protect the living standards of insiders, it might have a rather disastrous effect.

However, this would clearly be related to the level of basic income – a technical rather than a theoretical issue. A fairly high basic income – requiring a rather higher tax rate – would probably choke off labour supply sufficiently to have the desired effect. Since all income would be taxed, this would make even small amounts of work unattractive to the least skilled, since their pay after tax might seem insultingly low. Conversely, employers might be forced to extend the range of efficiency wages and insider jobs by upgrading various forms of production (investing in more efficient methods) so as to induce more labour to be supplied, rather than relying on cheap, unskilled labour-power.

Unfortunately, in the late 1990s the discussion of basic income (especially among political theorists) has focused too much on its ethical justification, especially as a result of Van Parijs's attempt to provide an innovative theory of justice with this principle at its core.[43] However, as Gough rightly points out, basic income is an institutional solution to certain strategic economic problems and policy dilemmas, not an ethical principle.[44] It must be justified by reference to its likely consequences, not its moral properties, and in competition with other systems for income maintenance and poverty prevention, such as the Australian structure of universal means tests and conditional benefits.[45]

Even so, there is nothing intrinsic to basic income that encourages people to substitute associational or communal unpaid work for low-paid formal labour-market activity. Indeed, in so far as basic income's rules legalize the present shadow economy, the idea seems to imply the opposite effect. Yet this may not be the case if it becomes an aim of social policy to stimulate and reward those forms of collective action that improve the quality of life of communities, and especially disadvantaged communities.

Here the role of local authorities is important. Instead of devoting substantial resources to 'creating real jobs' and 'defending local services', they might instead try to stimulate and support voluntary, communal schemes for improving neighbourhoods and the social environment.[46] Since there would no longer be limits on the financial rewards that could be given to participants, the old distinctions between 'voluntary' and formal paid schemes would become irrelevant. Local authorities' role would increasingly be to identify and sustain the initiatives of their citizens, rather than provide services and regulate their activities.

None of this would even address the other major problems of the globalized economic environment raised at the beginning of this chapter. Accelerated immigration (both legal and illegal) challenges social citizenship.[47] Basic income in one country would not be a stable long-term solution to these issues; it would mean that citizens enjoyed rights not available to other residents. Only if every human being were to be a bearer of this fundamental social right would a global system of citizenship be operationalized.[48] Until then, social citizenship remains in tension with human rights.

Conclusions

In recent years it has become clearer that the social counterpart of the free-market Utopia of unrestricted gainful exchange between bargain-hunting individuals is a bit like the Hobbesian state of nature: a war of all against all.

Hence attempts to promote mutual responsibility and reduce conflicts (i.e. some version of communitarianism) have become fashionable. Unfortunately for liberal democracy, first thoughts about this have pointed towards archaic paternalistic and authoritarian forms: traditional family values, the work ethic, punishment and forced labour.[49] Much of this is prescribed in the name of citizenship, as an attempt to make sense of the reciprocal element of social justice in a new globalized environment.[50] Added to this, of course, come stronger attempts to reduce immigration flows.

Yet the attractions of new choices opened up by globalization – more prosperity, opportunity, freedom and mobility for everyone in the world – are largely nullified by such national policies. It is understandable that the members of long-standing political associations, and especially hitherto successful First World states, should seek ways of protecting their national assets and cultures, and the standards of living of their citizens. Yet to do so in this way appears to be largely self-defeating, and not conspicuously successful. Young people quickly find ways to evade or frustrate these policies, and to enjoy the fruits of open markets and world travel.

In this chapter I have argued that several features of the new world economy make the traditional idea of labour-based reciprocity as the basis of social justice irrelevant and inappropriate. Actual conditions under the new international division of labour do not easily link paid work with national benefit systems. Yet there may be a case for privileging the living standards of some citizens over others, at least in certain national policies. If so, then more effective measures are likely to take the form of restrained competition, rather than compulsory reciprocity.

Whether or not the (largely fortuitous and skewed by generation as well as gender) possession of 'insider' job status can be justified theoretically, it is the defence of the assets and advantages associated with this status that has been the main focus of attempts to protect national prosperity against global competition.[51] An alternative approach that might link the defence of such assets to justice among members and the common good would be to abandon the pretence of simple reciprocity through the formal labour market, and focus instead on effective means of restraining competition which are consistent with fairness.

This analysis has tried to show how, once the problem has been redefined in this way, arguments about basic income as a policy measure are stood on their head. The problem becomes one of compensating people sufficiently to reduce their labour supply behaviour, while at the same time allowing them to participate and contribute to the common good. Basic income alone could not achieve this, but in combination with a few other measures it might be the only way to reconcile these otherwise divergent goals. Above all, it could be the basis of a realistic form of co-operation, based on limited but relevant reciprocity and effective restraint. Within this pragmatic system, a kind of distributive justice could be negotiated (democratically) between members.

Notes

* This chapter originally appeared in 1998 in *CRISP* 1 (1), 63–85, published by Frank Cass.
1. S. White (1995) 'Rethinking the Strategy of Equality: An Assessment of the Report of the Commission on Social Justice', *Political Quarterly* 66 (3), 205–10, and (1996) 'The Right to Work and the Right to a Basic Income', Paper given at a conference on Van Parijs's *Real Freedom for All*, University of Warwick, 4 May.
2. L. Mead (1986) *Beyond Entitlement: The Social Obligations of Citizenship*, New York: Free Press.
3. G. Brown (1997) 'Why Labour Is Still Loyal to the Poor', *Guardian*, 2 August, p. 19; T. Blair (1997) Speech to Labour Party Conference, *Guardian*, 11 October, p. 8.
4. A. Weale (1983) *Political Theory and Social Policy*, London: Macmillan; B. Jordan (1985) *The State: Authority and Autonomy*, Oxford: Blackwell.
5. White, 'Rethinking the Strategy of Equality'.
6. M. Rhodes (1996) *Globalisation and West European Welfare States*, Cambridge: Polity.
7. J. Dunn (1987) 'Citizenship in the Classical Tradition', *Political Issues* 9 (1), 17–41.
8. M. Olson (1982) *The Rise and Decline of Nations: Economic Growth, Stagflation and Social Rigidities*, New Haven, CT: Yale University Press; J.M. Buchanan (1986) *Liberty, Market and State: Political Economy in the 1980s*, Brighton: Harvester Wheatsheaf.
9. B. Jordan (1996) *A Theory of Poverty and Social Exclusion*, Cambridge: Polity.
10. K. Polanyi (1944) *The Great Transformation: The Political and Economic Origins of Our Times*, Boston: Beacon Press.
11. G. Esping-Andersen (1996) 'The Impasse of Labour-Shedding and Familialism', in G. Esping-Andersen (ed.) *Welfare State in Transition: National Adaptations in Global Economies*, London: Sage.
12. R. Solow (1990) *The Labour Market as a Social Institution*, Oxford: Blackwell.
13. Polanyi, *The Great Transformation*.
14. A. Gamble (1988) *The Free Economy and the Strong State*, London: Macmillan.
15. Brown, 'Why Labour Is Still Loyal to the Poor'.
16. B. Jordan, S. James, H. Kay and M. Redley (1992) *Trapped in Poverty? Labour-Market Decisions in Low-Income Households*, London: Routledge; E. Evason and R. Woods (1995) 'Poverty, Deregulation of Labour Markets and Benefit Fraud', *Social Policy and Administration* 29 (1), 40–54; K. Rowlingson, C. Whyley, T. Newburn and R. Berthoud (1997) *Social Security Fraud*, London: Policy Studies Institute.
17. B. Jordan (1995) 'Are New Right Policies Sustainable? "Back to Basics" and Public Choice', *Journal of Social Policy* 24 (3), 363–84; Jordan, *A Theory of Poverty*.
18. R. Freeman (1995) 'Welfare State Expenditures', Paper given at a Conference on the Social Costs of Transformations in Central Europe, Institute for Human Sciences, Vienna, 15 December.
19. F.F. Piven and R.A. Cloward (1972) *Regulating the Poor*, London: Tavistock; B. Jordan (1976) *Freedom and the Welfare State*, London: Routledge & Kegan Paul.

20. Rhodes, *Globalisation and West European Welfare States*.
21. T. Hammar (1990) *Democracy and the Nation State: Aliens, Denizens and Citizens in a World of International Migration*, Aldershot: Gower.
22. Jordan, *A Theory of Poverty*.
23. B. Jessop (1994) 'The Transition to Post-Fordism and the Schumpeterian Workfare State', in R. Burrows and B. Loader (eds) *Towards a Post-Fordist Welfare State?* London: Routledge.
24. Jordan, 'Are New Right Policies Sustainable?'
25. Jordan, *A Theory of Poverty*.
26. W. Kymlicka and W. Norman (1994) 'Return of the Citizen: A Survey of Recent Work on Citizenship Theory', *Ethics* 104 (2), 352–81; S. Mulhall and A. Swift (1992) *Liberals and Communitarians*, Oxford: Blackwell.
27. J. Straw (1997) 'Locked In, Shut Out', book review, *Guardian*, 20 November.
28. Jordan, *A Theory of Poverty*.
29. G. Hughes (1996) 'Communitarianism, Law and Order', *Critical Social Policy* 16 (4), 17–42; G. Hughes (1997) 'Radical Communitarianism, Community Safety and Social Justice', *Contemporary Political Studies* (Political Studies Association), pp. 273–85.
30. B. Jordan, M. Redley and S. James (1994) *Putting the Family First: Identities, Decisions, Citizenship*, London: UCL Press.
31. Jordan, 'Are New Right Policies Sustainable?'.
32. Brown, 'Why Labour Is Still Loyal to the Poor'.
33. Office for National Statistics (1997) *Social Trends, 1997* (General Government Expenditure by Function), London: The Stationery Office.
34. B. Jordan (1987) *Rethinking Welfare*, Oxford: Blackwell.
35. B. Jordan (1989) *The Common Good: Citizenship, Morality and Self-Interest*, Oxford: Blackwell.
36. W. Beveridge (1942) *Social Insurance and Allied Services*, Cmd 6404, London: HMSO; W. Beveridge (1944) *Full Employment in a Free Society*, London: Allen and Unwin.
37. C. Pateman (1995) 'Democracy, Freedom and Special Rights', John Rees Memorial Lecture, University of Wales, Swansea.
38. P. Van Parijs (1995) *Real Freedom for All: What (if Anything) Can Justify Capitalism?* Oxford: Clarendon Press.
39. T. Walter (1988) *Basic Income: Freedom from Poverty, Freedom to Work*, London: Marion Boyars; H. Parker (1989) *Instead of the Dole: An Enquiry into the Integration of the Tax Benefit System*, London: Routledge; Jordan, *The Common Good*; D. Purdy (1996) 'Jobs, Work and Citizens' Income: Four Strategies and a New Regime', European Institute Working Paper, 96/1, San Domenico di Fiesole, Italy: EUI; B. Barry (1993) 'Justice, Freedom and Basic Income', London: London School of Economics.
40. A. Gorz (1992) 'On the Difference between Society and Community, and Why Basic Income Cannot by Itself Confer Full Membership of Either', in P. Van Parijs (ed.) *Arguing for Basic Income*, London: Verso.
41. White, 'The Right to Work'.
42. J. Elster (1986) 'Comment on Van der Veen and Van Parijs', *Theory and Society* 15 (5), 709–22.

43. Van Parijs, *Real Freedom for All*.
44. I. Gough (1996) 'Justifying Basic Income?', *Imprints* 1 (1), 72–88.
45. T. Eardley, J. Bradshaw, J. Ditch, I. Gough and P. Whiteford (1996) *Social Assistance in OECD Countries*, London: Department of Social Security.
46. B. Jordan and M. Jones (1997) 'Communitarianism, Social Policy and Social Work', Exeter: University of Exeter.
47. R. Bauböck (1991) 'Migration and Citizenship', *New Community* 18 (1), 27–48; M. Breuer, T. Faist and B. Jordan (1995) 'Collective Action, Migration and Welfare States', *International Sociology* 10 (4), 369–86.
48. B.S. Turner (1993) *Citizenship and Social Theory*, London: Sage; M. Roche (1995) 'Citizenship and Modernity', *British Journal of Sociology* 46 (4), 715–33.
49. A. Etzioni (1993) *The Spirit of Community*, New York: Touchstone.
50. Blair, Speech to Labour Party Conference.
51. Esping-Andersen, 'The Impasse of Labour-Shedding and Familialism'.

CHAPTER FOUR

Should Talent be Taxed?[1]

STUART WHITE

1 Introduction: Unequal Talent as a Problem of Egalitarian Citizenship

Equality is a fundamental norm of citizenship. A central question of political philosophy concerns the implications of this norm for society's economic arrangements. According to one influential school of egalitarian thought, these arrangements must prevent citizens suffering material disadvantage through no fault of their own (centrally, disadvantage in access to income and wealth).[2] But differential brute luck in the genetic and/or social lotteries will leave citizens with highly unequal endowments of talent or ability, which in the right economic context will swiftly translate into highly unequal degrees of lifetime access to income and wealth. Thus, it is argued, economic arrangements must be consciously structured so as to prevent and/or correct for brute luck inequality in marketable talents.

Assume that this objective is indeed desirable. How can and should we try to achieve it? Undoubtedly a large part of the answer is: education. But even under a thoroughgoing regime of equal educational opportunity, significant inequalities in talents, and thus in earnings potentials, may remain, reflecting underlying genetic differences and the residuum of sociological effects on the distribution of talent that are probably ineliminable outside of a society that has abolished the family. How should an egalitarian society handle this residual inequality of talent? One idea that has received some attention is that of 'talent taxes' or, more exactly, of a system of talent-based taxes and subsidies.[3] Under such a system, the state would evaluate each citizen's earnings potential, compare it to the average, and then assign each citizen a tax or grant to correct for the difference between them. Is a talent tax the answer to the problem of unequal marketable talent? What are the potential merits of a talent-based tax/subsidy scheme? What are the potential problems? These are the questions I shall address in this chapter.

I begin, in section 2, by setting out the specific talent-based tax/subsidy scheme examined in this chapter: the egalitarian earnings subsidy scheme

(ESS). As I explain in section 2, ESS assigns to each citizen a special earnings subsidy or tax rate (so many pence per pound earned) so that his or her after-tax income–leisure schedule is identical to that of someone with average earnings potential. ESS appears to be a very well-targeted device for correcting for brute luck inequality in marketable talent. Section 3 outlines three further advantages to ESS: it is not obviously bad for economic incentives (to work or to invest in human capital); it implements an attractive conception of economic reciprocity; and, in contrast to talent-based *lump-sum* tax/subsidy schemes, it does not result in what has been called the 'slavery of the talented'. In section 4, I then consider three objections to ESS. The first objection is essentially one of incompleteness: while ESS corrects for unequal access to income and leisure, it does not by itself ensure equal access to income, leisure *and* work satisfaction. The second objection is one of feasibility: in the pure form presented in sections 2 and 3, ESS presumes a wildly unrealistic degree of knowledge about individual earnings capacities on the part of the state. The third objection is one of intrinsic desirability: in its practical, informationally realistic form, ESS would allegedly involve a stigmatizing public division of citizens into discrete ability groupings.

However, even if, in view of these objections, we must relinquish the idea of a strictly talent-based tax/subsidy scheme, are there other types of 'personal endowment'-based tax/subsidy scheme that could address talent-related inequalities? One intriguing pointer here is the childhood privilege tax recently proposed by Bruce Ackerman and Anne Alstott. Drawing on Ackerman and Alstott's discussion of this idea, section 5 briefly outlines and tentatively evaluates the option of a self-contained tax/subsidy scheme based on citizens' estimated degree of childhood privilege as a non-stigmatizing partial alternative to, and partial surrogate for, ESS. Radical egalitarian ideas of the sort discussed in this chapter are, of course, somewhat marginal in the contemporary politics of the advanced capitalist countries. Section 6 concludes with a brief discussion of this point and of whether we can expect any revival of interest in egalitarian conceptions of economic citizenship. My comments are tentative and incomplete, but, I hope, go some way to addressing the objection that reflection on egalitarian proposals has become a futile exercise.

2 Tackling Inequality of Talent:
The Egalitarian Earnings Subsidy Scheme

To help fix ideas, imagine that we have two persons, Alf and Betty. The maximum that Alf can reasonably be expected to earn in a full working year given his exogenously determined ability endowment is £25,000, while the maximum that Betty can reasonably be expected to earn over the same period given her endowment is £80,000.[4] Clearly, there is a significant inequality between Alf and Betty in earnings potential, and thus, in their accessible bundles of income and leisure. This is depicted in Figure 4.1 where Alf's trade-off between income and leisure, when working at his peak-ability wage rate (the highest wage rate he can reasonably be expected to command, given his ability endowment), is given by the line XZ, and Betty's trade-off is given by the line YZ.[5] All the combinations of income and leisure on line YZ, and in the space between lines XZ and YZ, are in principle accessible to Betty but not to Alf. Thus, working at their respective peak-ability wage rates, Betty gets more income than Alf for any given length of time worked; and if Betty takes a job below her peak-ability wage rate, perhaps because she finds a lower-paid job more intrinsically satisfying, she can still get more income than Alf for any given length of time worked, even if he still works at his peak-ability wage rate in a job that he finds rather unpleasant. Betty is thus better off than Alf in terms of opportunities for combining income, leisure and, probably, job satisfaction. Assuming that capability for well-being and agency increases with access to income, leisure and satisfying jobs, and at the same rates for both parties, then Betty's superiority in income–leisure space translates directly into a superiority in the space of capability. It is this inequality, deriving from the brute luck inequality in endowments of talent, that we wish to address.

How might we address this inequality? Imagine that the average maximum reasonable earnings potential in the society in which Alf and Betty live is £40,000.[6] We could now say: for every pound that someone with Alf's earnings potential (£25,000) actually earns, we will give him or her an earnings subsidy of 60p; and, for every pound that someone with Betty's maximum reasonable earnings potential (£80,000) actually earns, we will require him or her to pay 50p in tax. No subsidy is paid, and no tax is due, however, until each respectively chooses actually to work and earn some income; and the final amount of the subsidy or tax that each is eligible for will depend entirely on how much income he or she chooses to earn, though the *rate* of subsidy or tax per pound earned will remain the same for each of them regardless of how long or at what wage-rate they choose to work, being based on an estimate of their respective earnings potentials.

In terms of Figure 4.1, the effect of such a proposal is to shift Betty's peak-ability income–leisure schedule down from YZ to the broken line RZ, and to shift Alf's peak-ability income–leisure schedule, XZ, up to this same hatched line. The effect of the proposal is thus to give Alf and Betty the same peak-ability income–leisure schedule – the peak-ability income–leisure schedule of someone with their society's average maximum reasonable earnings potential. Thus, each will end up with the same level of after-tax income if each works at his or her peak-ability wage rate for a full working year. In addition, each will attain the same level of after-tax income for *any* length of time worked at their respective peak-ability wage rates. Putting the same point in reverse, each will have to work the same length of time at his or her peak-ability wage

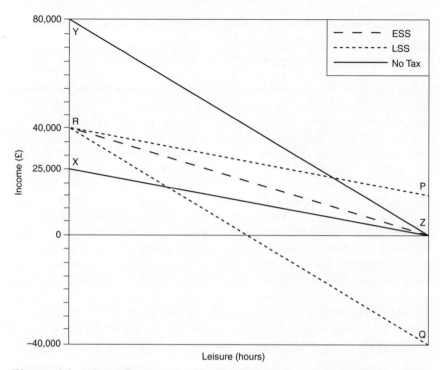

Figure 4.1 Alf and Betty under No Tax-Benefit System, LSS (Lump-sum Tax/Subsidy Proposal) and ESS (Egalitarian Earnings Subsidy Scheme)

rate as the other to attain the same level of after-tax income that the other achieves when working at this wage rate. Since their peak-ability income–leisure schedules now coincide, Alf and Betty have access to exactly the same set of income–leisure bundles, and to this extent have the same capabilities for well-being and agency.

This, then, is ESS, the essence of which may be captured by a simple function:

$$Y_i = (1 + s_i)W_i H_i \qquad (1)$$

where Y_i is the level of after-tax earned income of individual i, W_i is the individual's wage rate in whatever job he or she happens to be working in, H_i is the number of hours worked by the individual, and s_i is the subsidy rate applied to each pound that individual i earns. The formula for s_i itself may be simply given as:

$$s_i = (T^* - T_i)/T_i \qquad (2)$$

where T^* is the society's average maximum reasonable earnings potential over, say, a full working year, and T_i is the individual's own maximum reasonable earnings potential over this same period.[7] Where $T^* > T_i$, s_i will thus be positive; and where $T^* < T_i$, s_i will be negative (i.e. the individual will face an earnings tax).[8]

The egalitarian intuition underpinning ESS may be expressed as follows: in any society at a given time there is, we may imagine, an aggregate pool of earnings power. If we could set things up fairly to start with, we would naturally wish to endow each citizen with a right to an equal share of this pool of earnings power. Everyone would then get the same return for a given amount of labour. But nature and social contingency get in the way. ESS corrects for this. The taxes and subsidies it employs reallocate shares of the earnings-power pool so that if any two citizens exert themselves in work they will receive the same return. What could be fairer than that? I should emphasize, however, that ESS does not remove the need for other redistributive schemes to redress inequality in initial endowments of external wealth and/or inequality in other kinds of personal endowment that significantly affect citizens' life-chances independently of their earnings potential ('handicaps'). If these other redressive schemes are not up and running, then implementing ESS by itself could quite conceivably exacerbate the brute luck inequalities in well-being and/or agency that are our ultimate concern.[9] ESS should be seen, then, as one feature of an ideal egalitarian economic constitution, addressed to one specific inequality (brute luck inequality in marketable talent), and not as a fully sufficient system of egalitarian redress in its own right.

3 Advantages of the Egalitarian Earnings Subsidy Scheme

Incentives

Proposals for egalitarian redistribution are frequently objected to on the grounds that they will undermine incentives to work and invest in human capital. ESS, however, appears not to fare too badly in this regard. As far as work incentives are concerned, the effect of ESS is to give everybody the same peak-ability, after-tax, wage rate. Faced with this wage rate, some people will choose to work more than they would in the absence of any transfer scheme, while others will work less. The direction and extent of change for any given individual, talented or untalented, will depend on how the conventional substitution and income effects happen to balance out in that particular instance. The direction of the aggregate effect on labour supply, relative to a no subsidy/tax baseline, is theoretically indeterminate. As regards human capital, it is important to bear in mind that in estimating an individual's maximum reasonable earnings potential for purposes of assigning her an earnings subsidy/tax rate, we take into account what that person could potentially earn after undertaking the level of training that is reasonable given the person's underlying ability endowments. A naturally talented individual, who could earn a lot after undertaking all the training of which she is capable, can choose to forgo this training, but this will not affect her (relatively high) estimated earnings potential or the (relatively high) earnings tax she will have to pay. If she consequently earns well below her potential, she will end up with a relatively low level of after-tax income. While ESS suppresses differences in final incomes across the ability range, we thus see that it retains differences in final incomes between differentially educated people at a given level in the ability range, and so does not deprive people at any given level in the ability range of a material incentive to invest in human capital.

Egalitarian Reciprocity

Each citizen may be said to have a *contribution capacity*: his or her ability to contribute goods and services of value to the community. Realizing one's contribution capacity has two dimensions to it. The first has to do with the length of time one chooses to work. The second has to do with the value to the community of the service one chooses to provide when working for a given length of time. Someone who works a full working year, providing the highest-value service he can, given his endowment of ability, is fully realizing his contribution capacity. One chooses to realize one's contribution capacity to only a partial extent by choosing to work for less than a full working year and/or by choosing to provide a service to the community whose value is less than the highest-value service that one could provide.

Let us now introduce a simple principle of justice: egalitarian reciprocity. According to the principle of egalitarian reciprocity, two individuals who both realize their contribution capacities to the same extent – let us say they produce 80 per cent of the maximum value they could contribute over a given period – should, *ceteris paribus*, receive the same level of final income. The underlying intuition is that since each has made, within the bounds of his or her ability, an equal effort to benefit the community, each is deserving of equal reward from the community. Similarly, if two individuals choose to realize their respective contribution capacities to unequal extents, then they are deserving of proportionately unequal rewards, and thus, to proportionately unequal final incomes.

Now, so long as we are willing to accept that market-determined wage rates are an accurate measure of the value to the community of a given labour service (or we are willing implicitly to adjust the wage rates attached to specific jobs through job-specific taxes and subsides so that these rates correspond to our assessment of the value to the community of the relevant labour services),[10] then an ideal ESS will institute a distribution of final incomes that fully satisfies egalitarian reciprocity. For instance, under ESS all those who work a full working year at their respective peak-ability wage rates will get the same level of after-tax income, which will also be the highest level of income attainable in the community. On the assumption that wage rates are a true reflection of the value to the community of a given labour service, this outcome of an ideal ESS satisfies the requirement that those who fully realize their contribution capacity should receive the same (and highest) level of reward. On the other hand, if some individuals decide instead to work half a full working year at this same peak-ability wage rate, or to work a full year at 50 per cent of their peak-ability wage rate, they will all receive only half the after-tax income as compared with those who continue to work a full year at their peak-ability wage rate. Given the same assumption about the relationship between wage rates and the value of labour services to the community, this satisfies the requirement that those who choose to realize their contribution capacity only partially should receive a proportionately lower level of reward than those who realize their contribution capacity in full.

No Slavery of the Talented

There is a widespread view that talent-based tax/subsidy arrangements are in some way unfair to the talented. One more specific objection focuses on how this kind of scheme allegedly affects the respective income–leisure trade-offs of the talented and the untalented. According to this *work duration objection*, under a talent-based tax/subsidy arrangement the talented have to work longer hours than the untalented to obtain almost any given level of after-tax income. A second objection focuses on how such schemes allegedly affect the respective trade-offs between income and job satisfaction. According to this *unpleasant job objection*, under a talent-based tax/subsidy arrangement the talented are more likely than the untalented to have to work in jobs they find unpleasant in order to obtain a given level of income (or, to be more exact, a given combination of income and leisure). Put the two objections together, and we have the image of the talented sweating away for long hours in jobs they dislike, while the untalented bathe in the sun, or else use the benefits they receive to subsidize the taking of jobs that pay well below their peak-ability wage rates, but which they enjoy tremendously: the 'slavery of the talented'.[11]

These objections help us appreciate the difference between ESS and a more familiar lump-sum talent-based tax/subsidy proposal. Under the lump-sum tax/subsidy proposal (let us call it LSS), the state evaluates each person's maximum reasonable earnings potential, compares it to the average, and then assigns each individual a lump-sum tax or grant equal to the difference between them. Thus, if the average maximum reasonable earnings potential in the society in which Alf and Betty live is, as assumed above, £40,000 over a full working year, then, if we refer back to Figure 4.1, Betty would be liable under LSS to a lump-sum tax of £40,000 per year, while Alf would get a lump-sum grant of £15,000 per year. Working a full working year at their respective peak-ability wage rates, each is then constrained or enabled to attain an after-tax income equal to that which someone with average earnings potential would obtain when working at his or her peak-ability wage rate for this same length of time. This is illustrated in Figure 4.1,, where we see that with the move to LSS Alf's peak-ability income–leisure schedule shifts from XZ to PR, while Betty's shifts from YZ to QR; given these schedules, each will now end up with £50,000 *if* he or she works a full working year at his or her peak-ability wage rate.

The work duration objection, as defined above, is a perfectly valid objection to LSS. Looking back at Figure 4.1, we can easily see that for almost any level of after-tax income that is accessible to Betty, Alf can achieve that same level of income by working fewer hours than Betty. This is unfair to Betty.[12] But the work duration objection is completely defused by a switch to ESS. Under ESS, the talented and untalented face the same trade-off between income and leisure when both working at their respective peak-ability wage rates, or, indeed, when both working at any given percentage below their respective peak-ability wage rates. In terms of Figure 4.1, both Alf and Betty, working at (or at the same percentage below) their peak-ability wage rates, have to work the same hours to achieve any given level of after-tax income. So, in this particular respect, ESS clearly does not entail anything like the 'slavery of the talented'.

This leaves us with the unpleasant job objection. In the case of the LSS, I think this objection again applies. Because, under LSS, their peak-ability income–leisure trade-off is so poor relative to that of the untalented, the talented simply cannot afford to be as choosy as the untalented about the kind of jobs they are willing to take. To attain almost any level of income (or, more exactly, any combination of income and leisure) that is accessible to both parties under LSS, the talented have to work closer to their peak-ability wage rates than the untalented do. If we assume that the talented and the untalented have an equal probability of finding jobs which pay at or close to their respective peak-ability wage rates relatively unpleasant, then it follows that under LSS the talented will face, on average, a worse trade-off between income and work satisfaction than the untalented.[13] The talented are more likely to have to sacrifice work satisfaction, by doing an unpleasant job, to attain a given level of income (more exactly, to attain any given combination of income and leisure) than the untalented; or, to put the same point in reverse, they are likely to have to give up more income (or leisure) than the untalented to enjoy any given level of work satisfaction. For example, if we return once more to the case depicted in Figure 4.1, Alf could choose under LSS to take a satisfying job at 50 per cent of his peak-ability wage rate and still end up with an after-tax income of £27,500 per year. But if Betty took a similarly satisfying job at 50% of her peak-ability wage rate, she would end up with an after-tax income of exactly £0 – she would only just pay off her lump-sum tax liability of £40,000 per year. To attain the same level of after-tax income as Alf attains over a full working year when he works at 50 per cent of his peak-ability wage rate, she cannot in fact afford to take a job below 84 per cent of her peak-ability wage rate. Thus, Betty's opportunity to trade off income for work satisfaction, by working in satisfying jobs below her peak-ability wage rate, is much more limited than Alf's.

Precisely because it meets the work duration objection, however, I think ESS also meets the unpleasant job objection. As we have seen, ESS gives the talented and untalented the same income–leisure trade-off when they both work at their peak-ability wage rates. If, in order to avoid an unpleasant job, a talented individual then works at a certain percentage below her peak-ability wage rate, she will get a proportionately lower level of final income for any length of time worked (for example, if she works at 60 per cent of her peak-ability wage rate then, for any length of time worked, she will end up with 60 per cent of the final income she would have got working at her peak-ability wage rate). But under ESS exactly the same is also true of the untalented individual. If he works at a given percentage below his peak-ability wage rate because he finds his peak-ability job so unpleasant, he too will see his final income reduced by a proportionate amount for any length of time worked. Under ESS, the talented and the untalented are thus both free to take jobs below their peak-ability wage rates if they find lower-paid jobs more satisfying, but, for any given level of voluntary underemployment (employment at a given percentage below their respective peak-ability wage rates), they can expect the same reduction in final income. To go back to the previous example, if Alf takes a really satisfying job at 50 per cent of his peak-ability wage rate under ESS, he will end up with £20,000 if he works a full year in that job. If Betty takes a similarly satisfying job at 50 per cent of her peak-ability wage rate, then under ESS she too will end up with this level of after-tax income if she works the same length of time. Thus ESS appears to impose on a talented individual such as Betty exactly the same opportunity cost in terms of income (and/or leisure) for taking a relatively low-paid, but intrinsically satisfying, job as it does for an untalented individual like Alf. In this respect too, therefore, it does not look as if ESS can be said to entail the 'slavery of the talented'.

4 Problems with the Egalitarian Earnings Subsidy Scheme

No Guarantee of Equal Work Satisfaction

Although ESS does not generate any systematic inequality in access to income, leisure and work satisfaction between the talented and untalented, it certainly does not guarantee equality of access to all these goods across all individuals. Any two people under ESS will have access to the same combinations of income and leisure, but one of them, talented or untalented, may find jobs at or close to her peak-ability wage rate intrinsically satisfying while another, talented or untalented, may only find jobs some way from his peak-ability wage rate at all intrinsically satisfying (or, indeed, may find no jobs at all intrinsically satisfying). Thus, potentially significant inequalities in capability for well-being could remain under ESS even though, strictly speaking, it does not entail the 'slavery of the talented'. It is hard to say how severe this problem is likely to be in practice. Given universal access to a high level of education and training (assumed throughout this chapter), and assuming that everyone has a reasonably wide range of jobs open to them at or close to their peak-ability wage rate,[14] perhaps everyone will be able to find employment at or close to their peak-ability wage rate that is tolerably satisfying, or at least not positively unpleasant. But this is pure speculation (and, even if true, does not rule out some remaining degree of inequality in access to satisfying work and capability for well-being). Disadvantage in access to satisfying work can be seen as akin to a handicap and thus as something that ultimately requires its own scheme of compensatory transfers to run alongside ESS.

Imperfect Information

An ideal ESS scheme, reaping all the ethical advantages I have discussed above, would involve placing each individual along some continuum of earnings potential and then applying an appropriate, highly individualized rate of earnings subsidy/tax to every pound she earns. It would also require very exact assessment of just how far a percentage shortfall between a person's current wage rate and her maximum reasonable wage rate is due to occupational choice, and how far due to involuntary underemployment. The idea that a state, today or ever, could possess and effectively process this level of information is clearly in the realms of science fiction.[15]

It does not follow, however, that because we cannot introduce an ESS in its ideal form, we cannot institute a rough approximation of the scheme that would reap at least some of the ethical advantages associated with the scheme in its ideal form. At the risk of sounding a little like H.G. Wells or Aldous Huxley in the moments when they were writing parodies of Utopias, let me try to elaborate how this might conceivably work.

First, egalitarian social planners would have to institute a set of intelligence and capacity tests so as to divide people up into a relatively small number of ability groupings. Having left people in these groupings to go out and earn for a number of years, during which time the planners would collect data on their earnings performances, the planners would then use this information to arrive at some assessment of the groups' respective earnings potentials. The planners might, for example, specify the earnings potential for members of group X in terms of the mean or median wage rate at which members of group X have earned during the preceding years.[16] The planners would then assign each ability grouping a specific earnings subsidy/tax rate which the tax authorities would henceforth apply to every pound which members of these groups earned so as to equalize average earnings performance across the groups. In a very simple version of this kind of scheme we might, for example, divide the population into three subgroups: those whose ability and earnings potential is clearly and significantly below average; those whose ability and earnings potential does not clearly and/or significantly deviate from the average; and those whose ability and earnings potential is clearly and significantly above average. We would then give members of the first group an earnings subsidy on each pound earned, and members of the third group, a special tax on each pound earned, with those in the intermediate group (perhaps the vast majority of the population) receiving no special subsidy and paying no special tax. The feasibility even of this crude approximation of ESS is far from obvious, but with further reflection we might elaborate a workable approximation along these lines.

Stigma and Civic Inequality

'Egalitarianism' should not be understood as referring reductively to the resourcist egalitarianism with which we have been concerned thus far in this chapter – the egalitarianism that talks the language of income, wealth, jobs, taxation, and so on. Egalitarianism is properly understood in terms of a cluster of ethical commitments which include, but go beyond, this resourcist egalitarianism. Also important, for instance, is what we may call *civic egalitarianism*. A civic egalitarian aspires to a society in which, independently of holdings of wealth and income, of jobs, of abilities, of education, of gender, of race, of religion – the list could obviously go on – people are regarded by each other as being worthy of equal respect, and in which there is a rough parity of esteem among citizens.[17] This would be a society without regularized patterns of contempt and/or resentment between members of different social groups; in which one citizen does not prejudge, or seek to avoid, or do down, another because he/she belongs to a social group differentiated according to the sort of criteria I outlined a moment ago. Following ethical socialists such as R.H. Tawney, we might conceptualize the good society as one in which there is a healthy, mutually reinforcing symbiosis between civic and resourcist egalitarianisms: in which civic equality underpins, through the spirit of fellowship it engenders, resourcist egalitarian policies which, in turn, help to maintain the conditions for civic equality and fellowship; and in which we affirm resource equality and civic equality as independent, if mutually supportive, goods.[18]

The troubling challenge to ESS which we then have to address is simply this: by requiring the state publicly to categorize citizens into ability groupings in order to assign them appropriate earnings subsidy/tax rates, is it not likely that any practicable version of ESS will undermine the spirit of civic egalitarianism? Surely, the critic charges, the explicit public categorization of individuals on the basis of ability is bound to have a profound effect on the way in which citizens regard and interact with each other. Casting a wary eye back to the dystopias depicted by Wells and Huxley, we can picture a society in which highly taxed 'alphas' peer down with contempt at modestly taxed 'betas', who in turn peer down with contempt at heavily subsidized 'gammas', who themselves stare up in resentment at betas and, especially, alphas.[19]

There is, of course, no logical incompatibility between the idea that persons are to be regarded with equal respect and the idea that we should, to use George Akerlof's phrase, 'tag' individuals according to ability endowments.[20] Indeed, it is precisely because we endorse the principle of equal concern and respect at one level that we wish to equalize earnings potentials in the first place, and so get involved, via ESS, in the whole business of 'tagging'. The critic's claim is not one about the logical relations between these concepts, but a claim about the possible socio-cultural effects of public classification into ability groupings on the respect and esteem in which citizens hold each other. The claim is that their attitudes towards each other would change in ways that are incompatible with the kind of parity of esteem that is integral to civic egalitarianism. By so undermining the spirit of civic egalitarianism, ESS would deprive the citizens of a given society of an intrinsic communitarian good (the good of Tawneyesque 'fellowship'); might thereby jeopardize its own political stability over time; and, in the meantime, could well have a detrimental effect on the self-respect of less talented citizens and, in this way, serve directly to increase the inequality in capability that it is intended to reduce.

In response, a proponent of ESS can say at least two things. First, the introduction of such a scheme is politically feasible only if there is fairly widespread egalitarian sentiment in the community to begin with. Will this sentiment not work to neutralize the allegedly divisive and stigmatizing effects of explicitly splitting the citizenry up into discrete ability groupings? Second, there is an important distinction between ability in a comprehensive sense, and ability as it specifically affects earnings potential. One can, for example, have low earnings potential but still be a very talented parent or friend. The ability groupings characteristic of a practicable version of ESS relate, of course, to ability in the second, restricted sense, and there is no reason why people should regard these ability classifications as imparting a public judgement on individuals' abilities understood in the comprehensive sense.[21] Ultimately this disagreement may turn on the extent to which one thinks that there is an innate propensity for human beings to engage in invidious comparisons of themselves with others, to try to build up their sense of self-worth by displaying themselves not merely as good in some important respect, but as better than others in some such respect. If one is pessimistic on this point, then one will see ESS, in its practicable form, as offering too much rich material on which this regrettable human propensity can go to work. If one is more optimistic, then the two responses canvassed above will seem more persuasive. It is far from clear, then, that a practicable version of ESS is necessarily incompatible with civic egalitarianism; but a decisive rebuttal of this claim will depend on successfully defending a controversial view of human nature.

5 A Feasible Alternative? Ackerman and Alstott's Childhood Privilege Tax

Should we, then, simply give up on the idea of taxing talents? If so, we need not give up on the more basic idea of taxing citizens on the basis of their personal endowments (as opposed, say, to taxing them on the basis of their earnings performance or on the basis of their endowments of external wealth). There may be other forms of personal endowment taxation that are attractive in themselves and which may serve, in part, as feasible surrogates for ESS.

One possibility worthy of consideration, I think, is Bruce Ackerman's and Anne Alstott's recent proposal for a childhood privilege tax.[22] Ackerman and Alstott argue that individuals enter the marketplace (and, indeed, adult life more generally) on unequal terms in part because of unequal degrees of 'childhood privilege': 'Millions of Americans get a head start simply because they are born into privileged circumstances. Many others are disadvantaged during childhood and stay that way for life.'[23] As a partial corrective for this, they propose to phase in, over a number of years, a new tax which varies according to an individual's estimated degree of childhood privilege. The suggested measure of childhood privilege is the level and consistency of parental income in one's childhood years. Specifically, they propose that those whose parents had low incomes over many years be designated as underprivileged and that as adults they pay a low childhood privilege tax ($380 per year at 1996 prices), while those whose parents consistently had high earnings be designated as privileged and pay as adults a much higher tax ($3800 per year). Others who fall in between will have an intermediate tax liability. Ackerman and Alstott would hypothecate the funds from this privilege tax to finance a universal flat-rate state pension (of $670 per month). They would allow 'escape hatches' whereby those who are not initially deemed underprivileged but who make low incomes 'year after year' and who can show 'very significant economic hardship' would be eligible for a reassessment of their status.[24]

The precise details of the Ackerman–Alstott proposal matter less for our immediate purposes, however, than their basic (and innovative) idea. Putting to one side their specific idea of hypothecating the privilege tax to pay for a public pension, one can readily conceive of a completely self-contained system of taxes and grants/subsidies based on degree of childhood privilege. Those who are assessed as having had privileged childhoods would pay a tax into this scheme, while those who are assessed as having had underprivileged childhoods would receive a tax credit or income grant.[25] In the simplest version of such a scheme, the latter would receive a lump-sum income grant to compensate for childhood underprivilege financed by lump-sum taxes on those assessed to have had privileged childhoods. An alternative scheme – albeit one that moves further away from what Ackerman and Alstott propose – would link the privilege taxes and subsidies to earnings in the manner of ESS: those who are assessed as privileged would pay a special tax on each pound earned while those assessed as underprivileged would receive a special subsidy per pound earned. Being labelled as someone who has had a materially poor childhood is perhaps less stigmatizing (to the person so labelled) than being labelled as someone of 'low talent'. If so, we could perhaps get some of the benefits of ESS by means of an ESS-style childhood privilege tax/subsidy scheme without making unfeasible informational demands or jeopardizing the kind of equality desired by the civic egalitarian.

Some caveats should immediately be entered, however. First, modelling the childhood privilege tax/subsidy scheme after ESS makes good sense if our concern with childhood underprivilege is related only to how it affects a citizen's earnings potential as an adult. However, if we accept that the disadvantage associated with childhood underprivilege extends beyond diminished earnings potential,[26] it seems unfair to tie redressive subsidies and taxes entirely to earnings in the manner of ESS. For example, imagine that Claire and Derek both suffer diminished self-confidence due to a deprived childhood and that we wish to compensate them for the way this impairs *not* their earnings potential, but their general efficacy in formulating and pursuing personal projects. If we pay compensation for this disadvantage in the form of an ESS-style earnings subsidy, then we will end up giving more compensation to whichever of the two does the more work. This seems rather odd given that we are not in fact trying in this instance to compensate for sub-average earnings potential but for a quite different form of disadvantage (one that, by assumption, both suffer to exactly the same extent). Moreover, why should the burden of financing compensation for this specific disadvantage, quite independent of sub-average earnings potential, fall more heavily on the shoulders of privileged individuals who choose to work and earn a lot than on the shoulders of those privileged individuals who choose to work only a little? On balance, therefore, it may be desirable to modify an ESS-style version of the childhood privilege tax/subsidy scheme in the direction of the lump-sum version. But the choice as between the two is not, I think, an 'either/or' choice. A hybrid is conceivable in which the childhood underprivileged receive a modest lump-sum grant plus a special earnings subsidy, financed from a special tax (partly earnings-related, partly lump-sum) on those with privileged childhoods. In practice, pragmatic considerations might tell in favour of a simpler scheme – for example, a pro rata earnings tax (perhaps with a ceiling) for the privileged, financing a lump-sum grant for the underprivileged.

A second caveat concerns the level at which the childhood privilege taxes and subsidies are set. An obvious objection to the childhood privilege tax idea is that it will give parents an incentive to limit their earnings so that their children qualify for a subsidy, or at least escape a relatively heavy tax liability. Ackerman and Alstott have two main responses to this objection. First, they respond that if a parent is firmly in a particular earnings tranche (e.g. firmly in the high earnings tranche), then, *at the privilege tax levels they propose*, the present value of the costs incurred by relegating oneself to a lower earnings tranche for the required number of years to enable one's children to qualify for a lower privilege tax will offset the present value of the benefits to one's child from qualifying for this lower tax liability.[27] But what if a parent is capable of only just getting over the income threshold separating the underprivileged and the non-privileged (or the non-privileged and the privileged)? For a parent in this position, the cost of keeping his or her earnings under a threshold which he or she can anyway only barely surpass may be much less than the present value of the benefits to his or her child, in the form of diminished future tax liabilities, from having a parent under this threshold. This worry can be addressed, Ackerman and Alstott suggest, by keeping the relevant income thresholds defining privilege/underprivilege for any given cohort of children uncertain.[28] The income thresholds used to define degree of childhood privilege for a given cohort of children might be announced only when this cohort of children reaches maturity, and the thresholds applicable to this specific cohort adjusted from the previous cohort's thresholds to reflect the particular circumstances of the newly matured cohort. Thus, if a lot of parents reduced their labour supply and depressed their earnings, the thresholds defining privilege/underprivilege for their cohort of children would be correspondingly adjusted down. This method of setting the thresholds makes it more risky for parents to try to play the system: they have to trade off definite reductions in income and in their children's welfare now, in the form of reduced earnings, against future benefits to their children (lower tax liabilities) that are highly uncertain.

I think these responses to the parental incentives objection do bolster the case for a childhood privilege tax/subsidy scheme. But, as Ackerman and Alstott would admit, their overall response to the parental incentives objection is concessionary: it is acknowledged that incentive considerations will set an upper limit on the level at which the relevant taxes (or subsidies) are set. And, as regards the concerns of this chapter, this in turn will obviously affect the level of redress that such a scheme might offer for brute luck inequalities in earnings potential. If the upper limits on childhood privilege taxes/subsidies are quite low, then the level of redress offered will be correspondingly low, perhaps much lower than that which would be achieved under the ideal form of ESS. This is not necessarily a reason to reject the scheme, of course, but it does underscore the 'second-best' quality of the scheme as a means of redressing inequality of marketable talent.[29]

A final worry concerns whether the scheme might not be unduly stigmatizing, not to those receiving the subsidies or paying the taxes, but to their parents. If some children are labelled as having had underprivileged childhoods, might this not be a badge of shame to the parents concerned? Of course, if one does not regard such esteem effects as inherently worrying, one might use this point as the basis for a further argument against the incentives objection: parents won't slack up at work under a childhood privilege tax/ subsidy scheme, it might be argued, because they value the esteem that comes from having their children evaluated as having had the 'best' (or at least not the 'worst') kind of childhood. But some parents will try to earn as much as they can and they will still end up having their children designated as 'underprivileged'. If *these* parents suffer diminished esteem in their own and others' eyes under such a scheme, even though they have done their best for their children, then I think this is something that ought to worry the egalitarian. I am not sure how much of a problem it is in practice likely to be, but I would caution against dismissing it.

6 Conclusion: Prospects for Egalitarian Citizenship

Should talent be taxed? In spite of the apparent advantages of ESS in its pure form, the problems identified here suggest, on balance, that it may be desirable to attempt direct talent-based tax/subsidy schemes on the model of ESS. Moreover other forms of endowment-based tax/subsidy scheme, such as the Ackerman–Alstott proposal for a childhood privilege tax/subsidy scheme, may be part of a reasonable egalitarian economic constitution. And the theoretical model of ESS can perhaps still provide some assistance as we come to think in more detail about how more feasible endowment-based tax/ subsidy schemes such as this ought to be structured. Of course, any tax/ subsidy scheme of this kind is off the political agenda for the foreseeable future in countries such as the United Kingdom and the United States. Does this make consideration of such schemes a futile exercise? In closing I would like to address this challenge.

In response, it is worth first recalling how in the 1950s many people dismissed the anti-welfarist, anti-socialist writings of Friedrich Hayek as hopelessly anachronistic.[30] The world, it was confidently proclaimed, had moved decisively on from such mid-Victorian ideology to a new age of collectivism and 'planning'. But thirty years later Hayek's supposedly anachronistic ideas were helping to guide and inspire governments, in the United Kingdom and elsewhere, in their efforts to break with post-Second World War collectivism and planning. Hayek's ideas found a new and receptive audience because, as welfare capitalist societies entered a period of deep crisis in the 1970s, those ideas addressed a deeply and widely felt need for radical change. Looking ahead from where we are today, it is possible that currently unfashionable egalitarian ideas may likewise one day find a newly receptive audience. Technological change and the internationalization of trade may continue in the future to widen income inequalities between the skilled and the unskilled in the advanced capitalist countries, as they have in the recent past; and there may turn out to be limits as to how far we can limit the growth in these inequalities through remedial education and training; or limits as to how far more affluent citizens can escape their consequences through withdrawal into gated communities and more authoritarian policing of society at large. Though the nexus of causality is still far from understood, there is now a suggestive body of evidence that high levels of economic inequality have detrimental effects on the health of citizens in all income and social classes, and not merely on that of those in the most disadvantaged class.[31] Our understanding of the genetic determinants of life-chances is set to increase in the years to come, and there are already concerns about how employers and insurers might begin to use information on individuals' genetic endowments in their employment, pay and premium-setting decisions, discriminating more finely between those with good and bad endowments. Against the background of these developments, is it possible that we will see a renewal of interest in radical egalitarian ideas that seek not merely wider opportunity in the meritocratic sense, but *redress* for the disadvantages of natural and social fortune?

Notes

1. This chapter draws substantially on my 1999 article, 'The Egalitarian Earnings Subsidy Scheme', *British Journal of Political Science*, 29, 601–22, published by Cambridge University Press. Earlier versions of it were presented to workshops at the University of Exeter, Nuffield College, Oxford, and the Massachusetts Institute of Technology. I would like to thank Dario Castiglione, G.A. Cohen, Joshua Cohen, Cecile Fabre, Diana Gardner, David Halpern, Iain Hampsher-Monk, Leah Johnson, Erin Kelly, William Leblanc, David Miller, Alan Patten, Andy Sabel, Marc Stears, Peter Vallentyne, Frank Vandenbroucke, Ramon Vela, Steven Warner, Albert Weale, Ralph Wedgewood, Martin Wilkinson, Andrew Williams and Jonathan Wolff for their questions and comments on this topic. Needless to say, all remaining errors are my own.
2. See G.A. Cohen (1989) 'On the Currency of Egalitarian Justice', *Ethics* 99, 906–44.
3. See John Rawls (1974) 'Some Reasons for the Maximin Criterion', *American Economic Review, Papers and Proceedings* 64, 141–6, p. 145; John Rawls (1974) 'Reply to Alexander and Musgrave', *Quarterly Journal of Economics* 88, 633–55, pp. 654–5; Richard Musgrave (1974) 'Maximin, Uncertainty, and the Leisure Trade-Off', *Quarterly Journal of Economics* 88, 625–32, pp. 630–2; Ronald Dworkin (1981) 'What Is Equality? Part 2: Equality of Resources', *Philosophy and Public Affairs* 10, 283–345, pp. 311–12; Philippe Van Parijs (1995) *Real Freedom for All: What (if*

Anything) Can Justify Capitalism?, pp. 60–5, Oxford: Oxford University Press; and Brian Barry (1996) 'Survey Article: Real Freedom and Basic Income', *Journal of Political Philosophy* 4, 242–76, pp. 270–3. I have benefited from reading a longer version of Brian Barry's 'Real Freedom and Basic Income', a paper presented to a meeting of the London School of Economics Rational Choice Group, 22 November 1995. I shall refer to this paper below as 'Real Freedom and Basic Income B'.

4. What do I mean by saying that these are the maximums which they can *reasonably* be expected to earn? In part, I mean that in calculating their earnings potentials for purpose of specifying their subsidy/tax rate, we should disregard those high-paying jobs which Alf or Betty, given their ability endowments, might be able to get, but which they have an understandable reason of conscience for not wanting to do – for example, being a designer of new weapons systems. I further elaborate the notion of maximum reasonable earnings potential in note 14 below.

5. I am assuming that Alf and Betty can in principle work any length of time between zero hours per year and a full working year (so that their income–leisure schedule is continuous) and that wage rates are constant with length of time worked (so their income–leisure schedules are not kinked or curved).

6. £40,000 is not, of course, the average of £80,000 and £25,000, but we may imagine that there is at least one other person in this society who drags the average down to this level (Chris, let's say, who has a maximum reasonable earnings potential of £15,000).

7. Equivalently, one might express s_i as the difference between the societally average peak-ability wage rate and the individual's peak-ability wage rate, divided by the individual's peak-ability wage rate.

8. A potential problem with ESS that I shall abstract from in this discussion is that it is not necessarily self-financing. Even if we generously assume that everyone works at their peak-ability wage rate (i.e. that there is no underemployment), the sum of total tax liabilities and of subsidy entitlements will equate only if members of the talented and the untalented groups, optimizing against the income–leisure constraint that is now common to them, choose to work a number of hours that cause these two sums to balance out against each other. If they do not, we would have to move the tax/subsidy rates away from their first-best levels as here defined until the scheme came into budgetary balance; and the more we did this, the less attractive the scheme would become as a way of correcting for inequalities in marketable talent.

9. Imagine, for example, that there are two individuals, Dan and Edna. Dan has a much higher earnings potential than Edna, but also suffers from a debilitating physical handicap that limits his mobility. In a laissez-faire world without any tax–benefit system, Dan is to some extent compensated for his handicap by his high earnings potential. If we now introduce ESS without also introducing a scheme of compensation for handicaps, then we may well make Dan even worse off relative to Edna than he was in the laissez-faire world. I thank Peter Vallentyne for this point and for pressing me to clarify the place of ESS in relation to a complete scheme of egalitarian redistribution.

10. One might object that market wage rates are not always an accurate measure of the relative value to the community of labour services. Two things may be said in

response to this objection. First, some activities which we intuitively think are valuable might be better paid, and others which we intuitively regard as less valuable might be less well paid, if the distribution of purchasing power were more equal, as it would be under an ESS. Second, if, with a more egalitarian distribution of purchasing power, we still thought that certain activities were not paid in accordance with our judgement of their value to the community, then we would remain free as a community to supplement ESS with wage subsidies to those jobs we think are underpaid (taxes for those we think are overpaid). For further relevant discussion of the use of wage rates to assess the value to the community of labour services, see David Miller (1996) 'Two Cheers for Meritocracy', *Journal of Political Philosophy* 4, 277–301, especially pp. 284–90, 294–8.

11. See especially Dworkin, 'Equality of Resources', pp. 311–12, and Van Parijs, *Real Freedom for All*, pp. 60–5. I think that the work duration and unpleasant job objections offer the best construction of the 'slavery of the talented' idea, though neither Dworkin nor Van Parijs presents the idea in precisely these terms.

12. Of course, if 'overtime' is possible – working beyond the normal working week here assumed – then Betty is better off than Alf under LSS in the overtime range. The work duration objection to LSS does depend on the assumption that the lump-sum transfers are set to equalize income–leisure outcomes for a full working week where the operative notion of a full working week is itself at or towards the limit of what most citizens regard as acceptable. If the lump-sum transfers were set to equalize income–leisure outcomes for, say, half a full working week, then the objection would have much less force. Betty would be worse off than Alf at achieving income–leisure combinations in the lower half of the work range, but she would be better off than Alf in this respect in the upper half of the work range. Neither would be worse or better off than the other overall, within the range of what is taken to be an acceptable working week. My thanks to Jo Wolff for raising this point.

13. This disadvantage will be offset to the extent that the talented have, on average, better access to satisfying work at or close to their peak-ability wage rate. The objection is also subject to the same caveat as the work duration objection (see note 12).

14. This assumption may well be too strong. Particularly worrying is the possibility that some people may in fact have 'spiky' earnings profiles: these people, *who may be talented or untalented* (i.e. have earnings potential above or below their society's average), can do one job at their peak-ability wage rate and their next highest-paying job is at a wage rate substantially lower than this, say at 50 per cent of their peak-ability wage rate. If these people find their peak-ability jobs very unsatisfying, then, under ESS as we have thus far described it, they will face a very drastic trade-off between income and leisure on the one hand and work satisfaction on the other. To handle this problem, we would almost certainly have to amend our understanding of what constitutes an individual's maximum reasonable earnings potential, disregarding earnings spikes in determining each individual's appropriate rate of earnings subsidy or taxation for ESS (unless and until the individuals in question choose to work at the spikes). Brian Barry considers this problem in relation to LSS in 'Real Freedom and Basic Income B',

Section VIII. I thank Alan Patten for helping me to see how it also applies to ESS in its simplest form.

15. For a rejection of talent-based (lump-sum) tax/subsidy schemes on these grounds, see Barry, 'Real Freedom and Basic Income', pp. 270–3. See also Rawls, 'Reply to Alexander and Musgrave', pp. 654–5.

16. For related, but more developed, ideas, see John Roemer (1994) 'A Pragmatic Theory of Responsibility for the Egalitarian planner', in John Roemer, *Egalitarian Perspectives*, Cambridge: Cambridge University Press, pp. 179–96.

17. See David Miller (1997) 'What Kind of Equality Should the Left Pursue?', in Jane Franklin (ed.) *Equality*, London: Institute for Public Policy Research; and Debra Satz, 'Inequality of What and among Whom?', Paper prepared for delivery at the Annual Meeting of the American Political Science Association, San Francisco, September 1996.

18. See especially R.H. Tawney (1964 [1931]) *Equality*, London: Allen & Unwin.

19. See Aldous Huxley (1932/1994) *Brave New World*, London: HarperCollins.

20. See George Akerlof (1984) 'The Economics of "Tagging" as Applied to the Optimal Income Tax, Welfare Programs, and Manpower Planning', in George Akerlof, *The Economic Theorist's Book of Tales*, Cambridge: Cambridge University Press, pp. 45–68.

21. I owe these responses to Martin Wilkinson.

22. See Bruce Ackerman and Anne Alstott (1999) *The Stakeholder Society*, New Haven, CT: Yale University Press, pp. 155–77.

23. *Ibid.*, p. 160.

24. *Ibid.*, p. 170. Other features of the scheme that I shall set aside here, and which Ackerman and Alstott discuss, include the possibility of varying the rate of privilege tax so that it steadily rises and perhaps then falls with the individual's working age; finding a fair way to treat children of divorced and remarried parents; and finding a fair way to treat a single child versus a child in, say, a five-child family, where the parents in the two families have the same level of income.

25. Ackerman and Alstott's overall proposal would in fact be similar in its effect, given that they wish to combine a differentiated privilege tax with a corresponding cut in social security payroll taxes which fall disproportionately on the low paid (who, of course, tend to be underprivileged in the here relevant sense). Overall, the underprivileged will end up with more money in their pocket relative to the status quo, and the privileged with less.

26. As Ackerman and Alstott put it (*The Stakeholder Society*, note 10, p. 259), 'We are interested in the market advantages that privilege confers but also, more broadly, in its intangible social and psychological advantages.' The importance of market advantages in motivating the proposal is clear from the discussion at pp. 160–1 of how individuals' income attainments are correlated with parental income attainments.

27. See Ackerman and Alstott, *The Stakeholder Society*, p. 165, and note 33, p. 262.

28. *Ibid.*, note 33, p. 262.

29. I should also point out that the childhood privilege tax/subsidy scheme is not purposely designed to redress genetically based inequality in marketable talent as distinct from that which originates from familial/social background. Ackerman and Alstott do not think that genetic differences explain a great deal of inequality

in marketable talent, citing recent research which estimates that only 10–15 per cent of existing earnings inequality can be explained in this way. See Ackerman and Alstott, *The Stakeholder Society*, p. 162.

30. The parallel between the marginal standing of egalitarian thinking in the 1990s and radical free market thinking in the 1950s is also suggested by G.A. Cohen (1997) 'Back to Socialist Basics', in Franklin (ed.) *Equality*, pp. 29–31.

31. See Richard T. Wilkinson (1996) *Unhealthy Societies*, London: Routledge.

CHAPTER FIVE

Social and Cultural Integration in Civil Society [1]

RAINER BAUBÖCK

Civil Society and Its Contrasts

In this chapter I try to sketch a model of civil society that attempts to integrate different approaches and traditions of political thought. Most theories seem to grasp certain important aspects while neglecting others. I want to suggest that civil society can be best understood by specifying what theorists thought that it is not. We arrive at a workable conception of civil society by combining its negative contrasts. These are: barbarian societies, the state of nature, the family, the market economy, and the state.

Everybody agrees today that there is a boundary that separates civil society from the state. [2] What theorists today disagree about is whether civil society includes the institutions of the family and of the private enterprise. For example, Jean Cohen and Andrew Arato's influential account includes the private world of the family in the realm of civil society, while Ernest Gellner suggests that kinship is a principle of social organization just as opposed to that of civil society as state coercion. [3] I think Gellner is right on this point. Conversely, coming from a tradition of critical theory, Arato and Cohen are more sensitive to the necessity of maintaining a boundary between civil society and a capitalist economy, while Gellner emphasizes the contribution of economic growth to the spread of civil society in the Western world. It seems to be perfectly possible to combine these contrasts. Yet there are very few attempts at defining civil society that do this. [4]

The ancient contrast of civilization with barbarian societies and the Hobbesian contrast with the anarchical state of nature can be taken into account by internalizing both into a model of civil society. Civil society requires a common and shared public culture and a generalized practice of virtues of civility – that is, a willingness to use arguments and to listen to them in the pursuit of one's interests and to refrain from coercion. [5] A breakdown of 'civilization' occurs when citizens no longer speak a common language and share a common understanding of the rules of the game. A breakdown of civility occurs when violence becomes endemic in society or when people are ready to submit to illegitimate political authority. Even highly developed societies may relapse into a 'state of nature' if people no longer expect that their most fundamental interests and needs will be protected by the state. States of nature may develop on a micro scale in pockets of poverty and destitution such as in some of the urban 'ghettos' of Western societies, or on a macro scale when ethnic membership overrides common citizenship, as in the break-up of Yugoslavia.[6] While these contrasts are *alternatives* to civil society, the state, the market economy and the family provide contrasting *institutions* whose separation from each other creates a social sphere for civil society. Civil society can thus be understood as a precarious balance between these three institutions.

This suggests a triangular model of civil society in which the institutional ensembles of state, market and family form the corners.[7] A triangle opens a two-dimensional space and we can then understand civil society as the social sphere that emerges from a functional differentiation between the state, the market and the family. The greater the distance and the clearer the boundaries between the three institutional corners, the larger the area within which civil society can flourish. We may now distinguish between civil society in a wider sense as the total institutional ensemble in which state, market and family are kept in balance, and civil society in a narrower sense as the intermediate sphere different from all three institutional cornerstones of modern society.

There is one immediate objection which may be raised against this scheme. How can we assign equal weight to three institutions which are so different in nature? In some contexts the state may be seen as an actor, whereas markets are not actors but fields of interaction. Should we not therefore replace the term 'market' with enterprise? Both the family and the state are in certain respects collective social units and agents, but the scope of action of the state spans the whole society, while families are micro-collectives within societies. In order to avoid such confusion, it is important to insist that the model focuses on institutions, not organizations or agents. A social institution is a set of sedimented norms and rules for interaction. Institutions reproduce themselves by structuring social interaction according to their own rules. These rules are generally accepted as given by agents and shape their expectations. Institutions can thus appear to have a life and mind of their own.[8] They aim at a *longue durée* of self-perpetuation independently of the individuals and collectives that participate in them.[9] State, market and family are used as shorthand terms for such rules that structure social interaction and relations.

This raises the further question of where individuals fit into this model. Should we conceive of civil society from the perspective of methodological individualism as a social structure that must be ultimately reducible to individual actions and choices? Or should we alternatively think of it in the sociological tradition ranging from Durkheim to Luhmann's system theory that sees individuals and social phenomena as different kinds of reality so that individuals ultimately form only an external environment for the autopoietic operations of social systems? I would like to take no firm stance on either side. I think that social theory becomes richer if it allows us to focus on how institutions shape the interactions of individuals and are in turn reproduced by rule-conforming individual behaviour. In a differentiated society, institutions are highly specialized. Their rules correspond with certain roles that they attribute to individuals. Specialized institutions are blind to the total complexity of individuals; they perceive them only as agents in those roles which fit into the pattern of their rules. Institutions thus produce their own internal descriptions of what individuals are *for them*.

A democratic state perceives individuals primarily as citizens. The citizen role defines what all individuals can expect from the state and vice versa. There are of course other and more specialized roles such as those for professional politicians, civil servants, lawyers and judges, etc. But citizenship is the basic relation of membership that connects individuals to states, and structures their interactions by generalized legal rights and obligations.

In the economy, individuals encounter each other as bearers of preferences and needs for goods and services that are provided by others. A market mediates transactions between them by payments. The basic role of market participants is that of owners of money or of marketable goods, services and capacities. In contrast with the realm of the state, where the equality of citizen is also a substantial one, markets divide rather than homogenize individual roles into those of consumers, employers, owners of capital assets, workers, etc.

The family is the core institution in the modern sphere of intimacy. In contrast with the formalized interactions in the realm of the state and the market, where roles are to a considerable degree anonymous, as a family member the individual is a singular and non-exchangeable person. Relations are normally structured by face-to-face communication. The basic role of the private person is less abstract and formal than that of economic agents; it creates a sphere of exclusive interaction from which others may be shut out and it carries expectations of solidarity and generalized reciprocity among members. At the same time, the roles of family members are less equal than those of citizens; they are highly differentiated according to age, gender and degrees of kinship. There is an alternative way of labelling this corner of the triangle: instead of family we may also use the term 'private household'. This would put stronger emphasis on the exclusive nature of the sphere of privacy and would make clear that individuals with no relatives who live in single-member households still have a firm institutional location in this sphere (whereas the inmates of 'total institutions' such as prisons, military barracks or psychiatric hospitals are deprived of a place in society where they are respected as private persons). The family provides a model for wider communities of an ethnic type where membership is derived from (imagined) common descent, while the household is a model for regional communities that share a territory and its resources.

In many respects, social control is more pervasive in modern society than in pre-modern ones. The libertarian idea of autonomy as the minimization of social constraints on individual choices might have been adequate for the lonely pioneers at the American western frontier but certainly not for modern urbanized society. Our analysis of civil society as a balance between the three core institutions suggests a more sober view of the social bases of autonomy in modern society. It implies that none of their roles completely dominates the lives of individuals. One of the essential virtues of civil society is that it prevents the total subordination of individuals to the imperatives of a single type of institution. As each institution tends to recognize individuals only in their corresponding roles, encroachment on the sphere of influence of other institutions simultaneously diminishes individual autonomy. In civil society, individuals can switch between different roles and none of these roles defines them completely. The combination of their roles as citizens, economic agents and members of families and households increases opportunities for individuals and thus creates preconditions for 'positive liberty'. The boundaries between corresponding institutions maintain 'negative liberty' by protecting individuals from being fully exposed to a single set of rules that governs their prospects in life. This is true for all three kinds of institutions. Although individuals are recognized in their *singularity* in the sphere of informal and intimate relations, they are at the same time deprived of important public aspects of their identity. Thus, women who are reduced to their role as housewives are deprived of social recognition by fellow citizens and fellow employees.

The usual way to illustrate the idea of institutional differentiation is to characterize the internal modes of operation or the specific outputs of each institution or subsystem.[10] However, if we are interested in the balanced ensemble of institutions that can be characterized as civil society, we have to look at the boundaries that characterize social interactions as falling within a certain social sphere. The labels which I have chosen for these boundary distinctions can be explained as follows.

The distinction of political versus economic is straightforward. Interactions are political when they have to do with deliberation, decision-making or implementation of collectively binding decisions and economic when they allocate scarce goods or services between independent agents by means of exchange. The distinction between public and private that separates the state from the family has at least two different connotations. Public is, on the one hand, what is related to the public interest and the common good of a society, and, on the other hand, what takes place or is represented in a public space. This can be the physical space of a street or the virtual space of mass media and telecommunications. Conversely, interactions are private when they can be withdrawn from the public sphere. Private goods are withdrawn from public use, and private matters are those about which information need not be made public. The distinction between open and closed interaction that distinguishes the sphere of the family from that of the economy might seem even more confusing. By closed interactions I mean those which depend upon shared membership in a community. Open interaction occurs where the distinction between members and non-members is irrelevant and the rules are tailored for the interaction of anonymous individuals.

Figure 5.1 visualizes the conceptual distinctions introduced so far and illustrates a further interesting point that emerges from the triangular structure. It raises the question of how the opposite corner should be characterized from the perspective of each binary distinction. Is the family a political or an economic institution? Are market transactions private or public? Should the state be seen as a closed or an open sphere of interaction? The diagram deliberately suggests ambiguous answers to all these questions.

Families and households are basic units of consumption and production (mainly of labour power) for the economy, and much internal interaction within the family is geared to the external performance of its members in

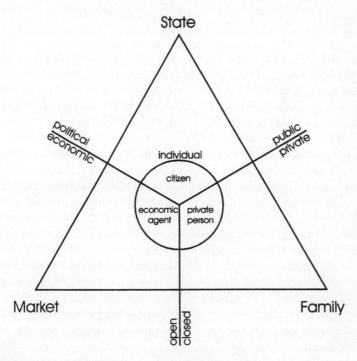

Figure 5.1 The Civil Society Triangle: Boundaries of Spheres and Roles of Individuals

markets. Family households have also been the basic units of the political system. Active citizenship was until not so long ago a privilege for male heads of households. Legal equality of genders has contributed to individualizing citizenship but the membership of minor children in the polity is still mediated by the family; their passive citizenship rights are largely exercised by parents on their behalf.

Markets are public spaces where private preferences are co-ordinated by exchanging private goods. Elsewhere I have suggested a more general distinction that explains the different nature of privacy in markets and in the family. Any kind of privacy is grounded in what is commonly called negative liberties. Yet such liberties can be conceived as the answer to two different questions. First, which of the actions and choices of others that affect me can I control because I am entitled to interfere with them? Second, which of my own actions and choices do I control because others are not permitted to interfere with them? The answer to the former question constitutes the realm of privacy in the household as a sphere of exclusive control from which others may be legitimately excluded. Market liberty is an answer to the second question; it establishes a sphere of non-interference where individuals are protected in their private property rights but interact in a public sphere from which no one who legally owns marketable goods, skills or money is excluded.[11]

Finally, modern democratic states are simultaneously open and closed institutions. The rule of law in constitutional democracy establishes an open structure for interactions. In contrast with the equality of siblings or spouses in the family, the equality of citizens is grounded in their anonymity before the law, which treats them as equals without regard for the person. In liberal states, citizens are tied to each other not by imagined bonds of common descent or of friendship (Aristotle's *philia*), but by sharing the same rights and a common dependency on protection by the law. Yet as democracies, liberal states are also inevitably closed. Any system of democratic decision-making has to distinguish between members and non-members. Although liberalism may overcome most internal exclusions from membership (based on gender, class, race, age and foreign origin or descent), it cannot fully overcome the external boundaries that separate permanent residents of countries from each other as members of different polities.

I have explained above that the differentiation between the roles of citizen, economic agent and private person provides opportunities for the articulation of individual autonomy. I now want to show that the partially overlapping boundaries provide a structure within which the second liberal core value of individual equality can be reasserted. Democratic and liberal theory has been haunted by the problem of how to reconcile an internal differentiation of society, which increases opportunities and thus autonomy exercised in individual choices, with the idea of moral equality of persons and of equal status of citizens in a political community. I contend that there are three different types of solution. Equality seems to have been greatest in segmentary societies where at the same time individual autonomy was virtually non-existent. The differentiation of social spheres, which is irreversibly connected with the emergence of urban civilizations, can be achieved in three different ways: by a corresponding separation of human populations, of the individual self, or of institutional spheres of interaction. The first of these solutions is best exemplified by the model of ancient democracy. Citizens could be free and equal in the republic only because the life-sustaining economic and domestic activities were carried out by slaves, women and *metics* who remained excluded from the polis. The second solution is a Rousseauian one which splits the individual into a private person and a public citizen. It avoids the hierarchical structure of the former only by projecting a similar hierarchy into the self: individuals have higher interests as citizens which check on their lower desires as members of families or economic agents.[12] A modern liberal solution implies no such hierarchy but simply a difference in the rules of interaction. The notion that individuals are equal in their moral capacities and as members of society gains in plausibility if everyone has a recognized place in each social sphere and no one is confined in his or her activities to one single sphere. The partially overlapping boundaries between spheres furthermore avoid the schizophrenic solution of dividing the individual – that is, the indivisible – into incommensurate selves.

Thus, for example, the intimate world of the family is not public and it is not open, but interactions between persons in this world not only are coded as intimate but also are structured politically and economically. As citizens, persons are bearers of rights towards the state, but also towards each other. Violations of these rights (e.g. by acts of violence against women and children) will open the sphere of the family to the legitimate intervention of the state. Similarly, relations within the family are economic. The internal division of labour in domestic work and child-rearing is connected to economic activities outside the household. Economic dependency of wives on husbands reflects and reproduces their unequal positions in gendered labour markets. The feminist critique of liberalism is therefore correct when it points out that the structure of contemporary liberal democracies is still in many ways based on Greek and Rousseauian solutions. Women and men do not have equal access to, and positions in, all three core institutions of modern society; and predominantly male activities in markets and in politics are perceived as socially more rewarding than raising a child or caring for elderly parents. However, the critique goes wrong when it asserts that the problem results from the very existence of boundaries and differentiated spheres.[13] The distinction between public and private has been historically associated with gender discrimination, but the only strategic perspective for female emancipation within modern society is to redefine this boundary so that the social construction of gender difference is no longer associated with this distinction. My contention is that the boundary is an essential precondition for individual autonomy in modern society and that it is indeed possible to modify it so that it no longer perpetuates gender inequality.

As this discussion has shown, the idea of civil society as a balance and boundary maintenance between the three core institutions is obviously not simply a descriptive, but also a normative one. It attributes positive value to functional differentiation while at the same time emphasizing that it is not guaranteed by the process of modernization but has to be constantly striven for and readjusted. There is a parallel with Michael Walzer's theory of justice as boundary maintenance between the distributive spheres of social goods.[14] However, in his book *Spheres of Justice,* Walzer does not give us a picture of a differentiated structure of modern society. He presents an open-ended list of goods with certain distributive properties. Society is in the last instance a community of shared meanings and moral values. It is differentiated only with respect to the plurality of goods and distributive norms, but still appears as a single community, where membership is the one overriding good for everybody.[15] My approach also differs from overly moralistic analyses of civil society which incorporate all its desirable virtues into its very definition. Larry Diamond suggests that organizations in civil society are concerned with public rather than private ends and, furthermore, do not act from a desire to capture state power, but from a concern for the public good.[16] This excludes not only the family and the firm from civil society, but also political parties in a competitive democratic system. Describing civil society in terms of the motivations of actors makes its scope not only exceedingly narrow but deprives the concept of most of its explanatory value. In my view, civil society is neither, as Diamond seems to suggest, a realm of Rousseauian political virtues, nor, as Gellner insists, an amoral social order where the pursuit of private interests creates public benefits.[17] What we should strive for is a description of civil society as a social *structure* which establishes *constraints* on the pursuit of private interests and provides *incentives* for individual and collective agents to develop habits of civility.

A normative implication of our image of civil society is that the unfettered dominance of one type of institution over another is a reason for critique and a likely cause of degeneration. This can be grounded in a liberal ethical theory which values equality and autonomy. A well-balanced structure of civil society is that institutional arrangement within modernity which increases the scope for individual autonomy for all members. It combines equal and substantial citizenship with voluntary transactions in markets that allow the realization of different individual preferences and with a sheltered sphere of privacy in which individuals are involved in intimate relations and chosen communities.

The neoliberal version of a capitalist market economy, which attacks the responsibility of government for social welfare, is a threat not just to the poor and unemployed, but to civil society in a much wider sense. Margaret Thatcher's famous remark that 'there is no such thing as society, there are only individuals and families' reflects this type of imbalance. The underlying idea is that the task of politics should not be the pursuit of the common good of society but merely the maintenance of order. The neoliberal ideology promotes an encroachment of the economy on the sphere of politics by claiming that markets can provide the best solutions for the provision of genuine public goods.

Neorepublican ideologies in the tradition of Rousseau attack civil society from the opposite side. They complain that economic and political liberalism has led to a proliferation of individual rights at the expense of duties towards the political community. Citizenship should be understood as an obligation,[18] or an office.[19] Some communitarian authors such as Alasdair MacIntyre lament the loss of an Aristotelian conception of public virtues which are shared and mutually affirmed within the political community.[20] Republican ideas of this sort may be either conservative or socialist in their tendency. Conservatives, for example, emphasize the obligations of recipients of public welfare benefits (such as workfare schemes for the unemployed) whereas left-wing republicans stress the obligations of political participation and advocate schemes of direct democracy.

Marxist theory and Soviet communism were a peculiar kind of alternative to civil society. On the one hand, they destroyed the autonomy of the market sphere by subjecting the economy completely to political decision-making. On the other hand, politics was seen as a mere element of the superstructure, which is largely determined by economic class interests. The socialist state was therefore not an institution where radical democratic experiments such as workers' councils could flourish. It was driven by the economic imperatives of industralization and administering a planned economy. In order to achieve this goal, the state was reduced to its coercive functions and all independent bases of civil society were destroyed.

The idea that the economy should not dominate political life and vice versa is quite common. However, is there also a danger emerging from the sphere of the family? Intuitively, one might think of phenomena such as nepotism, hereditary public office, or the rule of family clans, which are not commonly regarded as a threat in contemporary Western societies. Yet the more imminent danger lies in the symbolic transformation of the polity by ethnic nationalism or racist discrimination into an imagined family. The rules of communal closure of interaction which characterize the sphere of kinship and intimacy can infect political as well as economic life. In politics, this leads to the identification of the nation with a community of descent, or of culture transmitted only by descent and inaccessible to minorities and immigrants of different ethnic origins. In the economic sphere, ethnic and racial discrimination may exclude certain populations from access to higher education and from the more attractive segments of labour and housing markets. Where discrimination of this sort is pervasive, markets are usually not at all colour-blind but reinforce collective stigma by indirect mechanisms of segregation.

Civil Society as Associational Pluralism

So far I have elaborated only the wider concept of civil society, which emphasizes the necessary balance and boundaries between the institutions of the state, of markets and of the family. Figure 5.2 permits a second interpretation of civil society which is premised upon the first: civil society can be identified with the inner area of the triangle. This area grows with increasing the length of the sides (which operationalizes distance and boundary maintenance between institutions) and is maximized for a given perimeter when all sides are of equal length (which operationalizes balance). This second interpretation follows naturally from the idea that state, market and family are not institutions within civil society but mark its boundaries.

The inner area of the triangle can be understood as an energy field structured by magnetic forces emanating from the three poles. The orientation of a compass needle placed in this field is determined by its location and by the power of attraction of each pole. Similarly, the position of institutions of civil society determines their internal goals and rules. Figure 5.2 illustrates this idea:

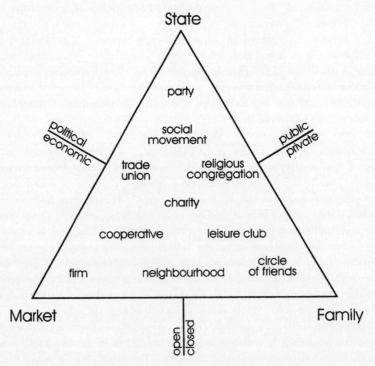

Figure 5.2 The Civil Society Triangle: Location of Associations

(a) The closer an institution comes to one of the corners, the stronger will be the impact of institutional rules and norms which are characteristic for that corner (political parties, firms, circles of friendship).

(b) Institutions which are located near the perimeter but at roughly equal distance from two corners will be under conflicting pressures (trade unions, religious congregations, neighbourhood communities). Their role in society is always open to challenge and may be affected by any minor redrawing of boundaries.

(c) The closer institutions are to the centre of the triangle, the greater their autonomy. Autonomy here refers to the opportunities of members to define for themselves the relevant goals and internal rules of their association (social movements, leisure clubs, co-operatives, charitable associations).

Associations in civil society do not just fill a social vacuum opened by functional differentiation between state, market and family. They mediate between individuals and these institutions in a dual sense of the word: by connecting them and by coming between them. Thus, circles of friends and clubs provide social milieux for 'marriage markets'. Social movements and, to a lesser extent, political parties enable citizens to become active in politics apart from their mere passive representation in parliament. Regular employment gives individuals access to consumer markets by providing them with income, and often also creates networks for new recruitment in the labour market (for family members or friends). Apart from these connecting functions, civil society associations also create a distance between individuals and the core institutions of modern society. In addition to the opportunities for switching between the roles of citizen, economic agent and family member, civil society also provides individuals with alternative and less demanding roles. Its associations and organizations offer some respite from the strains to which individuals are subjected in a competitive economy, a state regulating ever more aspects of social life and the burdens of family responsibilities. Companies that offer regular and long-term employment with some protection against lay-offs shelter wage earners from continuous exposure to the pressures of the labour market. For a broad middle class of employees, the workplace is also a social environment where they can gain recognition and make friends. Social movements and party organizations often create similar sheltered milieux where *group* representation relieves citizens from the difficult task of becoming politically active as *individuals*. Finally, leisure is not confined to family activities but can be spent in circles of friends or private associations.

I have so far refrained from giving any positive definition of civil society and have suggested that instead we explore what it is not. But once we have defined its external limits, we can see that there is indeed a specific principle which characterizes institutions within civil society and becomes stronger as we move towards the centre of the triangle. This principle is what Tocqueville called 'the art of association'. Civil society consists of a plurality of voluntary associations. That explains its attraction for normative liberal thought:

> The civil society, the liberals' greatest invention and deeply cherished by them, is the realm of interest and choice *par excellence*. It stands for the totality of relationships voluntarily entered into by self-determining individuals in the pursuit of their self-chosen goals.[21]

As Parekh points out, this separates civil society from the state, which is coercive because it monopolizes legitimate violence and is compulsory because membership is acquired at birth.

However, the separation is not perfect. Voluntary association can be fully realized only in civil society, but the idea also spills over into the realms of state, family and market. We can now understand that classical social contract theory was an attempt to ground the state's coercive and compulsory power in a principle that is more germane to civil society. Contractarian theorists thought that political authority is legitimate only if the state can be conceived of as a voluntary association of its citizens. A similar argument can be made about the family. While for Locke it was still quite obvious that, unlike the state, the family cannot be conceptualized as a voluntary association, this has become challenged in later liberal thought. Children cannot choose their own parents, but sexual partnership among adults is today seen as a matter of voluntary association between autonomous individuals.

A market economy is that set of institutions where the principle of voluntary association seems to apply to the fullest extent, and this explains why so many theorists have seen the market as the very core of civil society. However, the mere transaction of money, goods and services creates no association, but only ephemeral social ties. The principle might, then, be applied to the firm as an organization which operates in market environments. Wage labour is based on voluntary contract, but still it seems improper to call the privately owned enterprise a voluntary association. Workers may have few options but to sell their labour; they may be subjected to considerable coercion within the ongoing labour contract; and their 'membership' is disconnected from ownership rights. The model of voluntary association thus applies better to shareholders than to wage labourers. For the same reason, consumer or producer co-operatives come much closer to the core principle of civil society. In private firms, co-determination, workplace democracy, autonomous production units and similar models import organizational principles of civil society into the firm. Of course, they are introduced only if they also contribute to the economic targets of the enterprise by increasing labour productivity or helping to avoid disruptive union struggles. However, the very fact that such organizational techniques prove to be efficient in many cases shows a certain strength of civil society and demonstrates the mediating role of enterprises between civil society and the market.

We may thus conclude that civil society is, after all, not just the social space left unoccupied by states, families and markets. Voluntary association as the internal principle of civil society also becomes relevant for all three core institutions of modern society, although it is severely constrained by their respective tasks of allocating private goods, of enforcing collective decisions among territorial populations and of primary socialization and stabilizing intimate relationships. There is thus no binary distinction which separates civil society from these institutions in the same way as they are separated from one another. This is why there is also no substantive distinction between the wider and the narrow model of civil society.

What are the basic features of voluntary associations within the inner core of civil society? The minimum criteria for voluntariness in associations refer to entry and exit. Membership is acquired voluntarily – that is, neither by birth, nor automatically, nor under coercion – and members can leave the association freely. More far-reaching interpretations also involve some degree of internal democracy – that is, an equal voice for individual members in collective decision-making. Institutions located closer to the corners deviate from this ideal type of voluntary association in various ways, and especially so with regard to the criterion of internal democracy, which is frequently overridden by the functional imperatives that market, state or family establish for their performance.

A second important characteristic of civil society institutions is what we may call associational pluralism. None of the associations enjoys a monopoly in its field of activity.[22] There are always several associations which pursue similar targets and offer similar goods and services. Individuals may therefore choose among different associations. This is also a precondition of voluntary entry and exit.

Finally, associations in civil society generally lack the means of coercion or the capacity to dominate the life prospects of their members. As mentioned above, this contrasts with the rigid role requirements and the power of coercion exercised by the state, the family and in employment. Voluntary associations may be seen as a training-ground for citizens where they learn the virtues of civility.[23] Yet this is not due to some inherent characteristic derived from the collective goals of voluntary associations. What teaches people to resort to argument in trying to gain or retain fellow members for an association is the lack of coercive power over individuals and the lack of total dependency on the part of individuals. A further important implication of this is that individuals may simultaneously be members in many different associations. As Larry Diamond points out, multiple memberships in civil society enhance cohesion at the societal level because they may bridge cleavages of class, region, religion, ethnicity or political ideology.[24] Civil society is not plural in the sense of Furnivall's and M.G. Smith's analysis of colonial societies, with their rigid separation of ethnic communities forming a political hierarchy and interacting only in the marketplace.[25] Voluntary associations create a network in which individuals are nodes with multiple and optional connections between each other. This network of voluntary associations creates an open structure, overlying the patchwork of ascriptive communities.

It would be naive to deny that institutions of civil society can themselves become coercive. If they do, they normally imitate the models provided by the state or the family. There are religious sects that are more closed than families and political movements that organize themselves like armies. Agnes Heller and Ferenc Fehér have raised the even more troubling concern about micro-totalitarianism, which they find in 'biopolitical movements' and the censorship of free thought and speech by 'political correctness'.[26] However, as long as such movements have no other means at their disposal than public argument and symbolic action, they expose themselves to critique. Micro-totalitarianism presents a real danger when it is able to instrumentalize the state for its purposes (as McCarthyism did in the 1950s) or when it goes underground (as do radical political groups when they resort to terrorism). When it manifests itself within an open and well-balanced civil society, there is reasonable hope that it may be overcome.

In this way, the associational pluralism of civil society can be defended from a normative point of view as a social environment which promotes the flourishing of individual autonomy within the constraints set by the conditions of modernity.

Cultural Dynamics in Civil Society

Where does culture fit into this dual model of civil society? I will not add another attempt to the endless list of definitions of the term 'culture'. For our present purposes it is sufficient to understand that culture refers, on the one hand, to complex systems of symbols and ideas that human beings use in their communication and, on the other hand, to comprehensive ways of life or to societal communities whose members share a system of symbols and ideas. In a shorthand manner we may speak about culture as language and culture as community. Culture in the first sense connects individuals and groups in an open structure of communication. Because they belong to a single species, human beings can be (re)socialized in any language and any system of values. Culture in this sense is therefore unbounded within the human world and separates it only from other animals. Culture in the second sense, however, distinguishes individuals within human society by providing markers according to which they can be grouped into different categories. Cultural markers define boundaries of communities, such as ethnic identity, as well as internal status and tasks within each collective, such as gender roles. Some markers refer to features of the body, such as sex, race and age, but culture also produces its own markers, such as language, religion or ethnic tradition and origin.

Cultural anthropologists tend to look at societies as communities of different culture. However, there are alternative approaches in cultural anthropology which show that the boundaries between ethnic communities are not simply given by a threshold of cultural differences at which communication breaks down. Ethnic groups maintain their collective identities not in splendid isolation, but through the construction of boundaries that structure interaction and exchange between them.[27] In modernity, the identification of societies with homogeneous cultural communities has simultaneously become analytically obsolete and politically pervasive. Modern industrial societies can no longer be characterized and distinguished from each other as comprehensive ways of life. They are split into an endless variety of overlapping local, generational, class and professional milieux. None of these are self-sustaining cultural communities: they are all embedded in larger national or international cultural circles. On the other hand, there is a strong sense of community attached to certain religious and ethnic minority cultures, but these rarely coincide with societal boundaries marked by state borders and citizenship. I doubt whether any theory can give a coherent account of these confusing multi-layered and intersecting patterns of cultural community in modern societies. It might still be useful to consider whether the core institutions of civil society (in the wider sense of the term) create their own cultural dynamics of diversification or homogenization.

I want to propose the following hypotheses:

1 Modern states strive towards homogenization of populations with regard to standardized national cultures.
2 Contemporary market economy creates volatile and highly diversified patterns of consumer culture, which reach beyond national boundaries and may extend to global dimensions.
3 Family socialization reproduces or blends the more stable intergenerational cultural milieux or ethnic communities below the level of autonomous national minorities or sovereign states. Thus, each of the three core institutions has its peculiar dynamic (of homogenization or diversification) and its maximum range (global, national or subnational) within which this dynamic operates.
4 A weak civil society may lack any specific cultural dynamic of its own and simply reflect in its various associations the different tendencies emerging from markets, state and family networks. However, civil society may also become the sphere of an ongoing cultural discourse which is able to integrate all the different types of communities and cultural codes of communication.

National Homogenization of Culture

Gellner's theory of nationalism gives a convincing account of the fundamental difference between premodern and national culture.[28] In complex agrarian society, cultural difference between regions, religious groups and estates is a stabilizing element for political rule and is fully compatible with the organization of the economy. The societal structure thus provides incentives for the proliferation of cultural distinctions. Modern industrial economy rests on a completely different division of labour. It requires people who share a common basic education and are able to communicate with anonymous others about complex matters such as the technical details of a manufacturing process. Rather than being rigidly fixed in village traditions, modern men and women have to become mobile. The larger cultural space of the nation replaces for them the small-scale rural community as a place where they belong and are seen as belonging. However, neither the family nor the economic organization of capitalism is able to provide the cultural socialization required for an industrial economy. Wage labour needs some basic qualification before it enters the market. This task has to be left to the modern nation-state, which establishes a system of public education. The state is not just a *deus ex machina* providing the solution required by the market. States have their own agenda of internal and external maintenance of power which pushes them towards creating nations by cultural homogenization of the mass of population.[29] An historical explanation of how this miraculous convergence between cultural needs of states and markets came about should include the following elements. First, the internal victory of absolutism over the landed aristocracy was achieved by the centralization of administration throughout the territory. Second, some national languages were first standardized for the internal communication of the civil service. Third, since the French Revolution and the Empire of Napoleon I, armies of citizens have proved to be vastly superior in external conflicts with rival powers. The state, which had been a very remote presence in the lives of the rural mass of population, broke up the culturally and economically self-sustaining communities by its administration, its army and its schools.

Nonetheless, there are limits to the cultural homogenization of society. Modern nation-states have to be built from the territorial and cultural resources provided by premodern societies.[30] These are extremely heterogeneous, and different in different regions of the world. In the New World, states were built from scratch by massacring or colonizing local populations, and the dominant culture was simply transplanted in the same process. In some cases, territories had already been unified by absolutism and there was a long high cultural tradition ready to be transformed into a modern national culture (France may be the best example, but Japan could equally be mentioned). In other instances, the high culture was there, but the territory

106

still had to be politically united (German unification and Italian *Risorgimento*). Finally, in most parts of the world, states and national cultures had to be constructed simultaneously from a patchwork of territorially interlocked cultural and ethnic groups.[31] Once nation-building had been shown to be extremely successful on both shores of the North Atlantic, it became a universal model which could be adopted both by internal ethnic minorities and by colonized peoples in their struggles against oppression.[32] The outcome of the national transformation of modernity is therefore full of ambiguities.

On the global level, the former structure of empires and colonies has been replaced by the international system of independent nation-states. However, relations of dependency have thereby hardly diminished and, as the current proliferation of new and ever smaller states shows, this dynamic does not converge towards a stable equilibrium. On the state level, most states have remained *de facto* multicultural or multiethnic. There is hardly any state which satisfies the nationalist imperative of internal cultural homogeneity. (Iceland is sometimes quoted as an exception.) Even ethnic groups which were not strong enough to form independent states have often proved to be remarkably resistant to assimilation into the dominant culture. The reason for this is not the survival of pockets of pre-modernity but, on the contrary, the pervasive modernization of ethnicity in the framework provided by the nation-state. For groups with sufficient territorial concentration, struggling for some kind of autonomy within a given state is mostly much more attractive than surrendering to an arrogant national majority who will always treat them as second-class citizens. Yet in order to mobilize for this struggle and then also to administer partial autonomy, the ethnic group has to transform itself into a pseudo-nation. It needs its own intelligentsia, its own dictionaries and schools; it has to appoint its own representatives and to modernize the regional economy. This strategy of modernization has mostly worked quite well in cases of territorial linguistic minorities such as the Québecois or the Cataláns. It may, however, present a deadly dilemma for indigenous minorities, whose traditional forms of life may be destroyed by such modernization, which is at the same time their only chance of gaining recognition and protection as minorities.

Diversification and Globalization of Consumer Culture

Nationalism and the industrial revolution were at their origins closely related to each other. Nascent capitalist economies required not only secondary socialization of the mass of population in a standardized cultural idiom but also the external protection of national markets against powerful and more advanced rivals. But during more recent stages of modernity it has become ever more obvious that the cultural dynamic of markets is not bounded in the same way as that of states. Markets are parasitic on states and families with regard to the types of cultural communities that may emerge from them and with regard to the cultural material which they circulate,[33] but they can relate communities to each other and distribute this material within a much wider and potentially global range. I will briefly illustrate these two points.

Capitalist markets are disembedded (in Karl Polanyi's terminology). They require a structure of communication that is *open in social space* with regard to potential partners of interaction but *not open-ended in social time* with regard to the sort of ties they promote between individuals. Market interactions generate social bonds only as long as contractual obligations have not been fulfilled; they do not create transgenerational communities.

Participants in market transactions are disunited as competing producers and sellers, but are in a way united as consumers. Goods offered in markets are also cultural signifiers, and all those who buy and consume the same type of merchandise or services thereby share a certain culture. They appear as similar to each other if consumption takes place in a public space or if private consumption is no longer excluded from the eyes of the public. However, they need not interact with each other in private consumption and they do not participate actively in a culture by recombining or modifying its inventory of symbols. Their participation is only via the market mechanism that adapts supply to individual preferences as long as these translate into demand backed by purchasing power.

The shaping of such preferences is, however, obviously not independent of supply. Markets do not necessarily homogenize preferences. The common idea that commodity production necessarily standardizes cultural attributes and tastes is a misperception dating from what has been called the Fordist era of twentieth-century capitalism. The lowering of costs of production by standardization of products is not an inherent tendency of markets but only of a specific type of economic regime. Today, diversification of products and targeting of certain groups of consumers gives companies a competitive edge in many branches of the economy. In this sense, global market economies do not necessarily promote a global mass culture. However, they generate a non-participatory and consumerist type of culture which does not use cultural signifiers so as to exclude certain groups from consumption but instead combines them into newly synthesized styles that appeal to specific groups of consumers. World music may serve as an example. It uses different ethnic styles eclectically as an ingredient for a kind of music very far removed from its ethnic origins. Furthermore, the ethnic elements are not used to appeal to members from the respective groups but are meant to attract consumers anywhere else in the world.

International consumer markets produce mass culture not in the sense of inevitable standardization, but in the sense of increasing detachment of consumers from cultural communities where some participatory interaction between cultural producers and audiences is essential. However, the separation is not perfect. Just as consumer cultures are parasitic on ethnic and national ones, we may also say that certain communities, which are not constituted via market interaction, use commodities in order to identify their membership. Urban youth culture is the most obvious example. It is not buying sports shoes of the same make which brings together certain youths; rather, the brand serves them as a marker by which they can symbolize a particular lifestyle, recognize those who share it and distinguish themselves from rival peer-groups.

State-sponsored national culture and market-sponsored consumer culture are thus quite different in their structure and dynamics. The task of the former is to educate not consumers but producers and citizens. This requires considerable efforts from those who undergo cultural training in the institutions of basic or higher education and therefore makes for a much more participatory type of cultural community. National culture is also a kind of mass culture. Yet it is neither high in the sense of being accessible only to an elite, nor is it low in the sense of appealing only to a mass of consumers. Like consumer culture, it is also parasitic on other forms: it processes the traditions both of artistic high culture and of popular ethnic culture as raw materials from which to form a national language and an inventory of symbols and myths that can be used as markers of national identity.

National culture is essentially more exclusive than consumer culture. Communities which share a common language or history are not inherently inaccessible to outsiders. Languages can be learnt and histories can be enriched with those of minorities or newcomers. It is the exclusionary nature of the state that makes exclusive the culture which it transmits. In modern industrial society, a national culture becomes the most precious of all public goods provided by the state to its citizens, and it is jealously guarded by the intellectuals to whom its maintenance is entrusted. Language and history, though not in themselves exclusive, are used as markers in order to stake and to refute claims to the resources of state power necessary for cultural reproduction. It is therefore essential for national culture to provide markers which allow members and non-members to be distinguished. When a process of assimilation leads to a point where language, history or lifestyles fail to do so, religion or skin colour may well be used as relevant markers, and nationalism then becomes racist.

Family and the Reproduction of Cultural Milieux

The role of families in the transmission and reproduction of culture is different from both that of states and that of markets. The old controversy between primordial and situational or instrumental theories of ethnicity[34] appears greatly exaggerated once we consider this institutional specialization. Parents are the agents of primary socialization of children. Whatever can be regarded as primordial about cultural identities is created by the family and the family only. The first language we learn, the first customs we habitually accept without reflection, the first ideas about those with whom we share a common way of life – all this is not just learnt in the family but becomes part of our character and defines the kinds of person we are. Later in their lives, some people make choices or are compelled to adapt to cultural styles that diverge sharply from this original impregnation. However, after a certain age, such changes rarely undo the cultural programs of primary socialization. Entering a new consumer culture requires only a minimum of adaptation. Assimilating into a national culture, for example by adopting a new language for everyday communication, is more difficult, and involves intensive education and also some kind of retraining with regard to one's secondary socialization. But it can be done, provided there are sufficient facilities and incentives. Whether or not assimilation into a national culture is possible is, first of all, a matter of how open or closed it is towards outsiders. Primordial cultural impregnation does not *per se* determine a person's access to consumer culture or national culture, because these are manufactured rather than organically grown and do not usually become a part of a person's character. In modern mobile societies, primordial culture is, however, no longer autonomous and self-reproducing over generations. This remains largely invisible for national majority populations and can lead to the illusion that the family is still the essential transmitter of national culture and shapes corresponding national characters. It is the assimilation of immigrants or minorities which shows the linkage between family and state in the intergenerational transmission of culture. Although an adult person may never completely undo her primary socialization by assimilating into a new national culture, the latter may well become the dominant environment within which her children will be socialized.

Socialization in the family neither homogenizes cultural patterns, as does the school system, nor does it create perpetually new ones as do consumer markets; it reproduces relatively stable intergenerational milieux of class, region, religious or political affiliation and ethnicity. Social, geographical, ideological and cultural mobility in modern society tends to blur the boundaries and to undermine the stability of these milieux. Marital mobility is crucial because it may import a mix of milieux into the process of primary socialization and can thereby generate cultural synthesis at the level of primary socialization.[35] Women and, much more rarely, men who live with a partner from a very different cultural origin already experience a more thorough process of resocialization than those who merely change their residence or learn a new language. For children from mixed marriages, this experience may be a much more profound one that combines cultural affiliations at the deepest level of primordial identities. Families are thus not necessarily a conservative institution which shields cultural milieux over generations from volatile consumer culture and the homogenizing impact of school socialization. Depending on the rate of intermarriage and on the capacity of women to assert their own cultural background in mixed marriages, families may also become the agents of cultural evolution.

Our approach could also help to give a more plausible account of the 'ethnic revival' within modern societies. This often-noted phenomenon goes against much post-Second World War sociological theory of modernization as a transition from ascription to achievement and from particularism to universalism. Ethnic identity has definitely not been revived in Western society in its pre-modern forms of comprehensive and self-sustaining ways of life. However, it may well survive over many generations in cultural milieux sustained by family and kinship ties. This is often much easier for ethnic identities within an established national majority culture, where the pressure of assimilation does not reach into the spheres of private and intimate life. Thus regional identities have been kept alive or have been invigorated by the federal structure that many democratic states have. The end of the Fordist era of the capitalist economy with its trends towards the standardizing not only of products but also of lifestyles may have had a positive impact on the articulation of 'white majority ethnicity', too.

Ethnic minorities have been mostly under much stronger pressure to assimilate, which has undermined their simple intergenerational reproduction via household and family – that is, by maintaining a certain level of residential cohabitation and endogamy. Their only chance was to politicize ethnicity and to gain access to those resources of cultural reproduction which are monopolized by the state: school curricula, and official recognition of languages in courts, in public administration, in topographic inscriptions, etc. In modern society, ethnicity is thus either reproduced only via families and markets and thereby reduced to milieu culture, or mobilized politically in the sphere of the state, in which case it will be instrumentalized in conflicts over the division of power between groups.

Civil Society and Cultural Discourse

Cultural integration in civil society will, then, depend again on proper checks and balances between the dynamics of nation-building, market diversification and the intergenerational reproduction of primordial identities. Disintegration would result from either of these becoming dominant outside their proper institutional sphere. Is there also a specific cultural dynamic that characterizes civil society in the narrow sense namely its plurality of associations? At first glance this does not appear to be the case. Associations in civil society are characterized by their particularism and diversity of interests as well as of organizational forms. Some are merely transmitters of cultural dynamics generated within the core institutions. Others, such as religious congregations, have their own comprehensive system of values, the foundations of which transcend not just society but this world. This may immunize them against the impacts of cultural dynamics which we have discussed so far. They can thus themselves be powerful cultural institutions which define binding goals in life and interpretations of the world for their members, even within modern and largely secular societies. How could we then expect that all these different associations which share no common cause still jointly contribute to a common societal culture in a way that counterbalances the dynamics of state, market and family?

Nevertheless, I think that such an argument can be made. We may understand civil society as the sphere of cultural discourse in the sense suggested by Agnes Heller.[36] This is, once more, a normative rather than merely a descriptive idea. In ideal cultural discourse, no persons or groups perceive themselves as merely an object and no issue is excluded from becoming an object. There is no specific target or collective goal for cultural discourse apart from the ongoing conversation itself. It is an end in itself. People take part in it for the sake of communication. It would be wrong to attribute to cultural discourse what Habermas thinks is the essence of discourse itself: an implicit striving for consensus. Philosophers disagree about whether all communication has a hidden grammar referring to an ideal speech situation in which participants aim at rational consensus. Anyhow, at the surface level of actual discourse in civil society which interests us, a presumption of everyone's orientation towards consensus would not make sense. Participants in cultural discourse need not necessarily aim at convincing others of their view. They may as well aim at stating the irreconcilability of their perspectives with others. Mutually shared misunderstandings may be the outcome of a discourse. The only thing which unites participants is their very participation, their readiness to articulate their points of view. The relevant contrast is thus not with dissent, but with recourse to coercion. Cultural discourse is suspended when free speech and free association are restricted or when people are forced into compliance.

However, an open cultural discourse requires more than just the absence of repression. It cannot flourish within the core institutions of state, market and family and also within those associations of civil society which are primarily interested in identifying their membership and shielding their activities from external challenge. Cultural discourse transcends the boundaries of organizations, groups and institutions, and links individuals located in different positions. It brings together diverse publics by connecting separate discourses rather than by establishing one single overarching discourse.

This idea provides us with a third and final interpretation of civil society as a sphere where individuals communicate with each other as equal citizens but free from the constraints imposed by politics. Their communication is not necessarily oriented towards political deliberation which ultimately culminates in collectively binding decisions. And they are equal only as participants in the discourse, and not in the much more restricted sense of equality before the law. What this means is that citizens bring all their gendered, generational, religious, political, regional or ethnic identities into the discourse. They do not negotiate behind a 'veil of ignorance', but reveal in public who they are and what they stand for. This combines aspects of

Hannah Arendt's notion of activity by which people disclose themselves to their fellow-citizens and Iris Marion Young's concept of a heterogeneous public.[37] A valid critique of these two theories is that democratic politics requires instrumental and not merely expressive activity,[38] and a more homogeneous perspective than that which emerges from the combination of particular group perspectives. Instead of dismissing these ideas, we should consider whether they might only have been misplaced. Civil society could be their proper location. This interpretation of civil society goes beyond its description as an 'association of associations' and emphasizes the ties that an ongoing and open cultural discourse creates between individuals who are otherwise strangers for each other, disunited by their economic interests, or united only by their equal and mostly passive status of political citizenship.

A similar distinction between cultural discourse in civil society and political discourse oriented towards the polity can be found in John Rawls:

> Comprehensive doctrines of all kinds – religious, philosophical, and moral – belong to what we may call the 'background culture' of civil society. This is the culture of the social, not of the political. It is the culture of daily life, of its many associations.[39]

Rawls contrasts the non-public reasons advanced within this background culture with public reason, which is characteristic of a democratic polity:

> It is the reason of its citizens, of those sharing the status of equal citizenship. . . . Among the nonpublic reasons are those of associations of all kinds. . . . This way of reasoning is public with respect to their members, but nonpublic with respect to political society and to citizens generally. Nonpublic reasons comprise the many reasons of civil society and belong to what I have called the 'background culture', in contrast with the public political culture. These reasons are social, and certainly not private.[40]

The notion of cultural discourse modifies this statement only in one regard: The background culture of civil society is public in the sense that reasons are addressed not exclusively to members of associations, but also to a wider audience of citizens. This is how civil society establishes a common discourse beyond the boundaries of associations and social groups and yet different from that carried on in the political sphere.[41]

Ideal cultural discourse is open in the dual sense of being open-ended in time and non-exclusive. Political debates require gag rules in order to count the votes. There are no such rules for stopping an ongoing discourse in civil society. Its ebbs and floods and its dominant and neglected issues will be determined by the force of arguments, by the numbers and social positions of participants, and by the range of the media they use. Cultural discourse is also not inherently exclusive. Foreign citizens who live permanently outside a country cannot be permitted to take part in political decision-making without rendering democracy absurd. However, anybody, from anywhere in the world, may make a relevant comment in an ongoing cultural discourse. The rule of non-interference with the internal affairs of countries or of communities and associations within countries does not apply to cultural discourse. This is why it is not constrained by the particularism of groups and associations. That particularism becomes the very stuff which cultural discourse feeds upon. In a uniform and homogeneous society, cultural discourse is externally bounded. A lack of alternative perspectives will slow down and impede cultural evolution in such countries. Conversely, in a heterogeneous multicultural society where communities are highly segregated, discourse becomes internally bounded. In such 'plural societies' it is replaced by a mute division of labour between groups, by an ongoing struggle for increasing each group's share in political power, and by the policing of each community's frontiers of cultural identity.

This normative analysis of ideal cultural discourse has to be confronted with a Foucauldian diagnosis of actual discourses by which power is constituted and distributed throughout society. The two types of analysis are compatible with each other as long as one recognizes that the critical thrust of any analysis of discourses in modern society is derived from implicit normative ideas about alternative discourses which are open, integrative and liberating. The framework of liberal democracy certainly does not guarantee that cultural discourse will remain unaffected by the dynamics of markets, nationalism and small communities. However, it makes it possible to transcend these dynamics of cultural fragmentation or homogenization which emerge from the core institutions. This mere possibility is sufficient to make cultural discourse relevant as a normative idea which can then be turned critically against the observed biases, exclusions and constraints.

Figure 5.3 visualizes the interpretation of civil society as a sphere of cultural discourse by adding culture as a third dimension to the triangle. Cultural discourses contribute most to the integration of civil society when they unfold at a level where they escape the diversifying, standardizing and particularizing dynamics of markets, states and family socialization.

Conclusions

Civil society is a complex phenomenon by any description. The main reason why this is so, is that it is not, to paraphrase Rawls, a free-standing model of social life. It depends on its contrasts and it partially shapes these contrasting institutions according to its own image of associational life – a democratic state, a pluralistic market economy and equitable family relations of genders and generations.[42] This complexity and, most of all, the divergence of its cultural dynamics are more likely to generate conflict than a harmonious equilibrium. How can we expect anything as precarious as a balance between all these forces to make for social cohesion? Maybe the question itself is

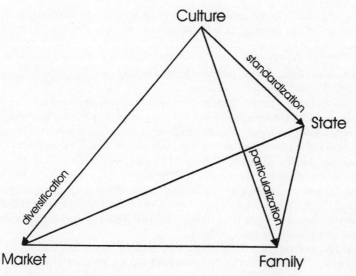

Figure 5.3 The Civil Society Tetrahedron: Cultural Dynamics of State, Market and Family

problematic. A civil society perspective helps to lower the level of our aspirations as to how much cohesion we can expect or even desire. It is a useful corrective for communitarian and republican ideas that call for integration through shared moral values or through the political obligations of citizenship. In civil societies the demands of citizenship are counterbalanced by the legitimate pursuit of particular interests, ideologies and identities.[43] Citizenship itself cannot remain a completely undifferentiated status of strictly equal individual rights and duties. The heterogeneity of civil society is reflected in the democratic polity where organized group interests, political and religious ideologies and cultural identities of national and ethnic minorities are articulated and pervasively shape the political agenda. We should not deplore this as a degeneration of politics. The most important demand of citizenship is to learn to cope with the plurality[44] that is continuously generated by civil society.

Notes

1. This chapter is an abbreviated and revised version of a longer essay called 'Social and Cultural Integration in a Civil Society', first published in Rainer Bauböck, Agnes Heller and Aristide Zolberg (eds) (1996) *The Challenge of Diversity: Integration and Pluralism in Societies of Immigration*, Public Policy and Social Welfare, vol. 21, Aldershot: Ashgate/European Centre Vienna.
2. This is not so in the earliest uses of the term, when civil society was identified with

the *res publica* or commonwealth and was contrasted with barbarian societies (in ancient Roman thought) or with an anarchical state of nature (in seventeenth-century English social contract theory).

3. Jean Cohen and Andrew Arato (1992) *Civil Society and Political Theory*, Cambridge, MA: MIT Press; Ernest Gellner (1994) *Conditions of Liberty: Civil Society and Its Rivals*, London: Hamish Hamilton.

4. A rare example is the following: 'The sociological variant of civil society refers to a space or arena between household and state, other than the market, which affords possibilities of concerted action and self-organisation' (Christopher Bryant (1993) 'Social self-organisation, civility and sociology: a comment on Kumar's "Civil Society"', *British Journal of Sociology* 44 (3), 397–401, p. 399).

5. According to Rawls, the duty of civility implies the willingness to comply even with imperfect constitutions and unjust laws within a nearly just society, a duty which is, however, suspended for permanent minorities who have suffered from injustice for many years (John Rawls (1971) *A Theory of Justice*, Cambridge, MA: Harvard University Press, p. 355).

6. On the re-emergence of barbarity in modern times see Claus Offe (1994) 'Moderne "Barbarei": Der Naturzustand im Kleinformat?', *Journal für Sozialforschung* 34 (3), 229–47.

7. A triangular model similar to the one which I will present here has been developed in research on welfare services. Drawing on analyses by Gershuny and Rose, Evers and Wintersberger suggested that states, markets, and households contribute in specific ways to social welfare. The point of their 'welfare triangle' is to argue that many organizations are characterized by a specific mix of principles related to the three corners. The so-called 'third sector' of voluntary non-profit-making organizations can thus be located at the centre of the triangle. My idea that civil society can be visualized in a similar way generalizes this earlier model. See Jonathan Gershuny (1983) *Social Innovation and the Division of Labour*, New York: Oxford University Press; Richard Rose (1985) *The State's Contribution to the Welfare Mix*, University of Strathclyde Studies in Public Policy, no. 140; Adalbert Evers, and Helmut Wintersberger (1990) *Shifts in the Welfare Mix: Their Impact on Work, Social Services and Welfare Policies*, Frankfurt am Main: Campus Verlag, and Boulder, CO: Westview Press.

8. Mary Douglas (1986) *How Institutions Think*, Syracuse, NY: Syracuse University Press.

9. See Anthony Giddens (1984) *The Constitution of Society*, Oxford: Polity Press.

10. Kenis and Marin suggest distinguishing markets, state, households and the so-called third sector in between them by the specific public, private or communal character of the goods which they provide (Patrick Kenis and Bernd Marin (1994) 'Managing Aids', unpublished manuscript, European Centre, Vienna).

11. Rainer Bauböck (1994) *Transnational Citizenship: Membership and Rights in International Migration*, Aldershot: Edward Elgar, pp. 224–6.

12. This hierarchical order of human activities and interests is at the core of Arendt's differentiation between labour, work and action (Hannah Arendt (1958) *The Human Condition*, Chicago: University of Chicago Press).

13. Kymlicka notes that the essential liberal distinction is that between the public–political and the private–social. This is a boundary different from the one

separating the private domestic sphere from the social spheres of markets and civil society. The latter is not grounded in liberal thought but shared by all major Western philosophical traditions (Will Kymlicka (1990) *Contemporary Political Philosophy: An Introduction*, Oxford: Oxford University Press, pp. 250–4). Kymlicka suggests that the feminist critique of this second boundary should lead us to define the right to privacy as an individual one rather than as a right of the family as a collective unit. However, this seems to give some plausibility to the accusations that liberalism is after all based on atomistic individualism – a claim which Kymlicka is at pains to reject by showing that the liberal conception of civil society presumes a natural sociability of human beings. What Kymlicka does not consider is the specific nature of intimate relations as opposed to voluntarily chosen associations in civil society. Stable intimate relations, even when freely chosen by adults, imply mutual dependency and build upon a kind of unconditional trust. Privacy rights of single persons within the family protect them against the burdens of this dependency and its potential encroachment on their individual integrity. They thus secure their autonomy within the family and their capacity to act independently outside the family. This is different from a right of privacy which is collectively exercised by the family and is meant to guarantee a protected space for intimate relations against the intrusion of the public sphere. Which right belongs to which category is often a matter of debate, and changes with the integration of feminist concerns into the liberal perspective. But the distinction itself is still essential. For example, in the contemporary liberal view, the right to abortion involves individual privacy rights of the women, whereas the right of parents to educate their children is one jointly exercised by the family. As feminist theories of care have emphasized, the mere assertion of individual rights can be destructive of intimate relations. The boundary which protects intimacy is therefore irreducible to individual privacy, but requires genuinely collective rights jointly exercised by partners cohabiting in a stable sexual relationship.

14. Michael Walzer (1983) *Spheres of Justice: A Defense of Pluralism and Equality*, New York: Basic Books.
15. In a later essay, Walzer has described civil society as a realm of associational activity where citizens learn the virtues of civility and toleration, but which still needs to be integrated by a democratic state (Michael Walzer (1992) 'The Civil Society Argument', in Chantal Mouffe (ed.) *Dimensions of Radical Democracy*, London: Verso).
16. Larry Diamond (1994) 'Toward Democratic Consolidation: Rethinking Civil Society', *Journal of Democracy* 5 (3), 4–17, p. 6.
17. Gellner, *Conditions of Liberty*, p. 137.
18. Adrian Oldfield (1990) *Citizenship and Community: Civic Republicanism and the Modern World*, London: Routledge.
19. Herman van Gunsteren (1998) *A Theory of Citizenship: Organizing Plurality in Contemporary Democracies*, Boulder, CO: Westview Press.
20. Alasdair MacIntyre (1981) *After Virtue*, Notre Dame, IN: University of Notre Dame Press.
21. Bikkhu Parekh (1992) 'The Cultural Particularity of Liberal Democracy', *Political Studies* 40 (special issue), 160–75, p. 163.

22. A monopoly for a single political party or the suppression of religious freedom by an established church are therefore indicators that there is no fully developed civil society. This is very different from Larry Diamond's suggestion that parties are beyond the pale of civil society because it is their inherent target to gain political power in the state. (In Diamond's approach, religious congregations would have to be similarly excluded if they look forward to salvation in the next world rather than orienting themselves towards the public interest in this one.)

23. Walzer, 'The Civil Society Argument'.

24. Diamond, 'Toward Democratic Consolidation', pp. 9, 13.

25. J.S. Furnivall (1939) *Netherland's India: A Study of Plural Economy*, Cambridge: Cambridge University Press; M.G. Smith (1965) *The Plural Society in the British West Indies*, Berkeley: University of California Press.

26. Ferenc Fehér and Agnes Heller (1994) *Biopolitics* (European Centre, Vienna), Aldershot: Avebury.

27. Fredrik Barth (ed.) (1969) *Ethnic Groups and Boundaries: The Social Organization of Culture Difference*, Oslo: Universitetsforlaget.

28. Ernest Gellner (1983) *Nations and Nationalism*, Oxford: Blackwell.

29. An aspect that is to some extent neglected in Gellner's account of nationalism.

30. Anthony D. Smith (1986) *The Ethnic Origins of Nations*, Oxford: Blackwell.

31. Ernest Gellner constructs from these various combinations of territory and culture a typology of four time zones of European nationalism (Gellner, *Conditions of Liberty*, pp. 113–18).

32. Benedict Anderson (1983) *Imagined Communities: Reflections on the Origins and Spread of Nationalism*, London: Verso Editions and New Left Books.

33. This is also true for the early stages of nationalism. Benedict Anderson's account of nationalism contrasts with Ernest Gellner's in that the former attributes much weight to the emergence of print capitalism. The newspaper and the novel are in Anderson's view the first mass commodities, the consumption of which creates the imagined community of the nation in the readers' minds (Anderson, *Imagined Communities*). However, the medium is not quite the message. The national awakening by these media requires, first, that masses be made literate by compulsory school education and, second, that the intelligentsia use these media to spread their ideas about political emancipation and economic modernization.

34. Nathan Glazer and Daniel P. Moynihan (eds) (1975) *Ethnicity: Theory and Experience*, Cambridge, MA: Harvard University Press; John Rex (1986) *Race and Ethnicity*, Milton Keynes: Open University Press.

35. Walzer registers only four kinds of modern mobility: geographical, social, marital and political (Michael Walzer (1990) 'The Communitarian Critique of Liberalism', *Political Theory* 18 (1), 6–23, pp. 11–12).

36. Agnes Heller (1996) 'The Many Faces of Multiculturalism', in Bauböck *et al.* (eds) *The Challenge of Diversity*.

37. Arendt, *The Human Condition*; Iris Marion Young (1990) *Justice and the Politics of Difference*, Princeton, NJ: Princeton University Press.

38. Mary G. Dietz (1995) '"The Slow Boring of Hard Boards": the Work of Politics', *American Political Science Review* 88 (4), 873–86.

39. John Rawls (1993) *Political Liberalism*, New York: Columbia University Press, p. 14.

40. *Ibid.*, p. 213.
41. Benhabib has criticized Rawls' theory for drawing too sharp a boundary between the public sphere and civil society and between political and social reason (Seyla Benhabib (1996) 'Towards a Deliberative Model of Democratic Legitimacy', in Seyla Benhabib (ed.) *Democracy and Difference: Contesting the Boundaries of the Political*, Princeton, NJ: Princeton University Press, pp. 74–7). She emphasizes that 'civil society is also public' (p. 76): its associations are constrained by constitutional principles and involve citizens in processes of political deliberation. My conception of cultural discourse also stresses the public side of civil society which transcends the particular interests of its associations but acknowledges also that this public sphere is not necessarily political. The role of citizens deliberating about the common good is but one among many different roles individuals may play in civil society.
42. Michael Walzer has developed a closely related argument (Walzer, 'The Civil Society Argument'). He dismisses four versions of the good life because of their singular focus on only one 'preferred setting' for realizing their ideal: Marxist socialism and market liberalism base their vision on the economy, republicanism on the democratic state, and nationalism on the national community. The civil society perspective is preferable to each of these because it partly denies and partly incorporates the concerns of the four other ideologies. Its usefulness is limited if it is meant to provide a complete alternative, but it can be used as a critical argument in the transformation of the dominant institutions of society.
43. See Claus Offe (1998) ' "Homogeneity" and Constitutional Democracy: Coping with Identity Conflicts through Group Rights', *Journal of Political Philosophy* 6 (2), 113–41, for an interesting argument about the different dynamics of conflicts about interests, ideologies and identities.
44. See van Gunsteren, *A Theory of Citizenship*.

PART TWO

Citizen Dispositions

CHAPTER SIX

Modus Vivendi *Citizenship*

DUNCAN IVISON

Introduction: *modi vivendi*

How much consensus or community spirit does a liberal democratic society need in order to establish and maintain the political goods that flow from social co-operation? And in answering this question, what follows for a conception of citizenship? One answer to this question is to argue for some form of liberal nationalism, suitably chastened by liberal principles, as providing an additional motivational thickening agent for citizens to adhere to the strenuous demands of a liberal theory of justice.[1] The difficulty such arguments face, however, is that at some point the liberal principles are either trumped by nationalist concerns (restricting the scope of citizenship rights, for example), and thus a liberal justification for doing so must be found, or are interpreted so expansively as to dilute the point of appealing to nationalism in the first place. I do not examine these important and complex arguments here. Rather, I want to examine the way in which liberals conceptualize deep social and political diversity in the first place, and then see what follows for a conception of liberal citizenship. If, as I suspect, many liberals (and republicans) are uncomfortable with an appeal to nationalism (however constituted), then other resources must be found for thinking about the relationship between citizenship and pluralism.

Given deep social and political pluralism, liberals are committed to generating the requisite commitment to co-operation from moral resources which do not presuppose (overly) controversial world-views. In doing so, they often dismiss alternatives as being either too thick with regard to their metaphysical foundations, or too thin with regard to their moral commitments. A version of the latter charge is often levelled against what Rawls calls a 'mere *modus vivendi*' between citizens as providing a suitably principled and stable basis for establishing 'constitutional essentials'. My aim in this chapter is to try to pursue the logic of a *modus vivendi* in a slightly different way than

Rawlsians, and in particular, explore its implications for a conception of citizenship. The gist of my argument is that however unattractive a *modus vivendi* seems as the basis for a political settlement at the level of a simple balance between competing conceptions of the good or interests, at the level of competing conceptions of the *right* it is unavoidable, and arguably desirable.

Consider two versions of *modus vivendi* compliance with political norms:

1 *A simple or static modus vivendi*: The parties are motivated to comply with political norms only where it is in their interest to do so, where 'interest' is narrowly defined in terms of the individual goods of the members or the norms and values of a particular group.

2 *A relational or dynamic modus vivendi*: The parties are motivated to comply with political norms where it is in their interest to do so, but (a) these interests include moral interests, and (b) *over time* the demands and practices of social co-operation may come to be seen as not only mutually advantageous but fair and reasonable. However, the content of 'fair and reasonable' is not dependent on an overlapping consensus on political values independent of the interests or conceptions of the good of the parties, or their concrete practices of interaction.[2]

My claim is that there is a space worth exploring *between* accounts of citizen compliance associated with a simple or static *modus vivendi* and those associated with more consensual ideals of deliberative public justification. My aim is to begin to outline the possibilities of a form of '*modus vivendi* citizenship' that is at least theoretically more attractive than is usually thought, especially from a Rawlsian perspective.

Why explore such possibilities? Doesn't it involve accommodating power or force to reason rather than standing back and criticizing such relations? This dichotomy is a false one. I presume that all human interaction is characterized by relations of power. All forms of social and political arrangements, then, are a kind of *modus vivendi*. Consensus is a critical idea but one necessarily open to question; one must ask what portion of nonconsensuality is implied in such a power relation, and whether that degree of nonconsensuality is necessary or not.[3] Consensus is not always a basis for understanding relations of power but is often a result of them.[4] This is not to say that human interaction is incapable of being constitutive of freedom. Rather, it means accepting a more complex relation between power and freedom. Individual and collective agents are governed in a multitude of discursive and practical ways. However, precisely because of the ubiquity of relations of power – the 'total structure of actions' bearing on the actions of agents who themselves are not wholly determined – the evasions and resistances they provoke are also ubiquitous. There is always a 'field of possibilities in which several ways of behaving, several reactions and diverse comportments' can be realized in relation to the 'governing of conduct'.

Freedom is not so much ignored in such an account as presupposed by it, although without the pretence of its ever being independent of relations of power.[5]

Citizenship and conflict

Albert Hirschman has distinguished between two kinds of conflict: either–or (involving non-divisible goods) and more-or-less (involving divisible goods).[6] The latter are easier to manage than the former. Marxism, for example, presents class struggle in terms of an either-or conflict. The development of the welfare state in market-based liberal democracies suggests that it is not quite as immune from mitigation and shifting compromise as Marxists have thought. However, Hirschman warns against the inverse of this tendency: asserting that there are no either–or conflicts left. This risks underestimating the depth of hatreds or differences that drive conflicts, or at least which are exploited, cultivated and manipulated by leaders and movements (he gives as examples the reunification of East and West Germany, and the former Yugoslavia; Rwanda and Northern Ireland also come to mind). Ethnic, linguistic and racial conflicts today often do seem to be either–or conflicts over non-divisible goods, especially when matters of political distribution and retribution are at the centre of them. Boundaries are drawn, for example, to maximize ethnic or linguistic homogeneity; rights and resources are distributed along ethnic/cultural lines (to ensure or undermine cultural and political power); and groups become locked into acts of pre-emptive 'preventive repression' against historical enemies.[7] But Hirschman is pressing a subtle point. However formidable they appear at first glance, these conflicts might have negotiable and contingent parts open to renegotiation and accommodation – for Hirschman, capacities closely related to those honed and practised in pluralist market relations.[8]

This last claim is interesting but controversial, and stems from a tradition of social theory emerging from the eighteenth century. Hirschman has written very perceptively about this period, and especially about the (positive) political by-products of the kinds of conflicts that occur in pluralist market societies. Note that this is a very different claim from those made by theorists who argue that markets are important because they provide the opportunity for citizens to become self-reliant and thus should displace positive welfare rights. Hirschman, rather, is interested in the effect that market-type interactions have on the way people perceive and cope with social conflict: namely, how demands for reform and injustice emerge and are dealt with (or not) through bargaining and compromise, and how assumptions about the necessity for 'definitive solutions' are gradually diluted. In the right conditions, moderation and constraint can emerge, paradoxically, as a by-product of social conflict.

I do not want to pursue Hirschman's specific claims in any detail here. But I do want to transpose certain elements of his hypothesis to the question of how citizens are meant to cope with disagreement as it is presented in contemporary political theory. Liberals must assume that clashes over beliefs and values in the public sphere can be converted into the more-or-less variety (or if not, avoided) and that liberal beliefs are best suited to providing a background consensus on the political arrangements and regulative principles of justice suitable for conditions of deep social and political diversity. I shall be examining this conception of consensus and its consequences for thinking about citizenship below.

I want to make two preliminary points. The first has to do with the conceptions of citizenship that we have inherited from the past. Conceptions of citizenship are closely related to conceptions of legitimacy and stability. Contemporary liberal political theory construes the relation between citizenship, consensus and stability in a particular way. In its contractual mode, it uses contractarian reasoning as a mode of practical reason to elicit shared common ground between diverse citizens and their conflicting conceptions of the good. Whereas for Aristotle and some parts of the republican tradition, a shared conception of the good *ipso facto* provided the standard of community spirit or consensus required to secure the benefits of political co-operation; for contemporary contractarians (and others), different grounds need to be found. Because of the way in which the problem is posed, it is difficult at times to imagine a means of coping with the deep diversity of contemporary societies except with reference to some kind of contractual device. The historical horizon of contemporary discussions of justice thus has interesting consequences for their accompanying accounts of citizenship. I do not provide a discussion of that horizon here, complex as it is.[9] But to expand the conceptual space in which citizenship is (re)thought in contemporary circumstances requires expanding our historical grasp of what it is we are thinking with.

The second preliminary point has to do with defining the conceptual scope of the chapter. The formal or legal question of what it is to be a citizen is often taken as separate from the question of what makes for a good citizen. This is analogous to the distinction between asking about the metaphysical nature of personhood as opposed to the nature of 'the good person'. The former, to borrow from Locke, is a forensic question, the latter something quite different. But these questions do, of course, become entwined (as in fact they did for Locke), and similarly, it is difficult to make a clean distinction between the two senses of citizenship. To be a citizen is always to be a citizen of some particular state. Citizenship is often thought of and evaluated according to universal criteria – for example, to do with basic rights or human dignity – but crucial aspects of its meaning remain (for better or worse) insistently particular.

What is it to be a good citizen? It depends. The question cannot be answered solely with reference to a catalogue of rights and responsibilities which accompany a certain legal status. What is of interest is the manner in which citizenship becomes a mode of expressing one's membership in a particular political community. By this I mean the way in which it *implicates* us in the public political culture of that community. We might not like the fact that it does, or the way that it does, or we might even deny that it does. But it does.

One way to see this is to consider different ways of conceptualizing political community, and to investigate the accompanying accounts of citizenship, in terms of what is implied or suggested as constituting good citizenship. I shall try to do this in what follows, albeit very generally. In particular, I want to focus on the extent to which citizens are meant to hold their interests and beliefs in a particular way, especially with regard to their consequences for others and for the community as a whole. Deliberation in the public sphere is significant because of the role it plays in liberal ideals of political community and ideals of democracy. Not only should 'public opinion' be the product of reflection and discussion in order to be able to supervise and check political power effectively,[10] but democratic deliberation is seen as a reasonable procedural means of accommodating deep social and political diversity and disagreement. Ideally, citizens in the public sphere are meant to pursue their interests and interactions with others in particular ways – most importantly, for liberals, in terms of a background framework which includes a commitment to liberal public ends. This citizen ethic is meant to bite into one's overall moral identity (that is, one's overall set of beliefs and interests).[11] The practice of political virtue is parasitic on our holding our beliefs and interests – and, importantly, those of others – in the right way. Failing the emergence of such a disposition, the goods of political interaction and co-operation can remain elusive.

Modes of Political Identification

Rawls supposes a pluralism of reasonable comprehensive doctrines in modern democratic societies, the result of the exercise of human reason within the framework of relatively free democratic institutions. By 'comprehensive doctrine' he means a doctrine that

> includes conceptions of what is of value in human life, and ideals of personal character, as well as ideals of friendship and of familial and associational relationships, and much else to inform our conduct ... it covers all recognized value systems and virtues within one rather precisely articulated system.[12]

People who disagree over 'comprehensive' religious, moral and political doctrines will have difficulty agreeing on a conception of justice to regulate the basic institutions of society, Rawls claims, if that conception depends in any significant way upon an acceptance of a particular comprehensive doctrine. A society in which people do not share a public conception of justice is not 'well ordered'.[13] His solution is complicated, but the gist is that reasonable people can come to support liberal principles despite their disagreement over comprehensive doctrines, by reaching an overlapping consensus on a *political* (i.e. not comprehensive) conception of justice.

I want to leave aside the larger questions about Rawls's theory for the moment, and focus instead on the idea of a 'reasonable comprehensive doctrine'. Are the disputes that dominate political life in Western democracies today really disagreements between 'comprehensive' doctrines? There are, of course, important disputes between quite self-contained and exclusionary world-views, such as between religious and secular fundamentalists. But the mode of political identification that Rawls's account presupposes seems too cleanly drawn. It underplays the extent to which political identities, in particular, are fundamentally interdependent in a number of complex ways. Relations of identity are held in place and constituted, in part, by perceptions of difference, and vice versa.[14] So as much as political identities often seem fixed in opposition to each other, the underlying structure is actually relational; difference is essential to identity because it provides the means for it to become fixed and distinct in the first place. Hence identities are vulnerable to processes of redefinition and counter-definition, and at least potentially unstable. This vulnerability can manifest itself in both responsive and resentful ways. It might provoke a critical responsiveness to 'otherness' previously thought intrinsically inferior or unworthy of tolerance.[15] Or it might intensify intolerance and even disgust for those entities or persons against which a 'true' identity defines itself and gains its sheen.

To notice how identity is constructed in this relational and oppositional way does not necessarily make it any easier to reshape or reform. But an appreciation of this interdependence promotes a wariness about strategies that attempt to dredge out of public life the cultural densities upon which identities and attachments depend.[16] Such strategies are vulnerable to accusations of bad faith or hypocrisy as they run up against the multiple sources from which citizens draw their sense of moral and political understanding. Public disavowal of metaphysics seems to invite the eventual exposure of unacknowledged dependencies upon metaphysical claims.[17] One side seeks to protect public life from metaphysical and 'visceral' inter-subjective judgements and attachments, while the other sees the very possibility of meaningful community to depend upon their admittance. For William Connolly, the only solution is to redraw a new form of *modus vivendi* between competing moral sources that does not pretend to have established a priori what counts as a genuine public reason. But such a *modus vivendi* should still aim to constrain these opposing views by promoting an 'ethos of engagement' between them and thus altering the sensibility within which questions of justice are considered – in part, it seems, by exposing their interdependency, hence contingency.[18]

What is of interest here is not so much Connolly's ideal of an ethos of engagement and 'critical responsiveness' between diverse cultural and political identities (the account of which raises a number of difficult questions),[19] but the characterization of contemporary pluralism that underlies it and the form that grounds for social and political community might possibly take. If there is both *more* overlap between cultural, ethical and political identities and sensibilities than is usually presumed and yet potentially *less* consensus or common ground available in contemporary societies, then upon what can an ideal of citizenship (and ultimately justice) take hold?

Public reason

The public sphere provides a framework within which a particular (liberal) mode of public expression or dialogue occurs. Following recent discussions, especially Rawls's, we can label this particular mode of expression as a form of *public reason*. Citizens engage in public reason when they reflect upon and contest reasons provided to justify the coercive power of the state in matters of basic justice.

Given deep diversity about conceptions of the good and the best way to live, the only way people can live together in complex societies is to find some way of living with each other's differences. For Rawlsians, this entails finding some way of justifying the legitimacy of political institutions and regulative norms of justice in terms that all (or at least the vast majority) can accept, given reasonable pluralism. Establishing the requirements of legitimacy is not necessarily the same as constructing agreement on basic rules of justice. This raises some tricky issues to do with the relation between legitimacy and an overlapping consensus on principles of justice.[20] A regime might be legitimate but not just. I shall assume that liberals are interested only in 'liberal legitimacy', and in so far as this is true, see *some* necessary connection between the conditions for legitimacy and principles of justice.

Consider two general modes of public justification: consensual and distributive.[21] Consensual modes of public justification provide reasons R which are reasons for each and every citizen to accept proposition P. Distributive modes of justification provide reasons Ra for citizen (or group of citizens) I; reasons Rb for citizen (or group of citizens) II, etc., where Ra is not necessarily the same as Rb (though they are directed at a proposition P). Distributive accounts, given their focus on interests (narrowly construed), have tended to be associated with theories of justice as mutual advantage. I continue to make such an association below to some extent, but note that the connection is not as straightforward as is often assumed.

We can characterize different forms of public deliberation which flow from these distinctions as well. A consensual mode of public justification implies that public debate will be characterized by a search for consensus on the regulative principles of the main political institutions of society. Desires and beliefs are thus subject to a filtering process designed to promote such a consensus, a process which involves the refining or 'laundering' of preferences.[22] Public reasons (suitably defined) are thus offered in the course of public deliberation, the purpose of which is either to *reveal* consensus on a regulative concept which the individuals of a given community (perhaps unknowingly) share, or to *construct* a consensus via procedures and principles which everyone accepts.

A distributive mode of public justification suggests that public debate will be characterized by the search for an optimal compromise with regard to given interests and preferences.[23] Public justification thus must appeal to what individuals, *given* these interests, would accept; political arrangements must suit these interests and not the other way round. Public reason, in so far as it acts as a constraint on self-interest, is simply what rational prudence suggests in contexts where the co-operation (or forbearance) of others is a condition of individuals' satisfying their preferences. Distributive modes of public justification thus take public reason as the lowest common denominator from which to justify basic political institutions – i.e. establishing a *modus vivendi*.

David Gauthier, for example, sees morality as the *product* of rational agreement, not vice versa.[24] What it makes sense for the contractor to agree to, on this account, is that the constraints of society must 'advance what one judges good' relative to a baseline of non-agreement.[25] Each must gain from co-operation in a way that they could not on their own. Society is thus a 'cooperative venture for mutual advantage'.[26] It provides a means of ensuring (through coercive sanctions) that others will not take advantage or free-ride on one's co-operative behaviour, as well as providing determinate norms of cooperation. The benefits of co-operation and the need for assurance and determinate norms provide agents with reasons to obey the norms of society; they are capable of being justified in this way to each rational agent who seeks to advance her good.

Now it is often suggested that distributive modes of justification fail to capture something essential about the nature of public justification. In theories of justice as mutual advantage, for example, the rational constraints that emerge from the amoral premises of rational choice are justified in so far as people lack the 'power irresistible' to ride roughshod over everyone else to get what they want. To paraphrase Rawls, 'to each according to their threat advantage' is not much of an account of public justification – though it is, of course, impersonal and impartial.[27] Consensual modes of justification, on the other hand, are meant to engage the interlocutors in a process of common deliberation which aims at a morally richer and more stable form of consensus, one that is reflective of people's *prior* equal moral standing and thus a different fit between the justification of rules and the motivation to obey them. The constraints of justice are not simply the product of co-operation but are reflected in the idea of agents seeing themselves as related to each other 'in a fundamental moral relationship expressed in mutual justification'.[28]

Before considering Rawls's argument more closely, note that Gauthier has recently elaborated his argument in interesting ways. He writes of a 'real but limited transformation of her own exercise of rationality in deliberation' when a citizen internalizes the 'right reason' (i.e. the public reason) of an authorized public person on matters which 'significantly affect the interactions of the citizens and the public goods available to them'.[29] The institutions established to structure interaction in order to promote mutual advantage 'embody the common good' of such a society, one tied to the enhancement of the individual goods of the members.[30] Such a constitution, in so far as it reflects agreement reached through 'reasoned interchange' and 'deliberative politics',

> offers each person the opportunity to advance whatever proposal he pleases, but requires him to submit it to the critical consideration of his fellows, so that its adoption depends on his being able to give it a reasoned grounding that must either speak equally to the life-plans of all the participants, or establish the parity of the proposal with similar and compatible proposals that, taken together, reflect equally their several life plans.[31]

As an ideal of justice, Gauthier admits, it is essentially negative; 'the virtue of the self-interested ... that curbs self-interest'.[32] But things can change. Bonds of mere convenience can grow into 'ties of mutual civic [though not necessarily personal] concern'. Public or civic friendship does not supplant the agreement needed for instrumental partnerships to constrain strategically rational actions for mutual benefit, but *supplements* it, 'with the further demand that the agreement assure equal respect'.[33] By this, Gauthier means that each respects the identity and aims of her fellows and willingly accords them 'equal place in their common affairs with her own'.[34] If each comes to see her share of benefits as 'fair and reasonable', then others become not merely accepted but regarded as 'friends ... as persons in whom one takes [a political or civil] interest'. Hence a constitution – the framework for structuring interaction to promote mutual advantage – becomes 'an affirmation of civic friendship, and not a mere treaty or compact of alliance'.[35] It comes to reflect the commitment of individual contractors to the equal value of those with whom they cooperate in political society.[36]

Gauthier emphasizes that he is not suggesting that 'deliberation' or 'reasoned interchange' is opposed to his well-known emphasis on strategic interaction, but that it is intended to supplement it (in the course of an argument concerning how a constitution comes to embody 'higher law'). The opposition between reason and force is a false one; 'reason and force coexist in all human interaction'. Deliberative agreement is thus 'strategic bargaining under full information',[37] proceeding from a baseline not necessarily of equality of condition but one in which there is a desire for mutual advantage, and which also 'invites' a desire to 'manifest civic friendship through the expression of equal respect'.[38]

For any theory of justice (or the state) grounded mainly on self-interest, a major problem is that it is not clear why people should be just or obey political norms when the cost of not doing so is less than compelling. In his major work *Morals by Agreement*, Gauthier argued that only someone with a settled disposition to act justly will be invited to join in co-operative ventures and that this provides a rationally compelling reason – grounded in self-interest – to adopt such a disposition. This argument, and the account of justice accompanying it, has been subject to considerable critical attention, not to be summarized here. But the moves discussed above would seem to confirm a suspicion that Gauthier is in search of extra-contractual help in securing the motivational and institutional stability of a political society organized around the principles of justice as mutual advantage.[39] For the purposes of this chapter, however, what is interesting is how the account of strategic interaction supplemented by ties of civic friendship provides a way in to thinking about alternatives to more 'consensual' modes of deliberative public justification. Gauthier rejects the viability of a simple or static form of *modus vivendi* as the grounds for a framework of political co-operation over time. But nor does he presume away the ubiquity of strategic behaviour in human, and especially political, interaction. He might not have captured everything there is to our traditional notions of moral obligation towards others, but his unwillingness to overestimate these notions seems right too. Does it provide a means of thinking about the possibilities of the dynamic or relational *modus vivendi* identified in section 1? And if so, is it really any different from consensual modes of public deliberation and what they demand of citizens? Before tackling these questions directly, consider Rawls's alternative account of the 'idea of public reason'.

Rawlsian public reason

For Rawls, the 'liberal principle of legitimacy' states that

> our exercise of political power is fully proper only when it is exercised in accordance with a constitution the essentials of which all citizens as free and equal may reasonably be expected to endorse in light of principles and ideals acceptable to their common human reason.[40]

'Common human reason' alone, however, does not converge on the necessary principles. It has to be focused on a specific set of questions and grounded in a specific political conception of justice and accompanying ideal and ethos of citizenship. Hence the account of public reason:

Public reason is characteristic of a democratic people: it is the reason of its citizens, of those sharing the status of equal citizenship. The subject of their reason is the good of the public: what the political conception of justice requires of society's basic structure of institutions, and of the purposes and ends they are to serve. ... Public reason is the reason of equal citizens who, as a collective body, exercise final political and coercive power over one another in enacting laws and in amending their constitution.[41]

So the ideal of citizenship imposes a duty of civility to 'explain to one another ... how the principles and policies they advocate and vote for can be supported by the political values of public reason'. This duty also implies a willingness to 'listen to others and a fair-mindedness in deciding when accommodations to other views should reasonably be made'.[42]

Public reasons are meant as reasons to be shared in the sense that they are reasons for each in virtue of being reasons for all.[43] The scope of public reason is crucial; they are distinct from 'non-public' reasons in so far as they invoke reasons acceptable to all and not just to a particular group. Public reason includes a 'set of guidelines of inquiry that specify ways of reasoning and criteria for the kinds of information relevant for political questions'.[44] These guidelines specify the modes of reasoning that may be used, and the types of considerations that may be appealed to, in discussing political questions. Thus public reason has 'special subjects'. It does not apply to the specifics of tax legislation, or the regulation of the environment, or the funding of the arts, but only to 'constitutional essentials' and matters of basic justice. This is not to say that we do not, in our 'personal deliberations', reason on the grounds of a whole range of 'background' philosophical, moral, religious, political, and cultural beliefs. But in the public forum, when proposing (or voting on) matters to do with constitutional essentials, citizens should observe the limits of public reason. We should not appeal to what we see as the truth of a particular philosophy, religion, or other 'comprehensive doctrine', but instead confine ourselves to 'plain truths, now widely accepted, or available, to citizens generally'.[45] A belief in the superiority of one's conception of the good is not a basis for what can be reasonably advanced as the grounds for society's basic political institutions.

Convergence on the idea of public reason *follows* the process of converging on the political conception of justice, or at least within a family of reasonable political conceptions of justice. And this seems problematic. For how can we prejudge the range of issues and disagreements citizens of democratic societies might want to pursue in the political arena on the basis of an agreement concerning basic constitutional principles? Surely it would be *through* some form of public reason that hope of citizens arriving at a proper 'overlapping consensus' (or some other form of agreement) on the political conception of justice would be realized. But Rawls seems to suggest that the trajectory goes the other way.[46] No configuration of institutional devices or 'invisible hand' mechanisms can conjure the right kind of consensus, argues Rawls, and so he proposes an ideal of citizenship that accompanies the political conception of justice: the 'political conception of citizens as free and equal' (and rational and reasonable). The 'fair-mindedness' of citizens thus includes the willingness to 'propose fair terms of cooperation that others as free and equal also might endorse', to act on these terms provided others do ('even contrary to one's own interest'), and a recognition of the burdens of judgement.[47]

Consider Rawls's contrast between the political conception of justice and a *modus vivendi* – which is 'political in the wrong way'.[48] Rawls's account of a *modus vivendi* is the simple or static account described above: an equilibrium point between two indifferent or hostile parties, analogous to a treaty neither party has a current interest in violating but will if circumstances and opportunities arise. A social consensus founded exclusively on political bargaining entails a form of social unity that is 'only apparent, as its stability is contingent on circumstances remaining such as not to upset the fortunate convergence of interests'.[49] If society is to be a fair system of co-operation, a simple balance between competing political and moral forces will not do.

So why should citizens honour the limits of public reason? Part of Rawls's response is that the requirement to act in accord with public reason is grounded in the fact that people are reasonable – that they have a higher-order motivation to act for public reasons (i.e. suggest and comply with 'fair political ideals'). The concept of the person, in other words, presupposes the particular form of practical reason required.[50] This hardly helps justify the priority of the right – the acceptance of public reasons as defined – to those who do not have the higher order desire in the first place. Two things could be said to follow from this. First, it appears as though Rawls is in fact appealing to a controversial conception of the person (based on particular meta-ethical and metaphysical claims) which undermines the stated aim of political liberalism to avoid such commitments. Second, if Rawls is not appealing to such a conception of the person, or to the truth of this conception of practical reason, then either his argument risks circularity or he thinks that an account of practical reason can be separated from comprehensive views and still be convincing to people who hold different conceptions of the good, or even truth. Rawls seems committed to some version of the latter; but this seems weak support for the strong claim that the political values *always* outweigh non-political ones in matters of basic justice.[51]

There might, for example, be very different accounts of where the boundaries between public and non-public reasons should be drawn, even accepting that abstracting from particular standpoints and agreement on basic political ground rules will be necessary for any kind of social co-operation given pluralism.[52] It is not a case of having to justify the right to those who reject any form of public reason or reasonableness whatsoever, but a case of having to justify the right to those who reject, for example, the particular distinction between the public and non-public at the heart of Rawls's account.[53]

Note that metaphysical, religious or 'green' speech is not actually forbidden in the public forum. Religious enthusiasts and believers in Gaia can proselytize and argue their case as much and as intensely as they like. The point, however, is that appeal to God or to Mother Earth will not – given reasonable pluralism – provide *the* grounds for the justification of the exercise of coercive political power over non-believers and other citizens. Some other, more neutral ground will have to be found; or so Rawlsians argue. Good citizens, in their interactions with each other, recognize the constraints imposed by the ideal of public reason in the public forum.[54]

But given deep diversity, a convergence on a single standard of public reason itself might be questionable. In other words, why presume that the fact of reasonable pluralism does not also apply to standards of right?[55] The greater the limits of public reason, the narrower the range of possible interpretations of principles admissible to the public sphere. And yet contemporary politics is increasingly characterized by demands for the expansion of this space, and for the recognition of diverse modes of political identification and thus diverse modes of public justification. This presses directly against Rawlsian strategies of constraining the scope of public reason for the sake of reaching an overlapping consensus on free-standing political values. If convergence upon a single public standpoint or standard is unlikely, we should expect to find a mix of different levels of agreement and points of convergence. Public reason itself, then, is pluralized.

Rethinking *modus vivendi* citizenship

For Gauthier, existing interests are the measure of the constraints of justice, albeit now with the proviso that these can evolve into (or at least alongside) an ideal of civic friendship over time. For Rawls, a political settlement grounded on interests is not enough, and what is needed is convergence on an ideal of a political conception of justice that can stand independently of citizens' conceptions of the good and which is rooted more deeply than mere constrained self-interest. I have been suggesting that Gauthier was right to be concerned whether interests alone could provide a basis for a desirable form of political settlement and accompanying ideal of citizenship, and also that we should be wary of tying an overlapping consensus on a free-standing political conception to the derivation of norms of public discourse and debate. The reason for this wariness is that such a conception is vulnerable to charges of either inconsistency (at worst, hypocrisy) or circularity; the conception of reasonableness underpinning public reason either has too much content, hence is more controversial than presumed, or has too little, hence is unable to carry the justificatory load. Reasonable citizens are reasonable either because they are liberal[56] or because they hold more or less coherent beliefs that draw upon a 'tradition of thought or doctrine'.[57] The former rules out too much, the latter too little.

But if one denies that liberal legitimacy needs to take the form of an overlapping consensus around constitutional essentials and an accompanying ideal of public reason, then what other terms of co-operation could be arrived at, given social and political pluralism? The problem is that the fact of pluralism cannot be allowed to dictate the terms of consensus too directly. If the terms are too thin, they risk being meaningless – or worse, simply entrenching and legitimating existing relations of power. But nor can they be simply pragmatic – a *modus vivendi* as it is usually meant – since then the parties remain ready to defect or free-ride given the opportunity, and any political arrangements dependent on such foundation would be fundamentally unstable.

The main assumption governing much of the analysis of the shortcomings of *modus vivendi* arrangements is that the interests of the parties remain static. Rationality is almost exclusively strategic and instrumental. *Modus vivendi* citizenship here just is the strategic pursuit of one's self-interest(s) via appeals to others' self-interest by conditional offers of forbearance or co-operation. If the paradigm of successful strategic interaction is the market, then political institutions are justified on the grounds of supplanting or constraining strategic interaction where this would be advantageous to everyone, compared to the non-cooperative baseline of an anarchic state of nature.

Put this way, a *modus vivendi* is obviously not very attractive. But consider the second model of *modus vivendi* mentioned above: the dynamic or relational *modus vivendi*. If we drop the account of comprehensive beliefs that Rawls provides, and the bracketing off of beliefs suggested in his idea of public reason, are we then really only left with the option of striking a static *modus vivendi*? Suppose a different starting-point for social interaction. The aim is not necessarily to provide reasons to co-operate that would motivate an amoralist (what could?), but rather to provide them to socialized beings who value social interaction and who draw on a diversity of moral sources to understand and justify the value of these interactions.[58] Thus agreements will often tend to be, in Cass Sunstein's phrase, 'incompletely theorized'.[59] But the fact that they co-ordinate does not mean that the agreements are automatically right or just. They can (and should) be subject to critique and scrutiny over time, including with reference to more general principles and ideals. My point is that a political settlement grounded on incompletely theorized agreement does not necessarily evolve into a wider overlapping consensus on political values, as presumed in consensual modes of public justification. Incompletely theorized agreements worry Rawlsians because it means that they are incompletely justified. But all political agreements, I want to argue – even ones to do with constitutional essentials and matters of basic justice – are incompletely justified, given the account of the relation between power and reason set out in section 1. Incompletely justified and mixed public reasons are the grounds of co-operation in conditions of socially and politically diverse liberal democracies.

But doesn't this give up too much? Wouldn't the lack of an overlapping consensus on a free-standing political conception create a motivational deficit on the part of citizens to co-operate and negotiate with each other, especially with the less powerful or less able? And even if it did manage to create a kind of consensus, would it be so thin as to be almost meaningless?

The key question, then, is how can citizens can be motivated to continue to negotiate and make compromises in the face of frequent disagreement and lack of convergence on a free-standing political conception. The possibilities canvassed here take the form of considering the ways in which citizens come to perceive and recognize each other through social and political interaction. If we drop the requirement to bracket our conception of the good in the public sphere, our task might seem to have been made even more difficult. How can citizens deliberate about matters of basic justice as bearers of thick conceptions of the good and particular interests and yet do so on equal terms – that is, recognize each other as worthy of equal concern and respect, and thus not simply impose their views on each other without much concern for reciprocity or mutual acceptability?

Brian Barry has argued recently that equal respect fails as means of establishing the grounds for mutually acceptable terms of cooperation because it does not *by itself* lead to the conclusion that disagreements over conceptions of the good should be resolved by retreating to neutral ground. Charles Larmore, for example, argues that the obligation of equal respect consists in our being 'obligated to treat another as he is treating us – to use his having a perspective on the world as a reason for discussing the merits of action rationally with him'.[60] Barry argues that this leaves open the possibility that as long as we argued that our conception of the good was *rationally* superior to others, and hence a proper basis for constitutional arrangements, dismissing other views (because they won't or can't acknowledge our rationally compelling argument) could be compatible with treating them with respect. Hence we need an additional sceptical proviso to move us to more neutral ground. The proviso acknowledges that we cannot in fact produce such a rationally compelling argument, and thus it would be unreasonable for us to insist on imposing our conception of the good on others.

But reasonable people will also disagree about the criteria for certainty. How does an epistemological claim get us out of moral trouble? It can't. Barry's criticism is searching, but the addition of the sceptical proviso misses the point. It does not follow from my not being able to persuade others to agree with my claim that I should be sceptical about that belief. Scepticism will not deliver us to neutral ground, any more than presupposing equal respect will. The important point about the limits of my being able to convince others is, rather, that I come to see and accept those limits in some way and that I refrain from imposing them on others *despite* my initial convictions about them.

The argument from equal respect in relation to citizenship might be useful if understood slightly differently. The challenge is not to presuppose a moral conception of respect for others (as I think most discussions do, including Larmore's) but to *move to it* in some way, in this case via a conception of political membership and the forms of interaction this implicates us in. The move is not necessarily to neutral ground but to terms of co-operation that are acceptable given citizens' beliefs and interests. The relationship that holds between citizens is one in which certain features about the diversity of world-views and beliefs are particularly salient. Equal concern and respect arises only when citizens recognize that the exercise of public reason presupposes access to the public sphere. But if public reason is plural rather than singular, then how are such deliberations carried out on equal terms?

The desire to justify ourselves to others is a powerful mechanism, but not conclusive, given a reasonable diversity of public reasons. It needs to be combined with something else. This something else can only be some additional incentives for the parties – especially more powerful parties – to remain committed to the pursuit of equal terms of co-operation in the face of continued disagreement. An acknowledgement of the basic preconditions for continuing deliberation would be part of any answer, as I have suggested above, but similarly is not conclusive. Expanding what counts as a public reason presupposes that the parties admitted to the public sphere are worthy of at least being listened to in their own terms. This in turn engenders consideration of the relations which are said to hold between citizens. The desire to impose beliefs without reference to others' convictions is loosened – not because of scepticism, but rather with the increasing recognition of not only the diversity, and often opacity, of others' beliefs, but the need to co-operate nonetheless. Over time, that is, citizens come to identify with the major institutions and practices of a society without necessarily seeing the reasons for doing so as akin to sharing the same values, ethnicity, language, culture or conception of the good.[61]

Other incentives, though less pristine, are also relevant. One motivation for continuing to identify with just institutions might be the desire to avoid the conditions that would lead to their being undermined. True, from the perspective of a purely self-interested agent, the costs of a significant proportion of society being alienated or excluded from the basic institutions might not be such as to motivate him to ignore his relative bargaining strength and refrain from taking advantage. But if we begin from an assumption of a slightly richer confluence of interests of citizens, as argued for above, then such an incentive can be understood in a different way. Citizens do not perceive each other merely as threats and thus interact *only* to secure advantage or pre-empt hostile attacks. Interaction, over time, breeds a wider and more diffuse array of sympathies that a purely strategic account of citizenship underplays. Thus the costs of social deprivation or conflict might come to be seen to threaten not only (or mainly) the individual goods of the parties, but the political good of a well-ordered society as a whole.

One source of responsiveness, of course, might indeed be the inability to justify current arrangements as they stand and thus the inability to tolerate living with the kinds of injustice this entails. The crucial element in this story is the manner in which the desire to justify ourselves to others interacts with the shifting horizons of the norms of public justification according to the *modus vivendi* struck between citizens on matters to do with the diverse moral sources of the good and the right. Here the explicit acknowledgment of the incompleteness of justification is, I believe, a virtue. It historicizes practices of justification to a certain extent. And it signals an openness to revisiting the particular configurations of good and right embodied in the background basic structures, institutions and norms of society. Being a good citizen means never thinking that the distance between justice and injustice is to be measured strictly in terms of fidelity to a justificatory ideal of deliberative consensus.

Acknowledgements

I am grateful to Iain Hampsher-Monk, Dario Castiglione and Catriona McKinnon for the invitation to participate in this project, and to the participants of seminars at Exeter and York for their helpful comments and discussion – especially Matt Matravers and Sue Mendus. I am particularly indebted to Matt Matravers for his generous help and the opportunity to read forthcoming work that touches on many of the themes of this chapter (especially in section 4). I am also very grateful to John Ferejohn for an illuminating discussion on the dynamic structure of *modus vivendi* arrangements.

Notes

1. For example, David Miller (1995) *On Nationality*, Oxford: Oxford University Press; Yael Tamir (1993) *Liberal Nationalism*, Princeton, NJ: Princeton University Press; from a republican perspective, Maurizio Viroli, (1995) *For Love of Country: An Essay on Patriotism and Nationalism*, Oxford: Oxford University Press.
2. My point is that a static *modus vivendi* may evolve into a dynamic *modus vivendi* and possibly other, thicker forms of social solidarity, but not necessarily in the way described by Rawls. Hence I also mean to distinguish my discussion from that of Charles Larmore in *Patterns of Moral Complexity* (1987, New York: Cambridge University Press), especially at pp. 122–30. Rather confusingly, at least for my purposes, he endorses a view of liberalism 'as *modus vivendi*', by which he means the

view that Rawls has now developed more explicitly in *Political Liberalism* (1993, New York: Columbia University Press).

3. Michel Foucault (1984) 'Politics and Ethics: An Interview', in Paul Rabinow (ed.) *The Foucault Reader*, New York: Pantheon Books, p. 379.

4. In addition to Foucault, see James Scott (1990) *Domination and the Arts of Resistance: Hidden Transcripts*, New Haven, CT: Yale University Press. For an exemplary discussion of this theme in relation to Habermas's critique of Foucault, see James Tully (1999) 'To Think and Act Differently: Foucault's Four Reciprocal Objections to Habermas's Theory', in S. Ashenden and D. Owen (eds) *Foucault Contra Habermas*, London: Sage, pp. 573–615.

5. Michel Foucault (1983) 'The Subject and Power', in Hubert Dreyfus and Paul Rabinow, *Michel Foucault: Beyond Structuralism and Hermeneutics*, Chicago: University of Chicago Press, p. 221; Scott, *Domination*, p. 111; Duncan Ivison (1997) *The Self at Liberty: Political Argument and the Arts of Government*, Ithaca, NY: Cornell University Press.

6. A.O. Hirschman (1995) *A Propensity to Self-Subversion*, Cambridge, MA: Harvard University Press, pp. 231–48.

7. See, for example, Russell Hardin (1995) *One for All*, Princeton, NJ: Princeton University Press.

8. Claus Offe is more pessimistic; cf. Offe (1991) 'Capitalism by Democratic Design? Democratic Theory Facing the Triple Transition in East Central Europe', *Social Research* 58, 865–92.

9. I have made an initial attempt at this in (1997) 'The Secret History of Public Reason', *History of Political Thought* 18, 125–47.

10. Charles Taylor (1993) 'Modernity and the Rise of the Public Sphere' in G.B. Peterson (ed.) *The Tanner Lectures on Human Values*, Salt Lake City: University of Utah Press, pp. 223–33.

11. For Rawls there are two relevant senses of identity: one's 'public' or political identity (which refers to the rights and duties one has a member of a political society), and what he calls a 'moral' or 'non-institutional identity', involving 'deeper aims and commitments', including 'non-political' aims and commitments (Rawls, *Political Liberalism*, pp. 30–1; henceforth *PL*).

12. *PL*, pp. 13, 175.

13. *PL*, p. 35.

14. William Connolly (1991) *Identity/Difference: Democratic Negotiations of Political Paradox*, Ithaca, NY: Cornell University Press, especially pp. 64–8.

15. On these possibilities, see William Connolly (1995) *The Ethos of Pluralization*, Minneapolis: University of Minnesota Press.

16. The metaphor is from Connolly (1999) *Why I Am Not a Secularist*, Minneapolis: University of Minnesota Press, p. 23.

17. See Connolly's discussion of Kant and Habermas in this regard; *Why I Am Not a Secularist*, pp. 29–46. Rawls's discussion of how comprehensive doctrines run afoul of public reason is relevant here; see below.

18. Connolly, *The Ethos of Pluralization*; *Why I Am Not a Secularist*.

19. For example, where does the motivation to treat each other with 'agonistic respect' or restraint come from? But see Connnolly, *Why I Am Not a Secularist*, especially pp. 39–46, 63–4, 157–61.

20. *PL*, p. 226; John Rawls (1995) 'Reply to Habermas', *Journal of Philosophy* 42, 175–6.

21. Here I am drawing on my 'Secret History of Public Reason'. The terms are adapted from Fred D'Agostino (1991) 'Some Modes of Public Justification', *Australasian Journal of Philosophy* 69, 390–414; Gerald Postema (1995) 'Public Practical Reason: An Archaeology', *Social Philosophy and Policy* 12, 64–73; and Gerald Postema (1995) 'Public Practical Reason: Political Practice', in Ian Shapiro and Judith Wagner Delew (eds) *Theory and Practice*, New York: New York University Press, pp. 348–52. They should not be blamed for how I use them here.

22. Robert Goodin (1986) 'Laundering Preferences', in J. Elster and A. Hylland (eds), *Foundations of Social Choice Theory*, New York: Cambridge University Press, pp. 75–102.

23. See David Estlund (1993) 'Who's Afraid of Deliberative Democracy?', *Texas Law Review* 71, 1453–60.

24. David Gauthier (1988) 'Moral Artifice', *Canadian Journal of Philosophy* 18, 385–418, and (1986) *Morals by Agreement*, Oxford: Oxford University Press.

25. David Gauthier (1998) 'Mutual Advantage and Impartiality', in Paul Kelly (ed.) *Impartiality, Neutrality and Justice: Re-reading Brian Barry's Justice as Impartiality*, Edinburgh: Edinburgh University Press, pp. 121–2.

26. John Rawls (1971) *A Theory of Justice*, Cambridge, MA: Harvard University Press, p. 4, quoted in David Gauthier (1993) 'Constituting Democracy', in David Copp, Jean Hampton and John E. Roemer (eds) *The Idea of Democracy*, New York: Cambridge University Press, p. 317.

27. Rawls, *A Theory of Justice*, p. 134.

28. David Gauthier (1997) 'Political Contractarianism', *Journal of Political Philosophy* 5, 134.

29. David Gauthier (1995) 'Public Reason', *Social Philosophy and Policy* 12, 37. Also Gauthier, 'Constituting Democracy', pp. 320–1, 326.

30. Gauthier, 'Constituting Democracy', p. 320.

31. *Ibid.*, p. 321.

32. *Ibid.*

33. *Ibid.*, p. 318.

34. *Ibid.*

35. So Gauthier admits that merely instrumental partnerships do not provide an adequate basis for the social bonds necessary for a society based on mutual advantage: '[W]ithout civic friendship, and the equal respect it engenders, some persons will almost certainly find themselves relatively disadvantaged by actual social arrangements, which they cannot be expected to accept willingly, so that the society will tend to be both coercive and unstable' ('Constituting Democracy', p. 321; n. 4, p. 332). Cf. Rawls on public reason and civic friendship in (1999) 'The Idea of Public Reason Revisited', in *John Rawls: Collected Papers*, ed. Samuel Freeman, Cambridge, MA: Harvard University Press, p. 579.

36. This formulation is from Matt Matravers, 'Contract and Sovereignty', unpublished.

37. 'We regard each bargainer as serving as an ideal representative of the particular person he will be in the social world to be shaped by the constitution on which all agree' (Gauthier, 'Constituting Democracy', p. 324).

38. Gauthier, 'Constituting Democracy', n. 12 , p. 333; Gauthier, *Morals by Agreement*, pp. 155–6, 201–5.

39. See especially Gauthier, 'Constituting Democracy', n. 4, p. 332, and n. 12, p. 333.
40. *PL*, p. 137. Note that Rawls has gone some way to respond to critics in 'The Idea of Public Reason Revisited'. I have tried to note the changes with regard to *PL* as best I can, but space prohibits a more complete analysis. Especially relevant for our purposes is Rawls's acknowledgement of a limited (as I understand it) pluralization of public reason, and his account of the 'wide view of public political culture'. The latter appears to create room for the introduction of comprehensive views into political debate in various ways (see especially pp. 591–4). But ultimately they derive their status as genuine public reasons only in so far as they can, in due course, be re-presented in terms of the political values alone.
41. *PL*, pp. 212–14.
42. *PL*, p. 217.
43. Postema, 'Public Practical Reason', pp. 69–71.
44. *PL*, p. 223.
45. *PL*, pp. 250–4.
46. Note that the 'depth and breadth' of an overlapping consensus not only extends to the *principles* of justice but 'goes down to the fundamental ideas within which justice as fairness is worked out' (*PL*, p. 149). But compare now 'The Idea of Public Reason Revisited' (pp. 581–8, 592–3), where room is given for the development of new and changing political conceptions of justice through public reason, as well as varying interpretations of them (see especially n. 35, pp. 586–7), within a family of conceptions rather than just one. But to be admissible, conceptions must still meet two sets of criteria, and these criteria are essentially those presented in *PL* (see pp. 581–5).
47. Rawls, 'Reply to Habermas', p. 134; see also the discussion of the 'criterion of reciprocity' in 'The Idea of Public Reason Revisited', pp. 578–9.
48. *PL*, pp. 39–40.
49. *PL*, pp. 147, 158–68.
50. *PL*, p. 30; cf. p. 148: 'No sensible view can possibly get by without the reasonable and rational as I use them.' For a helpful discussion of the complexity and problems raised by Rawlsian reasonableness, see Leif Wenar (1995) 'Political Liberalism: An Internal Critique', *Ethics* 106, 32–62.
51. *PL*, pp. 139–40.
52. Rawls insisted in *PL* that there is 'but one public reason' (p. 220); however, '[a]ccepting the idea of public reason and its principle of legitimacy emphatically does not mean ... accepting a particular liberal conception of justice down to the last details' (p. 226). Now he seems to accept a limited pluralization of public reason: 'the forms of permissible public reason are always several'; see 'The Idea of Public Reason Revisited', p. 583 and n. 46 above.
53. For example, J. Habermas (1995) 'Reconciliation through the Public Use of Reason: Remarks on John Rawls's *Political Liberalism*', *Journal of Philosophy* 42, pp. 129–30; S. Benhabib (1992) *Situating the Self*, Cambridge: Polity Press, pp. 99–100, 106–7; Bonnie Honig (1993) *Political Theory and the Displacement of Politics*, Ithaca, NY: Cornell University Press. Cf. Rawls, 'The Idea of Public Reason Revisited', n. 28, pp. 582–3.
54. Rawls now thinks that when debating fundamental political questions we can introduce comprehensive doctrines into political discussions, provided that 'in due

course, we give properly public reasons to support the principles and policies our comprehensive doctrine is said to support' ('The Idea of Public Reason Revisited', pp. 584, 591–4; see the definition of the reasonable citizen at p. 578).

55. On this point see Richard Arneson (1997) 'The Priority of the Right over the Good Rides Again', *Ethics* 108, 187–8; and Michael Sandel (1994) 'Political Liberalism', *Harvard Law Review* 107, 1782–9. Rawls now accepts, as noted above (n. 52), that the forms of permissible public reason are 'several'.
56. See the attributes of the 'reasonable person' at *PL*, pp. 81–6.
57. *PL*, pp. 59–60.
58. I am grateful to Matt Matravers and Sue Mendus for discussion concerning this formulation.
59. Cass Sunstein (1995) 'Incompletely Theorized Agreements', *Harvard Law Review* 108, 1735–6.
60. Larmore, *Patterns of Moral Complexity*, pp. 64–5. The discussion by Barry is in Brian Barry (1995) *Justice as Impartiality*, Oxford: Oxford University Press, pp. 175–6.
61. See Andrew Mason (1999) 'Political Community, Liberal-Nationalism, and the Ethics of Assimilation', *Ethics* 109, 261–86, especially at pp. 274–5. Rawls himself acknowledges that a *modus vivendi* concerning constitutional essentials can, over time, evolve into a more stable form of political settlement – that is, one grounded in an overlapping consensus on the values of the political conception – given the 'looseness' of our comprehensive views (see *PL*, pp. 159–72, 165–6). But it is not clear why such 'looseness' entails the development of an *overlapping consensus* around the political conception rather than a form of agreement closer to a dynamic *modus vivendi*.

CHAPTER SEVEN

Civil Citizens

CATRIONA MCKINNON

Introduction

Blueprints for good government and political practice are always accompanied by a set of assumptions about the characteristics and capabilities of those for whom the blueprints are drawn up. These assumptions will point to undesirable qualities – egoism, greed, cruelty – which political principles ought to restrain so as to make the shared lives of citizens tolerable, but also to desirable qualities necessary for stability and the maintenance of justice. Sets of such assumptions are normative accounts of good citizenship. What distinguishes an account of good citizenship from an account of the good person is its scope. An account of good citizenship addresses only those qualities necessary for the maintenance of the good polity, efficient political processes, and desirable forms of political organization. Even the most far-reaching account of good citizenship will not demand that good citizens be perfectly virtuous people; in fact, it can be seen as a desideratum of an account of good citizenship that it does not make this demand.[1]

The characteristics invoked in accounts of good citizenship vary widely: autonomy, independence, intellectual abilities, fraternity, reciprocity, patriotism, nationalism and religious convictions have all been invoked by different thinkers.[2] These qualities have been defended as aspects of good citizenship from the point of view of certain detailed and wide-ranging moral theories. Some philosophers have argued that the demands of citizenship described by such theories are incompatible with the search for principles which accommodate the deep and ineradicable differences between people. Such deep differences conflict with the expectations described by such accounts of good citizenship. Acknowledging the fact of deep difference means that we cannot legitimately expect a citizen to exhibit characteristics which are not of value from the point of view of his or her moral, religious, or philosophical beliefs.[3] The search for an account of good citizenship that does

144

not draw on moral, religious or philosophical theories is motivate
idea that political justification must avoid reference to such theories in its
take seriously the ineradicable fact of moral, philosophical and religious
diversity. On this view, we ought to aim for political principles which are
acceptable from the point of view of every reasonable person regardless of the
differences between such people. The exemplar of such an approach is John
Rawls's political liberalism, which starts by accepting 'the fact of reasonable
pluralism'.[4] Political liberals believe that the inevitability of a diversity of
reasonable comprehensive doctrines disqualifies appeal to any one moral,
religious or philosophical doctrine in an account of good citizenship.

According to Rawls, part of what it is for a person to be reasonable is for
her to exercise her sense of justice by engaging in public reason when
debating political matters with other citizens. Engaging in public reason has
various specific implications for how the good citizen ought to act which will
be explored shortly. Suffice it to say now that a discourse governed by public
reason is one in which no potential participant is excluded by virtue of her
moral, religious or philosophical commitments. Political justifications
governed by public reason address all reasonable people:

> The point of the ideal of public reason is that citizens are to conduct their
> fundamental discussions within the framework of what each regards as a
> political conception of justice based on values that the others can reasonably be
> expected to endorse and each is, in good faith, prepared to defend that
> conception so understood.[5]

There are two common and connected criticisms of accounts like Rawls's
which make engagement with public reason central to good citizenship. Some
critics claim that engaging in public reason requires skills and abilities beyond
the reach of most people – skills which, even if they were not beyond the reach
of most people, would nevertheless make the morally unacceptable
requirement that people abandon or ignore their most deeply held
commitments and beliefs.[6] The criticism has two aspects: first, that most
people are unequipped to engage in public reason, and second, that even if
most people were equipped to engage in public reason, it is not acceptable
that we ask them to do so, given the fact of reasonable pluralism.

The argument of this chapter will be that from the perspective of political
liberalism it is not implausible to assume that certain key skills of civility
necessary for engaging in public reason as a good citizen are within the reach
of most people; this will address the first aspect of the criticism. The damaging
misconception that Rawls's account of good citizenship turns on the
expectation that people abrogate their deeply held commitments and beliefs
underlying the second aspect of the criticism will also be questioned. I will
argue that acquiring the skills of civility enabling engagement in public
reason actually requires such commitments and beliefs.

Civility and Public Reason

Rawls conceives of persons as characterized by two moral powers: the capacity for a conception of the good and the capacity for a sense of justice. The capacity for a conception of the good is the capacity to conceive of ends as valuable and pursue them appropriately. Accepting the fact of reasonable diversity means accepting that the content of conceptions of the good will differ from person to person, and hence that clashes between them as they pursue these conceptions will be inevitable. We need principles of justice to adjudicate between these clashes. The capacity for a sense of justice makes possible the principled resolution of such clashes according to stable procedures against an enduring background of just institutions. Rawls characterizes a sense of justice as follows: 'A sense of justice is the capacity to understand, to apply, and to act from the public conception of justice which characterises the fair terms of social cooperation.'[7] A sense of justice is manifested in one's dealings with other citizens by meeting one's natural duty of civility.[8] Rawls's claim that we have a natural duty of civility does not place him in the natural law tradition: all Rawls means by the term 'natural duty' is a duty which does not presuppose an act of consent or promising.[9] Understanding what this duty is requires the isolating of some of the actions and attitudes it demands.

Good Faith

We have a natural duty of civility not to invoke the faults of social arrangements as a too ready excuse for not complying with them, nor to exploit inevitable loopholes in the rules to advance our interests. The duty of civility imposes a due acceptance of the defects of institutions and a certain restraint in taking advantage of them. Without some recognition of this duty mutual trust and confidence is liable to break down.[10]

One aspect of the duty of civility is a requirement that a person not take advantage of what she believes to be defects in laws to promote her own interests at the expense of the interests of others; in other words, to act in good faith. In all societies but those which are perfectly just, the law and social institutions will contain defects which allow for some to take unfair advantage of others. A good example is the practice of gazumping in house buying, which is illegal in Scotland but still legal in England.[11] When a buyer is gazumped, the vendor, and perhaps even the second buyer, may both fail to meet their duty of civility. Another example is noise nuisance. The noisy neighbour who genuinely believes that blaring music at all hours is fair to her neighbours will be rare. A more plausible explanation is that the noisy neighbour knows that this is unfair but simply does not care, in which case she lacks civility. A more controversial example is the verbal harassment of women by men in public places. Perhaps there are men who genuinely believe that this attention is welcomed by women. If so, they do not act in bad faith when they harass women – which is not to say that there is nothing else wrong with what they do, or that there are no grounds for legislation to prevent it.

The good citizen will consider whether what she proposes to do is legal only because of inevitable imperfections and loopholes in the law. If, in her judgement, her proposed course of action would be ruled out by a perfectly just system of law, she will not pursue it. The person who does pursue a course of action she judges to be legal only because of imperfections in the law acts in bad faith. Defining good citizenship in terms of action in good faith means that in the ideal society the choices of the good citizen are restricted not only by law, but also by her conscience. The duty of civility requires the exercise of judgement with respect to one's range of legal choices.

Obeying the law

In a state of near justice at least, there is normally a duty (and for some also the obligation) to comply with unjust laws provided that they do not exceed certain bounds of injustice.[12]

Another aspect of the duty of civility is the general duty to abide by unjust laws in nearly just regimes. Whereas the requirement to act in good faith relates to what is permitted in law, this aspect of civility relates to what is demanded by law. Rawls places great emphasis on stability as a political ideal: the good citizen will not break every law she believes to be unjust, because law-breaking is a serious attack on stability. Instead, the civil citizen uses democratic procedures and other legal methods – letter-writing, marches, campaigning and lobbying, etc. – to draw her fellow citizens' attention to unjust laws. But when all law-abiding, democratic measures have been exhausted, civility demands civil disobedience.

Civil Disobedience

Each person must decide for himself whether the circumstances justify civil disobedience, [but] it does not follow that one is to decide as one pleases. It is not by looking to our personal interests, or to our political allegiances narrowly construed, that we should make up our minds. To act autonomously and responsibly a citizen must look to the political principles that underlie and guide the constitution. He must try to assess how these principles should be applied in the existing circumstances. If he comes to the conclusion after due consideration that civil disobedience is justified and conducts himself accordingly, he acts conscientiously.[13]

At a certain point, and after all legal options have been exhausted, the injustice of a law will become intolerable for the good citizen, and civil disobedience towards, rather than the toleration of or law-abiding protest against, unjust laws becomes a requirement of good citizenship. Rawls conceives of civil disobedience as a form of address: with civil disobedience the good citizen appeals to the sense of justice of other good citizens. The point at which civil disobedience becomes a requirement of good citizenship, and so supersedes the requirement of obedience as an aspect of civility, must be a matter of judgement for the individual citizen.[14] The good citizen applies her understanding of fair principles of justice to her society as a whole to determine whether it is nearly just and thus whether any injustice is serious enough to warrant abandoning toleration of unjust laws in the name of civility.

Voting in Accordance with the Common Good

The final exercise of judgement demanded by the duty of civility places certain restraints on how a person should cast her vote. According to Rawls, there are two common conceptions of voting, both of which contravene the duty of civility. First, one might conceive of voting as a wholly private matter: the individual casts her vote in accordance with her interests by voting for the party or the measure that will best promote these interests. Second, one might conceive of voting as reflecting the agent's convictions about the good and the truth: the individual casts her vote for the party or the measure that best embodies her beliefs about the good and the truth, whatever these beliefs are. Rawls claims that

> Both views are similar in that neither recognises the duty of civility and neither respects the limits of public reason in voting on matters of constitutional essentials and questions of basic justice. The first view is guided by our preferences and interests, the second view by what we see as the whole truth. Whereas public reason with its duty of civility gives a view about voting on fundamental questions in some ways reminiscent of Rousseau's Social Contract. He saw voting as ideally expressing our opinion as to which of the alternatives best advances the common good.[15]

The duty of civility demands that when entering the ballot box, a person should be thinking neither 'What is best for me?', nor 'What do I most believe in?', but rather 'What is best for us, as a political community?'

Public Reason

Voting in accordance with an idea of the common good, acting in good faith, and making judgements about the appropriateness of obedience or civil disobedience are connected by the most fundamental aspect of the duty of civility: the requirement to engage in public reason when discussing political questions:

> The ideal of citizenship imposes a moral, not a legal duty – the duty of civility –
> to be able to explain to one another ... on fundamental questions how the
> principles and policies [one] advocate[s] and vote[s] for can be supported by
> the political values of public reason.[16]

A commitment to public reason colours and constrains the sorts of
considerations a person can put forward in a conversation with others about
questions of basic justice. Acknowledging that other people will inevitably
have views different from his about fundamental values and the good life, the
good citizen attempts to find reasons which he can offer to others as reasons
for them in a conversation about questions of fundamental justice. The ideal
of public reason ties together all the examples of civility given above in the
following ways:

1 Public reason rules out the appeals to pure self-interest needed to justify
   acting legally in bad faith and self-interested voting. A person whose
   self-interest does not coincide with mine cannot be expected to accept
   my self-interested reasons as reasons for her.
2 Public reason rules out appeal to beliefs about the good and the truth *per
   se* as reasons for others. The person who accepts the fact of reasonable
   pluralism accepts that other reasonable people will have views and values
   that differ from her own, and so reasons indexed to her full-blooded
   moral, religious or philosophical views will not be reasons for others who
   do not share her views. This rules out voting according to what she sees as
   the whole truth.
3 The assessment of whether a system is nearly just when considering civil
   disobedience requires thinking about how the system approximates to
   principles endorsed by public reason. This requires that a person engage
   with public reason in order to see whether the principles that govern the
   law are in fact principles endorsed by public reason.

For Rawls, public reason is an ideal because it is only by engaging in
public reason that we can arrive at stable, democratic principles expressing
equal respect for all.[17] It is important to note Rawls's distinction between the
ideal of public reason and the idea of public reason.[18] The idea of public
reason applies only to discussion of fundamental political questions in the
public political forum – that is, that forum consisting of judges (especially
supreme court judges), chief executives and legislators, and candidates for
public office. However, the ideal of public reason applies to discourse in this
forum and also to the thinking of citizens who are assessing whether officials
in the public political forum act according to the idea of public reason:

> When firm and widespread, the disposition of citizens to view themselves as
> ideal legislators, and to repudiate government officials who violate public
> reason, is one of the political and social roots of democracy, and is vital to its
> enduring strength and vigour. Thus citizens fulfil their duty of civility and

support the idea of public reason by doing what they can to hold government officials to it.[19]

The ideal, over and above the idea, of public reason is fundamental to democracy because it demands that citizens evaluate the performance of their legislators.

Clarifying how the duty of civility is met by exercising public reason when engaging in different sorts of political behaviour allows us to isolate the following four aspects of good citizenship:

1   The good citizen is aware that the views of others differ from her own, and that this is the inevitable result of the free exercise of reason, and 'the burdens of judgement'.[20]
2   The good citizen is willing and able to engage in public reason by offering reasons in political discourse which also count as reasons for reasonable others.
2a The good citizen is willing and able to empathize and identify with views unlike her own in order to assess whether the reasons she proposes to invoke in political debate are reasons acceptable to others, given their different conceptions of justice.[21]
2b The good citizen is willing and able to listen to the views of others expressed in good faith, and to accept the possibility that her own view might be mistaken in some aspects.[22]

Aspect 1 reflects a fact about the world which political liberals like Rawls purport to take seriously as their starting-point, the fact of reasonable diversity. Aspect 2 states the ideal of public reason. Aspects 2a and 2b describe the skills of civility necessary for successful engagement with public reason.

Civility is the ideal governing our interaction with others as good citizens who accept that political discourse about fundamental questions ought to be governed by public reason. The more diversity there is in society, the more restraint and effort the duty of civility requires. Civility requires that a person refrain from asserting her own beliefs about justice as decisive, that she take the time to listen to the views of others and consider whether her own views are flawed, and that she exercise imagination and understanding in trying to empathize with others and come to grips with their reasons. The more diverse the views we encounter, the more effort we have to make to listen, empathize and assess our own beliefs in a conversation about justice with others.

To return to the two objections mentioned earlier, it has seemed to some that deep diversity means that the duty of civility at the core of Rawls's account of good citizenship is either unrealistic or too demanding. The first objection is that people in conditions of deep diversity are not normally able to make the effort and exercise the restraint necessary for Rawlsian civility. In political debate, people are not capable of striving for empathy and identification. Political debate is and can only be a matter of conflict and contest. To expect anything else is psychologically unrealistic.[23]

The second objection is that, even if a person is in a position to acquire and exercise the skills of civility, it is unacceptable that she be expected to exercise these skills in political debate with others with whom she is in deep disagreement. These skills might be appropriate in discourse with others who share basic moral, religious or philosophical beliefs because in such cases the differences between people are closer to the surface. But it is not acceptable to ask a person to exercise these skills in discourse with others whose moral, religious or philosophical conceptions of the world fundamentally differ from and perhaps contradict her own. The demandingness of civility in conditions of diversity conflicts with deep commitments which are part and parcel of having a conception of the good.

These two objections can now be answered. In the next section I will address the first objection by tracing some connections between Rawls's account of the search for self-respect and acquisition of the skills of civility. In the section after that I will address the second objection by arguing that public reasons are available only to those who retain their deep convictions and commitments.

Acquiring the Skills of Civility

> Without [self-respect] nothing may seem worth doing, or if some things have value for us we lack the will to strive for them. All activity becomes empty and vain, and we sink into apathy and cynicism. Therefore the parties in the original position would wish to avoid at almost any cost the social conditions that undermine self-respect.[24]

The claim that self-respect is 'perhaps the most important primary good'[25] is common to both *A Theory of Justice* and *Political Liberalism*. In Rawls's theory, primary goods are all-purpose means to a diversity of life plans; they are the goods it is rational to want whatever else one wants.[26] The principles of justice distribute these goods.

The self-respect-related good that appears on the list of primary goods is 'the social bases of self-respect'.[27] Aspects of the basic structure of society – social structures, distributions of goods, forms of social organization – can promote or impede the development of self-respect. Rawls's recommendations for the distribution of liberty, opportunity, power and income and wealth are all informed by an understanding of how different distributions of these goods represent different patterns of opportunity for self-respect.[28] Self-respect has a central role in the justification of principles in both *A Theory of Justice* and *Political Liberalism*. Rawls defines self-respect as follows:

> [Self-respect] first of all ... includes a person's sense of his own value, his secure conviction that his conception of the good, his plan of life, is worth carrying out. And second, self-respect implies a confidence in one's ability, so far as it is within one's power, to fulfil one's intentions. When we feel that our plans are of little value, we cannot pursue them with pleasure or take delight in their execution. Nor plagued by failure and self-doubt can we continue in our endeavours.[29]

The just society is in part a society in which the institutions of the basic structure distribute other primary goods so as to maximin opportunity for the development of a sense of self-worth, and confidence in one's abilities to pursue one's plans.[30] By looking at how one develops these two aspects of self-respect, we can see how the skills of civility are acquired.

Rawls says that the development of self-respect depends upon: '(1) Having a rational plan of life, and in particular one that satisfies the Aristotelian principle; and (2) finding our own person and deeds appreciated and confirmed by others who are likewise esteemed and their association enjoyed.'[31] I shall refer to the conditions in which we enjoy the esteem of those we esteem as 'the conditions of reciprocal esteem'. Satisfaction of the 'Aristotelian principle' in a person's rational life plan matters for her self-respect because of how it enhances her existence in the conditions of reciprocal esteem. Rational life plans support self-respect only if they contain ends consistent with the Aristotelian principle.[32] The principle is that, 'other things being equal, human beings enjoy the exercise of their realized capacities (their innate or trained abilities), and this enjoyment increases the more the capacity is realized, or the greater its complexity'.[33] Rawls's example of someone meeting the Aristotelian principle is a person able to play both chess and draughts but who prefers to play chess because of the superior demands it makes on her abilities. Anyone satisfying the Aristotelian principle develops and refines the talents and assets which promote ends forming part of her rational plan of life. By focusing on the social aspect of the Aristotelian principle we can understand the connection between the development of self-respect and the skills of civility. Rawls refers to this aspect of the Aristotelian principle as its companion effect.

> As we witness the exercise of well-trained abilities of others, these displays are enjoyed by us and arouse a desire that we should be able to do the same things ourselves. We want to be like those persons who can exercise the abilities we find latent in our nature.[34]

The claim that self-respect depends on the pursuit of rational life plans that satisfy the Aristotelian principle introduces a social element into the account of self-respect in two ways. First, being in a position to witness displays of talent and so be prompted, as the companion effect states, to emulate these displays ourselves normally requires some form of association with others. This association need not be formal, overly intimate or especially prolonged. But it must be close enough for us to witness the exercise of others' well-trained abilities, and the effect they have on others. Second, satisfying the Aristotelian principle matters for self-respect because such satisfaction is likely to prompt the esteem and respect of others, and a person's receipt of the esteem and respect of others is conducive to her respecting and esteeming herself. Again, association need not be formal, intimate or prolonged, but only close enough for others to witness our displays of talent and so experience the companion effect for themselves.

When associations play these roles, they provide the conditions of reciprocal esteem. These conditions are self-replicating. A person whose self-respect is supported by the esteem and admiration of others will have the self-worth and confidence to truly recognize and admire the efforts of others, thus giving support to their self-respect. 'One who is confident in himself is not grudging in the appreciation of others.'[35]

The connection between the search for self-respect and the skills of civility can now be made. A person's association with others in pursuit of self-respect requires that she be accepted by those others. Acceptance can take the form of anything from formal initiation to mere tolerance of the person's presence, either of which are adequate for observing the exercise of developed talents and experiencing the companion effect. But even in an association in which co-operative activity is central to membership, participation is well defined, and the bonds of shared beliefs and values are strong, there will nevertheless be differences between associates, who are never clones of one another. This means that a prospective associate must adapt her behaviour in different ways for different extant associates, which requires that she gauge each member's point of view. To do this, prospective members must acquire and exercise two key skills of civility: acknowledgement of difference, and empathy. Gaining the self-respect-related benefits of the conditions of reciprocal esteem not only depends on the fact of a person's association with others, but also depends on her learning from established members so as to emulate them and prompt the esteem of her newly acquired peers. This suggests that association requires another key skill of civility: the ability to listen to others and to accept the possibility of modifying a view in the light of others' views.[36]

The claim that to benefit from association with others we must realize that their views differ in part from ours, be sensitive to these differences, and be attentive to what they do and say so as to emulate whatever prompts the esteem of others, is intuitively appealing. Those who arrogantly talk over others, ignore their views, fail to recognize their differences and so insult and offend them are likely to find themselves excluded from associations to which they aspire.[37] Importantly, this is as much true for a neofascist hate group or religious cult as it is for a university debating society or amateur theatre company. All else being equal, the would-be neofascist will not gain acceptance if he insults the leader, fails to defer to the leader's familiars, or fails to identify the nuances of the group norms – the right things to say and do – and act according to them.[38] This shows that civility is not a 'thick' value which can be defended only from the point of view of a comprehensive liberal moral theory. Of course, some groups will lack civility altogether. Groups whose members abuse one another, or whose leaders humiliate and dictate to members, are not schools for civility. But neither are they schools for self-respect, which depends on a person maintaining a sense of his own status. A liberal society committed to securing opportunity for all should ensure for citizens the freedom to leave such groups.

The skills of civility are learnt in associations of every stripe; they are the skills necessary for navigating acceptance by those from whom one differs. A person lacking these skills has a psychological handicap, and is likely to find association with others difficult and traumatic. Admittedly, not all of us exercise these skills all the time. Some of us may use these skills to gain acceptance to an association, master the appropriate norms, rise to the top of the tree, and have no more use for civility. The skills of civility, like all skills, may be used instrumentally. But a person who abandons civility once she achieves the position she aspires to is likely to find that she can no longer secure the co-operative efforts of others necessary for the successful pursuit of her interests. Thus however much it might gall her, even the most self-seeking person would do well to practise civility towards others. Breakdowns of civility are perhaps most common in associations such as families, which have not been sought out by their members. Here the bonds of membership go very deep and can sustain temporary disruptions to civility. Most of us have to exercise these skills every day in the voluntary associations supportive of our self-respect, and we do so without thinking. Ascertaining the views of others, listening to them and learning from their differences are a fundamental part of social life as it benefits self-respect. Without the skills of civility we would find ourselves shunned, avoided and ignored, and inevitably suffer damage to our self-respect.

Once we accept the importance of self-respect and the account of its development in associational life, then we have a plausible story to tell about how people come to acquire the skills of civility. Furthermore, by making opportunity for self-respect a primary good, we ensure conditions in which the skills necessary for good citizenship can be acquired as a side-effect of the search for self-respect. Making the skills of civility key to good citizenship does not require that individuals have virtuous dispositions or especially good intentions; all it requires is that they care about their own self-respect. Distributions of primary goods which maximin opportunity for self-respect also distribute opportunities for the acquisition of skills that can be put to use both in the pursuit of our own self-respect, and in support of principles of justice which ensure that opportunities for self-respect continue to be given a just distribution.

Personal Commitments and Public Reason

Reflection on the relationship between any associational life and acquisition of the skills of civility means that the objection relating to the demandingness of civility must be recast. If the connections just outlined between self-respect, associational life and the skills of civility hold, then the brute claim that exercising the skills of civility is damaging would imply that association with others is damaging because successful association with others requires the exercise of these skills. This is implausible. On the contrary, exercising the skills of civility to achieve association with others and develop self-respect is central to well-being.

Instead of the idea that there is something objectionable about the exercise of the skills of civility *per se*, the objection must be that the way in which Rawls expects people to exercise these skills as citizens is objectionable. Consider David Miller:

> people who, say, belong to a certain church or are members of an ethnic community may not see these memberships and the value-commitments that go with them as even potentially open to revision – they are definitive, for these people, of their personal identity. The problem is to see why people whose identities are encumbered in this way should give priority to an unencumbered citizen identity which, as we saw, entails restricting the pursuit of their private goals within the bounds set by the principles of justice.[39]

Rawls's account focuses on exercising the skills of civility to engage in public reason to address fundamental political questions. The principles of justice endorsed by public reason support a maximin distribution of opportunity for self-respect, and in this sense support all citizens' well-being. Miller's objection is not that the distribution of goods recommended by the principles of justice is itself damaging to anyone's well-being, but rather that participation in a justificatory debate about these principles governed by free public reason makes unacceptable demands of certain people. These demands are to engage in public reason by exercising the skills of civility not only with respect to other members of the associations to which a person belongs, but also with respect to others with whom the person is not in association, and with whom she may be in deep disagreement. Widening the scope of civility to include others from whom we will inevitably differ creates the demand to engage in public reason. In what sense is this unacceptable?

The objection turns on the nature of political society as a form of association. As we have seen, political liberalism takes as its starting-point the fact of reasonable diversity. In that case the objection is that it is unacceptable to expect those in political society with one another to exercise the skills of civility towards one another, given that their association is characterized by ineradicable diversity, however reasonable. The thought is that the differences between people in this diverse association are so deep that the imagination, empathy, listening skills and admissions of fallibility that are needed for civility are too demanding. Understanding the objection that deep differences defeat civility requires thinking carefully about what it is to have a conception of the good.

To have a conception of the good is to have a set of beliefs and values reflecting what one takes to be of importance in human life, where these beliefs and values are informed by comprehensive religious, moral and philosophical doctrines.[40] The objection is that such fundamental beliefs and values carry with them a level of commitment which is in tension with the restraint, effort to empathize and listen, and admission of fallibility demanded by the duty of civility. For example, if a person sincerely believes that what gives a human life meaning is the worship of God in the Catholic faith, then she cannot be expected to understand atheism, to consider whether her reasons, informed by her Catholicism, are acceptable to atheists, or to accept that atheistic objections to her reasons might give her cause to amend her views. Part of the point of her views is that atheists make a grave mistake in denying the existence of God and failing to take up appropriate worship. Admittedly, 'Catholics versus atheists' is an extreme example, but it is supposed to illustrate the point that genuine conceptions of the good, sincerely held, demand total commitment. To ask people to compromise these commitments by exercising the skills of civility in the name of public reason is to ask them to abrogate their most deeply held commitments, and this is unacceptable.[41] According to this objection, political discourse characterized by (non-violent) interpersonal clashes and conflict is preferable to politics characterized by civility-as-restraint and mutual accommodation: clashes and conflicts are a sign of psychological health.[42]

This demandingness objection has it that the fact of reasonable diversity in political society, combined with reflection on what it means to have a conception of the good, makes civility across clusters of conceptions of the good too demanding, although civility within churches, ethnic communities, perhaps nations of patriotic citizens, is still possible. Many comprehensive doctrines informing conceptions of the good will share important features: different religious faiths will share a history and a commitment to God; different left-wing movements will share objectives and goals; different caring professions will share experiences and expectations. The objection has it that civil communication aiming at public reasons is possible, even desirable, across conceptions of the good in such clusters, for no one need give up fundamental beliefs – in God, equality, or the value of patience – to participate in intra-cluster debates. But to ask for shared reasons which straddle the spectrum of conceptions of the good, so as to make inter-cluster discourse possible – even when this spectrum is limited by criteria of reasonableness – is to ask people to find reasons unrelated to their most deeply held beliefs, and to ask them to accept that these beliefs might, in fact, be wrong. The objection is that this level of dissonance and denial is likely to cause damage to any person who attempts it, and should not be part of an account of good citizenship.

This is a serious objection. If public reason and cross-pluralism civility make damaging demands of individuals, then political liberals ought to rethink their accounts of good citizenship. Fortunately, the demandingness objection is not successful because it trades on a misconception of public reason as a form of denial, or amnesia.

The ideal of public reason does not require of citizens that they somehow pretend that they lack the religious, moral or philosophical commitments they actually have, or that they try to forget these commitments or deny them when engaging in fundamental political discourse. Instead, the ideal of public reason acts like a filter for those committed to it. A person committed to public reason considers whether the reasons yielded by her sincerely held conception of justice (part of her conception of the good) could also serve as reasons for others with different, but just as sincerely held, conceptions of justice. If the person believes that her reasons pass this test, these reasons are admissible in basic-justice debates, and she has acted as a good citizen.[43] It is important to note that this case of public reason is procedural. Good citizens are asked to submit their justice-related reasons to the test of public reason to determine whether they could serve as reasons for others. So long as a person makes a genuine effort to do this, regardless of the reasons she eventually endorses, she acts as a good citizen. Of course, this makes some intellectual demands of citizens, but people can be educated to meet these demands, and in fact meet them in their associational life.[44] All accounts of good citizenship which demand that the citizen think for herself place some intellectual demands on people. The important question is, which of these demands are most acceptable given the fact of reasonable pluralism? I submit that thinking about how one's reasons appear to others is less demanding than the accounts of citizenship requiring, for example, adoption of a particular religion or the regulation of life according to ideals of autonomy.

The minimal demands of Rawls's account of citizenship are made clear in his discussion of 'the proviso' with respect to the idea of public reason. The proviso is 'the injunction to present proper political reasons' in political debate.[45] The proviso allows that

> Reasonable comprehensive doctrines, religious or nonreligious, may be introduced in public political discussion at any time, provided that in due course proper political reasons – and not reasons given solely by comprehensive doctrines – are presented that are sufficient to support whatever the comprehensive doctrines introduced are said to support.[46]

The proviso allows for the possibility of introducing comprehensive moral, religious or philosophical doctrines into political debate so long as these comprehensive reasons are also at some point presented as political reasons, having been subjected to public reason. This means that a person who finds the scope of civility demanded by public reasoning particularly hard to accept can start by introducing into political debate reasons informed by her comprehensive views, given the understanding that these comprehensive reasons must at some point be made into public reasons. Rawls sees the proviso as beneficial for stability and equality: allowing comprehensive reasons into political debate only if at some point they are also presented as political reasons shows public reason in action, thus providing an example for those who find the norm of public reason particularly hard to adopt. This process reaffirms the nature of the political society as a constitutional democracy constructed from public reason and thereby fosters and sustains civility among citizens who see the ideal of public reason being approximated.

However, the main point is clear. Rawls states that public reason may be exercised by applying it to reasons yielded by comprehensive moral, religious or philosophical doctrines so as to turn them into political reasons. In that case, public reason and the skills of civility which make its exercise possible would not be available to a person who lacked, forgot or ignored her conception of the good. Far from asking people to deny their most fundamental beliefs, or distance themselves from their commitments, civility actually requires that people explore these commitments and beliefs so as to assess which of them might serve as public reasons fit for invocation in political debate. On Rawls's account, a person alienated from all beliefs and commitments constitutive of a comprehensive conception of the good would be unable to engage in public reason. Civility is defeated by apathy and anomie, not comprehensive commitment.[47]

Of course, this is not to say that the good citizen has privileged access to methods for determining which of her reasons also qualify as public reasons. According to Rawls, all that civility demands is that the good citizen make a genuine and sincere effort to consider whether her reasons could also be reasons for others, given her acknowledgement of their difference and her attempts to empathize with those differences. In order to assess whether the reasons she believes are suitable as public reasons are indeed fit for political discourse, the good citizen has to admit the possibility that she might be wrong, and listen to the opinions of others to determine whether she is in fact wrong.[48] Admitting that it is possible that one might be wrong is not tantamount to abandoning one's beliefs, or even having one's faith shaken.[49] The only way to discover the content of public reason is actually to engage in the process of applying the skills of civility to a consideration of one's own reasons as potential reasons for others with whom one is in political community. Political justification is a practice actually undertaken by civil citizens.[50]

Conclusion

This account of the skills of civility as the key to good citizenship characterized by public reasoning does not rely on unrealistic assumptions about the skills people are likely to have. The skills of civility are skills necessary for the development of self-respect. Neither is this account of good citizenship too demanding. Good citizenship does not require that one give up one's deeply held beliefs and commitments. Instead, it asks that one examine these beliefs and commitments in a spirit of empathy with others, given one's acceptance of their difference, and invoke in political debate only those reasons which one genuinely believes can also serve as reasons for others in political debate.

One final problem relates to the distinction between skills and dispositions. The argument of this chapter has focused on acquisition of the skills of civility, but, it might be objected, there is no justification of the demand that people exercise these skills in pursuit of good citizenship. We may be persuaded that people have the capacity for good citizenship, but on what grounds do we expect that they will be disposed to exercise these capacities?

The problem of motivating good citizenship is a problem in any account of good citizenship. The argument of this chapter suggests that in the pursuit of their self-respect people acquire and exercise the skills of civility in association with others. Thus, the problem of motivation can be recast as a question of why people should extend the scope of civility beyond those with whom they associate and who are similar, to those with whom they will inevitably differ. At this point, some philosophers argue that a shared nationality is vital to motivate this extension of scope. But there is another way to explain why radically different people owe one another civility. Public reason demands that the skills of civility be exercised so as to produce reasons that count as reasons for every reasonable person. Every reasonable person deserves political justifications invoking such reasons because every reasonable person has reasons of her own, and demands reasons from others. The justification of the demand that the scope of civility be extended to reach those from whom we differ on moral, religious or philosophical matters is that regardless of our differences we are all creatures who give and demand reasons. A person who has the skills necessary for a reason-based conversation with different others but who refuses to exercise these skills makes a mistake. The mistake she makes is not to ignore a fact about the other, but to fail to adopt the attitude towards the other that she would expect the other to adopt towards her. Our common status as reason-giving and reason-demanding beings justifies the demand that in political association we ought to widen the scope of civility so as to make public reason the currency of political justification.

Acknowledgements

Thanks are due to Iain Hampsher-Monk, Cécile Laborde, Jamie Munn and Steve Smith for their helpful comments.

Notes

1. Arguing that republican constitutions are the best means to international peace in *Perpetual Peace*, Kant famously claimed that people must 'create a good organisation for the state ... and ... arrange it in such a way that their self-seeking energies are opposed to one another, thereby neutralising or eliminating the destructive effects of the rest. And as far as reason is concerned, the result is the same as if man's selfish tendencies were non-existent, so that man, even if he is not morally good in himself, is nevertheless compelled to be a good citizen. As hard as it may sound, the problem of setting up a state can be solved even by a nation of devils.' (Immanuel Kant (1970) *Perpetual Peace*, in Hans Reiss (ed.) *Kant's Political Writings*, Cambridge: Cambridge University Press, p. 112.)
2. These characteristics have historically, and on the whole, been associated with men only, although John Stuart Mill is a laudable exception. On autonomy and independence as key to good citizenship, see Immanuel Kant, *The Metaphysics of Morals, The Theory of Right Part II: Public Right* (in Reiss (ed.), *Kant's Political Writings*). On intellectual abilities, see John Stuart Mill (1991) *Considerations on Representative Government*, New York: Prometheus Books; on women and citizenship, see Mill (1988) *The Subjection of Women*, Indianapolis: Hackett Publishing Company. See also Immanuel Kant, 'An Answer to the Question "What is Enlightenment?"' (in Reiss (ed.), *Kant's Political Writings*). On reciprocity, see Bill Jordan 'Justice and Reciprocity', this volume, Chapter 3. On patriotism, see Alisdair MacIntyre (1984) 'Is Patriotism a Virtue?', *The Lindley Lecture*, University of Kansas, and Margaret Canovan 'Patriotism Is Not Enough', this volume, Chapter 14. On nationalism see David Miller (1995) *On Nationality*, Oxford: Clarendon Press. On religious convictions, see John Locke (1983) *A Letter Concerning Toleration*, Indianapolis: Hackett.
3. See Norman Daniels (1996) *Justice and Justification: Reflective Equilibrium in Theory and Practice*, Cambridge: Cambridge University Press; Stephen Macedo (1990) *Liberal Virtues*, Oxford: Clarendon Press, and (1995) 'Liberal Civic Education and Religious Fundamentalism: The Case of God v. John Rawls', *Ethics* 105, 468–96; William Galston (1995) 'Two Concepts of Liberalism', *Ethics* 105, 516–34, and (1991) *Liberal Purposes: Goods, Virtues and Diversity in the Liberal State*, Cambridge: Cambridge University Press.
4. 'This pluralism is not seen as a disaster but rather as the natural outcome of the activities of human reason under enduring free institutions' (John Rawls (1993) *Political Liberalism*, New York: Columbia University Press, p. xxiv).
5. Rawls, *Political Liberalism*, p. 226.
6. See Richard C. Sinopoli (1995) 'Thick-Skinned Liberalism: Redefining Civility', *American Political Science Review* 89 (3), 612–20; David Miller (1995) 'Citizenship and Pluralism', *Political Studies* 43 (3), 432–50.

7. Rawls, *Political Liberalism*, p. 19. The capacity for a sense of justice – 'the duty of justice' – is also central to Rawls's position on good citizenship in his earlier work (1971) *A Theory of Justice*, Oxford: Oxford University Press, pp. 115, 334.

8. Rawls, *A Theory of Justice*, p. 115.

9. See Patricia Smith (1998) *Liberalism and Affirmative Obligation*, New York: Oxford University Press. See also my (forthcoming 2000) 'Rescue, Community and Perfect Obligation', *Res Publica*, 6, 105–16.

10. Rawls, *A Theory of Justice*, p. 355.

11. 'Gazumping' occurs when buyer A makes an offer to the vendor, which is accepted, but then buyer B makes a higher offer, which the vendor accepts in preference to A's offer. The practice is illegal in Scotland because the vendor's acceptance of a verbal offer is recognized as a contract.

12. Rawls, *A Theory of Justice*, p. 355.

13. *Ibid.*, p. 389.

14. *Ibid.*, pp. 363–82. For a different account of civil disobedience as good citizenship, see Ronald Dworkin (1977) 'Civil Disobedience', in *Taking Rights Seriously*, London: Duckworth.

15. *Ibid.*, pp. 220–1.

16. Rawls, *Political Liberalism*, p. 217.

17. Stability and equality are the two key values of political justification for Rawls. On stability, see *A Theory of Justice*, pp. 177–82, 219f, 454f, and *Political Liberalism*, pp. xviif, 38f, 65f, 142f, 143f. On equality, see *A Theory of Justice*, pp. 19, 100–8, 329, 505f, 504–12, and *Political Liberalism*, pp. 19, 79, 81, 109, 289.

18. John Rawls (1997) 'The Idea of Public Reason Revisited', *The University of Chicago Law Review* 64 (3), 761–807.

19. *Ibid.*, p. 769.

20. The burdens of judgement arise because of inevitable disagreements about what constitutes evidence and how evidence is to be weighed; the indeterminacy of clear answers to hard questions; differences of biographical experience and normative commitments; and the need to prioritize certain values over others (Rawls, *Political Liberalism*, pp. 56–7).

21. 'To respect another as a moral person is to try to understand his aims and interests from his standpoint, and to present him with considerations that enable him to accept ... constraints on his conduct' (Rawls, *A Theory of Justice*, p. 338).

22. 'The ideal of democratic citizens trying to conduct their political affairs on terms supported by public values that we might reasonably expect others to endorse ... expresses a willingness to listen to what others have to say and being ready to accept reasonable accommodations or alterations in one's view' (Rawls, *Political Liberalism*, p. 253). Accepting the consequences of the burdens of judgement also explains this requirement of public reason.

23. This objection can be supplemented with the claim that Rawls's account of good citizenship covertly employs a comprehensive liberal ideal of citizenship; the idea is that political liberalism smuggles comprehensive values in 'by the back door'. This common criticism is found in many places. See Miller, 'Citizenship and Pluralism'; Joseph Raz (1990) 'Facing Diversity: The Case of Epistemic Abstinence', *Philosophy and Public Affairs* 19 (1), 3–46. A particularly subtle version of this criticism is in Onora O'Neill (1997) 'Review of Rawls' *Political Liberalism*', *Philosophical Review* 106 (3), 411–28.

24. Rawls, *A Theory of Justice*, p. 440.

25. *Ibid.*, p. 440. See also pp. 92, 107, 443, 543–5, and *Political Liberalism*, pp. 106, 203, 318, 319.

26. Rawls, *A Theory of Justice*, p. 62; *Political Liberalism*, pp. 178–90.

27. Rawls, *Political Liberalism*, p. 181.

28. 'Self-respect depends upon and is encouraged by certain public features of basic social institutions, how they work together and how people who accept these arrangements are expected to (and normally do) regard and treat one another. These features of basic institutions and publicly expected (and normally honoured) ways of conduct are the social bases of self-respect' (Rawls, *A Theory of Justice*, p. 319).

29. Rawls, *A Theory of Justice*, p. 440. For more on self-respect, see Robin S. Dillon (ed.) (1995) *Dignity, Character and Self-Respect*, New York: Routledge; Jean Hampton (1993) 'Selflessness and Loss of the Self', in E.F. Paul, F. Miller and J. Paul (eds) *Altruism*, Cambridge: Cambridge University Press; Thomas E. Hill Jr (1991) *Autonomy and Self-Respect*, Cambridge: Cambridge University Press; Catriona McKinnon (1997) 'Self-Respect and the Stepford Wives', *Proceedings of the Aristotelian Society* 97, 325–30; David Sachs (1981) 'How to Distinguish between Self-Respect and Self-Esteem', *Philosophy and Public Affairs* 10 (4), 3–18.

30. 'The maximin rule tells us to rank alternatives by their worst possible outcomes; we are to adopt the alternative the worst outcome of which is superior to the worst outcomes of the others' (Rawls, *A Theory of Justice*, pp. 152–3).

31. Rawls, *A Theory of Justice*, p. 440.

32. Rational life plans are those suited to the individual's actual talents, given what she knows of those talents. See Rawls, *A Theory of Justice*, p. 417.

33. *Ibid.*, p. 426.

34. Rawls, *A Theory of Justice*, p. 428. For a critique of Rawls's account of how self-respect depends on achieving ends in accord with the Aristotelian principle, see Robert Yanal (1978) 'Self-Esteem', *Noûs* 21, 363–79, and Larry L. Thomas (1978) 'Morality and Our Self-Concept', *Journal of Value Inquiry* 12, 258–68.

35. Rawls, *A Theory of Justice*, p. 441. See also Daniel Brudney (1997) 'Community and Completion', in Andrews Reath, Barbara Herman and Christine M. Korsgaard (eds) *Reclaiming the History of Ethics: Essays for John Rawls*, Cambridge: Cambridge University Press.

36. See Rawls on 'the morality of association', *A Theory of Justice*, pp. 468–9.

37. See Sarah Buss (1999) 'Appearing Respectful: The Moral Significance of Manners', *Ethics* 109, 795–826.

38. See Nancy Rosenblum (1998) *Membership and Morals: The Personal Uses of Pluralism in America* (Princeton, NJ: Princeton University Press). Shklar's wonderful discussion of the social value of hypocrisy also invokes skills similar to the skills of civility: Judith Shklar (1984) 'Let Us Not Be Hypocritical', in *Ordinary Vices*, Cambridge, MA: Belknap Press. For a related discussion of the importance of protecting conventions of politeness and concealment, see Thomas Nagel (1998) 'Concealment and Exposure', *Philosophy and Public Affairs* 27 (1), 3–30.

39. Miller, 'Citizenship and Pluralism', p. 438. See also Iris Marion Young (1989) 'Polity and Group Difference: A Critique of the Ideal of Universal Citizenship', *Ethics* 99, 250–74.

40. Rawls defines a conception of the good as 'a more or less determinate scheme of final ends, that is, ends we want to realise for their own sake, as well as attachments to other persons and loyalties to various groups and associations. These attachments and loyalties give rise to devotions and affections, and so the flourishing of the persons and associations who are the objects of these sentiments is also part of our conception of the good. We also connect with such a conception a view of our relation to the world – religious, philosophical, moral – by reference to which the value and significance of our ends and attachments are understood. Finally, persons' conceptions of the good are not fixed but form and develop as they mature, and may change more or less radically over the course of life' (*Political Liberalism*, pp. 19–20).

41. Rawls expresses the objection as follows in 'The Idea of Public Reason Revisited': '[The] objection insists that we should always present what we think are true or grounding reasons for our views. That is, the objection insists, we are bound to express the true, or the right, as seen from our comprehensive doctrines' (p. 799).

42. The objection is not developed in this way by David Miller. See instead Sinopoli (who develops the objection in the name of John Stuart Mill), 'Thick-Skinned Liberalism'; see also the section of Macedo's 'Liberal Civic Education and Religious Fundamentalism' entitled 'What Good Is Political Liberalism?'

43. 'I have assumed throughout that citizens affirm comprehensive religious and philosophical doctrines and many will think that nonpolitical and transcendent values are the true ground of political values. Does this belief make our appeal to political values insincere? It does not. . . . That we think political values have some further backing does not mean that we do not affirm those values or affirm the conditions of honouring public reason' (Rawls, *Political Liberalism*, pp. 242–3).

44. The Final Report of the Advisory Committee on Education for Citizenship in Britain specifies a list of skills and abilities, including empathy and tolerance, that citizenship education is supposed to inculcate in children.

45. Rawls, 'The Idea of Public Reason Revisited', p. 784.

46. *Ibid.*, pp. 783–4.

47. Nancy Rosenblum also sees anomie as the biggest threat to good liberal citizenship, and builds her case for the toleration and promotion of the maximum amount of diversity in associational life upon this reflection (Rosenblum, *Membership and Morals*, esp. pp. 21, 31, 33, 104, 328, 331, 334, 349, 351, 362, 363). See also Galston, *Liberal Purposes*; he claims that 'The greatest threat to children in modern liberal society is not that they will believe in something too deeply, but that they will believe in nothing very deeply at all' (p. 255, cited in Rosenblum, *Membership and Morals*, p. 31).

48. 'The ideal [of public reason] . . . expresses a willingness to listen to what others have to say and being ready to accept reasonable accommodations or alterations in one's own view. Public reason further asks of us that the balance of those values we hold to be reasonable in a particular case is a balance we sincerely think can be seen to be reasonable by others. Or failing this, we think the balance can be seen as at least not unreasonable in this sense: that those who oppose it can nevertheless understand how reasonable persons can affirm it. This preserves the ties of civic friendship and is consistent with the duty of civility. On some questions this may be the best we can do' (Rawls, *Political Liberalism*, p. 253).

49. A point often emphasized by John Stuart Mill, especially in *On Liberty*; see H.B. Acton (ed.) *Utilitarianism, Liberty, Representative Government*, London: Dent, chapter 2.

50. 'It is inevitable and often desirable that citizens have different views as to the most appropriate political conception; for the public political culture is bound to contain different fundamental ideas that can be developed in different ways. An orderly contest between them over time is a reliable way to find which one, if any is most reasonable' (Rawls, *Political Liberalism*, p. 227).

CHAPTER EIGHT

Motivating Liberal Citizenship

MARK PHILP

I

Prior to the end of the eighteenth century, although it was quite common for writers on politics to value citizens and their contribution to politics, it was far more rare for them to think that democratic governments were desirable or viable. Only at the time of the American and French Revolutions did mass participation come to be seen as a politically feasible and worthwhile aspiration. In France, in particular, demands for democratic citizenship were fuelled by the belief that social distinctions could be overcome by each person becoming an equal member of the sovereign legislature, thereby becoming both sovereign and subject. This coupling, which drew on the classical republican tradition, linked citizenship to an ideal of civic virtue involving a passionate commitment to political activity and a willingness to subordinate personal interests to the common good. In the immediate aftermath of the Terror this ideal was widely repudiated, but in subsequent decades, especially in the work of Constant and Tocqueville, a more subtle understanding emerged of the place of political participation in securing liberties within the modern democratic republic:

> The danger of ancient liberty was that men, exclusively concerned with securing their share of social power, might attach too little value to individual rights and enjoyments. The danger of modern liberty is that, absorbed in the enjoyment of our private independence, and in the pursuit of our particular interests, we should surrender our right to share in political power too easily. The holders of authority are only too anxious to encourage us to do so ... [but] to renounce it, Gentlemen, would be a folly like that of a man who, because he only lives on the first floor, does not care if the house is built on sand.[1]

For Constant and Tocqueville, the civic virtue of the classical republic was neither desirable nor possible within the modern state; yet for both, political participation (what Constant called 'political liberty') remained essential as a constraint on those who ruled. Moreover, both recognized that such participation was not automatically forthcoming and had somehow to be motivated

> even when the people are satisfied there is much left to do. Institutions must achieve the moral education of the citizens. By respecting their individual rights, securing their independence, refraining from troubling their work, they must nevertheless consecrate their influence over public affairs, call them to contribute by their votes to the exercise of power, grant them a right of control and supervision by expressing their opinions; and, by forming them through practices for these elevated functions, give them both the desire and the right to discharge these.[2]

The underlying insight here, that participation is vital to safeguard the rights and liberties of citizens but that the exercise of these rights and liberties may undermine the motivation for participation, has continuing relevance for liberal democratic theory.[3] Rights against the political sphere must be combined with duties in that sphere, in a way which protects the rights without undercutting the motivation to meet the duties. Following Constant, theorists of liberal democratic citizenship have continued to wrestle with the tensions between the individualistic and atomized culture of capitalist states, and the perceived need to motivate citizens to participate in the political institutions of their states so that their rights against the state remain secure.[4] In recent debates, theorists of citizenship have acknowledged that motivating participation has been further complicated by the value pluralism and multiculturalism which increasingly characterize most modern liberal-democratic states.[5]

The framing of our understanding of citizenship in this way, as involving a tension between the private lives we want the state to protect and the need to motivate public participation in politics so as to guarantee that protection, has considerable merit. Not least, it starts from a parsimonious account of people's personal interests and motivations, couples this with some hypotheses about the necessary conditions for stable, orderly and benign political rule, and then argues about how these can be combined. In contrast, many republican theories have presented democratic participation as a good or end in itself, thereby uncoupling it from the functional role it plays, directly and indirectly, in the preservation of private or personal concerns and widening the gap between the demands of civic virtue on the one hand, and the actual beliefs and interests of the average citizen of the modern state on the other.[6] With the aim of generating a less ambitious account of citizenship, this chapter takes as its starting-point the initial insight of Constant and Tocqueville and asks what threshold level of citizen involvement is required to sustain stable, orderly and legitimate rule in democratic states and to prevent authoritarian or arbitrary government.[7] In the third section of the chapter, I distinguish three types of motivation for political participation and show how far they are able to motivate the minimum I identify as required for democratic political rule. In the final section, I question one aspect of Constant's insight, and argue that a theory of citizenship might be considerably more parsimonious in its demands than much recent democratic theory is inclined to accept.

My concern here is to identify a threshold conception of citizenship: one which identifies the minimum demands that must be made of citizens within modern liberal democratic states, in contrast to the more ideal-regarding and normative accounts of citizenship, which face serious motivational difficulties. In doing so, I must set aside two further dimensions of citizenship and democratic theory which were prominent in twentieth-century accounts: namely, the material preconditions for effective citizenship; and theories of institutional design. That is, I leave open the issue of what social, educational and economic resources are necessary to equip individuals to play the part of citizens, and what types of institutional framework are appropriate to democratic states. These issues are important, but I regard the question of the demands of citizenship and the issue of the motivation required to meet these demands as more fundamental. I also acknowledge that by seeing citizenship in these relatively functional terms I am ignoring other grounds for giving prominence to equal citizenship – such as considerations of justice or welfare. In contrast to much modern republicanism, the position I defend does not seek a high degree of association between a theory of democratic citizenship on the one hand, and a theory of the good society on the other: the former is a necessary part of the latter, but it is not identical with it.[8]

II

Citizenship describes a form of standing in politics, one which accords the individual the right to be ruled politically – that is, in accordance with the legitimated procedures or principles of the political domain.[9] Civil and personal rights are not identical to those of citizenship, since they can be accorded to persons who do not have citizenship, but, for Constant, certain political liberties (which are the rights component of citizenship) are necessary to safeguard these other civil and personal rights. At the heart of citizenship lies the right of individuals and/or groups to make demands on their political institutions and to hold their rulers responsible for their actions in office. To deny groups and individuals these rights is to deny them citizenship and its associated standing in politics and is to rule them coercively or paternalistically, not politically.[10] States ruled in such a way can be orderly and (sometimes) stable, but they achieve these ends by methods which are not legitimated by those ruled.[11] On this view, democratic politics provides its citizens with a distinctive 'standing' – one which involves certain basic rights with respect to the political domain, together with certain responsibilities. Although different democratic states operate with differing conceptions of this standing and its responsibilities, the role which politics plays in the authoritative resolution of conflict ensures that the demands made of citizens are broadly similar.

The rights which citizens are accorded in democratic politics place constraints on how citizens may act in that sphere. If a citizen makes representation or seeks in some other way to influence the political process and its outcomes, the right to do so is predicated on the implicit acknowledgement of a duty to abide by the accepted procedures of the political process, their spirit, and their outcome. Such 'procedural duties' are entailed by the exercise of certain rights within the polity, but they are not duties to exercise these rights. However, even relatively parsimonious theories of citizenship, like Constant's, insist that there must also be some responsibilities to exercise these rights, so as to sustain a culture of accountability for those who occupy positions of political power and trust. Two complex issues arising from this claim are whether this is really a 'duty', and whether it must apply to all who have political standing. The idea behind these 'participatory duties' is that the political system must be able to elicit the participation of its citizens, both in the formal institutions of the system, such as elections, sitting on juries, and so on, and in the broader sense of sustaining a political culture which links the citizen on the street to those who exercise public office.[12]

Two basic forms of both procedural and participatory duties can be identified. Procedural duties concern both:

(a) individuals' or groups' dealings with holders of public office, where norms of political propriety must be sustained; and
(b) individual or group responses to the output of the political system, such as laws and agreements, and their public stand on procedures.

In the former case, we are concerned with 'vertical' relations between citizens and the institutions and offices of the state. States which allow citizens to make representation to those in office without acknowledging the rules and norms of the political process create the conditions for extensive corruption – corruption which stems from individuals seeking to use illegitimate means to achieve desired outcomes (such as threats, bribes, and so on), and from élites seeking to secure and sustain their hold on power by gaining the support and compliance of groups through illegitimate means – as through patron-client relations or by violating norms for the appointment of public officials in order to build a political machine. In the second case – 'output-abidingness'–the concern is that groups and communities should acknowledge the legitimacy of the political procedures and comply with the letter and spirit of the agreements negotiated through these procedures. In such activities, the focus is not on a binary, formally defined, vertical relationship between citizens and public officials so much as on the less formal 'horizontal' responsibilities to one's fellow citizens who are subject to the same norms or rules. Keeping to the spirit of one's agreements involves not free-riding on others' compliance, and not raising questions about the legitimacy of the process as a tactical move to gain advantage over those who comply without complaint. Theories of citizenship certainly recognize that in neither case is such behaviour always illegal, but nor is it in keeping with the spirit of political negotiation and compromise, and to deny such responsibilities is effectively to seek a benefit beyond that which they can derive from, and legitimate within, the political process. We may call these 'horizontal' responsibilities because the benefit we forgo by complying is one which we could have gained only by free-riding on other citizens' procedural restraint;[13] whereas the vertical cases are those in which the citizen or group seeks illicit preferential access to resources or influence over decisions by in some way suborning those whose political office gives them control of these resources or decisions.

Those who insist on the continuing significance of participation have identified two different areas of importance:

1   There is engagement in activities to which one has a right by virtue of one's citizenship – such as in voting, making representation, involvement in interest-group activities, joining and acting in political parties, writing letters to newspapers and MPs, and in demonstrating, performing jury service and so on. (A duty to participate is a duty to participate within procedural constraints. The two types of duties are analytically distinct since, while a right to participate may entail duties when it is exercised, it is a distinct question as to whether we have a duty to exercise that right. Motivating compliance with procedural duties may draw on resources different from those that are required (or are available) to motivate compliance with participatory duties.)[14]

2   Theories of citizenship have also drawn attention to the importance of civic culture among those subject to political rule – what we might think of as a form of 'social capital',[15] which exists among citizens outside the directly political arena and provides a background of trust, shared information and political intelligence. This culture is seen both as motivating the more formal participation in the system, and as sustaining the accountability of politicians.

Both types of participation play a central role in Tocqueville's writing. The first is evident in his eulogy to American townships in the 1835 volume of *Democracy in America*, where it is seen as central to the preservation of a spirit of liberty – by which he meant the ability to resist encroachment on liberty by political authorities. The second animates the 1840 volume, which dwells on the corrosive effects of individualism on the political system and on the willingness of citizens to cede ever greater areas of responsibility to an increasingly centralized and bureaucratic state.[16]

Tocqueville's discussion in his second volume, in which he sees secondary associations as central to the exercise of individual liberty and to the formation of a public identity and a civic spirit among citizens, defends one side in a long-standing argument concerning civic culture.[17] The other side, the Spartan variant espoused by Rousseau, takes the sole unit of participation and identification to be one's *patrie*, with secondary associations being seen as wholly inimical to the formation of the general will. The division between Tocqueville, who emphasizes the benefits of associations with respect to the state, and Rousseau, who emphasizes the costs, revolves around the issue of how far membership of civil society and its various associations produces a consistent identification with the norms of the political domain, either directly (because of the way that participation enlarges the scope of one's interests) or by default (through the sheer proliferation of interests and the inability of any particular interest to gain ascendancy over all others),[18] rather than threatening to make the political process hostage to the strongest societal interests – as in Adam Smith's comment that 'People of the same trade seldom meet together, even for merriment and diversion, but the conversation ends in a conspiracy against the publick.'[19] While horizontal forms of participation are critical for the development of group identities and social capital, loyalties to a group do not necessarily lead to a more general form of *civitas*.

This fundamental point of disagreement has recently taken a new form, focusing on the problems generated by the presence of different systems of communal value and cultural life coexisting within the bounds of the liberal democratic state. When communities demand collective rights to protect their distinctive cultural values and practices, they effectively deny that their standing as citizens within the modern 'procedural republic' adequately protects their concerns.[20] Indeed, one feature of these debates has been to insist that such cultural differences pose a different order of problem than do individualism or interest-group conflict. On such a view, whereas conflict over distributive issues is in principle positive-sum, is negotiable and can be organized within a common framework of rules, conflict involving the politics of identity is zero-sum, non-negotiable and resistant to shared political procedures and practices. If communal identity is a constitutive feature of individual identity, framing the person's deepest 'dispositions and motives', then it will profoundly affect whether group members can recognize the legitimacy of extra-communal procedures and rules. On this view, identity trumps citizenship.

Theories of the material preconditions for democracy and of institutional design may try to find ways of rectifying structural imbalances caused by deep ethnic or social divisions – but it is unlikely that institutional design can always resolve such conflicts, not least because the procedures which generate and validate new institutional structures and patterns of redistribution themselves rely on the very procedural compliance and participation which ethnic or social divisions can make impossible. However, our concern here is with the responsibilities of citizens within democratic systems (whose institutional design may vary widely); and such a theory should be able to show what demands democratic systems must make on their citizens and whether these are more or less easily met. Having clarified these demands, I turn to the analysis of three distinct motives for citizens' compliance to see how far each is able to meet the procedural and participatory demands of the modern democratic state.

III

We can distinguish, loosely, three different types of motivations for compliance with political norms: *modus vivendi*, civic virtue, and mixed or multiple motivation.

Modus vivendi compliance occurs where the motive for compliance is the benefit which accrues to individual or group interests.[21] Conformity to political norms is, then, conditional on those norms offering an interest-maximizing strategy for the individual or group.[22] This need not mean narrow, self-interest maximizing, since the ends the individual pursues may involve group, or even global, altruism.[23] But it does imply that the interests or values which are maximized are identified independently of the norms and values which structure the rules of the political domain. Without that condition, we would be solving the problem of motivation by definition. Nor does *modus vivendi* require that citizens comply only where they judge that a specific act of compliance is strictly interest maximizing. On the contrary, acknowledgement of the role played by threshold judgements and co-ordination problems helps us see that compliance may be forthcoming not because the norms of the political system are accepted, nor because conformity with them maximally serves the groups's interests, but because non-conformity is not available as a strategy since a certain threshold for collective action would need to be crossed before the norms could be challenged.[24] But in each case, in so far as the motive for compliance in politics is given by these interests and values, our standing as a citizen is playing no role in our willingness to meet its demands; we accept or reject such demands wholly on the basis of their compatibility with our existing values or commitments. This may not pose a problem where a society is marked by a high degree of consensus on values and where the state's institutions and procedures are wholly congruent with such values. But state-building, the development of capitalist economies, democratization and modernization have combined to ensure that most modern nation-states are marked to varying degrees by atomism, value pluralism and/or group and ethnic conflict, and under such conditions there can be no assumption that individuals or groups will find any degree of fit with the procedural constraints which their political orders require of them in the pursuit of their ends.

The potential and limitations of *modus vivendi* compliance can best be seen with reference to the different responsibilities we have identified. Although in cases of atomism[25] we might anticipate widespread non-compliance, in fact compliance can be produced simply by ensuring that sanctions for non-compliance are seen as effective. Citizens' behaviour may be procedure abiding because the state is able to control its officers and to punish those who fail to comply with procedural norms.[26] Similarly, horizontal – or outcome – compliance may also be generated by the state's willingness to impose costs on defectors. Moreover, individuals and groups may also find it in their interests to support such activity on the part of the state even though this makes it more likely that their own defection (if and when it occurs) will be successfully punished (thereby further increasing the incentives for compliance).

Where there is extensive group conflict, however, procedural compliance is much more difficult to motivate, not least because communities often offer individual members some insulation from sanctions by the state, especially when the state is perceived as hostile to the group. Despite the tendency among political theorists to treat ethnic conflict as fundamentally different from class conflict, it seems likely that whenever the individual's identity (whether class or ethnic) is rooted in a solidaristic community and is coupled with an antagonistic relationship to the state, we would find something very like a politics of identity – and a similar willingness and ability (because communal solidarity facilitates collective action)[27] to mobilize to elude state sanctions. At the other extreme, élite groups with close relationships to the state will also be able to avoid sanctions, and have few incentives not to exploit their position to their advantage.

While procedural compliance may be differentially elicited under *modus vivendi* depending on whether the social order tends more to atomism and individualism than to group conflict, in neither case is participation easily motivated. In group conflict cases, if participation is elicited only when it is interest maximizing, and if it is procedure abiding only when *that* is also interest maximizing, it is probable that participation will be destabilizing. Under atomism it is unclear what the incentives for voluntary participation could be – hence the adoption in some states of enforcement mechanisms, such as penalties for non-voting, or against those resisting jury service. Moreover, there seem to be no incentives for the broader, horizontal forms of participation we have identified, not least because there are (by hypothesis) few group structures or associations upon which such participation could ride.

This conclusion needs some qualification: the concern to protect and promote one's interests does not necessarily militate against political participation. There may be less participation under a stable political order, since free-riding really does look costless; and for different reasons, participation will be perceived as unproductive where there is a highly coercive, authoritarian state. But acts of protest against, for example, blatant cases of corruption, fraud or insouciance towards civil rights by some section of the political élite might be generated by *modus vivendi* motives if the potential gains are large and the threshold for collective action is shown to be securely crossed – perhaps by the example set by some other group, not similarly motivated, such as the judiciary or the police. Getting out from under corrupt patrons may be in our interests, and acting to do so may also be an interest-maximizing strategy if it can be shown to be safe (and the incentives increase if staying under them can be shown to have escalating costs). One important insight this offers is that collective acts of resistance to derelictions of public duty, or to authoritarian states, may be motivated wholly or largely by self-interest – if the behaviour of others is able to signal that such behaviour is both low cost and has a high potential return. For example, individual acts of resistance to authoritarian regimes may, if rigorously penalized, prompt few imitators. But examples of unpenalized opposition may prompt others to add their voice; and once there are a few, then many more may treat this as a sign that they can oppose without penalty. The diverse thresholds for collective action in a population may allow a rapid snowballing effect to follow from a relatively minor incident. The downside is that virtuous compliance can unravel in a similar type of spiral. If a trust or honour system of time-keeping and in-lieu-leave operates in a firm and new management attempts to formalize certain procedures, such as clocking in and sick leave, the sense of fair play on which the old practices (and much else besides) rested may be rapidly eroded, leaving a very low level of institutional virtue.[28]

So the conclusion we should draw is that where citizens are motivated by nothing more than a *modus vivendi*, the greatest danger to political stability arises where lip-service to participatory demands masks group or identity conflicts. In cases of atomism, *modus vivendi* may motivate procedural compliance but is unlikely to motivate participation. However, the case for saying that the political system is thereby rendered unstable rests on the view that it risks subversion from élites within the order or from group forces outside. I return to this case in section IV, below.

Civic virtue is a central concept within the classical republican tradition. It refers to the citizen's desire to further the public good over his or her own private ends.[29] The emphasis is on virtue because it refers to an ingrained disposition to serve the polity or *patrie*, and to the fact that citizens recognize the demands of citizenship as delimiting their other concerns. Because private interests are admitted only when they are compatible with or actively shaped by one's civic concerns, it is sometimes difficult to establish that the agent is acting from civic virtue rather than from compatible private-regarding motives.[30] As a result, civic virtue is most easily recognized in situations where the individual's independent interest in conformity is weak – because of the costs imposed on the agent. Analytically, we can say that we have a case of virtuous conformity where it is the agent's commitment to his or her citizenship, as defined by the rules and principles of the political order, which makes the difference in determining her conformity with those principles. That is, civic virtue requires that it be the person's commitment *qua* citizen which motivates his or her compliance in the face of incentives, *qua* individual, to defect. This does not require that citizens act wholly without concern for how others act: civic virtue is not the same as unthinking self-sacrifice, but it does require that the virtuous citizen does not set the threshold for others' compliance entirely by prudential criteria. Citizens cannot rationally be indifferent to outcomes and must assess the costs of complying where others do not (they might, for example, face certain death, financial ruin or reprisals against their families, and it is implausible to think that the virtuous citizen must regard these costs as negligible and to hold that they cannot sometimes outweigh the benefit to the public good which the citizen is likely to bring about – which in some cases must be very small indeed). Individual interests can, then, have some weight, but virtuous citizens are those whose commitment to their citizenship and to political norms takes them beyond an immediate calculation of their interests, and where it is that commitment which motivates them to act in support of those norms – so that it is their commitment to their values and principles *as citizens* which motivates their compliance.

In cases where general compliance is not going to be forthcoming or where it is extremely improbable that it will be, where the potential costs of compliance are exorbitant, and where the contribution we can hope to make is small, then we may have to say that civic virtue has become dispropotionately costly and that citizenship has become impossible – since the demands it makes can be reasonably rejected. In such circumstances we might get acts of heroism or instances of great personal courage, but the need for this – in cases of domestic politics – is often an indication that the political order is too weak to be independently effective, which then makes it difficult for us to think of them as instances of civic virtue.[31]

Unlike *modus vivendi*, civic virtue motivates both compliance and participation across the full range of citizenship demands. But within the republican tradition, it tends to do so by giving overriding weight to the person's political standing over all other identities, by suggesting an inevitable tension between private interests and the demands of the common good, and by believing that a process of political education is essential to ensure that the appropriate degree of identification with the polis and the common good is achieved. The tradition draws on an understanding of politics as a fragile achievement for which the highest personal sacrifice can be asked, and in which the citizen's other interests and commitments are accorded little or no weight (since the sustaining of the republic is seen as a necessary condition for achieving these other ends). However, as writers as early as Montesquieu recognized,[32] in the more plural and complex world of the modern state, in which the unity and face-to-face character of the classical republic has been lost, it is not easy to see how to motivate this degree of commitment. Indeed, on Marx and Engel's account, it is wholly irrational to believe that we could do so:

> What a terrible illusion it is to have to recognise and sanction in the rights of man, modern bourgeois society, the society of industry, of universal competition, of private interest freely pursuing its aims of anarchy, of self estranged natural and spiritual individuality, and at the same time to want to annul the manifestations of the life of this society in particular individuals and simultaneously to want to model the political head of that society in the manner of antiquity.[33]

It seems that we would have to reject many relatively standard features of the modern state, such as pluralism, a flourishing civil society and economy, and the right to pursue one's own conception of the good as one sees fit, to secure the appropriate levels of civic virtue. This is not to say that it is never possible to generate such civic virtue: in *extremis*, during wars or in situations of high international tension, for example, nationalism or patriotism may result in high levels of public participation and commitment; but this is neither a common situation nor an ideal one. State-led nationalism – and state-led forms of cultural unity more generally – threaten to increase political solidarity and conformity only by decreasing the extent to which citizenship remains the basis for claims *against* the political order (as indeed Marx and Engels suggest). The problem of citizenship in liberal democratic orders is one of ensuring that there is compliance with political procedures, while sustaining some sort of 'civic' control on the institutions and officials of the state and defending the sanctity and security of the private concerns and interests of citizens. Small-scale, homogeneous, face-to-face communities might have enough solidarity to ensure that citizens are committed to the common good in a way which sustains compliance, critical distance and individual security, but modern states, for the most part, do not.[34]

Broadly speaking, this was the basis on which Constant repudiated the tradition of ancient liberty, and if there is a case to be made for civic virtue (and against Constant), it must be one which shows that modern liberal democratic states cannot remain resiliently stable without this degree of mobilization. But the strength of Constant's characterization of the problem of citizenship is that it suggests that if liberal democratic states cannot survive without civic virtue, then it is also the case that they cannot remain both democratic *and* liberal if they have to rely on its generation. The argument must shift from showing that liberal democracies as we know them need civic virtue, to showing that the very ideal of a liberal democracy is flawed. Rather than embracing this course we might do better to look elsewhere for an understanding of the form of compliance required by modern democratic states.

One alternative to civic virtue is the idea of over-determined compliance, which arises where the interests or values of the individual and the group endorse compliance in broad terms (while also providing limits to that endorsement) but where this is supported by some degree of independent commitment to the norms of the political domain so that, within limits, compliance is not dependent on securing the optimal advantage.[35] Something like this case can be recognized in the more recent work of Rawls, under the heading of 'overlapping consensus'. In contrast to the particularist and irrationalist approach to political unity adopted by nationalists and patriots (including many republicans), Rawls's account looks for a grounding in political values and the values of public reason. His approach is especially attractive because he recognizes that the values of public reason need not be treated as wholly free-standing universals (which would imply the irrelevance of one's particular citizenship), but can be recognized as emerging only through the particular practices and shared experiences of a political community. Consequently, what public reason demands is a local question, albeit one informed by the desire to ensure the highest and most general standard of justification. That is, it is not simply an empirical issue of what passes muster for public reason around here, but it also involves a judgement to the effect that what counts as public reason does so for the right reasons. Our citizenship, then, gives us access to institutions, shared practices and deliberative arenas; it requires us to act in these spheres in accordance with a common set of political values and standards of public reason, and we develop our understanding of our responsibilities as citizens through our participation in institutions and practices regulated by public reason which enable us to recognize our obligations to other citizens and to accept the necessity for procedural rules to govern the formation of law and public policy.

There is a worry here about boot-strapping. The values which grow out of participation seem also to be necessary to frame that participation in the first place – or participation will be opportunistic and will undermine attempts (if such exist) to appeal to public reason. How do we get from a default position of *modus vivendi* to one of self-restraint in line with public reason without implicitly presupposing the presence of the latter in the former? Rawls does not acknowledge this problem. He believes that the connection between the two motives (our personal and/or communal values and our commitment to public reason) will tend to be positive, and increasingly so, unless disrupted by external factors (such as war, natural disasters, etc.). For example, he sketches a story of the transformation from a *modus vivendi* through a constitutional consensus to an overlapping consensus.[36] In a constitutional consensus, the constitution satisfies certain liberal principles, but these principles are not deeply grounded in a shared public conception of society and the person, although they are affirmed as substantive principles. Rawls believes that, over time, liberal principles of justice, initially accepted reluctantly as a *modus vivendi* and adopted into a constitution, tend to shift citizens' comprehensive doctrines so that they at least accept the principles of a liberal constitution. ... Simple pluralism moves towards reasonable pluralism and constitutional consensus is achieved.[37]

However, in part because a constitutional consensus is 'a consensus taken literally', it lacks the conceptual resources to guide the interpretation and amendment of the constitution.[38] The search for such resources drives us from a constitutional consensus to a deeper and broader consensus on the principles which should structure the political domain.

This is an optimistic picture, although it is not without foundation: as we have seen, where compliance is widespread, continued compliance becomes relatively frictionless, and we can follow Hume in thinking that it can become increasingly so.[39] Moreover, we may draw on a range of accounts of virtuous mechanisms in social institutions which help us to understand how people can come to an institution with one set of interests and develop a different set through their participation – or can come to make war and stay to make peace.[40] However, we need to recognize that such arguments might not apply with equal force to the different types of citizen responsibilities we have identified.

The strongest case for participation leading to the inculcation of a sense of obligation to other participants and to conduct which conforms to procedural rules and public reason is one which focuses on procedural norms. In this case no assumption needs to be made about virtuous motives *prompting* participation – since we can accept that self-interest can motivate participation in the procedures. Instead, we can focus on the mechanisms by which this self-interest is gradually transformed through such participation so that those involved come to recognize the legitimacy of a range of rules and procedures and come increasingly to justify their demands with reference to public reason, thereby engaging in a self-laundering of preferences. Where the weight of the account rests is a matter of judgement: we might emphasize the inherent rationality of communicative action or the transformative effects of free public reason; we might recognize that the capacity of the state to enforce its procedural rules creates incentives for a degree of conformity which eventually becomes habitual; or we might run some combination of the two accounts. Nor do we have to insist that such effects can be guaranteed; in some conditions the absence of trust between parties will be so great that the incentives to defect from a procedure will be far greater than those to conform, and the suasive effects of the procedure will never have a chance to operate. But the fact that these mechanisms do not always operate does not detract from the fact that they sometimes do, and sometimes very powerfully, and that they tend to operate most powerfully in politics where social and political conflict is not extreme and where there is stability in institutions and trust or transparency in decision procedures.[41]

While conformity with procedures can become routine in situations where groups and individuals have an independent interest in seeking to influence the activities of the state, it is less obvious that vertical participation does so (since it demands time and effort and it is not similarly motivated), and it is equally open whether horizontal forms of participation will have positive rather than negative political consequences. Procedural compliance might be self-reinforcing in the way Hume implies, but does such compliance necessarily encourage virtuous participation in other areas of the system? Because procedural compliance supervenes on attempts to get the political system to respond to our interests and concerns, so that we become guided by procedures and public reason in the pursuit of these specific concerns, it does not follow that we are further motivated to bear responsibilities which we have no independent interest in bearing, nor that our involvement in the groups, subcultures and associations of civil society will necessarily have any positive implications for our attitudes towards or involvement in the political arena. One linking element may be that horizontal participation might stimulate groups to seek to influence the political system, thereby drawing them into the virtuous cycle of procedural compliance. But a great deal depends on how these groups and associations define themselves with respect to the state and the political process. Groups which define themselves in zero-sum terms will simply lack the basic trust required for positive identification with political norms to get off the ground, as will groups who define themselves against the state – as when the state is seen as inevitably tied to a particular religion and the group is grounded on an alternative set of religious commitments. It is difficult to identify the range of factors within a community or subculture which may result in high rather than low levels of identification with the norms and procedures of the political process, but it is certain that horizontal participation does not necessarily encourage either vertical political participation or 'virtuous' identification. Indeed, there are clearly possibilities for perverse disjunctions between the two dimensions of civic duty: for example, where conformity to procedural norms has become increasingly habitual and unreflective, it may become less firmly and independently motivated, and when participation in one's local community and culture is working to reinforce one's more local value system, we may see a covert slide to *modus vivendi* compliance.[42] Where the motives which underpin conformity become increasingly fragile, others' expectations about the resilience of conformity become correspondingly unfounded, with the result that observers can come to overstate dramatically the stability of an order only to find that relatively minor conflicts throw it into question.

IV

If we follow the distinctions drawn in this chapter, it seems clear that a virtuous cycle which delivers an overlapping consensus may be quite narrow in its effects, applying to areas in which we have an independent interest in influencing the state but having no necessary knock-on effects for participation or compliance in other areas of the political system. As we have seen, horizontal participation does not necessarily issue in vertical participation; sports clubs and choirs may remain sports clubs and choirs, with no broader spin-off for the political culture. Moreover, even where procedural compliance is high, more extensive virtuous participation can be difficult to motivate – not least, prosaically enough, because for most citizens, the costs of vertical participation are high relative to the rewards.[43]

There remains, then, a nagging doubt that we cannot meet Constant's and Tocqueville's anxieties that liberal democratic systems need a level of participation from their citizenship which they find extremely difficult to motivate even where they achieve high levels of procedural compliance and a reasonably wide agreement on political principles. On their accounts, there would remain the problem, even in the most auspicious of circumstances, of resiliently motivating the type of participation which is necessary for sustaining liberal civic cultures within modern, pluralist states, and there is still more of a problem where circumstances are not so auspicious. Moreover, the attempt to recruit Rawls to help solve this difficulty cannot be accounted a success; he too has problems motivating participation. This leaves us with the question as to whether in fact liberal democracies are inherently flawed, or whether the difficulty lies in the way we have framed the problem.

Constant's view, that surrendering our political liberty to those who rule is also to surrender our civil liberty, seems indisputable. Acton's adage about power corrupting is unlikely to become outdated – not least because, as Madam Mao is reputed to have said, while the exercise of power is delightful, the exercise of absolute power is absolutely delightful. What is less clear is whether the only recourse for liberal democracies is for citizens to share equally in the duties associated with political liberty. Many of those writing on citizenship assume that we are looking for both a form of standing and a set of responsibilities which attach to all. Similarly, Tocqueville's concern with individualism led him to think in terms of an alternative type of culture, in which all participate. In both cases, the solution is seen as involving all citizens in some way – hence the sense among contemporary theorists of liberal democracy of the continuing relevance of both Constant and Tocqueville.[44] There is, however, an alternative view – one which avoids insisting on widespread citizen virtue, without collapsing into a defence of élite democratic theory. This view has two components: a willingness to break the connection between rights and duties of participation; and a tolerance for a division of labour in the scrutiny of the state.

This alternative view emphasizes the importance of procedural rights and responsibilities, but recognizes that while the right to participate must be sustained, it need not be seen as a general duty for all citizens. Clearly, those who do participate have corresponding procedural responsibilities, but on this view there is no sense of a general civic obligation to participate. We might take the view that some minimal level of participation, such as voting in elections or performing jury service, is desirable – but we might equally hold that the responsibility or moral duty to undertake these tasks attaches not to those who have citizen rights but to those who, in addition, have the requisite level of knowledge or interest, a willingness to stay informed, and the ability to think through and exercise the responsibility with a degree of objectivity and intelligence. Although the right to participate is general (because it needs to be to preserve liberty), no general duty to participate flows from one's citizenship.[45] On this account, a citizen who wishes to live an utterly private life of religious devotion, and who disdains all political involvement, remains, nonetheless, a citizen – since her standing vis-à-vis other citizens is secured by a system of rights, and she has the right to participate if she chooses; but she is not to be seen as failing her citizenship by not participating. If, however, she seeks legislation to promote her particular world-view, she has clear procedural responsibilities which constrain both the means she can use and the ends she may reasonably pursue.

This view could be challenged by various ideals of citizenship, but I have eschewed this approach in favour of the more parsimonious line of approach which asks about what demands citizenship must make to secure stable liberal democratic political institutions, and from that perspective we need only ask whether this reduced theory of citizenship is adequate to this task. Of the four dimensions of civic duties which we identified, this reduced theory most plays down the third – that is, vertical participatory responsibilities: voting, making representation, joining political parties, demonstrating, and in general ensuring that those in power remain answerable to the views and interests of those whom they rule, together with specific civic responsibilities such as jury service. On the face of it, reducing the emphasis on these functions would seem to invite the very abuses of power which Constant and Tocqueville feared. The assumption is flawed, however, because it ignores the possibility that these functions may be served by other institutions or groups where there is no equivalent motivational problem.

The anxieties intimated by Constant and detailed in Tocqueville's eloquent account of the dangers of individualism (and the associated absence of horizontal forms of participation) may be allayed to a considerable extent, less by the activities of citizens and more by the professionalization of politics and its scrutiny – something which Tocqueville himself suggests in his account of the judiciary and the legal profession.[46] On this basis, Constant's implicit assumption that one is dealing with two groups – citizens and élite[47] – needs challenging. It needs challenging because of a wide range of mediating players and institutions between citizens and the political élite which serve both to set constraints on the élite and to overcome collective action and threshold problems for ordinary citizens. Organizations, institutions, networks, norms and hierarchies all render the behaviour of others more predictable and allow threshold judgements to be made with greater confidence. The emergence of information networks can also help generate and sustain a public sense of political propriety, which constrains leaders seeking to redefine those standards to their advantage. Equally, the existence of an effective judiciary and system of law enforcement works as much to assure procedural compliance on the part of the élite as among the citizenry. The same is true for the wide range of intermediary political and quasi-political institutions such as lawyers, professional watchdogs, journalists, commentators, academics and the intelligentsia. Moreover, the motives of these men and women need not be disinterested or altruistic. What matters is that there are mechanisms in operation for the enforcement of professional standards – since these create the same kind of *modus vivendi* incentives for compliance as are present among the more atomized citizenry, although the tighter, more face-to-face character of these intermediary groups and subcommunities makes enforcement of collective norms rather easier to sustain once it is established.[48] When Przeworski answers the question 'Who guards the guardians' by referring to 'those forces in civil society that find it in their self-interest', he overstates the extent to which such interests among the people at large can be organized and underestimates the importance of intermediary institutions in ensuring that there are groups which have both the interest and the capacity to exercise scrutiny.[49]

Alternatives to reliance on citizen participation can be found in a range of institutions and practices mediating between the formal political system and the broader political culture and society: the press, the judiciary and law enforcement system, professional systems of audit and control, and a wide range of interest groups and watchdogs which are involved in the ongoing reaction to and scrutiny of government policy and the administration of the political system more widely. These groups can substitute in part for the role which classical republicans ascribed to an active citizenry, and can do so without demanding exceptional virtue.[50] These institutions provide their members with employment and with personal incentives to work effectively in the public interest. There is no problem motivating their participation and, although they may require guidance and reminders of their responsibilities within the political domain, there are formal and informal mechanisms to exert such pressure, coupled with their need, in a democratic and open society, to sustain their own accountability and standing with the public.

The two elements which militate against the subversion of these intermediary institutions by those in power, or by those within who come exclusively to pursue their own ends, are transparency in the political process and a context of institutional pluralism. The former makes accountability more easily enforced; the latter offers a situation in which institutions are partly in competition with each other so that each has incentives to ensure that their own standards are unimpeachable and that others are similarly constrained. Indeed, the arguments which I have used for the way in which *modus vivendi* motives may be transformed through procedural involvement and the need to defend proposals in public also apply in the case of such agencies in their interaction with the political system. In both cases the motives which bring people into the political system, or into the social and civic institutions associated with politics, may be various, but these institutions shape their members' behaviour and preferences. The ethos of an institution takes on new life as it is imparted to and interpreted by new members, but this takes place within a broader context of institutional pluralism in which the ethical integrity of the institution and its practitioners remains open to question by competitors, by the political institutions with which they interact, and by the members of the public whose interests they affect. The professionalization of the law, the civil service and, to at least some degree, the media gives people the opportunity to make a career out of some of the most important forms of participation, but it also gives them a range of responsibilities to fulfil. Of course, there are risks: the judiciary may become out of touch with public attitudes; we may develop an unimaginative, obstructive and inefficient administrative service, or a sensationalist and irresponsible mass media.[51] Although on the one hand we should not underestimate these dangers, on the other hand we should not think that we can guard against them only by developing a mobilized citizenry, since competition between mechanisms for public scrutiny and for maintaining transparency and accountability ensures that it will always be in the interests of other groups or institutions within society to take up the challenge.

Moreover, there is no puzzle about what is to motivate political participation on the part of members of the public when their interests are affected by such institutions since we need not look beyond self-interest. Citizens can act self-interestedly with respect to challenging the activities of the government, or these other institutions, such as the press, cause and interest groups, political parties, the police, the judiciary, etc. And these institutions must defend their conduct (in so far as they can) by reference to their responsibilities, procedures, and their ethos more broadly; but their defence must be conducted in public and according to standards of public reason. Liberal democratic political systems can, then, accept that there is no general duty to participate on the part of citizens, so long as those with grievances can find institutions which can represent and resolve those grievances in terms of a defensible public reason.

Two areas of this account may generate concern among political theorists. The first concerns how genuinely pluralistic liberal democratic societies are. Critics of Dahl's original account of democracy, for example, argued that the fact of the matter is that there is unequal access to resources for collective mobilization, and that liberal democratic societies are consequently not truly pluralistic – hence Dahl's later acknowledgement of 'polyarchy'. However, the account I offer here is not Dahlian. My concern is with *institutional* pluralism, not with pluralism in the social order. In contrast to the view that there is a widespread need for virtuous political participation on the part of citizens to act as a bulwark against forms of tyranny, I am arguing that a plurality of institutions, together with a climate of transparency, can serve instead and can draw support from citizens who use these diverse institutions to express grievances against their treatment by the political system. What is required is not equal capacities for mobilization among diverse citizen groups, but facilitated individual access to these institutions. It is possible to build in certain types of protection for individuals and access to institutions through basic forms of institutional design, and/or by the creation of more ad hoc scrutiny bodies and complaints procedures, and by the provision of free legal advice. In each case we can promote the capacity of citizens to defend their civil rights against government by creating access to institutions which have an interest in protecting those rights and a responsibility to account for their activities publicly.

The second concern voiced with respect to pluralism concerns the unequal standing of ethnic minorities, women and other groups. Again, however, the concern is to ensure the protection of civil rights – and the kinds of mechanism I have outlined, when rooted in a culture which demands public accountability and the defence of procedures in terms of public reason, should provide an equal defence of those rights. That said, certain groups may feel that a procedural republic of this form will fail to do justice to those who have been victims of past injustice and discrimination – that is, those who need more than equal standing in order to rectify past abuses. Such a claim is best understood as invoking an argument for there being certain necessary material, cultural or social prerequisites for equal citizenship – and that a group's historical experience has left them without adequate access to these prerequisites. There is no need for the account developed here to reject such claims, nor do they compromise its parsimonious character. There may be certain types of disadvantage which must be overcome for people to be able to act effectively as equal citizens, but, if there are, they will certainly not be more numerous than would be those required, for example, by an account demanding civic virtue. Moreover, I do not argue that liberal democracies are always viable, irrespective of their historical record or their treatment of their minorities. The much more circumspect claim I make here is that liberal democracies may have resources in their institutional pluralism for ensuring that widespread individualism or a lack of participation do not render them unviable as political orders, and that where horizontal participation takes the form of attempts to turn the political system to the advantage of one or other group, institutional pluralism may play a similarly constraining role – thereby curtailing despotism from both above and below.

Acknowledgements

My thanks to Erica Benner, Selina Chen, Matthew Clayton, Jerry Cohen, Tom Christiano, Bob Goodin, Des King, David Miller, Alan Patten, Philip Pettit and Adam Swift for comments on earlier versions of this chapter.

Notes

1. Benjamin Constant (1988) *The Liberty of the Ancients Compared with That of the Moderns*, in Biancamaria Fontana (ed.) *Political Writings*, Cambridge: Cambridge University Press, p. 326. On Tocqueville, see L. Siedentop (1979) 'Two Liberal Traditions', in A. Ryan (ed.) *The Idea of Freedom*, Oxford: Clarendon Press.
2. Constant, *The Liberty of the Ancients*, p. 328.
3. Despite Mill's rather puzzling failure to recognize the importance of participation as a source of constraint on power in his *Representative Government*; see H.B. Acton (ed.) *Utilitarianism, Liberty, Representative Government*, London: Dent.
4. See, for example, the classical statement of the rise of citizenship rights by T.H. Marshall (1950) *Citizenship and Social Class*, Cambridge: Cambridge University Press, and the extensive discussion of theories of citizenship by Desmond King and Jeremy Waldron (1988) 'Citizenship, Social Citizenship and the Defence of Welfare Provision', *British Journal of Political Science* 18, 415–43; David Miller (1995) 'Citizenship and Pluralism', *Political Studies* 43 (3), 432–50; and Will Kymlicka and Wayne Norman (1994) 'Return of the Citizen: A Survey of Recent Work on Citizenship Theory', *Ethics* 104 (2), 352–81. See also the collection of essays, which includes Kymlicka and Norman, edited by Ronald Beiner (1995) as *Theorizing Citizenship*, Albany: State University of New York Press. See also Michael Sandel (1984) 'The Procedural Republic and the Unencumbered Self', *Political Theory* 12, 81–96, and Benjamin Barber (1984) *Strong Democracy: Participatory Politics for a New Age*, Berkeley: University of California Press.
5. On which, see especially Will Kymlicka (1995) *Multicultural Citizenship*, Oxford: Oxford University Press.
6. The same motivational problem holds true even for non-Aristotelian accounts of the value of civic participation, such as Q. Skinner (1997) *Liberty before Liberalism*, Cambridge: Cambridge University Press, since even if civic participation is in general instrumental to securing liberty, it does not follow that it is always, or indeed ever, in my interests to act virtuously.
7. I do not discuss the criterion for democratic stability at any length, my concern being more with the way that arguments about the quality of democratic rule are linked to claims about the part citizens must play in a democracy. Nor am I assuming that stability is something which is either present or absent. On the contrary, I take it that it is a matter of degree, and is also linked to the question of the cost of democratic rule – for example, how much it has to invest in enforcement, or to what extent it relies for its stability on producing a range of outcomes and how far these outcomes are relatively easily produced. There is no straightforward answer to the question of what renders democratic rule stable; my concern here is mainly to indicate what type of citizenship seems to be required at

a minimum, and to argue that we should be wary of arguments which rest the responsibility for stability wholly on the civic virtue of their citizens. See, for example, Adam Przeworski *et al.* (1995) *Sustainable Democracy*, Cambridge: Cambridge University Press, especially part I, chapters 3 and 4, and the striking, but not wholly persuasive, comment made about the Brazilian voter who reputedly waited two hours to cast his vote in the presidential election, and having done so, said, ' "Now I have done my share. The rest is theirs." Anyone concerned with the quality of democracy will see such a political system as greatly impaired. And the question of whether such democracies can last remains open' (p. 64).

8. The requirement that the account of democratic citizenship should preserve political stability and individual liberty, however, does place considerable constraints on how far the political order could be at variance with people's conceptions of justice or welfare. At the same time, as will be made clear below, the demands of citizenship may place constraints on how far individuals or groups can insist on their particular conceptions of the good in the face of the disagreement of others – so that the theory of citizenship must contribute to a theory of the political principles which must regulate citizens' actions in the public domain. The connection between these issues is discussed in T. Nagel (1990) 'Moral Conflict and Political Legitimacy', in J. Raz (ed.) *Authority*, Oxford: Blackwell pp. 300–24 (first published in *Philosophy and Public Affairs* 16 (3) 1987). See especially p. 302: 'arguments that justify may fail to persuade, if addressed to an unreasonable audience; and arguments that persuade may fail to justify. Nevertheless, justifications hope to persuade the reasonable, so these attempts have a practical point: political stability is helped by wide agreement to the principles underlying the political order.'

9. I discuss the basis for this view more fully in (1997) 'Defining Political Corruption', *Political Studies* (special issue on political corruption) 45 (3), 436–62. A very much earlier version of the argument in this section can be found in my (1998) 'Citizenship and Integrity', in Alan Montefiore and David Vines (eds) *Integrity*, London: Routledge.

10. Groups such as children may lack rights to full civic 'voice', but they are the recipients of political concern, and their interests can be represented in the political domain and in the various institutions of the state.

11. Clearly, there are issues concerning what proportion of a population has to be ruled in this way – but there remains a clear distinction between a democratic state seeking wide public legitimation and an autocratic state seeking at best a very narrow legitimation sufficient to maintain its control over the means of coercion. See also above, note 10.

12. Hence Constant's and Tocqueville's belief that a system may fail because, despite procedural compliance, the lack of participation results in despotism; compare Alexis de Tocqueville's fears for the rise of individualism in (1946) *Democracy in America*, vol. 2, trans. H. Reeve, revised F. Bowen and P. Bradley, New York: Knopf.

13. Formally, of course, free-riding is costless: the free-rider problem is precisely one in which 'it is possible for an individual to . . . benefit from whatever amount of the good is provided without contributing to its production costs'. A problem arises because if every member is a free-rider then no public good will be provided, and where only some free-ride, their activity violates a broader sense of fairness within

the political system, and the 'game' can deteriorate into a form of chicken, with potentially disastrous effects. See, for example, Michael Taylor and Hugh Ward (1982) 'Chickens, Whales and Lumpy Public Goods: Alternative Models of Public Goods Provision', *Political Studies* 30 (3), 350–70, and Philip Pettit (1986) 'Free-Riding and Foul Dealing', *Journal of Philosophy* 83, 361–79.

14. We can, however, recognize mixed motives. See the more extensive discussion of this issue in the last two sections of this chapter. See also Robert Goodin (1995) *Utilitarianism as a Public Philosophy*, Cambridge: Cambridge University Press, chapter 3.

15. Cf. James S. Coleman (1990) *Foundations of Social Theory*, Cambridge, MA: Harvard University Press, pp. 300–21.

16. Tocqueville, *Democracy in America*, volume 1, part I, chapter 5, and volume 2, part II, chapter 2.

17. In this tradition see, for example, the litany of community participation reeled off by Robert Putman in his eulogy to the civic spirit of the northern Italians: 'neighbourhood associations, choral societies, cooperatives, sports clubs, mass based parties' in Robert Putman (1993) *Making Democracy Work*, Princeton, NJ: Princeton University Press, p. 173.

18. Which, Madison argues, is the virtue of republican (that is, representative) government with a large and diverse citizenry; see Alexander Hamilton, James Madison and John Jay (1788/1964) *The Federalist Papers*, no. 10, New York: The New American Library of World Literature.

19. Adam Smith (1976) *The Wealth of Nations*, Oxford: Clarendon Press, p. 145. In a similar vein, Mancur Olson argues, in his (1982) *The Rise and Decline of Nations*, New Haven, CT: Yale University Press, that special interest groups, subcommunities and organizations with limited *civitas* (i.e. limited engagement or commonality of interest with the broader community of citizens) which play a major participatory role in the institutions of the state can have extremely destructive effects on the political system.

20. Sandel, 'The Procedural Republic'. See also Will Kymlicka (1995) *Multicultural Citizenship: A Liberal Theory of Minority Rights*, Oxford: Clarendon, and his edited collection (1995) *The Rights of Minority Cultures*, Oxford: Oxford University Press, and, more generally, Iris Marion Young (1990) *Justice and the Politics of Difference*, Princeton, NJ: Princeton University Press; Anne Phillips (1995) *The Politics of Presence*, Oxford: Clarendon, and John Rawls (1993) *Political Liberalism*, New York: Columbia University Press.

21. Drawing on Rawls's *Political Liberalism*, p. 147.

22. See Nagel, 'Moral Conflict and Political Legitimacy', who identifies this as a 'convergence' theory of political legitimacy – that is, one looks for 'a possible convergence of rational support for certain institutions from the separate motivational standpoints of distinct individuals' (p. 303).

23. For example, where compliance is conditional on the solution maximizing my community's security or welfare; or where it is conditional on, for example, minimizing global ecological damage. The ends may be worthy; what *modus vivendi* indicates is that we treat the pursuit of our ends as of prime importance, and where we stick to political rules and norms we do so only because doing so serves those ends.

24. Cf. Mark Granovetter (1978) 'Threshold Models of Collective Behaviour,' *American Journal of Sociology* 83, 1420–43. Granovetter has also pointed out that because a person's threshold is 'simply that point where the perceived benefits to an individual of doing the thing in question exceed the perceived costs', two people with different beliefs, preferences and intensity of preferences may nonetheless end up with the same threshold. Hence the phenomenon of strange partnerships on the barricades. This conclusion is important because it underlines that we cannot assume that just because collective action takes place there must be a single, widely shared norm prescribing that action; there may be no norm, just a fortuitous conjunction of self-interested calculations, or there may be many norms which serve to different extents to weight judgements of acceptable probability in such a way that collective action becomes possible.

25. That is, where there is a breakdown of collective or communal norms and value systems and where each individual's identification and pursuit of his or her ends takes place without reference to the norms and values of some larger social unit.

26. This does not mean punishing every offender – just doing enough to ensure that the vast majority of the people perceive the costs of non-compliance to outweigh its benefits.

27. Cf. Michael Taylor (1988) 'Rationality and Revolutionary Collective Action', in Michael Taylor (ed.) *Rationality and Revolution*, Cambridge: Cambridge University Press.

28. See A. Gouldner (1954) *Patterns of Industrial Bureaucracy*, New York: Free Press, and the discussion in Gary J. Miller (1992) *Managerial Dilemmas*, Cambridge: Cambridge University Press, pp. 207–10.

29. Richard Dagger's suggestion that 'someone expresses civic virtue when he or she does what a citizen is supposed to do' (Dagger (1997) *Civic Virtues: Rights, Citizenship, and Republican Liberalism*, Oxford: Oxford University Press, p. 13) fails to distinguish behavioural conformity and types of agency. As we have seen, doing what a citizen is supposed to do may be variously motivated. The crucial point is that the citizen is committed to serving the public good – and to putting his or her duties as a citizen before all other concerns. In Nagel's lucid formulation this position is a 'common standpoint' theory of legitimacy, which asks us to evaluate institutions on the basis of a common moral motive which makes no reference to our own interests. See 'Moral Conflict and Political Legitimacy', pp. 303–4.

30. Goodin's argument that there may be no need to distinguish between motives where there are many possible motives which could have led to an act runs very much contrary to the republican project. It does so because within the classical republican tradition, the compatibility of motives which Goodin hypothesizes is not seen as a naturally occurring phenomenon. If we find Goodin's hypothesis more plausible than, say, Machiavelli's, then we will not see the need for civic virtue. Cf. Goodin, 'Do Motives Matter?' in *Utilitarianism as a Public Philosophy*.

31. This is why Machiavelli talks about civic virtue only within the already constituted republic; the *virtù* of the legislator is of a different order, and is more like virtue in the international arena where, clearly, heroism in the service of the state vis-à-vis other states may indicate internal strength rather than weakness – but it is still not easy to motivate.

32. Hence, for all his love for ancient republics, Montesquieu clearly believed that they could not be created in the modern commercial societies of his day.
33. Marx and Engels, *The Holy Family*, cited by Patrice Higonnet (1998) *Goodness beyond Virtue: Jacobins during the French Revolution*, Cambridge, MA: Harvard University Press, p. 1.
34. Although face-to-face communities *might* have enough solidarity, it is also likely that they will have it at the expense of critical distance.
35. See Nagel, 'Moral Conflict and Political Legitimacy', pp. 304–5, on a similar attempt to mix 'convergence' and 'common standpoint' theories.
36. Cf. Rawls, *Political Liberalism*, pp. 158–68.
37. *Ibid.*, pp.163–4.
38. *Ibid.*, p. 165.
39. David Hume (1902 [1751]) *Enquiry Concerning the Principles of Morals*, ed. Selby Bigge, Oxford: Clarendon Press, IX, ii, 283.
40. For example, Pascal's famous argument for how one develops a belief in God once one has determined that it is in one's interest to have such a belief. See Jon Elster's discussion in (1984) *Ulysses and the Sirens*, revised edition, pp. 47–54, Cambridge: Cambridge University Press, pp. 47–54, and Joshua Cohen (1994) 'A More Democratic Liberalism', *Michigan Law Review* 92, 1503–46.
41. Trust can be seen as an alternative to transparency since they serve the same purpose of legitimating the outcome of procedures – either through their intrinsic authority or through the fact that the participants can themselves assess the fairness of the outcomes. In either case, groups which defect from the agreements they have negotiated find it difficult publicly to legitimate their action – and there is correspondingly more chance of others supporting the enforcement of agreements by the state. Of course, one then faces the problem of explaining where this trust comes from – see, for example, Martin Hollis (1998) *Trust within Reason*, Cambridge: Cambridge University Press.
42. For example, nationalist political parties in a multinational state may, while acknowledging the legitimacy of the national constitution and its political procedures, act in ways which serve to consolidate their popular support while eroding their supporters' identification with the broader political system.
43. If we try to reduce the costs of participation, we risk rendering it so empty that it could not plausibly serve as a bulwark against political oppression; if we attach differential rewards to it, we threaten to turn the political arena into a struggle for access to and control over the distribution of such rewards.
44. Hence also the tendency of those drawing on Constant and Tocqueville to understate the more élitist aspects of their work.
45. John Dunn's 'Political Obligations and Political Possibilities' is one of the few works to break with the assumption that political obligations must be conceived of as owed equally by all citizens and to think through the implications of a division of political duties: in John Dunn (ed.) (1980) *Political Obligation in Its Historical Context*, Cambridge: Cambridge University Press.
46. See *Democracy in America*, volume 1, part II, chapter 8.
47. Or, indeed, Tocqueville's suggestion that democratic society tends towards a stark opposition between the mass and a very small élite.
48. Although, it must also be said, such face-to-face communities also make vicious

conduct easier to sustain, once it is established – and the crucial question becomes one of how far the 'community' is open to influence and scrutiny by other groups, and what standards of conduct these other groups sustain. Thus a corrupt police force will be difficult to break open if all the control institutions are corrupt, but substantially easier if they are 'clean'.

49. A. Przeworski (1991) *Democracy and the Market*, Cambridge: Cambridge University Press, pp. 25–6.
50. See Tocqueville's similar argument for the role of the judiciary and lawyers – even if, with hindsight, we can see that it is possible to overdo one's confidence in any one particular professional body.
51. On which see Robert M. Entman's salutary (1989) *Democracy without Citizens: Media and the Decay of American Politics*, Oxford: Oxford University Press.

PART THREE

Identity

CHAPTER NINE

Equality of Recognition and the Liberal Theory of Citizenship

ALAN PATTEN

The concept of citizenship provides a lens through which many problems in political theory can be fruitfully examined. In part, this reflects the statist context in which much political theorizing occurs. The state remains the basic unit of politics, and the concept of citizenship neatly sums up the standard relationship between the individual and this basic unit. But citizenship is also important to political theorists because it points to a number of distinct but interconnected questions that must all be kept in mind in considering many issues of political morality.

A theory of citizenship involves answers to at least three distinct questions. The *membership question* asks: Who is to be given the status of citizen? Are all adults residing on the territory of the state to be regarded as citizens, or only some subset of them? If only a subset, then on what basis is the subset to be defined? The *entitlement question*, in contrast, enquires into the rights and entitlements that are conferred on an individual by virtue of his or her having the status of citizen. If I am a citizen, what does this entitle me to in the way of non-interference, or positive support and recognition, from my fellow citizens, either directly or provided through the medium of the state? The third question is the *responsibility question*. What responsibilities, dispositions and identities are expected of a person by virtue of having the status of citizen? If I am a citizen, what dispositions am I expected to develop and exercise, and what identity or identities, if any, should I share with my fellow citizens? In short, the first question concerns who is to be considered a full member of the community, the second concerns what one can claim in virtue of being a full member, and the third concerns what the community expects of one as a full member.[1]

A persuasive theory of citizenship is one which gives plausible answers to each of these questions, taken one by one, and which can show that the three answers given are mutually compatible and supporting. Debates about citizenship have often focused on just one of these questions. For example, T.H. Marshall's famous mid-twentieth-century essay 'Citizenship and Social Class' is usually associated with the entitlement question: he wanted to argue that the status of citizenship had come to imply not just civil and political rights but also social rights.[2] Sometimes, however, debates about citizenship have addressed all three questions at once and have been concerned with the coherence and mutual compatibility of the three answers. For instance, the eighteenth-, nineteenth- and early twentieth-century debates about the suffrage centred on whether one could consistently answer the three questions in the following way. To the membership question, the answer was that virtually all adults should have the status of full citizen. To the entitlement question, the answer was that this status entails a set of political rights, including the right to vote in parliamentary elections. And to the responsibility question, the answer was that someone who has the right to vote is expected to display political virtues such as independence, sound judgement, impartiality and public-spiritedness. Conservative critics of extension of the suffrage argued that these three answers are mutually incompatible: the people to whom it was contemplated giving the vote, they thought, could not be expected to display the required virtues.

A *liberal* theory of citizenship gives answers that are informed by liberal values to each of the three questions and gives some account of how the three answers cohere together which makes reference to the operation of liberal social and political institutions. I will assume, without really exploring the issue, that a liberal response to the membership question would give to virtually all minimally competent adults residing on the territory of the state for some minimal length of time the opportunity to be citizens or full members of the community. The assumption here is that any attempt to justify denying citizenship to significant categories of residents by reference to liberal theory is almost certainly bound to fail.

My aim in this chapter is to employ this three-dimensional framework to explore the relationship between liberal citizenship and what is often termed the 'politics of recognition'.[3] Modern societies are typically characterized by a diversity of ethnic, linguistic, national, gender, sexual and religious identities and affiliations. To some extent, liberal theory's response to this diversity or 'identity-pluralism' (as I shall term it) is clear. A liberal view of citizenship embraces freedoms of conscience, speech and association, and rights to non-discrimination and equal opportunity, that go part of the way towards accommodating the demands arising from identity-pluralism. But there is also a set of issues concerning what can be termed the 'character of the public sphere' that is less clearly addressed in liberal theory. As we shall see below, these include questions relating to political boundaries, the language and symbolism of public institutions, and the contents of school curricula, public broadcasting, and so on. On all these issues, groups defined by their identity make claims to recognition that must be addressed, in some way or another, within a liberal theory of citizenship.

The main tendency in liberal theory has been simply to ignore recognition claims of these kinds. In John Rawls's influential account of liberalism, for instance, there is no consideration of the implications for liberal citizenship of national or linguistic diversity, nor is there direct consideration of recognition claims based on ethnic, sexual or gender identity.[4] The assumption seems to be that the political community is characterized by national and linguistic homogeneity and that such forms of pluralism as are found in the community (for instance, diversity of 'conceptions of the good') are best addressed through a standard schedule of liberal rights and freedoms such as those mentioned earlier. Another common response of liberals to recognition claims is to invoke some variant of the principle of neutrality. On this view, liberal citizenship abjures the politics of recognition because of its commitment to state neutrality between the various identities and visions of the good life found amongst citizens.

This chapter will argue that a liberal theory of citizenship should include a principle of equal recognition requiring the public sphere to be equally reflective of the different identities found among citizens of the community. With this thesis in mind, the argument will unfold in three stages. In section I, I examine the idea and importance of recognition and formulate the principle of equal recognition. Section II then looks at why such a principle is a plausible part of a liberal answer to the entitlement question. This involves explaining why it is a principle that should be endorsed within a liberal account of citizenship and showing why a liberal approach that simply ignores recognition claims, or dispenses with them by an appeal to the doctrine of state neutrality, is inadequate. The final section of the paper, section III, explores how far, and under what conditions, the proposed answer to the entitlement question is compatible with an acceptable liberal answer to the responsibility question. Here I will address the significant worry that recognition of a diversity of identities in the public sphere will discourage the formation of the common political identity, or sense of common citizenship, that is necessary for a successful liberal polity.

I

What I shall term the *principle of equal recognition* is addressed to a series of issues – largely ignored in mainstream liberal theory – relating to the character of the public sphere. These include controversies over the drawing of meaningful political boundaries, the contents of school curricula, and the languages and symbolism employed by the state and major institutions of civil society.[5] It is commonly supposed that although liberal theory tells us much about what the state should do and not do within a given set of boundaries, it has nothing to say about how those boundaries themselves ought to be drawn. In the same way, although it is obvious that the public sphere will have to be conducted in certain languages, and will make use of a set of symbols (in preambles, on flags, in official documents and ceremonies, etc.), many people suppose that a liberal political theory has nothing distinctive to say about how decisions about language, symbols, and so on should be made. For some, the liberal position on these issues is simply to allow the majority to decide on the basis of its own preferences and outlook.

In recent years, however, political theorists have become increasingly sensitive to the ways in which constructions of the public sphere can unequally advantage different people.[6] A standard example is the designation by the state and major institutions of civil society of certain dates in the calendar as public holidays and days of rest.[7] In most Western countries, the choice of these days reflects the identity and practices of the historic Christian majority. Christmas, Easter and Sundays are all accorded a special status that is not enjoyed by the important dates on the calendars of other religions. This way of constructing the public sphere gives Christians advantages that are not enjoyed by others.

One advantage is that the choice of these particular holidays and days of rest can be taken as a form of public *symbolic affirmation* of the value of the Christian way of life and identity that is not enjoyed by other religions.[8] A second is that the choice of these particular days *accommodates* the practices associated with Christianity in a way that is not true for other religions. Whereas the calendar is arranged in such a way that most people are not working, and are not at school, at times when major Christian rituals and celebrations take place, it can be more difficult to fit the practices of other religions into the standard Western work and school week. Finally, as a consequence of the first two advantages enjoyed by Christians, they enjoy a third advantage as well: the choice of holidays and days of rest associated with Christianity *promotes* the maintenance and reproduction of the Christian community from generation to generation. Because of the public affirmation, and the accommodation of the practices, existing members are encouraged to remain within the community and it is relatively more attractive for new members to join.[9]

Decisions about boundaries, languages, school curricula, and so on can unequally advantage people with different identities and affiliations in much the same way. Consider, for instance, some group A, whose members share a distinctive culture, have a sense of themselves as constituting a group, and aspire to be self-governing as a group. Imagine, further, that political boundaries could be configured in such a way as to allow As to be predominant within a political unit. Such a configuration not only would fulfil the desire of As to be self-governing but also would make it more likely that As will be able to live under laws that reflect the commitments of their own distinctive culture. By contrast, if the configuration of boundaries left As living in a much larger political unit dominated by Bs, then the laws of that unit would be less likely to reflect the distinctive A culture, and the aspiration to self-government of As would be frustrated. Depending on how boundaries are configured, then, the A identity may be accommodated to a greater or lesser extent. *A*s may also feel symbolically denigrated if boundaries are configured in such a way as to reflect the majority *B* culture and identity but not their own. And if *A*s are disadvantaged with respect to the goods of accommodation and symbolic affirmation, this may have knock-on effects over time for their capacity to reproduce themselves as a group. It may be relatively more attractive for newcomers, or even present members of *A*, to assimilate into the larger *B* society.

Decisions about what language or languages to offer public services and conduct public business in can also unequally advantage different people. The decision, for instance, to make some language *L* the sole language of the public sphere accommodates the linguistic needs of those who speak *L* but clearly does not accommodate the needs of those in the community who have difficulty speaking *L*. Such a decision may also be considered a symbolic affirmation of *L* (and an *L*-speaking identity) vis-à-vis other languages and language-based identities in the community, and it may work to promote the *L* community over time at the expense of other language groups. A similar analysis might be offered with respect to choices about school curricula: particular decisions about what histories and religions to teach, what texts to read, and so on can accommodate the outlook and commitments of some groups in society more than others, and can affirm and promote certain identities at the expense of others.[10] In these contexts and others, the way in which the public sphere is constructed can represent a significant advantage or disadvantage to different people according to their identity, tastes, cultural affiliations, and so forth.

I shall say that an identity is 'recognized' in the public sphere when the institutions of the public sphere are designed in such a way as to fit or reflect the character of that identity to at least some degree. What exactly this relation of 'fitting' or 'reflecting' amounts to will depend on the aspect of the public sphere being considered. In considering the boundaries of the state, for instance (for example, the boundaries and salience of federal units), the relevant identities will be those which are associated with a desire for collective self-government (for instance, national identities). Recognition of such an identity would involve creating institutional-jurisdictional space in which groups having such an identity can be self-governing as a group (or at least, can be in the majority within some political unit). Recognition of a language-based identity, by contrast, involves offering public services and transacting public business in the language in question. And recognizing other kinds of identities might involve designing a school curriculum that included narratives and texts reflecting the experiences of those sharing those identities.

Two or more identities are recognized 'equally' when the same kinds of institutional-jurisdictional resources and spaces that are devoted to the recognition of one identity are also devoted to the recognition of the other(s). Thus, if for example there are two national identities having adherents within some region, one reflecting an attachment to that region, the other to the state as a whole, then equal recognition might involve some kind of devolutionary or federal arrangement. Under such a scheme, those with the regionally based identity and those with a pan-state identity would both enjoy some (roughly equal) degree of self-government with members of the group with which they identify. Equal recognition of two or more linguistically based identities would involve offering comparable services and conducting business of roughly equal importance in each of the languages in question. And so on.

Notice that the conception of equality being asserted here is broadly 'resourcist' rather than 'welfarist'.[11] That is, equal recognition in the public sphere is a matter of achieving a certain distribution of institutional space and capacity, such as time devoted in the curriculum, public services offered in a certain language, fora for collective decision-making, etc. Equality is not a matter of the degree to which individuals are successful at transforming those institutional resources into a feeling of affirmation, into accommodation of their cultural needs, or into cultural survival. Depending on their circumstances and outlook, some individuals will be more efficient at transforming a given level of institutional resources into these outcomes than others.[12]

II

Having explained what I mean by 'equal recognition in the public sphere', let me now turn to the question of whether, and on what basis, a liberal account of citizenship ought to include a principle of equal recognition as part of its answer to the entitlement question. We have been seeing that alternative constructions of the public sphere can advantage different people to different degrees. Whether or not the state is unitary or federal, to recall just one example, makes a considerable difference to different individuals depending on whether they have a pan-state identity or identify (wholly or partly) with a regionally based national minority. It influences the degree to which their needs and goals are accommodated in the public sphere, the extent to which they feel symbolically affirmed or denigrated, and the extent to which the group they identify with is able to reproduce itself as a group over time.

The fact that goods such as accommodation, affirmation and promotion are at stake in thinking about the character of the public sphere makes it problematic simply to ignore recognition claims in setting out a liberal account of citizenship. Because alternative constructions of the public sphere entail different distributions of advantage and disadvantage, people can legitimately expect decisions about the character of the public sphere to be informed by some framework of justification.

Even if recognition claims should not be ignored, however, it is possible that the response most in keeping with liberal political morality would be to reject them. As was observed earlier, one doctrine often associated with liberalism is that of state neutrality. According to this doctrine, the state should be rigorously neutral between the different conceptions of the good life prevalent among its citizens. This requires that it not introduce policies, or design institutions, with a view to accommodating, affirming or promoting any particular conception of the good life (or, we might add, any identity associated with such a conception), but should instead seek to withdraw as far as it can from the cultural field. On this view, the best way to address the fact of identity-pluralism is to divorce the public sphere from questions of culture and identity as much as possible.

It is easy to be sympathetic with the doctrine of state neutrality, particularly when it is noticed that the alternative – the positive recognition of various different identities – is likely to be crude and incomplete at best. For one thing, we can rarely be confident that *all* the different identities seeking recognition can in fact be granted that recognition; avoiding recognition altogether, where this is an option, avoids the problem of creating insiders and outsiders and weakens the symbolic denigration associated with non-recognition.[13] Also, any scheme of public recognition will most likely, as a practical matter, need to impose some minimal size requirement and/or discriminate between established or historic identities and those associated with newcomers and immigrants. But of course these discriminations have a degree of arbitrariness to them which is hard to defend, and it may seem preferable just to take the state out of the business of recognition altogether by adopting some kind of neutrality requirement.

Another reason why it might be best to avoid recognition arises out of the observation that identity groups are almost always internally heterogeneous. The danger is that any particular attempt to recognize some identity will involve specific ideas and narratives relating to what somebody with that identity is like – ideas and narratives that may not, in fact, be shared by everyone belonging to the identity group. Referring to gay and African-American identities in contemporary America, for instance, K. Anthony Appiah worries that

> the politics of recognition requires that one's skin color, one's sexual body, should be acknowledged politically in ways that make it hard for those who want to treat their skin and their sexual body as personal dimensions of the self.[14]

One final argument against recognition claims draws attention to the fact that some identity groups are oppressive or illiberal in character. They involve practices that are harmful to, or subordinating of, some of their own members (e.g. female members), or they promote hatred or intolerance towards other groups in society. In some cases, the liberal state might tolerate the existence of such groups – if they are not seriously harming anyone – but it is not at all clear that a liberal state should ever positively recognize them, if that means reconfiguring the public sphere in such a way as to better fit or reflect the group's identity

These arguments do not seal the case against positive recognition, however. Even if restraint should be exercised in recognizing illiberal groups, it does not follow that recognition should also be withheld from groups squarely within the boundaries of liberalism or from non-ideologically defined groups such as those based on language. Just as the harm principle sets limits to liberal toleration without obliterating it altogether, it might also set limits on liberal recognition that still leave considerable scope for recognition claims. As far as the other objections to recognition are concerned, it is important to keep in mind that non-recognition is often impossible. There will always be contexts in which the state and other institutions of the public sphere cannot help but recognize at least one identity, or there is compelling reason for it to do so; this is likely to be the case for decisions about school curricula, public boundaries, state symbols, and the language of the public sphere. It is in such contexts, where universal non-recognition is not really an option, that the principle of equal recognition in the public sphere becomes most salient.

This last point is unlikely to persuade some of the most committed proponents of liberal neutrality, however.[15] Defenders of neutrality are fond of the distinction between 'neutrality of effect' and 'neutrality of justification' or 'intent'. Whereas neutrality of effect forbids the state's policies and arrangements from having the effect of favouring or disfavouring any particular conception of the good life, neutrality of justification or intention only prohibits the state from justifying its policies and arrangements by reference to the superiority or inferiority of particular ways of life (or, more weakly, the goal of promoting particular ways of life). The observation that recognition is, in some contexts, impossible to avoid may imply that neutrality of effect is impossible but it in no way rules out neutrality of justification. So long as the state does not justify its policy of recognizing some identities but not others by reference to the supposed superiority or inferiority of the different identities in question, neutrality of justification is not violated. A scheme of recognition designed to accommodate, affirm and promote otherwise marginalized identities, by contrast, arguably does violate the constraint. It seems to pick out certain identities as worthy of attention and intervene with the intention of accommodating, affirming and promoting those identities.

To respond properly to this last formulation of the neutralist objection to recognition claims, it is necessary to ask why a liberal account of citizenship ought, in the first place, to include a principle of equal recognition as part of its answer to the entitlement question. The answer, I would like to suggest, is deceptively simple. A basic liberal commitment is to the ideal of treating citizens as equals – treating them, as Ronald Dworkin puts it, with 'equal concern and respect'.[16] This abstract commitment to equality, in turn, implies something more concrete about the way in which resources and opportunities are distributed through the design of public institutions. It implies that there is a prima facie reason to design institutions in such a way as to ensure that resources of value to citizens are distributed equally. If we know only that some valuable resource is to be distributed in a way that respects citizens as equals, it is hard to see how any distribution other than an equal one could possibly be justified.[17]

The argument of the previous section showed that recognition is something that is typically of value to citizens. Recognition of one's identity is valuable in the sense that it can accommodate one's identity-related needs, work as a form of symbolic affirmation, and promote the maintenance over time of the identity-group. Recognition is also something, we have seen, that can be distributed more or less equally, depending on how the public sphere is configured. In the light of these considerations, it is hard to see how the abstract idea of liberal equality could be consistent with anything other than the principle of equal recognition. All else being equal, equal respect for citizens means designing a public sphere that equally distributes identity-related institutional space and capacity.

The 'all else being equal' qualifier in this formulation is not trivial. Liberal equality will sometimes require the state to distribute more of some particular resource to certain people to offset the disadvantages they face as a result of their natural and social handicaps and endowments. According to Rawls, liberal equality is also compatible with resource inequalities if such inequalities work to the advantage of the less well off. Of more direct relevance to equal recognition in the public sphere, the qualifier might also permit inequalities in the distribution of some resource if they are offset by compensating inequalities in the distribution of other resources. For example, the state might declare only a subset of the languages spoken by its citizens to be 'official' but then financially compensate the speakers of non-official languages for the disadvantages they face.[18]

The principle of equal recognition, I am suggesting, is a simple requirement of the liberal ideal of treating people as equals. For liberals, each citizen's life matters, and matters equally. There is thus no reason why the public sphere ought to be configured in a way that devotes more attention to the cultural identity of some citizens than it does to the identity of others. To ignore this requirement would be to show less than equal respect for the lives of some citizens in the community. Or at least it would do so in the absence of some story about compensation for endowment deficits, or about inequality working to the benefit of the less well off, or about the offsetting presence of some compensating inequality (or so on). Even if such a story can be told with respect to some particular recognition claim, the principle of equal recognition still establishes a baseline against which the inequality must be justified.

This egalitarian perspective on the principle of equal recognition explains, I think, why the neutralist objection to certain recognition claims is misplaced. This perspective worries, as we have seen, that the politics of recognition will violate neutrality of justification by picking out certain identities as worthy of attention and intervening with the intention of accommodating, affirming and promoting those identities. On the view I have been sketching, this objection fails because the recognition claims in question are not being justified by any assumptions concerning the inferiority or superiority of various identities or by reference to any principle that the identities in question ought to be accommodated, affirmed or promoted as much as possible. Rather, the justification of those claims appeals to the ideal of liberal equality. Where recognition claims are justified, it is by the principle that the public sphere should accord just as much institutional space and capacity to one group's identity as it does to others'.[19]

III

So far I have been focusing on the entitlement dimension of liberal citizenship and, in fact, on just one aspect of this dimension – namely, what a liberal citizenship has to say about the character of the public sphere in a context of identity-pluralism. I have argued that the ideal of liberal equality requires a liberal answer to the entitlement question to embrace a principle of equal recognition in the public sphere. According to this principle, the public sphere should be configured in such a way as to provide the same kinds of institutional spaces and capacities to different identities prevalent in the community. Thus, for example, the principle requires that public services be provided, and public business transacted, in minority languages and not just the language of the majority, that institutional-jurisdictional spaces be carved out (through federalism or devolution, for instance) in which national minorities can be self-governing, and that the curricula of public schools reflect narratives and experiences of minorities (be they religious, ethnic, racial, or so on), and not just those of the majority.

As we saw at the beginning of the chapter, however, a complete theory of citizenship cannot just content itself with answering the entitlement question. It must also consider what I termed the responsibility question and give some account of how its answers to the various questions are mutually compatible and supporting. It is now time to turn to the responsibility question and confront a natural suspicion that many readers will have about the picture of liberal citizenship being drawn so far. This is the suspicion that the heterogeneous public sphere that is implied by the principle of equal recognition will be unable to generate the common sense of citizenship, and the set of citizen dispositions and virtues, that are likely to be part of any plausible liberal answer to the responsibility question. In short, the consistent application of the principle of equal recognition is likely to generate too much social fragmentation and too little sense of common purpose or mutual solidarity to be a workable part of liberal citizenship.[20]

It is worth noting in passing that essentially the opposite charge is sometimes made against equal recognition in the public sphere by cultural nationalists. Equality in the public sphere, they argue, ignores the profound social pressures that crush some vulnerable identity groups and lead to the hegemony of others. Only by abandoning equal recognition, and putting the institutional resources of the state behind an endangered cultural identity can such an identity have any hope of survival. I do not propose to consider this kind of objection here, except to observe that it presupposes that it is (sometimes) acceptable for the state to upset equality in order to promote cultural survival. If this is true, then considerations of cultural survival will have to be balanced against the principle of equal recognition (analogously, perhaps, to the way in which claims of individual need sometimes have to be balanced against claims of material equality). Whatever we decide about this matter, however, it still seems important to consider the principle of equal recognition as part of a liberal account of citizenship, if only to have a clearer idea of what is being given up when policies of cultural nationalism are adopted.

Let us return, however, to the responsibility question and begin by noting that most liberals are now wary of giving an overly complacent answer to it. Liberal theorists no longer think (if they ever did) that liberal institutions will run themselves or will operate very effectively or endure for very long if citizens are animated entirely by self-interest. The success of free institutions, they now agree, depends crucially on the degree to which citizens are animated by certain dispositions and virtues.[21] For free institutions to operate successfully, citizens need, for instance, to exercise self-restraint and toleration. Citizens must also exemplify the virtue of 'reasonableness': they must show a willingness to settle political disagreements by appeal to reasons that are acceptable to others rather than through recourse to coercion.[22] Free institutions depend, in addition, on the willingness of citizens to accept certain burdens and sacrifices for the sake of the common good. They must be willing to vote, to maintain a minimal degree of knowledge about current events, and to speak out and demonstrate against injustice. They must even be prepared, in extreme circumstances, to risk their lives to preserve the institutions of their freedom.[23]

The worry about the politics of recognition is that it will lead to a fragmented public sphere in which citizens are not encouraged to develop these and other virtues and dispositions that are part of a plausible liberal answer to the responsibility question. Providing institutional space and capacity to different identity-groups, according to this view, will encourage individuals to associate with fellow group members rather than mixing freely with a cross-section of all citizens, and it will foster a narrow, factional identification with the group and its causes rather than with the common purposes of the community as a whole. To the extent that this is true, the liberal answers to the entitlement and responsibility questions are in conflict, and something will have to give. Since watering down the liberal answer to the responsibility question (for instance, denying that a common sense of citizenship is necessary) does not seem to be a viable option, this would seem to suggest that our earlier answer to the entitlement question might need to be revisited.

For ease of reference, let us call this the 'fragmentation objection' to incorporating a principle of equal recognition into the liberal account of citizenship. For the remainder of this chapter, I want to consider the fragmentation objection. I will argue that, to a considerable extent, the objection is overstated. It is a mistake to think that rejecting equal recognition will necessarily diminish the social fragmentation of many societies characterized by identity-pluralism. In many cases, in fact, it is likely to exacerbate social fragmentation. Moreover, strong attachments to particular identities and identity-groups are not necessarily fragmenting, *if* they are accompanied by an attachment to the whole as a context in which difference flourishes. In fact, an appropriate liberal response to the tension between our earlier answers to the entitlement and responsibility questions may, after all, be to revise the answer to the responsibility question. This would not involve watering down the virtues and dispositions that are expected of the liberal citizen but would mean strengthening and elaborating them to include a disposition to recognize and affirm difference. That said, we cannot be certain that citizens would in fact develop this disposition in the context of a heterogeneous public sphere. To this extent, the fragmentation objection cannot be refuted outright, and institutional design should always be approached with an eye on both the entitlement and the responsibility questions.

The first problem with the fragmentation objection, then, is that it is seldom formulated in a comparative perspective. Proponents of the objection implicitly assume that the challenge of forging a common political identity can be resolved by holding the line against recognition claims. This assumption ignores the possibility, however, that it is the underlying fact of identity-pluralism that makes the sense of common citizenship difficult to achieve in many contexts, not policies which seek to affirm, accommodate and promote difference on an egalitarian basis. It ignores the possibility that social diversity might have become so profound and divisive in a particular society that it will be difficult to achieve a shared civic identity under *any* model of the public sphere.

In fact, in many cases the rejection of equal recognition will only make it more difficult to foster a common political identity and the associated set of liberal virtues and dispositions.[24] Minority groups that feel excluded and denigrated by the configuration of the public sphere are hardly likely to feel a shared sense of citizenship with the majority, whose identity is comfortably affirmed in the design of the public sphere. It is true that the institutional separatism called for in some proposals animated by the principle of equal recognition may work against the development of a common political identity. But perceived social exclusion also discourages the formation of such an identity. When a group's language, or nationality, or symbols and narratives are excluded from the public sphere, its members are unlikely to develop more than an attenuated and highly conditional identification with the community as a whole. Many will not develop even a weak identification with the community but will be drawn to forms of political extremism and fundamentalism that oppose more radically the norms of the majority culture.

To this argument it might be objected that unequal recognition is more likely, *in the long run*, to promote the formation of a shared sense of political community. In the short run, the argument concedes, the perception of social exclusion may well embitter minority identity-groups against the broader community, but new generations will face a variety of incentives to assimilate into the majority, and this sense of exclusion will gradually fade away. But this rejoinder ignores the resilience of many identities and attachments. It is true that non-recognition will sometimes encourage assimilation. As we saw earlier, one of the goods associated with recognition is 'promotion of identity': recognition in the public sphere helps an identity group to maintain and reproduce itself over time. But assimilation is rarely complete,[25] and, for those who do not assimilate, the fact that fellow group-members are choosing to assimilate only adds to the sense of alienation from the majority community. There are, of course, some historical examples of more or less complete assimilation, but these seem less likely to be repeated today, given the heightened salience of identity in contemporary society. And even where assimilation does occur along some objective cultural dimension (such as language or religious belief), there is often a residual, but significant, identity difference that resists assimilation (think, for instance, of how the Irish identity has survived the decline of the Irish language or how a Jewish-American identity has been maintained despite significant secularization within the Jewish population).

One problem with the fragmentation objection, then, is that it seems overly optimistic about the prospects for generating a common political identity by rejecting recognition claims. Even if it is true that equal recognition will contribute to social fragmentation, it may be that a policy of non-recognition designed to promote assimilation would have a similar, if not more destructive, effect.

At the same time, the fragmentation objection may also be overly *pessimistic* about the prospects for developing a shared civic identity in a regime of equal recognition. Critics of the politics of recognition tend to assert that the public expression of a particular identity by social groups is necessarily in conflict with their affirmation of a more universal civic identity.[26] This assumption ignores, however, an important possibility. It seems possible *both* to identify with a distinctive language, nationality, set of symbols and narratives, and so on, *and* feel excited about, and proud of, living in a political community in which one's fellow citizens have very different outlooks, identities and attachments, each of which is given expression and affirmation. Indeed, these attitudes not only are consistent but also can be continuous with one another. It can be in virtue of the fact that one's own group specificity is recognized and affirmed in the public sphere that one's attachment to the political community as a whole is strengthened and extended: one identifies with the larger community *as* a context which is hospitable to one's own particularity as well as the particularity of one's neighbours.

The experience of immigration and multiculturalism in countries such as Canada and the United States shows how this combination of attitudes need not be a merely theoretical possibility. Upon arrival in their new country, immigrants often gravitate towards neighbourhoods of major urban centres where they can access social networks dominated by members of their ethnic group. Critics of multiculturalism sometimes point to this tendency as evidence that multiculturalism and high levels of immigration risk undermining social unity by fragmenting the community into a patchwork of ethnic enclaves. But it is striking just how often immigrants in this context report a strong sense of patriotism towards the larger political community.[27] They come to affirm their new community as a context in which they can, to some extent, enjoy and express their group specificity and at the same time take advantage of the opportunities afforded by the larger society. The modern cosmopolitan city is another example of how such attitudes can be continuous with one another. For many people, one of the undeniable attractions of large cosmopolitan centres is their extreme social diversity. People feel excited and proud about living in a context in which so many different identities and ways of life are jostling for attention and expression in a single urban space. Their attachment to the local community partly grows out of the possibility they have of throwing themselves into specific group identities alongside others who are doing the same.

The best theoretical response to the fragmentation objection may, in fact, not be to reject recognition claims but to think through more fully the kinds of virtues and dispositions that should be expected of liberal citizens. This would not mean watering down the liberal answer to the responsibility question to the point where no shared civic identity is expected at all. Rather, it involves making it more explicit that one expectation we ought to have of liberal citizens is a disposition to acknowledge and affirm difference. Just as liberal citizens are expected to develop virtues of toleration, reasonableness, and so on, they also need to foster an ability and readiness to perceive when their neighbours have identities and attachments different from their own, and a willingness to support and uphold arrangements which provide for equality among the bearers of different identities and attachments. Most of all, perhaps, they need to have a political identity that is partly defined in terms of the positive project of constructing a public sphere that is hospitable to different group identities and affiliations. When the liberal answer to the responsibility question is fleshed out in this way, it is less obviously in tension with an answer to the entitlement question that incorporates a principle of equal recognition. Equal recognition, it is true, will encourage the formation of a heterogeneous public sphere in which people attach considerable importance to their specific group memberships. But this centrifugal tendency is counterbalanced by an identification with the political community as a context in which one's particularity is expressed and acknowledged on an egalitarian basis.

So the fragmentation objection may be at once overly optimistic and overly pessimistic. It may be overly optimistic about the possibility of constructing a common political identity in a context where the recognition claims of various minority groups are rebuffed. At the same time, the objection may be overly pessimistic about the possibilities for constructing a shared political identity in the context of a heterogeneous public sphere in so far as it does not consider the possibility that liberal citizens might develop a shared civic identity defined around the project of making a community that is hospitable to difference.

Still, I do not think we can reject the fragmentation objection just on the basis of these two responses. It *may be* that, in the long run, unequal recognition outperforms equal recognition in terms of generating a common political identity of some kind. This strikes me as an essentially empirical question that cannot be answered a priori or in isolation from particular contextual considerations. Similarly, it *may be* that a strong and reliable disposition to acknowledge and affirm difference will not tend to develop under certain configurations of the public sphere. Separate school boards for speakers of different languages are one concrete example of how a principle of equal recognition might take institutional shape in a multilingual community. But it is an open question – much dependent on specific contextual considerations – whether a strong and reliable disposition to acknowledge and affirm difference, or a common civic identity, would develop in the context of a public sphere characterized by such a high degree of institutional separatism. Similar questions are often raised about attempts to accommodate minority nationalisms through federal or devolutionary arrangements.[28] We do not yet know – and what we do know needs to be thoroughly modulated according to local circumstances – whether, and to what extent, self-government arrangements for national minorities tend to erode the shared sense of common citizenship required for a successful liberal polity.

This last formulation of the issue points to the importance of paying careful attention to details of institutional design in seeking to reconcile the demands of the entitlement and responsibility dimensions of citizenship. A liberal reconciliation would no doubt involve a civic education programme and other institutional strategies designed to promote a form of intercultural integration that does not amount to assimilation.[29] We cannot say, in advance, how far such a reconciliation will be possible without attention to specific context. What does seem unlikely, however, is that the fragmentation objection would block *all* attempts to incorporate greater equality of recognition into the liberal idea of citizenship. Although in certain specific contexts equal recognition may exacerbate social fragmentation to an even greater degree than unequal recognition would, in other contexts the opposite will be true. And in some contexts, perhaps, it will be possible to dispose citizens to acknowledge and affirm social differences and see themselves as engaged in a shared project of making a political community that is hospitable to those differences. Where this is true, equal recognition can be continuous with a strengthened sense of common citizenship. A central challenge for theorists of liberal citizenship will be to devise institutional strategies that allow this last outcome to be realized as widely as possible.

Notes

Many thanks to colleagues and students who commented on earlier versions of the paper in a variety of settings. Thanks also to SSHRC and to FCAR for grants supporting my research.

1. Strictly speaking, a theory of citizenship, as I am characterizing it, would need to be complemented by a theory of residency, a theory of permanent residency, and so on. Each of these kinds of status raise questions of membership, entitlement and responsibility that parallel the questions posed by a theory of citizenship.
2. T.H. Marshall (1965) 'Citizenship and Social Class', in *Class, Citizenship and Social Development*, New York: Anchor.
3. See, for example, Taylor's essay of that title (Charles Taylor (1994) 'The Politics of Recognition', in Amy Gutmann (ed.) *Multiculturalism and the 'Politics of Recognition'*, Princeton, NJ: Princeton University Press).
4. John Rawls (1971) *A Theory of Justice*, Cambridge, MA: Harvard University Press, and (1993) *Political Liberalism*, New York: Columbia University Press.
5. I shall generally use the term 'public sphere' to denote 'state and major institutions of civil society'. Examples of major institutions of civil society include private broadcasters, hospitals, airlines, universities and major department stores.
6. Iris Marion Young(1990) *Justice and the Politics of Difference*, Princeton, NJ: Princeton University Press, chapters 4, 6; Yael Tamir (1993) *Liberal Nationalism*, Princeton, NJ: Princeton University Press, chapter 2; Will Kymlicka (1995) *Multicultural Citizenship*, Oxford: Oxford University Press, chapter 6, section 1.
7. Kymlicka, *Multicultural Citizenship*, pp. 114–15; cf. Veit Bader (1997) 'The Cultural Conditions of Transnational Citizenship: On the Interpenetration of Political and Ethnic Cultures', *Political Theory* 25 (6), 771–813; Joseph Carens

(1997) 'Two Conceptions of Fairness: A Response to Veit Bader', *Political Theory* 25 (6), 814–20.

8. The costs of denying someone public affirmation are well brought out in Taylor, 'The Politics of Recognition', pp. 25–6.

9. Taylor, 'The Politics of Recognition', pp. 40, 58–9, emphasizes the importance to some cultural groups of reproducing their community from generation to generation.

10. See the subtle discussion in Susan Wolf (1994) 'Comment', in Gutmann (ed.) *Multiculturalism and the 'Politics of Recognition'*.

11. For this distinction, see Ronald Dworkin (1981) 'What Is Equality? Part I: Equality of Welfare', *Philosophy and Public Affairs* 10 (3), 185–246, and (1981) 'What Is Equality? Part II: Equality of Resources', *Philosophy and Public Affairs* 10 (4), 283–345.

12. Taylor, 'The Politics of Recognition', tends to oppose a difference-blind, neutrality-based interpretation of equal recognition to an interpretation that emphasizes the pursuit of collective goals such as cultural survival. The resourcist metric of equal recognition being proposed in this chapter falls somewhere between these two extremes. It avoids difference blindness in so far as it advocates a heterogeneous public sphere with institutional spaces and capacities reflective of the different identities prevalent in society. At the same time, it does not promise cultural survival to any identity group – it promises only that any such group can enjoy the same kinds of institutional spaces and capacities in the public sphere to which other identity groups have access. In my view, an interpretation of equal recognition that guarantees cultural survival is vulnerable to the objection that cultural survival is sometimes put at risk because of choices made by group members themselves to revise, reinterpret or even reject their commitment to the group (for a good statement of this objection, see Jürgen Habermas (1994) 'Struggles for Recognition in the Democratic Constitutional State', in Gutmann (ed.) *Multiculturalism and the 'Politics of Recognition'*, pp. 130–2). It is also vulnerable to something like the 'expensive-tastes' objection that Dworkin ('What Is Equality? Part I') develops against welfarist metrics of equality more generally (for discussion of this objection in the context of debates concerning cultural protection, see Alan Patten (1999) 'Liberal Egalitarianism and the Case for Supporting National Cultures', *The Monist*, 82 (3), 387–410).

13. Thanks to Marc Stears for this point. See also Anne Phillips (1997) 'Why Worry about Multiculturalism?', *Dissent*, Winter, 57–63, p. 60. An example of this difficulty might be found in the debate about religious schooling. In principle, it might be possible to establish equal recognition of all major religious denominations by giving each the opportunity and resources to establish their own public schools. In practice, however, some religious groups are likely to be too small or geographically dispersed to be able to support a viable school system. Non-recognition is arguably less denigrating in a context where no religion is recognized than where some are recognized and others are not.

14. K. Anthony Appiah (1994) 'Identity, Authenticity, Survival: Multicultural Societies and Social Reproduction', in Gutmann (ed.) *Multiculturalism and the 'Politics of Recognition'*, p. 163.

15. The argument summarized in this paragraph is made in Harry Brighouse (1998)

'Against Nationalism', in Michel Seymour (ed.) *Rethinking Nationalism*, Calgary: University of Calgary Press, pp. 374–8.

16. Ronald Dworkin (1977) *Taking Rights Seriously*, London: Duckworth, p. 180.

17. As Dworkin expresses it, liberals are committed to a 'principle of rough equality', according to which 'resources and opportunities should be distributed, so far as possible, equally, so that roughly the same share of whatever is available is devoted to satisfying the ambitions of each'. 'Any other general aim of distribution,' he adds, 'will assume either that the fate of some people should be of greater concern than that of others, or that the ambitions or talents of some are more worthy, and should be supported more generously on that account.' (Ronald Dworkin (1978) 'Liberalism', in Stuart Hampshire (ed.) *Public and Private Morality*, Cambridge: Cambridge University Press, p. 129.) This principle of equality is further elaborated and refined in Dworkin, 'What Is Equality?', Parts I and II.

18. For a proposal along these lines, see Jonathan Pool (1987) 'Thinking about Linguistic Discrimination', *Language Problems and Language Planning* 11, 3–21, and (1991) 'The Official Language Problem', *American Political Science Review* 85 (2), 495–514.

19. Wolf, 'Comment', also argues that recognition claims can be grounded in equal respect rather than in comparative judgements about the worth of various cultures.

20. In many ways, this objection can be traced back to Mill's famous discussion of multination states, in which he worries that they will be unable to foster and sustain the virtues and dispositions needed to support a regime committed to liberal justice and representative democracy (J.S. Mill (1991) 'Considerations on Representative Government', in *On Liberty and Other Essays*, Oxford: Oxford University Press, chapter 16). For other statements of the objection, see, for instance, Will Kymlicka and Wayne Norman (1994) 'The Return of the Citizen', *Ethics* 104 (2), 352–81, p. 306 (who cite a number of other authors); David Miller (1995) *On Nationality*, Oxford: Oxford University Press, pp. 139–40; Ronald Beiner (1995) 'Introduction: Why Citizenship Constitutes a Theoretical Problem in the Last Decade of the Twentieth Century', in Ronald Beiner (ed.) *Theorizing Citizenship*, Albany: State University of New York Press.

21. Michael Sandel (1984) 'The Procedural Republic and the Unencumbered Self', *Political Theory* 12 (1), 81–96; Charles Taylor (1989) 'Cross-Purposes: The Liberal/Communitarian Debate', in N. Rosenblum (ed.) *Liberalism and the Moral Life*, Cambridge: Cambridge University Press; Ronald Dworkin (1989) 'Liberal Community', *California Law Review* 77 (30), 479–504; Steven Macedo (1990) *Liberal Virtues*, New York: Oxford University Press; William Galston (1991) *Liberal Purposes: Goods, Virtues, and Duties in the Liberal State*, Cambridge: Cambridge University Press; Rawls, *Political Liberalism*; Kymlicka and Norman, 'The Return of the Citizen'; Jeff Spinner (1994) *The Boundaries of Citizenship*, Baltimore: Johns Hopkins University Press, pp. 45–9; Alan Patten (1996) 'The Republican Critique of Liberalism', *British Journal of Political Science* 26 (1), 25–44.

22. Macedo, *Liberal Virtues*; Rawls, *Political Liberalism*; Kymlicka and Norman, 'The Return of the Citizen'.

23. For a fuller account of the 'liberal virtues', see Macedo, *Liberal Virtues*; Galston, *Liberal Purposes*; and Kymlicka and Norman, 'The Return of the Citizen'.

24. As Spinner aptly puts it (*The Boundaries of Citizenship*, p. 59), 'Liberalism is partly founded on the realization that the quest for uniformity in some areas will lead to more divisiveness, not more harmony.' See also Bhikhu Parekh (1991) 'British Citizenship and Cultural Difference', in Geoff Andrews (ed.) *Citizenship*, London: Lawrence & Wishart, p. 195.

25. See Will Kymlicka (1996) 'Social Unity in a Liberal State', *Social Philosophy and Policy* 13 (1), 106–36, pp. 127–8.

26. See, for instance, Beiner, 'Introduction: Why Citizenship Constitutes a Theoretical Problem', pp. 10–11.

27. See, for instance, Kymlicka, 'Social Unity in a Liberal State', p. 119, and (1998) *Finding Our Way*, Toronto: Oxford University Press, chapter 1.

28. For discussion, see, for instance, Kymlicka and Norman, 'The Return of the Citizen', pp. 307–9; Kymlicka, *Multicultural Citizenship*, chapter 9; and Kymlicka, *Finding Our Way*, chapter 13.

29. On multicultural civic education, see Yael Tamir (1995) 'Two Concepts of Multiculturalism', in Yael Tamir (ed.) *Democratic Education in a Multicultural State*, Oxford: Blackwell.

CHAPTER TEN

The Challenge of Reimagining Citizenship and Belonging in Multicultural and Multinational Societies

JAMES TULLY

Introduction

In *Strange Multiplicity: Constitutionalism in an Age of Diversity* I suggested one way in which a sense of belonging could be reimagined for multicultural and multinational societies.[1] This involves, first, seeing the diverse cultural and national identities of citizens as overlapping, interacting and negotiated over time. Drawing on Wittgenstein, we can say that identities are 'aspectival'. Second, reimagining belonging involves realizing that the cultural and national identities that are worthy of respect often require some form of acknowledgement or recognition in the public life and institutions of a society in order to secure a sense of belonging. The actual forms of acknowledgement or recognition are various and mutable, and they must be worked out by citizens and their representatives by means of democratic discussions, agreements and periodic reviews.

Rather than repeating my suggestion here, I would like to approach it from a slightly different path. I wish to discuss the role that the democratic freedom of citizen participation plays in engendering a sense of belonging and the complex forms this freedom takes in multicultural and multinational societies, the freedom not only to participate in accord with one's cultural and national identities when they are publicly recognized (as I stressed in *Strange Multiplicity*), but also to participate in the ongoing contests over how these are to be acknowledged, recognized and accommodated. I do this in the following sections: section 1 deals with the traditional republican or democratic freedom of participation of citizens; section 2 discusses three characteristics of identity politics; section 3 covers three types of demands for recognition; section 4 concerns who decides which identities are worthy of recognition, and by what procedures, in multicultural and multinational societies; and section 5 considers the sense of belonging and identity-related security that is engendered by participation in the public discussions over forms of public recognition and participation in institutions that accord recognition.

1 Freedom and Citizenship

Let us recall the main features of the freedom of citizens before employing it as a form of critical reflection on our contemporary problem of belonging in multicultural and multinational societies. Citizenship is defined in terms of two concepts: 'free peoples' and 'free citizens'. A collection of humans becomes, or takes on the identity of, a 'free people' by virtue of governing themselves by their own laws over time. This activity of self-rule is described by Quentin Skinner in the following manner:

> [It is] a system in which the sole power of making laws remains with the people or their accredited representatives, and in which all individual members of the body politic – rulers and citizens alike – remain equally subject to whatever laws they choose to impose on themselves.[2]

As we can see, there are two co-equal principles involved in being a 'free people': the rule of law (rulers and citizens alike remain equally subject to the law) and self-rule (rulers and citizens impose the laws on themselves). These two co-equal republican principles of 'constitutionalism' and 'popular sovereignty' have been accepted by liberals such as John Rawls and Jürgen Habermas as the basic principles of 'democratic legitimacy' in the contemporary age.[3]

This characterization of a 'free people' is internally related to the second concept, that of 'free citizens'. A 'free people' subject themselves to the law through their own participation. That is, they are 'free citizens' just in so far as they have a voice in their form of self-government. In Quentin Skinner's phrase, they 'impose the laws on themselves'. To be a 'free citizen' it is not sufficient simply to be a member of a free people. It is necessary to participate in some direct or indirect way in the exercise of political power: to be an 'active' citizen. If members do not have a voice in the way in which political power is exercised, and thus power is exercised over them without their say, 'behind their backs', as in the market or bureaucratic organizations, then they are, by definition, 'subjects' rather than 'free citizens'.

The ideal of 'free citizens' is, in its most utopian formulation, as Quentin Skinner explains, 'that all acts of legislation duly reflect the explicit consent of every member of the body politic as a whole'.[4] For well-known reasons, this ideal is unrealizable in practice, especially in the large and complex political associations of today, where participation is mediated, represented and indirect. Nevertheless, the underlying point remains valid. A member of a free people becomes a 'free citizen' only in so far as she not only has the opportunity to participate in some way or another, but actually participates. This is not to equate 'individual freedom' with the activity of political participation, as Quentin Skinner warns.[5] Rather, it is to say that there is another aspect or dimension of freedom which consists precisely in the activity of participation itself. This is, as Hannah Arendt put it, 'civic freedom' or the 'freedom of citizens'.[6]

The freedom of citizen participation is certainly the means of 'maintaining' and 'protecting' our 'individual liberty', as Quentin Skinner argues, but it is also, and just as importantly, the way we become, or take on the identity of, citizens.[7] That is, just as a 'free people' is a collective achievement (the bringing into being and sustaining of a self-governing people over time), so too is citizenship an achievement – something that is brought into being through its exercise. For republicans and democrats, citizenship is not equated with a set of rights and duties, as is often the case for liberals, nor is it sharing in a national identity, as is often the case for nationalists. It is an achievement acquired through engaging in the multitude of activities of imposing the laws on ourselves. Citizenship, therefore, is an identity that we acquire by being 'free citizens', by engagement in the institutions of self-rule of a free people.

Recall now the three main features of our identity as citizens. First, it is a form of self-awareness and self-formation that one comes to acquire through engagement with others in the public spheres where the exercise of political power is discussed and negotiated. Second, a specific form of self-consciousness is acquired through participation: the awareness of oneself as a member of, and as belonging to, the political association. Now, this sense of belonging to the political association is, as Habermas puts it, not only the awareness of ourselves as equal subjects of the constitutional rule of law. This alone, he stresses, is insufficient to generate solidarity and loyalty among the members of modern political associations. It is necessary also to foster the awareness of ourselves as, in some sense, the agents or authors or editors of those laws. This is what we mean by self-rule or popular sovereignty.[8] But this condition of 'democratic legitimacy' can be made good only if the members of the association have some sort of say in the way political power is exercised over them through the laws, because it is precisely this activity of civic freedom which does in fact create, or make good, the awareness of the laws as 'self-imposed', rather than as imposed 'non-democratically', 'behind our backs'.

Third, the form of participation which is necessary for the constitution of citizen identity is 'having a say' or being 'in on' the public dialogues and negotiations over how and by whom political power is exercised. We can thus say that citizenship is intersubjective and dialogical (a form of identity we achieve in public dialogues with others). According to the classic humanist heritage, the public dialogues and negotiations over the public good in which we become free citizens and free peoples exhibit the following three features.

First, public dialogues are the exercise of practical, not theoretical, reason. They involve persuasion, enquiry, negotiation, information seeking, deliberation, rhetoric and eristic.[9] Second, they are 'agonic' in character: citizens and rulers compete for, and endlessly dispute over, forms of mutual recognition and rule in accordance with the shared principles of freedom, equality and distinctness. Third, political dialogues are always 'negotiations', not 'consensus'. Any agreement is partial or conditional to some extent; open to reasonable redescription and challenge. An element of reasonable disagreement, of non-consensus, and so of dissent, contestation, renegotiation and compromise attends any agreement as a kind of 'permanent provocation'. An openness to always to listen to the other side – *audi alteram partem* – and to negotiate a revisable accommodation, rather than to aim at an unconditional consensus, is at the heart of the exercise of public reason.[10]

In sum, citizenship is an identity that members acquire through exchanging reasons in public dialogues and negotiations over how and by whom political power is exercised. 'Having a voice' in these activities of discussion and negotiation generates bonds of solidarity and a sense of belonging to the political association. The self-governing association one identifies with by virtue of becoming a citizen through such participation is what we call a 'free people', or 'free peoples' in multinational associations. Since the public discussions are marked by competition and disagreement – by 'negotiation' in the classic sense – it cannot be anything they agree on that gives citizens an identity and holds them together. Rather, it is nothing more or less than participation in the activities of public dialogue and negotiation themselves.

It follows from this account that citizen identity and belonging are not acquired by the mere possession of constitutional rights and duties, or by agreements on comprehensive goods or values, a shared national identity, fundamental principles of justice, or by agreements on a set of universal procedures of validation. It is not that some of these conditions of constitutional democracy in a nation-state are not necessary or important. Liberals and nationalists are right about this. Nevertheless, there are two reasons why these principles, procedures, shared goods and so on cannot adequately account for citizenship. First, as Hannah Arendt famously argued, they are the background conditions of citizenship, not the activity of citizenship.[11] These conditions derive from one principle of a 'free people', the 'rule of law'. They need to be complemented by the other principle, self-rule: that free citizens are subject only to those conditions that 'they choose to impose on themselves'.

The second reason these conditions are insufficient is that citizens, rulers and theorists disagree over them. They are always open to question, reasonable disagreement, contestation, deliberation, negotiation and amendment over time, in the course of a free people imposing them on themselves. They are not only the conditions of free political dialogue and negotiation but also what those negotiations are often *about*. This is what classical democrats mean when they say politics is in the realm of '*negotium*', not '*otium*'. As a result, the conditions of citizenship are not fixed, but are open to discussion and debate by free citizens in the course of imposing them on themselves. This is the only way that the two principles of a 'free people' – constitutionalism and popular sovereignty – can be treated as co-equal.[12]

So, engaging in the agonic and interminable public discussions and negotiations, both *within* and *over* the conditions of citizenship, constitutes and sustains our identities as 'free citizens' and generates the sense of belonging to a 'free people'. In the public discussions, citizens 'disclose' the identities they wish to see recognized, and others 'acknowledge' these and respond, either by agreeing or disagreeing, or by advancing demands for recognition of their own. Conversely, when these activities of '*citizenization*' are unavailable or arbitrarily restricted, the members of a political association remain 'subjects' rather than 'citizens' because the laws are imposed on them without their 'say'. The association is then experienced as 'alien and imposed', as a structure of domination that is both 'unfree' and illegitimate'. Subjects turn to other communities of democratic discussion and dialogue available to them, centred on their language, culture, ethnicity, nationality, gender, sexual orientation and the like. As a result of being in on *these* local discussions, they identify with *this* community rather than the larger political association. In these fora, they debate how they can reform the larger political association so that they can 'get in' or how they can 'secede' from it. The larger political association tends to instability and disintegration. It is then held together, if at all, by force, fraud and the management of interests rather than the bonds of solidarity created by free citizenship.

Now, in a well-ordered constitutional democracy, many avenues of participation are readily available. Citizens can participate both directly and indirectly in political dialogues: directly in a variety of public spheres, local initiatives, referenda, consultative meetings, the manifold local and global struggles for the establishment of public norms across the private sector, political parties, elections to local, regional, federal, national and supranational representative bodies, public service, interest groups, dissent, protest, and civil disobedience; and indirectly, through relations of critical trust with their elected representatives, public servants, courts, 'intermediary' organizations, and, especially, in public discussions facilitated by radio, television, print media and the Internet.

Nevertheless, in seeking to engage in the public dialogues and negotiations in these ways, the identity-diverse members of contemporary societies claim to experience arbitrary constraints that block their free participation, and thereby disable them from becoming free citizens. These constraints are the prevailing 'norms of intersubjective public recognition' they must follow in order to participate and be recognized *as* citizens. The prevailing norms of public recognition define the identity of citizens. Multicultural and multi-national citizens claim that the prevailing norms unjustly constrain participation in two different ways. They misrecognize or exclude the linguistic, cultural, gender-related and other identities of some of the members, and they impose, and assimilate them to, an alien identity (the identity of the dominant culture, gender, etc., under the guise of being a neutral liberal identity or a shared uninational identity). These members experience the norms of citizenship as alien and imposed, rather than self-imposed. They are treated as 'subjects' rather than 'citizens'; unfree in the very activities in which they are supposed to constitute themselves as free citizens and free peoples. These challenges to dominant norms of citizen-identity are what we call 'identity politics' and 'struggles for recognition'.

Now that I have sketched out a democratic conception of citizenship, I would like to describe briefly, in the next two sections, what I take to be the three relevant characteristics of identity politics and the three main types of struggle over recognition. Then we will be in a position to see how these demands can be approached and negotiated from our perspective of citizenship and belonging.

2 Three Characteristics of Identity Politics

'Identity politics' or the 'politics of recognition' is a concept that has come into common use to describe a wide range of political struggles which occur with increasing frequency and constitute one of the most pressing political problems of the present age. 'Identity politics' refers to struggles for the appropriate forms of political recognition and accommodation of the following kinds: the freedom of expression of individuals, immigrants and refugees, women, gays and lesbians, linguistic, ethnic, cultural and religious minorities, nations within and across existing nation-states, indigenous peoples, and Islamic and other non-European cultures and religions against Western imperialism and Eurocentrism.[13]

The forms of recognition and accommodation sought are as various as the struggles. Feminists and gays and lesbians demand formal equality and equal respect for their identity-related differences in opposition to dominant patriarchal and heterosexist norms of private and public conduct. Minorities seek different forms of public recognition, representation and protection of their languages, cultures, ethnicities and religions. Immigrants and refugees struggle for the rights of citizenship but also for freedom from assimilation to a dominant culture and language. Various models of regional, federal, confederal and independent forms of self-government and self-determination are advanced by suppressed nations and indigenous peoples. Nation-states in the Arab world and Third World aim to overcome the continuing Western cultural imperialism of the international system of nation-states and the processes of economic globalization. Many of these demands are for legal and political recognition not only within existing nation-states, but also in supranational associations such as the European Union, international law, at the United Nations and by the creation of novel 'subnational' and 'transnational' institutions.[14]

As these examples illustrate, the types of struggle are very different (to say nothing of the individual cases of each type), and they are not always or exclusively concerned with identity. Moreover, these types of struggle for recognition all have histories which pre-date by centuries the emergence of the concept of 'identity politics'. Nevertheless, they are referred to as 'identity politics' because they often exhibit three characteristics in the present which render them significantly similar to each other and significantly different from their past forms.

First, what makes these struggles so volatile and intractable is their 'diversity'. Identity politics is not a politics of many separate, bounded and internally uniform nations, cultures or other forms of identity, each seeking separate and compatible recognition and political associations, even though leaders often portray them in this manner and employ powerful processes of assimilation to eliminate internal differences. Rather, demands are articulated around criss-crossing and overlapping allegiances: indigenousness, nationality, culture, region, religion, ethnicity, language, sexual orientation, gender, immigration and individual expression. A minority nation or language group demanding recognition from the larger political association often finds minorities, indigenous peoples, multicultural citizens or immigrants within it who also demand recognition and protection. Feminists find that their identity-related demands are crossed by national, linguistic, cultural, religious, immigrant and sexual orientation differences among women, and nationalist and culturalist movements find in turn that women do not always agree with men. Members of a minority seeking recognition against an intransigent majority along one identity-related difference will have cross-cutting allegiances due to other aspects of their identity they share with members of the other side.[15]

It does not follow from the absence of separate, bounded and internally uniform identities that identity politics is dissolving through its own fragmentation, or that, as a result, humans can now relegate identity to the 'sub-political' realm and agree on principles, rights and institutions unmediated by identity-related differences. Quite the contrary. The increasing diversity and insecurity of identity-related differences fuel the demands for their political recognition and protection. What does follow is the now commonplace observation that any identity is never quite identical to itself: it always contains an irreducible element of alterity. Identity is multiplex or aspectival. Accordingly, 'diversity', or the multiplicity of overlapping identities and their corresponding allegiances, is the first characteristic of identity politics.[16]

Nevertheless, this 'hybridization' should not be treated as if it were *the* fundamental characteristic, even though it is the fundamental *experience* for some people, especially those living in exile or multicultural cities. It is certainly possible to bring a group of people to agree together in defence and promotion of one aspect of their identity, such as language, nationality or indigenousness, across their other identity-related differences, and this identification can be sustained for generations (as, for example, ranking one's Scottish identity prior to British, Sami prior to Norwegian, Catalonian prior to Spanish). What the multiplicity of overlapping identities entails is a second characteristic of identity politics: the priority granted to one identity, the way in which and by whom it is articulated, and the form of public recognition and accommodation demanded are always open to question, reinterpretation, deliberation and negotiation by the bearers of that identity.

An identity negotiated in these all-too-human circumstances will not be fixed or authentic, but it can still be plausible rather than implausible, well supported rather than imposed, reasonable rather than unreasonable, empowering rather than disabling, liberating rather than oppressive. That is, it will be a mutable and ongoing construct of practical and intersubjective dialogue, not of theoretical reason on one side or unmediated ascription on the other. Consequently, identity politics consists of three processes of negotiation which interact in complex ways: (a) among the diverse members of a group struggling for recognition; (b) between them and the group(s) to whom their demand for recognition is made; and (c) among the members of the latter group(s) (whose identity comes into question as a result of the struggle, whether they like it or not, as, for example, men, heterosexuals and members of dominant cultures and language groups discover).

The third and most elusive feature of identity politics is the concept of 'identity' itself. It is not one's theoretical identity, what one is as a matter of scientific fact or theoretical reason. It is one's practical identity, a mode of being in the world with others. A practical identity is a form both of self-awareness and of self-formation. It is a structure of strong evaluations in accord with which humans value themselves, find their lives worth living and their actions worth undertaking, and the description under which they require, as a condition of self-worth, that others recognize and respect them. A practical identity is also relational and intersubjective in a double sense. It is acquired and sustained in relation to those who share it and those who do not. Any practical identity projects on to those who do not share it another identity, the non-X, who, in reciprocity, seek mutual recognition and respect for their identity, which is seldom the one others project on them. This is why negotiation and agonic contestation are so fundamental to identity politics.[17]

As we have seen from the first characteristic, for most people there will be several overlapping practical identities. They will be a member of the human race, a man or a woman, a member of a religion and an ethnic group, a member of one or more language and cultural groups, a national of one of more nations, and so on. In so far as these identities are valued, they are a matter not of third-person ascription or projection but of first-person normative practices of self-consciousness and ethical formation, such as consciousness-raising in feminist movements, the acquisition, use and care for a language, culture, religion, community or nationality with others, and so on, *and* of third-person recognition, respect and, at its best, affirmation and celebration.

The injustice and unfreedom distinctive of identity politics follow from these three characteristics. Individuals and groups are thwarted in their attempts to negotiate and gain reciprocal public recognition and accommodation of their practical identities as part of their citizen-identity. Their identities are misrecognized or not recognized at all in the dominant norms of public recognition. Instead, an alien identity is imposed upon them, without their say, through processes of subjectification, either assimilating them to the dominant identity or constructing them as marginal and expendable others.[18] While ethnic cleansing and genocide are the most extreme and horrendous cases,[19] there is a multiplicity of types of misrecognition and corresponding injuries, and of appropriate forms of recognition.

It is now widely acknowledged that participation in the intersubjective negotiation of identity, the security of these processes of identity formation, and the acknowledgement, recognition and respect of these by others, are the prerequisites of the sense of self-worth of individuals and groups which empowers them to become free, equal and autonomous agents in both private and public life. As a result, the demeaning and disrespect of their identities through sexism, heterosexism, racism, nationalist, linguistic and culturalist chauvinism, the pseudo-scientific ranking of cultures, languages and polities in stages of development, with Europe and the United States at the apex, and the imposition of dominant cultures through processes which destroy identities and assimilate or marginalize individuals and groups are not only unjust, but also undermine the self-respect, and hence the very abilities, of the people concerned not only to resist these injustices but also to act effectively even if they opt to assimilate. This causes the well-known pathologies of oppression, marginalization and assimilation: lack of self-respect and self-esteem, alienation, trans-generational poverty, substance abuse, unemployment, the destruction of communities, high levels of suicide and the like.[20]

3 Three Types of Demand for Recognition

Struggles to overcome an imposed identity and to gain public recognition of a non-imposed identity through the three processes of negotiation mentioned above are not normally direct challenges to the principles of twentieth-century democratic politics: freedom, equality, respect for diversity, due process, the rule of law, federalism, mutual respect, consent, self-determination and political, civic, social and minority rights. These principles are appealed to by both sides in identity politics: to condemn the imposed identity and to justify the recognition of a identity-related difference on one side and to defend the established norms of citizen-identity on the other. Of course, these principles are interpreted and applied in different ways, but it is seldom the principles themselves that are in dispute. For example, gay and lesbian couples often demand to be treated equally to heterosexual couples, women to men, indigenous peoples to other peoples of the world who enjoy rights of self-determination, a suppressed nation to other nations, a suppressed language group to dominant language groups, immigrants to other citizens, Muslims to Christians.

The objection is that these principles are not interpreted, applied and acted on either in a difference-blind manner, as liberals often claim, or in accordance with a national identity which all citizens share equally, as nationalists often claim. Rather, they are employed in a manner that is partial to the identity-related differences of the well-to-do, the able, heterosexuals, males, and members of the dominant linguistic, cultural, ethnic, national and religious groups; and, conversely, in a manner that is biased against the practical identities of others. The solution is not to try to apply the principles in an impartial manner or in accordance with a common national identity in all cases, for in many cases this is not possible. Politics and public life have to be conducted in some languages or other, in accord with some modes of overt and covert conduct or other; statutory holidays, elections and the like will fall on some religious holidays; some versions of history will be taught in the educational systems and embodied in the public narratives and iconography; and so on. The suggestion is rather to interpret and apply these principles in a *difference-aware* manner: one which is not partial to any particular identity at the expense of others but is based on mutual respect for the diversity of identities of the sovereign citizens of the association, so that there is a genuine 'parity of participation'.

This suggestion has been controversial because it introduces a second aspect of equality. One standard aspect of equality is that all citizens should be treated equally in the sense of being 'impartial' or 'indifferent' to any and all identity-related differences. Members of a political association may cultivate their practical identities in private and voluntary associations but the government remains impartial with respect to them. While accepting this aspect of equality as legitimate, defenders of identity politics have challenged its applicability in many cases. As we have just seen, in many cases it is impossible to be impartial in this sense. When this is the case, it is necessary to take into account another aspect of equality: that is, to treat the reasonable identity-related differences involved with equal respect. To take a simple example, one person one vote, yet hold the campaign and voting in different languages where numbers warrant. Or, in the case of the European Union, publicly recognize eleven languages of participation, yet also give due recognition to other 'lesser-used', but support-worthy, languages. It is now fairly widely accepted that there are these two senses of the concept of equality that need to be taken into account.[21]

Many liberals have agreed and have reconceived liberalism along these lines.[22] Several nationalists have reconceived national identity along the lines of diversity and public negotiation.[23] In so doing they have made liberalism and nationalism more sensitive to the complex conditions of belonging in culturally diverse societies. This does not mean that each and every identity-related difference gains equal recognition and accommodation. That would be impossible. It means that demands for recognition should be accorded equal *consideration* in order to determine whether they are worthy of respect, and those that are should be given *due* recognition and accommodation. The assurance that demands for recognition will be given public consideration, even where the struggle for due recognition fails, is itself a powerful condition of engendering a sense of belonging, as I argue below.

Before we examine this maxim of identity politics in the following section, it is necessary to mention briefly the three types of demand to which it is designed to apply.

The first type of demand is for 'cultural diversity': the mutual recognition and respect for identity-related differences in the cultural sphere. All types of identity politics involve demands to negotiate the ways in which some members of a political association are currently disrespected and misrecognized in the broad sphere of cultures and values where they first learn and internalize their attitudes towards others. The aim, first, is to expose and overcome racism, sexism, ableism, ethnocentrism and Eurocentrism, sexual harassment, linguistic, cultural and national stereotypes, and other forms of overt and covert diversity-blind and diversity-partial speech and behaviour. Second, the objective is to foster awareness of and respect for diversity in all areas of society so that all members can participate on the basis of *mutual respect*. This type of demand standardly calls for curriculum reform, training in cultural diversity at work, and, most important, the democratic negotiation of diversity-sensitive equity policies and standards in the public, private and voluntary sectors.[24]

The second type of demand is for multicultural and multiethnic citizenship. These are demands to participate in the public institutions and practices of contemporary societies in ways that recognize and affirm, rather than misrecognize and exclude, the diverse identities of citizens. Women's movements, gays and lesbians, and linguistic, cultural, ethnic and religious minorities wish to participate in the same institutions as the dominant groups but in ways that protect and respect their identity-related differences: for example, to have some schooling in their minority languages and cultures, access to media, to be able to use their languages and cultural ways in legal and political institutions and at work (whether one is Muslim in France or

Surinamese in The Netherlands), to reform representative institutions so they fairly represent the identity diversity of the population, to have day-care facilities so that women and single parents can participate on a par with heterosexual males, to be able to speak, deliberate and act in public in a different voice, to have same-sex benefits, to observe a religious or cultural practice in public without discrimination, for constitutional charters of rights to be interpreted and applied in a diversity-sensitive manner, to establish minority and group rights where necessary, and so on – so that all citizens and minorities can participate equally, but not identically, with others.[25]

The third type of demand is for 'multinational' constitutional associations, or what might be called constitutional associations of more than one 'free people'. These are demands to establish autonomous political and legal institutions separate in varying degrees from the larger political association. Here, suppressed nations within multinational societies and indigenous peoples argue that the proper recognition of their identity *as* nations and *as* peoples entails that they have a right of self-determination: a right to govern themselves by their own laws. They may exercise this right either by determining a new federal or confederal relation within the existing constitutional association of which they are a part, or, if this meaningful exercise of self-government is blocked, by secession and the establishment of an independent nation-state. It is only by these means of self-government, they argue, that they are able to protect and live in accordance with their identity – their nationality and their indigenousness – and be 'free peoples'. If they are constrained to participate in the institutions of the dominant society, then they are misrecognized (as minorities within the dominant society rather than as nations or peoples), and their identity-related differences will be overwhelmed and assimilated by the majority.

This third type of demand became increasingly familiar in the latter part of the twentieth century. The response is often the suppression of the demand, and either assimilation or an armed conflict that ends in secession. However, the struggles have also given rise to experiments in the 'federalization' of multinational political associations – that is, regional autonomy, subsidiarity, dispersed and shared sovereignty, and flexible federal and confederal arrangements. Spain, Belgium, the United Kingdom, Canada-Quebec and the European Union itself are all examples of this kind of experimentation.[26] And, in Norway, Canada, the United States, Australia, New Zealand and South America, the struggles of indigenous peoples to overcome internal colonization and gain recognition as 'free peoples' are giving rise to experiments in new forms of indigenous self-government and federalism with the larger, surrounding non-indigenous governments, such as the Sami Parliament in Norway.[27]

The third type of struggle is the most complex because it brings into play the full diversity of overlapping identities and three processes of negotiation characteristic of identity politics. Those making the demand must persuade their own internally diverse members, through public dialogue and consultation, that they are not a province, region or minority of some kind, as the current form of recognition has it, but a distinct nation or people. They must also persuade the majority society, with all its internal diversity, and then persuade it to enter into negotiations to change the current constitutional relation to some form of greater autonomy and lesser association. As these negotiations take place, they almost always provoke the two types of demand for the recognition of cultural diversity and multicultural citizenship within and often across the nation or people demanding recognition. The diverse citizens within, such as linguistic minorities and multicultural immigrants, wish to ensure that their identity-related differences will not be effaced in the new institutions of self-government by a policy of either impartial liberalism or uniform nationalism. Yet cultural diversity and multicultural citizenship have to be recognized and accommodated in a form which does not infringe too deeply, or undermine, the identity of the nation or people, for this is the reason self-governing institutions of nationhood are demanded in the first place.

Given these conditions of identity politics in multicultural and multinational societies, let us now ask who decides, and by what procedures, in order that a sense of belonging can be generated and sustained.

4 Who Decides and by What Procedures so that a Sense of Belonging is Nurtured?

The central questions of identity politics are, first, who decides which identities of the members of a political association are unjustly imposed and which are worthy of recognition and accommodation? And, second, by what procedures do they decide and review their decisions? The response to the first question marks a democratic revolution in political thought in the twentieth century. It is no longer assumed that the identities worthy of recognition, and so constitutive of citizen identity, can be determined outside the political process itself, by theoretical reason. It is now widely assumed that the identities worthy of recognition must be worked out by the citizens themselves, through the exercise of practical reason in negotiations and agreements. In John Rawls's famous phrase, the question is 'political not metaphysical'.[28]

There are several reasons for this. The first is that there was a significant emphasis on democracy or the sovereignty of the people in both theory and practice in the latter half of the twentieth century – that is, on our first principle of self-rule. In theory, *quod omnes tangit* (what touches all must be agreed to by all), one of the oldest principles of Western constitutionalism, has been revived and given dialogical reformulation as the principle of democratic legitimacy: 'only those norms can claim to be valid that meet (or could meet) with the approval of all affected in their capacity as participants in a practical discourse'.[29] As I mentioned at the outset, the sovereignty of the people to reach agreements among themselves on the basic norms of citizenship of their political association through deliberation is said to be a principle equal in status to the constitutional rule of law.

In practice, there has been a proliferation of practices of democratic negotiation of the conditions of membership of a vast and increasing range of associations, from private- and public-sector bargaining to democratic constitutional change, international agreements and evolving institutions of cosmopolitan democracy.[30] In virtually every organization of human interaction and co-ordination, disputes over the prevailing relations of intersubjective recognition are referred to democratic practices of polling, listening, consultation, negotiation, mediation, ratification, referenda and dispute resolution. Moreover, new disciplines of negotiation, mediation and dispute resolution have developed in universities to train experts in 'getting to yes' and to reflect critically on the burgeoning practices of democratic participation and negotiation.[31]

The second reason stems from the negotiated character of identity politics. It is the people themselves who must experience an identity as imposed and unjust; they must come to support a demand for the recognition of another identity from a first-person perspective; and they must gain the mutual recognition, respect and support of others who do not share the identity. All this requires discussion and negotiation by the people involved in the three processes of negotiation mentioned in the first section – not of élites and representatives alone. On this account, a proposed identity counts as an identity only if it has come to be embraced in this democratic and dialogical manner, and it is recognized only if it has come to be affirmed by others in the same fashion. If an identity is advanced by a political élite without popular deliberation and support, and if it is recognized by another élite or an unelected court without passing through democratic will formation in the broader society, then it is not likely to be supported on either side. That is, it is not likely to be seen as an identity on one side or as worthy of respect in practice on the other. It will tend to be experienced as imposed, and the struggle for recognition will be intensified rather than resolved.

The third reason follows from the diversity of overlapping identities in any political association. When a demand for the recognition of an identity-related difference is advanced, it is necessary to ensure that this demand has the support of those for whom it is presented and, second, that it does not silence or suppress another identity-related difference equally worthy of recognition. The only way this can be ensured is for the people affected to have a voice in the proceedings. People must be able to advance alternative formulations of the demand which take into account the diversity of the people demanding recognition; others must be able to raise their objections to it and defend the status-quo or respond with counter-proposals; and others must be able to advance demands of their own that would otherwise be overridden. As a result of considerations of this kind, another principle of classic accounts of public dialogue was reintroduced into late twentieth-century politics: *audi alteram partem* (always listen to the other side).[32] The democratic negotiations of identity politics, accordingly, are not the dyadic dialogues of traditional theories of recognition, but, in Rawls's phrase, 'multilogues'.[33]

The fourth reason is that such popular-based negotiations provide stability and a *sense of belonging* for the right reasons. A struggle for recognition signals that a norm of public recognition by which citizens co-ordinate their interaction has been disrupted somewhere in the system of social co-operation comprising the society as a whole. If the dispute is not resolved, it can lead to anything from disaffection to secession. Negotiations open to citizens and trusted representatives provide a new or renewed norm of recognition that is stable because the people who must bear it have had a say in its formulation and have come to see that it is well supported (even when they do not all agree with it). They identify with it. This is the sense of belonging appropriate to a democracy.

There is one important limitation to the maxim that struggles for recognition must be worked out through negotiations among the people affected. In many cases of identity politics, those demanding the recognition of their identity-related differences are minorities. If their demands are put not only to the discussion of all but also to the decision-making of all, their fate is placed in the hands of the majority. Yet this is precisely the injustice they are trying to overcome with their demand. Democratic discussion and negotiation are necessary for the four reasons given above. However, it is not necessary for the final decision on a question concerning a minority to be made by a majority or by a consensus of all affected. The former is unfair to the minority, and the latter is Utopian.

Democratic discussions need to be placed in the broader reflective equilibrium of the institutions of the rule of law: representative governments, courts and the legal, constitutional and international law protection of human rights. If a demand for recognition is fully and openly discussed, supported and agreed to by the majority of the minority making the demand (applying *audi alteram partem* within); if it is well discussed and well supported by the other people affected and to whom it is addressed; if it accords with or can be shown plausibly to be an improvement on existing legislation, minority rights and international covenants; if it finds support in representative institutions and their committees of inquiry; or if the courts rule in its favour, then any of these institutions of the rule of law, depending on the particular case, can and should make the decision, even if there is an organized and vocal opposition to it by a segment of the majority affected. However, they should make the decision only on the condition that it is open to review and reconsideration in the future. Prejudices against different identities run deep within the dominant identities of contemporary individuals and groups, and they are supported by sedimented structures of political and economic domination. Discussion and deliberation can bring people around to see their own prejudices to some extent, but in the real time and context of politics the force of argument needs to be supplemented by the force of law in cases where the majority has a political or economic interest in upholding the biased form of recognition in dispute.

The second question is 'what are the procedures by which the people, in conjunction with their legal and political institutions, negotiate and reach agreements over disputed identities?' The widely proposed answer is again 'democratic': the correct procedures are the exchange of reasons *pro* and *contra* in public negotiations. The basic idea is that an identity will be worthy of recognition and respect just in so far as it can be made good to, or find widespread support among, those affected through the fair exchange of reasons. A fair exchange of reasons will determine which identities are reasonable, and so worthy of recognition, and which are unreasonable, and so either prohibited or at least not publicly supportable.

The conditions for the fair exchange of reasons are themselves contested by theorists and negotiators, but the following are commonly included. A member (individual or group) of a political association has the right to present demands to modify the forms of public recognition, and the others have a duty to acknowledge the demand and enter into negotiations *pro* and *con* if the demand is well supported by those for whom it is presented, the reasons for it seem plausible and the demand takes into account the concerns of others affected by the norm in question; the interlocutors in the negotiations treat each other as free and equal and accept that they are bearers of other practical identities which deserve to be treated with due respect; and any resolution should rest as much as possible on the agreement of those affected and should be open to periodic review. If the dominant members refuse to enter into negotiations, or drag their feet endlessly in the negotiations and implementation, then those making the demand have the right to engage in civil disobedience to bring them to negotiate in good faith.

These are roughly the minimum conditions of mutual recognition and reciprocity which ensure that a discussion is not biased towards any particular cultural identity from the outset. Muslim, atheist, indigenous, male and female interlocutors will interpret 'free and equal' in dissimilar yet reasonable ways (ways which the others will see initially as unfreedom and inequality), but, since this sort of disagreement is precisely what identity politics is about, it is not possible to filter out these differences at the outset without prejudging which identities are worthy of recognition. Of course, in the actual context of particular cases, further conditions are usually accepted by the interlocutors.[34]

The exchange of reasons over the recognition of identities can be classified into two types: those which aim at mutual understanding of, and those which aim at mutual agreement on, the identities in dispute. In the first type of exchange the interlocutors aim to understand the identities in question from the point of view of those who bear them and seek recognition. To gain mutual understanding it is necessary to listen to the reasons why a particular identity is important to the group advancing it, even if these are not reasons for others. An ethnic, religious, cultural or linguistic minority, a nation or an indigenous people, will have reasons for embracing their identity that derive from that identity. These internal reasons will not be reasons for supporting their demand as far as the other members of society are concerned. However, they will be important to the other members in understa ling why the identity is so important to them; why the members of the minority can agree to pledge allegiance to the political association only if this identity is secure.

Misunderstanding, stereotyping and deep cleavages will prevail in multicultural and multinational societies as long as these internal reasons are not exchanged in public as a basis for mutual understanding among identity-diverse citizens. Citizens need to know not only that there are culturally different others in the association, or wanting to get in, as a matter of fact. They need also to gain some understanding of those different cultural identities, the narratives in terms of which they have meaning and worth for their bearers, and so on.

As we know from classical accounts of dialogue, through these exchanges citizens are able to move around and see to some extent their shared political association from the identity of other cultures, nations, sexual orientations, and so on. In the course of this movement they become aware on reflection of their own identities as partial and limited like those of the others. Moreover, the interplay of internal reasons unsettles the prejudices and stereotypes internal to their own practical identities. That is, these practical conversations foster a new, shared citizen identity among the interlocutors – an identity that consists in the awareness of and respect for the diversity of respectworthy identities of their fellow citizens and of the place of one's own identity among the diversity of overlapping identities. This shared identity of diversity awareness is precisely the citizen identity appropriate to, and capable of holding together, multicultural and multinational political associations.

The second type of exchange of reasons aims at reaching agreement on which identities are worthy of recognition and how they are to be accommodated, as well as which should be prohibited. These reasons cannot appeal to particular identities, for they need to convince other interlocutors who do not share that identity and its internal reasons, even if they understand and respect it. Exchanges aimed at reaching agreement, therefore, search for reasons that identity-diverse citizens can share. These 'shared' reasons are various.

Mutual respect for individuals and minorities, toleration, freedom, equality, autonomy, community, human rights, and so on are reasons shared by most. The basic conditions of the discussions themselves rule out certain identities: those that are incompatible with respect for others. Reaching agreement, then, is a process that involves searching for these sorts of shared reasons, interpreting and applying them *pro* and *con* the identities in dispute, and working towards an agreeable form of mutual recognition and institutional accommodation of the identities, or aspects of identities, that are shown to be justifiable and supportable.

The forms of recognition and accommodation of identities they negotiate from time to time will constitute their shared multicultural and multinational identity as citizens of the same association. This is an identity they will all have reasons for supporting, not despite their identity-related differences, but rather because it gives due recognition to their diverse identities and it is always open to renegotiation. As I mentioned in the introduction to this chapter, it is their engagement in the ongoing discussions over this complex shared identity that binds them together as an association and gives them a sense of belonging.[35]

5 Belonging and Ongoing Struggles over Recognition

I would like to conclude with one final point about this sense of citizen belonging. I believe that a sense of belonging is engendered more by engagement in struggles over recognition than by the actual end-state of gaining this or that form of recognition. A necessary feature of belonging is that the society is open to these kinds of struggles over recognition – that is, that citizens and representatives are free to make demands to amend the rules of recognition, and other citizens and representatives acknowledge these demands and respond to them in various ways. This intersubjective and agonic activity of demand and acknowledgement in itself, quite apart from the achievement of formal recognition, engenders a sense that one is acknowledged and respected by others – even those who disagree strongly – and so nurtures a sense of identification with the larger society. The aim is thus not to discover the definitive and just forms of recognition (which, given the mutable character of practical identities, is a chimera) but to ensure that the norms of public recognition are always open to question, discussion and amendment over time. There are several reasons for this.

First, the agreements on norms of recognition are 'overlapping' rather than transcendent.[36] The interlocutors do not transcend their practical identities and reach agreement on an identity-blind norm. They exchange internal and shared reasons from within their practical identities, moving around to some extent to the perspectives of others, and reach agreements on an identity-sensitive norm of recognition. One of the most important discoveries of identity politics is that people with very different cultural, religious, gender and linguistic identities can nevertheless reach overlapping agreements on norms of public recognition, such as charters of individual and group rights and obligations, as long as these are formulated, interpreted and applied in an identity-sensitive manner.

Second, overlapping agreements do not conform to the ideal of a consensus. They are negotiated, provisional and contextual settlements which involve compromise, an element of non-consensus, and hence require review and revision after implementation.[37] The reasons for this derive from the three characteristics of identity politics. Recall that in a struggle for recognition there are three simultaneous processes of negotiation and they influence one another. As the interlocutors proceed, the rule of *audi alteram partem* is applied again and again by diverse individuals and groups whose identities are affected by the proposed form of recognition, demanding that their identities in turn are given due recognition and accommodation in the agreement. It is unreasonable to assume that each could receive the recognition they believe they deserve on the basis of their internal reasons alone. Such a recognition would be possible in principle only if identities were separate, bounded and homogeneous. Since they are multiple, overlapping and contested, their due recognition involves a complex back-and-forth accommodation and mutual compromise. Therefore, the agreement will be an attempt to give each legitimate claim its due recognition, and this will always involve compromise. It will be a complex 'accommodation', like the Northern Ireland Accord. In an agreement of this complexity, there is always, and unavoidably, reasonable disagreement.[38]

Take the example of an indigenous people (such as the Sami) demanding recognition and accommodation of their identity as a people. Once their demand is taken seriously and negotiations entered into, the non-indigenous governments affected by their proposed recognition present their internal and shared reasons for modifying the form of recognition sought. Others raise demands that their own rights and identity-related differences not be overlooked in the negotiations. These demands come both from within the indigenous community itself, by members who disagree with the negotiators, and from the non-indigenous communities affected by recognition. Compromise is unavoidable. In a struggle for recognition in British Columbia, Canada, for example, negotiations among the Nisga'a indigenous people, the provincial government and the federal government included presentations by over fifty third parties, took fifteen years to complete and the agreement is over 200 pages long.[39]

Moreover, negotiations take place in real time and under real constraints. Not all voices will be heard and not all compromises will be acceptable to all. The identities of the participants in the discussions will be shaped by the unjust relations of power that are held in place and legitimated by the contested form of recognition. Therefore, they will exchange reasons in unequal and asymmetrical ways in the negotiations. Rhetoric too will play a role.[40] In some cases a court or representative body will not unreasonably bring the negotiations to a (provisional) close. The dissenters they override may turn out on reconsideration to have been right after all. Any agreement can be interpreted in different ways, and this gives rise to disagreements over the institutions that are supposed to implement the agreement, and over the way those institutions operate. As they experiment with the implementation of the agreement over time, conflicts will develop in practice that they did not foresee in the negotiations. (For example, a group right established to protect a minority from domination and assimilation by the larger society may turn out to give the minority too much authority over the identity-related differences of its members.) In addition, the change in identities brought about by interacting in the new relations of recognition will itself alter their view of the agreement. By this time a new generation will enter into the negotiations, and bring generational differences with it. For these reasons, an agreement is always provisional and must be open to ongoing review and revision in light of experience with its institutionalization.[41]

Furthermore, a great deal of what is going on in struggles over recognition is not aiming at recognition so much as it is making public displays of the intolerability of the present form of recognition and publicly displaying another form of recognition. The other members of the society acknowledge this and respond in kind. It is an 'agonic' to-and-fro activity of mutual disclosure and mutual acknowledgement. Although this agonic game of disclosure–acknowledgment falls short of formal recognition, it is far from trivial. It is a means of discharging resentment at the present structure of recognition: displaying how a member would like to be seen by and relative to the other members; and generating a sense of pride in the disclosed identity (as a minority or a nation). Even when the others respond by denying recognition and putting forward another form of recognition, or defending the status quo, this degree of acknowledgement makes the minority feel a part of the larger society. These contestatory exchanges generate levels of self-respect and self-esteem among the members demanding recognition (in contrast to the standard view that recognition alone generates self-respect and self-esteem). And engagement in these games, although serious, involves a play element, like all competitive games, which helps to explain their persistence.[42]

Finally, the practical identities of the people engaged in struggles for recognition change in the course of the three processes of negotiation themselves. Nothing has changed more over thirty years of identity politics than the identities of men and women, immigrants and old-timers, indigenous and non-indigenous persons, Muslims and Christians, Arabs and Westerners, Europeans and non-Europeans, cultural minorities and majorities, hetero-sexuals and homosexuals, and so on. Part of this identity modification is the acquisition, through interaction with others, of a shared identity based on the reflective awareness of the diversity of identities of others and of the partiality of one's own. This shared identity does nothing to lessen their attachment to their practical identities and to the great struggles for their recognition. But it puts these in a different light. Their practical identities are now seen as partial, somewhat mutable, and overlapping with the similarly partial and somewhat mutable identities of others with whom they contend for forms of mutual recognition and accommodation.

Consequently, identity politics should not be seen as struggles for the definitive recognition of an authentic, autonomous or self-realizing identity, for, as this survey has shown, no such fixed identity exists. Rather, because the identities in contention are modified in the course of the contests, the aim of identity politics is to ensure that *any* form of public recognition is not a fixed and unchangeable structure of domination, but is open to question, contestation and change over time, as the identities of the participants change. Hence, identity politics is about the freedom of diverse people and peoples to modify the rules of recognition of their political associations as they modify themselves.[43] Consequently, belonging is related to freedom and acknowledgement, more than to recognition.

Notes

1. James Tully (1995) *Strange Multiplicity: Constitutionalism in an Age of Diversity*, Cambridge: Cambridge University Press.
2. Quentin Skinner (1998) *Liberty Before Liberalism*, Cambridge: Cambridge University Press, p. 74.
3. John Rawls (1995) 'Reply to Habermas', *Journal of Philosophy* 92 (3), 132–80; Jürgen Habermas (1995) 'Reconciliation through the Use of Public Reason', *Journal of Philosophy* 92 (3), 109–31.
4. Skinner, *Liberty before Liberalism*, p. 30.
5. Ibid., p. 74, n. 38.
6. Hannah Arendt (1977) 'What Is Freedom?', in *Between Past and Future*, Harmondsworth: Penguin.
7. Skinner, *Liberty before Liberalism*, p. 74, n. 38; Quentin Skinner (1984) 'The Idea of Negative Liberty: Philosophical and Historical Perspectives', in R. Rorty, J.B. Schneewind and Q. Skinner (eds) *Philosophy in History*, Cambridge: Cambridge University Press.
8. Jürgen Habermas (1996) *Between Facts and Norms*, trans. William Rehg, Cambridge, MA: MIT Press.
9. David Walton (1998) *The New Dialectic: Conversational Contexts of Arguments*, Toronto: University of Toronto Press.
10. Quentin Skinner (1994) 'Moral Ambiguity and the Renaissance Art of Eloquence', in *Essays in Criticism* 44 (4), 267–92, and (1996) *Reason and Rhetoric in the Philosophy of Hobbes*, Cambridge: Cambridge University Press, pp. 138–80.
11. Arendt, 'What Is Freedom?'
12. Anthony Laden (2000 forthcoming) *Reasonably Radical: Deliberative Liberalism and the Politics of Identity*, Ithaca, NY: Cornell University Press.
13. Jürgen Habermas (1994) 'Struggles for Recognition in the Constitutional State', in Amy Gutmann (ed.) *Multiculturalism*, Princeton, NJ: Princeton University Press.

14. Tully, *Strange Multiplicity*; Alain-G. Gagnon and James Tully (eds) (forthcoming 2001) *Struggles for Recognition in Multinational Societies: Spain, Belgium, the United Kingdom and Canada in Comparative Perspective*, Cambridge: Cambridge University Press; Abdellah Hammoudi (ed.) (2000 forthcoming) *Universalizing from Particulars: Islamic Views of the Human and the United Nations Declaration of Human Rights*, London: Taurus.

15. Homi K. Bhabha (1994) *The Location of Culture*, London: Routledge.

16. Andrew Linklater (1998) *The Transformation of Political Community*, Cambridge: Polity.

17. William Connolly (1995) *The Ethos of Pluralization*, Minneapolis: University of Minnesota Press.

18. Hammoudi (ed.), *Universalizing from Particulars*, pp. 1–20.

19. David E. Stannard (1992) *American Holocaust: Columbus and the Conquest of the New World*, Oxford: Oxford University Press.

20. Will Kymlicka (1991) *Liberalism, Community, and Culture*, Oxford: Clarendon.

21. Charles Taylor (1994) 'The Politics of Recognition', in Gutmann (ed.) *Multiculturalism*, pp. 25–74.

22. Laden, 'Constructing Shared Wills'.

23. Charles Taylor (1993) 'Shared and Divergent Values', in G. Laforest (ed.) *Reconciling the Solitudes*, Montreal and Toronto: McGill-Queens University Press, pp. 155–86.

24. Seyla Benhabib (ed.) (1996) *Democracy and Difference: Contesting the Boundaries of the Political*, Princeton, NJ: Princeton University Press; James Tully (1999) 'The Agonic Freedom of Citizens', *Economy and Society*, 28 (2), 161–82.

25. Will Kymlicka (1995) *The Rights of Minority Cultures*, Oxford: Oxford University Press, and (1995) *Multicultural Citizenship*, Oxford: Oxford University Press.

26. Gagnon and Tully, *Struggles for Recognition*.

27. Royal Commission on Aboriginal Peoples (1996) *The Report of the Canadian Royal Commission on Aboriginal Peoples*, 5 volumes, Ottawa: Supply and Services.

28. John Rawls (1993) *Political Liberalism*, New York: Columbia University Press.

29. Jürgen Habermas (1994) 'Discourse Ethics: Notes on a Program of Philosophical Justification', in *Moral Consciousness and Communicative Action*, trans. Christian Lenhardt and S.W. Nicholsen, Cambridge, MA: MIT Press, p. 66.

30. Paul Hirst (1994) *Associative Democracy: New Forms of Economic and Social Governance*, Cambridge: Polity; David Held, Daniele Archibugi and Martin Kohler (eds) (1998) *Re-imagining Political Community: Studies in Cosmopolitan Democracy*, Cambridge: Polity.

31. John Urry (1998) *Promoting Deliberative Democracy: Listening within Limits*, Cambridge: Cambridge University Press.

32. Skinner, *Liberty before Liberalism*, pp. 15–16.

33. Tully, *Strange Multiplicity*, pp. 99–116.

34. For an attempt to specify the conditions in a case of negotiating secession, see Supreme Court of Canada (1998) *Reference re Secession of Quebec*, File 25506, 20 August (www.droit.umontreal.ca/doc/csc-scc/en/rec/index.html).

35. Tully, *Strange Multiplicity*, pp. 183–212.

36. Rawls, *Political Liberalism*, pp. 133–73.

37. Richard Bellamy (1999) *Liberalism and Pluralism: Towards a Politics of Compromise*,

London: Routledge; David Hoy and Thomas McCarthy (1994) *Critical Theory*, Oxford: Blackwell, pp. 203–69.

38. Rawls, *Political Liberalism*, pp. 56–8; Anne Phillips (1997) 'Why Worry about Multiculturalism?', *Dissent*, Winter, 57–63; Iris Marion Young (1997) 'The Complexities of Coalition', *Dissent*, Winter, 64–9.

39. Nisga'a Nation (1998) *The Nisga'a Final Agreement*, with the Nisga'a Nation, the Federal Government of Canada and the Government of British Columbia, Victoria, BC: Ministry of Aboriginal Affairs.

40. Iris Marion Young (1996) 'Communication and the Other: Beyond Deliberative Democracy', in Benhabib (ed.) *Democracy and Difference*.

41. James Tully (1999) 'To Think and Act Differently: Foucault's Four Reciprocal Objections to Habermas', in D. Owen (ed.) *Foucault contra Habermas: Continuing the Critical Dialogue*, New York: Sage.

42. James Tully (2001 forthcoming) 'Freedom and Disclosure in Multinational Societies', in Gagnon and Tully (eds) *Struggles for Recognition*.

43. Tully, 'The Agonic Freedom of Citizens'.

CHAPTER ELEVEN

Must Europe be Belgian? On Democratic Citizenship in Multilingual Polities[1]

PHILIPPE VAN PARIJS

'Let us once again cast a glance upon Belgium, our constitutional "model state", the monarchical El Dorado with the broadest "democratic" basis, the university of the Berlin statesmen and the pride of the *Kölnische Zeitung*.' Thus starts an article published by Karl Marx in the *Neue Rheinische Zeitung*.[2] Most of the article is devoted to documenting the growth of poverty and crime in the *Modellstaat Belgien*, the allegedly exemplary 'model democratic state of Belgium', and it persuasively suggests that whatever its economic performance, there is a seamy side too to liberal capitalism. Although Marx's article could have been published under the title I rather frivolously proposed for this contribution, my purpose is rather different from his; and no doubt in contrast to what his answer would have been, I am already warning you that my answer will be yes. Sounding more ludicrous, the claim I shall thereby be making is likely to arouse less concern than if in the question 'Belgian' had been replaced by 'German', or 'French', or 'British', or even 'Dutch'. Moreover, what I shall invite you to take seriously as a desirable institutional future for the European Union is not – arrogantly – Belgium's current Ego, but, as it were, its Super-Ego; not its present institutional structure, but what I believe it must urgently be moving to.

More specifically, what I shall do in the bulk of this chapter is sketch two fundamental challenges to which Belgium's institutions need to respond in a coherent way. Finding such a response is by no means obvious, if only because the two challenges seem to generate conflicting demands. But the very survival of the country and – what is more important – the preservation of the combination of extensive freedom and generous solidarity which the country was able to develop, along with its neighbours, in the course of the twentieth century, hinge on identifying and implementing such a response. Very schematically, the discussion of possible responses to the first challenge will show how the demands of democratic citizenship foster the territorial partition, along linguistic lines, of what constitutes the last plurilingual sovereign remnant of the Habsburgs' multilingual empire. But if citizenship is not to become vacuous in a globalized market, I shall next argue – even more briefly – in connection with the second challenge, that we must resist this democratic impulse and attempt to restructure the country's institutions so as to make them lean but powerful, and durably compatible with the massive autonomy of essentially unilingual regions. With this as background, I shall finally suggest that the European Union as a whole, though coming from the opposite direction, as it were, increasingly faces the same predicament, and I shall sketch how an analogous response needs to be thought about and put into place.

The Democratic Challenge

The first challenge can be presented in many ways. I shall adopt the version given to it by John Stuart Mill in an ominous passage of the sixteenth chapter of *Considerations on Representative Government*. After having sympathetically noted that 'the Flemish and the Walloon provinces of Belgium, notwithstanding diversity of race and language, have a much greater feeling of common nationality than the former have with Holland, or the latter with France', Mill pronounces his famous (near) indictment of multilingual democracies:

> Free institutions are next to impossible in a country made up of different nationalities. Among a people without fellow-feeling, *especially if they read and speak different languages*, the united public opinion, necessary to the working of representative government, cannot exist. The influences which form opinions and decide political acts are different in the different sections of the country. An altogether different set of leaders have the confidence of one part of the country and of another. The same books, newspapers, pamphlets, speeches, do not reach them. One section does not know what opinions, or what instigations, are circulating in another. . . . For the preceding reasons, it is in general a necessary condition of free institutions that the boundaries of governments should coincide in the main with those of nationalities.[3]

Leaving out a number of nuances and qualifications, I shall give Mill's claim the following stark formulation: 'No viable democracy without a linguistically unified demos.' This claim I shall here simply call *the democratic challenge*.

For a long time, the process described by Mill was hardly noticeable in Belgium, basically because the country was ruled, north and south, by a French-speaking élite. But it is now in full swing. Let me just mention three indicators.[4] While the watching of Flemish TV by Walloons has always been very low, the watching of the French-language Belgian channels by Flemish viewers is now also down to 0.7 per cent of their TV time.[5] Even in Brussels, 85 per cent of francophones say they never read a Flemish newspaper.[6] And between 1954 and 1993, controlling for distance, the probability of moving from a Walloon commune to a Flemish commune or vice versa has dropped from one-half to one-third of the probability of moving from one commune to another within the same region.[7]

'The outcome', as sociolinguist Kas Deprez puts it, 'is that a genuine Belgian we-feeling is no longer possible.'[8] Or again, in the equally Millian formulation of political scientist Wilfried Dewachter, 'The country's other community is practically a foreign people. It is rather difficult for a political system to keep functioning satisfactorily with such mutual ignorance and hence such lack of mutual understanding of the two halves of the country.'[9] No one who has been following Belgian politics in recent decades can deny that this is an increasingly serious problem. No one who has read Mill's analysis can fail to suspect that this problem does not arise from an idiosyncratic defect of Belgium's populace, but is paradigmatic for all multilingual democracies. With about 6000 living languages in the world, with 211 sovereign states to accommodate them, and with formal democracy slowly gaining ground, the problem is definitely worth more attention than the traditional focus on the 'standard' case of unilingual democracies has encouraged.

What can be done about it? How can Mill's condition of a unified demos be fulfilled? Before we consider what can plausibly be regarded as the only four options, it is important to tease out a crucial ambiguity in the formulation I have given to our democratic challenge. As was neatly brought out in a controversy between Dieter Grimm and Jürgen Habermas about the European Union's democratic potential, a 'unified demos' can be understood either as a 'homogeneous ethnos' or as a 'common forum'.[10] In the former interpretation, which can plausibly be traced back to Carl Schmitt,[11] democracy is viable only for a homogeneous people, one which needs to possess not 'racial purity', but a shared culture and identity. Language matters here as a central component of a people's culture. In the second interpretation, which I shall take to be the best construal of Mill's thought, democracy is viable only for a communicating people, one which may not share a single culture or identity in any thick sense, but which possesses a common space for discussion and decision-making. Language matters this time simply as a medium of communication. As the linguistic conditions for a common forum are likely to be less stringent than the linguistic conditions for a homogeneous ethnos, this clarification may turn out to be crucial if one is not unnecessarily to foreclose some otherwise promising options.

Generalized Unilingualism

The most obvious way of meeting Mill's condition for a viable democracy consists in adopting a single language throughout the country. There is no doubt that other countries have successfully pursued this strategy. Thus, in

1789, French was the mother tongue of less than 50 per cent of the population then living in the territory that now forms France. There is no doubt that parts of Belgium's political élite were tempted to adopt an analogous strategy, toughly expressed in a quotation often attributed to Charles Rogier, one of Belgium's first prime ministers (1847–52) and a powerful liberal politician throughout the first half-century after Belgium's independence:

> The first principles of a good administration are based on the exclusive use of a language and it is obvious that the Belgians' sole language must be French. To achieve this outcome, it is necessary that, for a while, all civil and military functions should be entrusted to Walloons and Luxemburgers: in this way, being temporarily deprived of the advantages attached to these functions, the Flemings will be forced to learn French, and the Germanic element will be gradually destroyed in Belgium.[12]

I should add that at the time there was no lack of high-minded justifications for this tough approach. Friedrich Engels, for one, did not think much of the defence of weaker languages and cultures:

> By the same right under which France took Flanders, Lorraine and Alsace, and will sooner or later take Belgium – by that same right Germany takes over Schleswig; it is the right of civilisation as against barbarism, of progress as against stability.[13]

And Mill himself cannot be said to have lacked sympathy for this first way of meeting the democratic challenge he so forcefully formulated:

> Experience proves that it is possible for one nationality to merge and be absorbed in another: and when it was originally an inferior and more backward portion of the human race, the absorption is greatly to its advantage. Nobody can suppose that it is not more beneficial to a Breton, or a Basque of French Navarre, to be brought into the current of the ideas and feelings of a highly civilised and cultivated people – to be a member of the French nationality, admitted on equal terms to all the privileges of French citizenship, sharing the advantages of French protection and the dignity and prestige of French power – than to sulk on his own rocks, the half-savage relic of past times, revolving in his own little mental orbit, without participation or interest in the general movement of the world. The same remark applies to the Welshman or the Scottish Highlander, as members of the British nation.[14]

Yet Belgium did not follow this path. Why not? Basically because there were sufficiently numerous powerful and organized Flemish people who saw that it was in their collective interest to claim equal rights for their own language, or at any rate for a language far closer than French to their native dialects. There were therefore two competing processes of linguistic nation-building and one of them lost to the other. On one side, there was the central authority of an industrializing country with a strong interest in expanding an educated and mobile workforce through a linguistically uniform administration, army and –

above all – school system. This is the basic mechanism at work in the process famously described by Ernest Gellner as a transition from Kokoshka to Modigliani, from a linguistic map of Europe that looks like a mess of coloured patches to one in which nearly uniform surfaces are neatly separated by thick black lines representing political boundaries.[15] On the other side, there is the struggle to gain official recognition within a restricted area for a language so far unrecognized. To use Benedict Anderson's illuminating metaphor,[16] this works as a tariff, a customs barrier: to the people coming from the centre, the local people can now say, 'Do come, trade, work, administer here, but henceforth you'll need the humility to learn to speak our language rather than expect us to speak yours.' This amounts to the erection of new borders, to the drawing or strengthening of new lines, which does not prevent Modiglianization but forces it to operate on a smaller scale. In this case, unlike many others, the resistance won. And it is right that it should have won. Why? The answer is not straightforward. There is, after all, no lack of efficiency-based, and even equality-based, arguments in support of linguistic homogenization, of countries bulldozing out of existence their minority languages. My condoning of resistance does not rely on any alleged right for languages to survive, or on the assumption that we owe it to our ancestors to preserve their culture, or even on the aesthetic value of linguistic diversity. There are, I believe, only two types of arguments which can carry significant weight. One is consequentialist and relates to the long term. The other is justice based and concerns the transition period only.

There are undoubtedly strong efficiency advantages associated with the ease of communication and movement which linguistic homogeneity makes possible. But there are two effects of linguistic diversity which may plausibly, under some circumstances, more than offset these advantages. Given the nature and reach of present-day media, linguistic diversity is the firmest, and increasingly the only serious protection of cultural diversity, and the latter permits a diversity of experimentation in private and collective life, from which the general interest may well, in the long run, benefit. Second, in an increasingly globalized world, linguistic diversity is the firmest, and increasingly the only serious, brake on the mobility of people. It is in this sense a precious population stabilizer, at any rate if one regards massive migrations as undesirable, whether because of migration's propensity to dislocate local communities or because of its jeopardizing the economic and political viability of institutionalized solidarity. The first of these two arguments is rather speculative, while the second is contingent on a specific view of what counts as a good or just society. Both apply only to cases in which it is a less widely spread language that is losing ground.

The second, justice-based type of argument does not have those limitations, but it is necessarily restricted to the short term: it relates to what unavoidably happens in the transition from a situation of linguistic diversity within a territory to one in which one of the pre-existing languages is imposed as the official language. Having a mother tongue different from the one adopted as the official language puts one at a multiple disadvantage. People in that position have to bear the heavy cost of acquiring proficiency in a foreign language. They are handicapped, relative to natives of the official language, in economic and political competition. Most seriously perhaps, their self-respect is under pressure as a result of the subordinate, inferior status given to something as deeply associated with themselves (in other people's eyes and their own) as their mother tongue. Admittedly, this injustice is limited to the transition period: native French-speaking Bretons and native English-speaking Irish people do not suffer from it. But if the transition is short, owing to some vigorous unilingualism policy, the injustice is very acute. And if the transition is milder, it will affect many generations. Admittedly too, the injustice could in principle be alleviated in various ways (though it seldom is in any of them). The native speakers of the dominant language could pick up at least the full financial burden of language learning. Reverse discrimination measures could secure fairer access to jobs and promotions for the speakers of the dominated language. But even if the cost of learning were fully compensated and discrimination fully neutralized, there would remain the serious prima facie injustice associated with the unequal respect manifested in the sharply unequal public recognition of the official and the subordinate languages. Of course, all things considered, this justice-based argument may sometimes need to give way – for example, if the linguistic community concerned is very small – but it provides nonetheless the strongest and most general reason for condemning linguistic assimilation and justifying resistance to it.

Whether or not it is to be condemned, there is in any case no one in Belgium today, however attached to national unity, who still believes that this first strategy is the way to go – not even in the other direction. After all, over 60 per cent of Belgium's population now have Dutch as their mother tongue, and it is estimated that they produce about 70 per cent of the national product. But even a very timid attempt by the Flemish regional government to erode slightly the francophones' rights to receive administrative documents in French in six communes around Brussels has been met by fierce resistance, indeed was the subject of an official complaint to the Parliamentary Assembly of the Council of Europe on the ground that it violated the fundamental rights of a minority. Hence, we might as well forget generalized unilingualism. Too bad! It would have been so simple.

Generalized Bilingualism

The second strategy for meeting a bilingual society's democratic challenge consists in banking on bilingualism. It comes in two variants, profoundly different from one another, but both bound to fail, basically because of the conjunction of the same two trivial empirical facts: (a) For two people to communicate with one another, it is enough that one of them should know the other's language. (b) Learning a foreign language is a hard, costly job, and getting unmotivated children or teenagers to learn a foreign language is a hopeless project.

In the soft or liberal version, bilingualism is required of the territory without being required of the people. This means that the administration, the courts, the political assemblies and above all the schools are required to function in either language throughout the country, depending on what the preferences of (a sufficient proportion of) the local population happen to be. However, this soft bilingualism is just a milder, slower, more covert but no less inexorable form of generalized unilingualism. This is so because of a process perceptively described by Jean Laponce: the more kindly people behave towards one another, the more savagely languages treat each other.[17] Languages can coexist for centuries when there is little or no contact. But as soon as people start talking, trading, working with each other, courting each other, having children together, one language gradually drives out the other. The formal equality of Belgium's two languages, officially recognized in 1898, did little to slow down the Frenchification of Brussels and other Flemish cities in the early part of the twentieth century. Spreading from the urban centres, the 'oil stains' steadily kept growing as a result of parents choosing the 'best' schools for their children and mixed couples choosing the 'easiest' language for internal communication. Hence, the hard, authoritarian, centralized, deliberate, top-down Gellner-type mechanism and the soft, liberal, decentralized, spontaneous, bottom-up Laponce-type mechanism are simply two very different ways of achieving in the end the same outcome, the gradual extinction of a linguistic community.

The same cannot be said about the hard, authoritarian version of bilingualism, the only one that takes bilingualism seriously as it requires the people, not only the territory, to become bilingual. To enforce a widespread real competence in the second language, one might think, for example, of making it a strict condition for graduating from secondary school or entering higher education of any sort, or a prerequisite for applying for all public-sector jobs, possibly even some private-sector jobs, throughout the country, whether or not the performance of the job is likely to involve a significant use of the second language. Jules Destrée, the historical leader of the Walloon and socialist movement, considered this possibility:

> It is in Brussels that the fabulous theory of full bilingualism was born. Belgium is a bilingual country, hence all Belgians must be bilingual. By teaching French to the Flemings and Flemish to the Walloons, we shall achieve genuine national unity.

His assessment is unambiguous: 'This theory is imbecilic.'[18] This fierce hostility is not hard to understand. First, on the background of the asymmetrical, soft bilingualism that was prevailing in Belgium in Destrée's time, it is clear that hard bilingualism would give a systematic advantage to Flemings, the natives of the dominated language, whose competence in the dominant language was (and still is) far greater than the Walloons' competence in Dutch. Second, Destrée could not fail to be aware of the massive, indeed prohibitive, cost of motivating and teaching pupils, of motivating and training a sufficient number of teachers, for the learning of a language which there is little point in learning since the others will anyway be learning theirs. We are thus back to the double empirical fact mentioned at the start of our discussion of generalized bilingualism: it provides the fundamental reason why its hard version too is an unpromising prospect.

Non-territorial Separation

Let us not despair yet. For as we continue exploring the space of logical possibilities, we shall have no difficulty identifying a third straightforward way of satisfying Mill's condition of a linguistically unified demos. It consists in gathering all the people who speak the same language, wherever they live throughout the country, into a political entity, a *Gliedstaat*, and in devolving powers massively to this level. This is an extreme version of an idea put forward at the beginning of the twentieth century by Karl Renner, an Austrian social democratic thinker and politician who became president of Austria after the Second World War. In his remarkable *Das Selbstbestimmungsrecht der Nationen*, he tried to work out in detail – presumably for the first time in history – democratic institutions for an irreducibly multinational state.[19] What he proposed was a combination of territorial federalism and what he called personal federalism. Each of the eight nations within the Austro-Hungarian empire (Germans, Czechs, Poles, Hungarians, Slovenes, Slovaks, Croats, Italians) were to be given their own parliament and granted full autonomy in matters of culture, education and at least some aspects of social policy, with matters of common interest settled through negotiation between the representatives of the various nations.

The Austro-Hungarian Empire soon fell apart, and Renner's scheme was therefore never tried in the context for which it was meant. But various forms of non-territorial federalism were tried elsewhere, for example in Estonia in 1925, in Cyprus in 1960 and in South Africa in 1984, never with great success. The only place where it subsists is precisely in Belgium, in the limited but still quite recognizable form of its federalism of communities: next to its three regions – Flanders, Wallonia and Brussels – Belgium has three communities – Flemish (comprising all inhabitants of Flanders and the Dutch-speakers of Brussels), German (comprising the 60,000 inhabitants of a handful of German-speaking communes in the east of Wallonia) and French (comprising all the other inhabitants of Wallonia and the French-speakers of Brussels). The very fact that Belgium is still in trouble shows that this scheme has not fixed matters. But this might be because the variant of non-territorial segmentation it has adopted is not radical enough. It is easy to think – and some people do – of further expanding the powers of the communities, at the expense of either the regions or the federal government. One might also think of simultaneously and massively expanding the territory whose inhabitants can belong to either community, more precisely by making it possible not only for the inhabitants of Brussels (as is the case now), but also for those of the country's other two regions (Flanders and Wallonia), to be members of either the French or the Flemish community. What the existing weak version of non-territorial federalism cannot achieve, perhaps this more radical version could.

Not much reflection is needed to conclude that it could not. A first intrinsic difficulty can be compactly phrased in terms of a dilemma between linguicide and apartheid. For there can be a soft, choice-based conception of membership in a community, and a hard, ascriptive one. In the former interpretation, each household is free to choose the community it belongs to, as reflected, for example, in the choice of a school for its children. But there is then no reason why the weaker community should not feel under permanent threat – exactly as in the case of soft bilingualism, though with a major proviso: with economically unequal communities, the conversion speed from one community to the other may be further increased, as membership of the richer community is likely to bring with it a number of material advantages, but it may also be slowed down or reversed if the community with the weaker language is the more affluent one.[20]

There is of course a way of avoiding the strains generated by the fear of losing ground. It consists in depriving households of the right to choose which community they belong to. This is exactly what the hard version of non-territorial federalism does: which community you belong to – and hence which school you and your children attend, which health insurance package you receive, which sports facilities you have access to, which family law you are subjected to, etc. – is strictly determined by your native tongue. As one's native tongue is hardly less a matter of arbitrary luck than one's racial features, and as membership of different communities can be associated with very unequal packages of entitlements, it is clear that this ascriptive variant of far-driven non-territorial federalism is no less repugnant than the racial version of it imagined for South Africa in 1984.

This dilemma between (soft) linguicide and (linguistic) apartheid constitutes only one of two decisive difficulties for the strategy of non-territorial separation. The second one stems from the irreducibly spatial nature of any coherent, comprehensive project for a political community. There is a tremendous structural strain inherent in any set-up in which distinct political communities elaborate and discuss their own projects separately and then need to negotiate and compromise with each other on countless issues, because they happen to share the same territory. For this reason, too, non-territorial separation is not very promising after all as a strategy for addressing our democratic challenge. Is there any other candidate? Reluctantly, we must conclude, only one: territorial separation.

Territorial Separation

Underlying the rejection of each of the previous three options, there is the assumption not only that languages must be protected, but also that their protection requires some sort of territoriality principle to be enforced. With some minor qualifications, this thesis is the central message of Laponce.[21] It also provides a plausible explanation for why relations between linguistic communities have on the whole been significantly better in Switzerland than in Belgium, Canada or Spain, let alone in Sri Lanka, East Timor or Kosovo.[22] The territoriality principle amounts to telling any newcomer (whether by birth or immigration), 'Whatever your mother tongue, you are welcome to settle here. But if you do, you will have to learn the local language, which will be the exclusive language of public administration, of political communication and most importantly of publicly subsidized education.' Once this principle is firmly in place, our democratic challenge can be met through a massive devolution to suitably demarcated regions, or even at the extreme, by the territorial partition of the country. In contrast with non-territorial separation, there is here no dilemma between linguicide (languages are entrenched) and apartheid (all inhabitants of a territory belong to the same political community, with equal social and economic rights), nor does the irreducibly spatial dimension of projects and policies constitute a problem if boundaries are sensibly drawn.

For this solution to work smoothly, however, one obviously requires a significant degree of pre-existing linguistic homogeneity. For 99 per cent of Belgium's territory, this is not too bad, precisely because the territoriality principle has been in place, with some significant exceptions, since the language legislation of 1932. Regional unilingualism was then adopted for most of the territory outside the national capital, as a compromise between soft and hard bilingualism, to which, for the reasons sketched above, Flemings and Walloons were, respectively, bitterly opposed. The exceptions made by the 1932 compromise were the source of further trouble. Some of them were later erased, most prominently in 1962, when the borders were permanently fixed, instead of left alterable in the light of the linguistic census, and in 1969, when the Université Catholique de Louvain, Belgium's largest French-language university, was expelled from the Flemish town of Leuven in which it had been located for over five centuries. But the main exception persists. As Jules Destrée put it, 'When separatists are asked what will be done, in case of partition, with Brussels and the Congo, they are very embarrassed, and this is indeed the big stumbling-block of any fully separatist scheme.'[23] Congo has since taken care of itself – in this respect at any rate – but what about Brussels? Has its linguistic situation evolved so deeply in recent decades that it no longer constitutes a stumbling-block? I believe it has, and that the future lies, in this respect, neither in an absorption of Brussels, along with Wallonia and possibly the Grand Duchy of Luxemburg, into a redrawn Belgique; nor in a 'reconquest' of Brussels by Flanders; but in a full recognition of the increasingly *sui generis* nature of 'the people' of Brussels. Rather than filling out the crucial details of this territorial devolution scenario, which I regard as the best response to Mill's challenge in the Belgian context, I shall now turn, far more briefly, to the second challenge.

The Redistributive Challenge

This second challenge can be formulated in very general terms by stating that a number of major, irreversible trends, most of them closely connected to so-called 'globalization', have been converging to turn states increasingly into firms. States can no longer count on 'their' capital, 'their' workers or 'their' consumers, but they have to compete with each other to attract or retain savings and investment, skilled labour and the willingness to buy their products. As the pressure stemming from this competition intensifies, the pattern of public expenditure that can be sustainably achieved by each state is bound to be deeply modified. In particular, its ability to reduce the income inequalities that emerge from the operation of the market will be dramatically curtailed.[24] This is the second challenge, which I shall call the *redistributive challenge*.

This is not the place to dwell on the general nature of the underlying trends, their causes and consequences. I shall restrict myself to indicating why the challenge would take a particularly acute form were Belgium to fall apart, taking as a point of departure the following paradoxical fact. Among Belgium's eleven provinces (five in Flanders, five in Wallonia, and the region of Brussels), the province of Brabant wallon, to the south of Brussels, is at the same time the richest and the poorest. It is the richest in terms of average household income as recorded for income tax purposes. It is the poorest in terms of GDP per capita. The explanation is not that, since the Clabecq steel works were downsized, the province's biggest employer is one whose productivity might be suspected of being abysmally low, namely my own university. It is rather, quite simply, that the province in which one works need not be the province in which one lives. Therefore, many people who are currently earning high incomes in Brussels, or have done so in the past, can easily choose to retire in Brabant wallon or to commute daily into Brussels. Since Brussels is completely surrounded by the Flemish region, the many people who do such commuting either by car or by train – and many commute from more remote Walloon provinces too – travel every day through the three regions which territorial partition would make formally autonomous.

This paradoxical fact and its explanation should suffice to enable you to imagine how acute fiscal competition would be in the vicinity of Brussels – and with efficient transport, the area within daily commuting distance of Brussels can easily comprise half Belgium's population and three-quarters of its GDP – if each of Belgium's three regions was given a great degree of fiscal autonomy, and even more so if they became as independent of each other as EU member states can be. Firms can choose to settle or relocate in any of the three regions while hardly modifying the distance from their employees' residences or their business partners' sites. Households can also choose to stay in, or move to, any of the three regions, without a major impact on distances from their jobs, relatives or friends. There is therefore much to gain from a sharp and resolute lowering of tax rates in order to lure prosperous businesses and affluent taxpayers – and much to lose from sticking to high rates. It would therefore not take long for the fiscal competition triggered by fiscal autonomy to unravel the elaborate and comparatively generous redistribution systems slowly built up over the course of Belgium's history. The termination of trans-regional solidarity as a result of the partition process would thus be compounded by a rapid erosion of intra-regional solidarity.

Of course, in principle nothing would prevent autonomous regions from striking deals with one another in order to organize inter-regional redistribution and protect intra-regional redistribution at the levels that would have prevailed in the absence of partition. But the limits and fragility of such confederal system are notorious. The authors of the *Federalist Papers* observed the workings of the confederal constitution of the United (Dutch) Provinces of their time and were not impressed:

> Such is the nature of the celebrated belgic confederacy, as delineated on parchment. What are the characters which practice has stamped upon it? Imbecility in the government; discord among the provinces; foreign influence and indignities; a precarious existence in peace, and peculiar calamities from war. It was long ago remarked by Grotius that nothing but the hatred of his countrymen to the house of Austria kept them from being ruined by the vices of their constitution.[25]

There is no reason to expect a twenty-first-century Belgian confederation to be any less 'imbecile' than the 'belgic confederacy' of the eighteenth century pilloried in the *Federalist Papers*.

A Four-Pronged Package

Although far more would need to be said to show how serious this second challenge is and how hopeless it would be to try to tackle it through intergovernmental deals, enough has been said for us to see the emergence of a threatening tension. On the one hand, one cannot have a viable democracy in a multilingual society – this is the democratic challenge. On the other hand, one cannot have generous redistribution in a small open economy – this is the redistributive challenge. To make democracies more unilingual, and thereby alleviate the first difficulty, one needs to devolve power to linguistically more unified territories. But the more one decentralizes redistributive powers, the tighter the economic constraints on redistribution, and hence the more acute the second difficulty. In a multilingual area, therefore, here lies an undeniable tension, an unavoidable trade-off between smooth democratic functioning and generous intra- and inter-regional solidarity. But there are also ways of softening the trade-off. Imagining, implementing these ways is what I view as Belgium's central task in the years ahead. The guiding idea must be to strengthen the linguistic significance of borders while weakening their socio-economic importance.

More specifically, what is needed in the case of Belgium is a coherent package of reforms including at its core the following four:

(a) vigorous protection of the linguistic integrity of Flanders and Wallonia (though not of Brussels);

(b) a reform of (key sectors of) Belgium's welfare state that combines a central collection of resources with capitation grants to the three regions, each in charge of the conception and management of its own health and education systems;

(c) a reform of the electoral system that induces vote pooling across the linguistic border, instead of perpetuating the current state of affairs, in which unilingual parties fish for votes in only one of the two communities; and

(d) the gentle fostering of a common forum of discussion, which will increasingly be not in French (the common medium in the past and the majority language in Brussels), or in Dutch (the majority language in Belgium), or in German (the third national language and the majority language in the European Union), but in the emerging first universal lingua franca.[26]

I am convinced that this is also the sort of (four-pronged) package that Europe will, *mutatis mutandis*, increasingly need. In a nutshell, my diagnosis is as follows. On the one hand, the pressures of fiscal and social competition will build up, as savings, consumer demand, firms and highly skilled professionals become increasingly mobile. On the other hand, the strains arising from so-called asymmetric shocks and divergence within an economic and monetary union will start making themselves felt as regional specialization deepens, without labour migration providing an adjustment mechanism – as it does in the United States – because of Europe's linguistic diversity and the importance (argued for above) of preserving the latter. In this context, the need will develop for massive and systematic transfers across the borders of the EU's member states – at least if Europe does not want to perform even more poorly than the United States does today in terms of (freedom-friendly) solidarity. However, such transfers will only prove sustainable only (a) if they are consistent with the unilingual (sub)national polities' claim to organize the fine structure of their solidarity systems as they see fit; (b) if they take a very simple form that minimizes moral hazard while preserving autonomy, typically capitation grants to governments or citizens, centrally funded out of a common tax base; (c) if they can rely on electoral institutions that structure the political game at EU level along ideological rather than national lines, and (d) if they can be discussed and justified in a common forum of discussion using a language understandable all over Europe.[27]

Belgium is coming from a situation in which redistribution was operating at the global level, but without adequate recognition of the consequences of having two separate democratic spaces. The task is to accommodate this separation adequately, while preserving the sustainability of global solidarity. In Europe, separate national democratic spaces have been recognized all along, but redistribution is not (more than marginally) organized at the global level. The task is to create the conditions for global solidarity, while protecting the autonomy of separate national democratic forums. For such global solidarity is required if the redistributive challenge is to be met under contemporary conditions. And if the democratic challenge is to remain satisfactorily met, this must go hand in hand with protecting linguistically homogeneous territories and their autonomy. It is therefore not surprising that the set of conditions spelt out above in the European case should bear close resemblance to the policy package advocated earlier in the Belgian case. If Belgium can successfully adopt such a package, then it will make it far more credible that Europe can and must move in this direction too.[28]

This should have clarified in which sense it may not be altogether ludicrous to claim that Marx's *Modellstaat Belgien* will soon deserve to be, if not 'the university of the Berlin statesmen', at least a model worth thinking about and being inspired by for those who believe in the importance of preserving not only multilingualism and democracy but also social justice in today's Europe. So, must Europe be Belgian? In this rather qualified, somewhat far-fetched sense, yes indeed it must.

Appendix: Belgium: a few dates

1585   Reconquest of Antwerp by the Spanish army, key event for the division of the Low Countries between the Republic of the United Provinces in the north (later to become the Kingdom of the Netherlands) and the southern provinces, which will remain under Habsburg rule for another two centuries

1795   Invasion of Belgium by the French revolutionary army and annexation by France

1815	Incorporation of Belgium into the Kingdom of The Netherlands (Treaty of Vienna)
1830	Independence from The Netherlands. French chosen as the sole official language
1839	Recognition of Belgium's independence at the cost of part of the provinces of Limburg (Maastricht) and Luxemburg (to become the Grand Duchy) (Treaty of London)
1893	Universal male suffrage
1898	Official equality between French and Dutch as official languages
1899	First country to introduce proportional representation
1930	First Dutch-language university (Ghent)
1932	Official unilingualism in Flanders and Wallonia
1954	Last expansion of the territory of Brussels (nineteen communes)
1962	Recognition of the fixity of linguistic borders, tempered by 'facilities' in a number of communes
1968	Decision to transfer the Université Catholique de Louvain out of Flanders and partition of the Christian Democratic Party (the other national parties will follow in 1972 and 1978)
1970	Creation of the communities and regions
1993	Official transformation of Belgium into a federal state (new constitution promulgated on 17 February 1994)

Notes

1. This contribution was prepared within the framework of the inter-university research project 'The New Social Question' (Belgian Federal Government, Prime Minister's Office, Federal Office for Scientific, Technical and Cultural Affairs). Earlier versions were presented as a Visiting Fellow's talk at All Souls College, Oxford (May 1998) and at the conference 'The Historical Perspectives of Republicanism and the Future of the European Union' (Siena, 23–27 September 1998). A slightly different version appears in a festschrift in honour of Claus Offe (Karl Hinrichs, Herbert Kitschelt and Helmut Wiesenthal (eds) (2000) *Contingency and Crisis: The Politics of Institutional Design in Advanced Capitalism and Post-socialism*, Frankfurt am Main: Campus Verlag).

2. Karl Marx (1848) 'The "Model State" of Belgium', in K. Marx and F. Engels (1977) *Collected Works*, vol. 7, London: Lawrence & Wishart, p. 333.

3. John Stuart Mill (1861/1991) 'Considerations on Representative Government', in *On Liberty and Other Essays*, ed. J Gray, Oxford: Oxford University Press; emphasis added.

4. None of these is perfect, as there are no suitable comparable data that would enable us to put the putative trends in perspective. The underlying trend is of course supposed to relate to the knowledge of each other's language. But the last census which was allowed to collect and publicize linguistic data took place in 1947. A survey of February 1999 (by INRA Marketing Unit, Brussels, on behalf

of the association TIBEM: Tweetaligheid in beweging – Bilinguisme en mouvement) gives some clues as to where Belgium stands and where it is going. Thus, when the answer to the question 'Can you speak the other national language correctly?' is broken down into three age groups, the following pattern emerges. The percentage of subjects with Dutch as mother tongue who say they can speak French correctly rises from 15 per cent in the older category (55 or older) to 31 per cent in the 35–54 age group and to 35 per cent among the 15- to 34-year-olds. The percentage of francophone subjects who say they can speak Dutch falls from 19 per cent among older people to 12 per cent in the 35–54 age group and 4 per cent among the 15- to 34-year-olds. These survey results are somewhat misleading, mainly because the sample used significantly over-represents the Brussels area (about 1 million people, mostly francophones), in which the francophones' knowledge of Dutch is far higher than in Wallonia (about 3½ million people). However, correcting this bias would further depress the level of the second curve, but could hardly affect its slope. Both the proportion of Flemings who learnt French and the proportion of francophones who learnt Dutch have practically doubled from the older to the younger group, but whereas, among those who have learnt a second national language, the proportion of those who say they can speak it correctly has increased somewhat among the Flemings, it has dramatically decreased among the francophones, presumably because many of them chose to learn English as their second language, and Dutch only as their third language.

5. BRTN (February 1996) *Continukijkonderzoek*, Brussels: BRTN Studiedienst.
6. Fondation Francophone de Belgique (December 1997) *Étude sur l'identité francophone en région de Bruxelles-capitale*, Brussels, p. 23.
7. Michel Poulain and Michel Foulon (1998) 'Frontières linguistiques, migrations et distribution spatiale des noms de famille en Belgique', *L'Espace Géographique* 1, 53–62, pp. 55–6.
8. Kas Deprez and Louis Vos (eds) (1998) *Nationalism in Belgium: shifting identities, 1780–1995*, Basingstoke: Macmillan.
9. Wilfried Dewachter (1996) 'La Belgique d'aujourd'hui comme société politique', in A. Dieckhoff (ed.) *La Belgique: la force de la désunion*, Brussels: Complexe, p. 136.
10. Dieter Grimm (1995) 'Does Europe Need a Constitution?', *European Law Journal* 1 (3), 282–302; Jürgen Habermas (1995) 'Remarks on Dieter Grimm's "Does Europe Need a Constitution?"', *European Law Journal* 1 (3), 303–7.
11. Carl Schmitt (1926), *Die geistesgeschichtliche Lage des heutigen Parlamentarismus* (2nd edn, 1963), Berlin: Duncker & Humblot, p. 14.
12. As already shown by the Flemish historian Willems (Leonard Willems (1902) 'Over twee antivlaamsche brieven toegeschreven aan Minister Rogier', in *Verslagen en Mededeelingen der Koninklijke Vlaamsche Academie voor Taal- en Letterkunde*, Gent: A. Siffer, pp. 59–69), the sole source for this quotation is a Dutch-language lecture given in Ghent in 1866 by one Frans Gerard; the first part of the quotation there appears only in indirect speech, while the second part is only an interpretation of Rogier's thought by the author of the lecture. This has not prevented the passage from being quoted (generally in French) as authentic up to the present day: see, for example, Paul De Ridder (1988) *Het andere Brussel: een afrekening met vooroordelen*, Wommelgem: Den Gulden Engel, p. 106; Staf Beelen,

Laurent De Poorter, Philippe Haeyaert and Chris Vandenbroeke (1993) *Geschiedenis van de Vlaamse ontvoogding*, Deurne: MIM, p. 19; Marleen Brans (1993) 'High-Tech Problem Solving in a Multi-cultural State: The Case of Brussels', *Dutch Crossing: A Journal of Low Countries Studies* 49, 3–28, p. 25; etc. Nor does it prevent it from expressing what many members of the French-speaking bourgeoisie more or less secretly thought, including possibly Rogier himself, who in 1847 felt he had to publicly deny in Parliament that he intended to 'walloniser les Flandres' (Willems, 'Over twee antivlaamsche brieven', p. 57).

13. Friedrich Engels (1848) 'The Danish–Prussian Armistice', in Marx and Engels, *Collected Works*, vol. 7, p. 423.
14. Mill, *Considerations on Representative Government*, pp. 294–5.
15. Ernest Gellner (1983) *Nations and Nationalism*, pp. 139–40, Oxford: Blackwell.
16. Benedict R.O. Anderson (1993) 'Nationalism', in Joel Krieger (ed.) *The Oxford Companion to the Politics of the World*, Oxford: Oxford University Press, pp. 615–17.
17. Jean A. Laponce (1984) *Langue et territoire*, Québec: Presses Universitaires de Laval (English translation: (1987) *Languages and Their Territories*, Toronto: University of Toronto Press); (1993) 'Do Languages Behave Like Animals?', *International Journal for the Sociology of Language* 103, 19–30; (1996) 'Minority Languages in Canada: Their Fate and Survival Strategies', in André Lapierre, Patricia Smart and Pierre Savard (eds) *Language, Culture and Values in Canada at the Dawn of the 21st Century*, Ottawa: Carleton University Press.
18. Jules Destrée, Jules (1923) *Wallons et Flamands: la querelle linguistique en Belgique*, Paris: Plon, p. 127.
19. Karl Renner (1918) *Das Selbstbestimmungsrecht der Nationen, in besonderer Anwendung auf Oesterreich*, Leipzig and Vienna: Franz Deuticke.
20. For this reason, a federalism of communities provides an imaginable mechanism (the only one under present conditions) for a reconquest of Brussels by Flanders (whose GDP per capita is nearly 30 per cent higher than that of Wallonia). See Philippe Van Parijs (1999) 'Just Health Care and the Two Solidarities', Harvard Center for Population and Development Studies, Working Paper 99.03 for a sketch of how it would work.
21. Laponce, *Langue et territoire*.
22. In a country such as Switzerland, writes for example Alexandre Papaux, judge at the court of the canton of Fribourg, 'it is absolutely necessary to determine the territorial domains of each language and to protect autochthonous linguistic communities, whether or not they are threatened, in their traditional spreading areas. For the persistence of national languages cannot conceivably be guaranteed without ascribing to each an exclusive territory' (Alexandre Papaux (1997) 'Droit des langues en Suisse: état des lieux', *Revue Suisse de Science Politique* 3 (2), 131–4, p. 133.)
23. Destrée, *Wallons et Flamands*, p. 182.
24. For a vivid description of the transformation of states into firms, see Susan Strange (1992) 'Ethics and the Movement of Money: Realist Approaches', in B. Barry and R. Goodin (eds) *Free Movement*, Hemel Hempstead: Harvester Wheatsheaf. The extent to which 'globalization' is a novel phenomenon and the extent to which it is inimical to the thriving of large welfare states are hotly debated issues (for useful overviews, see, for example, Geoffrey Garrett (1998) 'Global Markets and

National Politics: Collision Course or Virtual Circle?', *International Organization* 52, 787–824; Frank Vandenbroucke (1998) *Globalization, Inequality and Social Democracy: A Survey*, London: Institute for Public Policy Research; Fritz Scharpf (1999) 'The Viability of Advanced Welfare States in the International Economy: Vulnerabilities and Options', Cologne: Max Planck Institute for the Study of Societies). But even those who support the view that investors do not necessarily dislike big welfare states cannot deny that, if they are to cope with the new context, the latter will be under pressure to reshape themselves in such a way that, whenever there is a marked conflict, the concern with a fair distribution will have to yield to the concern with competitiveness.

25. Alexander Hamilton, James Madison and John Jay (1788/1964) *Federalist Papers*, New York: The New American Library of World Literature.

26. The first of these four components has been motivated at length above; the second is further spelt out in Philippe Van Parijs (1999) 'Just Health Care and the Two Solidarities', Working Paper, Harvard Center for Population and Development Studies, 99.03; the third is presented and defended in Philippe Van Parijs (forthcoming 2000) 'Power-Sharing versus Border-Crossing in Severely Divided Societies', in Steven Macedo and Ian Shapiro (eds) *Designing Democratic Institutions*, New York: New York University Press, 217–33; and the last is laterally vindicated in Philippe Van Parijs (2000 forthcoming) 'The Ground Floor of the World: On the Socio-Economic Consequences of Linguistic Globalisation', *International Political Science Review* 21 (2), 217–33. All four are developed in a book in progress under the provisional title *La Dynamique des peuples et les exigences de la justice: la Belgique comme avenir de l'Europe*.

27. Following Grimm ('Does Europe Need a Constitution?' pp. 295–6), Kymlicka rightly stresses the importance of the language factor for the possibility of European democracy (Will Kymlicka (1999) 'Citizenship in an Era of Globalization: Comment on Held', in Ian Shapiro and Casiano Hacker-Cordón (eds) *Democracy's Edges*, Cambridge: Cambridge University Press). But his resulting pessimism can be justified only if he overlooks much of political life in multilingual countries – that is, in most countries in the world. 'Put simply,' Kymlicka writes, 'democratic politics is politics in the vernacular. The average citizen only feels comfortable debating political issues in their mother tongue. As a general rule, it is only elites who have fluency with more than one language, and who have the continual opportunity to maintain and develop these language skills, and who feel comfortable debating political issues in another tongue within multilingual settings' (p. 121). For unilinguals, and in particular for unilinguals in unilingual countries, this will sound only too plausible. But in the majority of countries, which happen to be multilingual, many people have no option, if they want to participate in national politics at all, but to do it entirely, or mainly, in a language different from their mother tongue. Some of them are even pretty good at it. Think of Nelson Mandela. True, such active political participation at the national level is restricted to an élite. But is it more than an élite that feels 'comfortable debating political issues' even in its mother tongue? Learning the tone, concepts and tricks which make for effective participation in 'one's own' mother tongue is hardly less difficult than learning another language to which one is frequently exposed anyway. More seriously, the people whose mother tongue is

different from the common political medium are at a serious disadvantage in political communication and competition, and this constitutes an undeniable source of unfairness which cannot easily be remedied. But this should not be a decisive objection either to EU-wide democracy, provided the teaching of a common second language can be effectively and widely organized. As is made clear in his reply to Grimm, Habermas believes the EU's Continental member states should manage that (Habermas, 'Remarks on Dieter Grimm's "Does Europe Need a Constitution?" ', p. 307). So do I.

28. That Belgium's constitutional endeavours have a wider relevance for Europe and beyond is often noted by foreign observers. For example, the Canadian political scientist Kenneth McRay warns that 'if [Belgium's] arduous search for a stable, plurilingual society were to fail or to be abandoned, this would be a loss not only for Belgium and for Europe generally, but also for other plurilingual and multilingual societies that pursue the same difficult quest' (K.D. McRay (1989) 'Plurilingual States and Capital Cities', in Els Witte (ed.) *Het Probleem Brussel sinds Hertoginneda*, Brussels: VUB, p. 205). The German sociolinguist Coulmas claims that Belgium's transformation into a federal state 'may eventually prove to be conducive to European integration in an unforeseen manner. Although King Baudouin contends that the new constitution guarantees a solid national state and excludes any form of separatism, many Belgian politicians see it as weakening the state. And this is just, some people think, what the [European] community needs' (Florian Coulmas (1991) 'European Integration and the Idea of a National Language: Ideological Roots and Economic Consequences', in Florian Coulmas (ed.) *A Language Policy for the European Community*, Berlin: Mouton de Gruyter, p. 3). Finally, the British political scientist Vernon Bogdanor interprets both Belgium and the European Union as 'quasi-federal' attempts to make a multinational community viable, while noting that 'the success of the European Union, like that of Belgian federalism, must remain a matter of some doubt' (Vernon Bogdanor (1997) 'Forms of Autonomy and the Protection of Minorities', *Daedalus* 126 (2), 65–87).

PART FOUR

Patriotism

CHAPTER TWELVE

Republicanism, Ethnicity and Nationalism*

MICHAEL IGNATIEFF

There have been three great episodes of nation-building during the twentieth century, and each has something to teach us about whether republican traditions of citizenship can be transplanted from their North Atlantic home to new nations with different civil societies and political histories; in other words, whether republican citizenship is possible in multiethnic post-communist, post-imperial societies.

The first such episode of nation creation at Versailles dismantled the empires of the Romanovs and the Habsburgs and created the highly unstable multiethnic nations of Central Europe and the Baltic states. These were unstable because they had little or no experience of the institutions of republican self-rule, and a weak civil society. The social actors necessary for self-rule – professional middle classes, lawyers, bureaucrats, commercial bourgeoisie – were insufficiently numerous to create a stable political class. The inertial tendency of these states in the inter-war years was towards autocracy, ratified by plebiscite. The second source of instability was their inability to create equal citizenship for all ethnic minorities. The Versailles settlement had imposed on these new states specific treaty obligations to safeguard minority rights.[1] This was supposed to prevent democracy from degenerating into ethnic majority tyranny. But it did not. Instability arose from within, by majoritarian tyranny – for example, the official persecution of Polish Jewry in the inter-war period; and from without, by irredentist agitation by foreign powers on behalf of 'their' minorities. The supposed 'plight' of the German minorities in the Czech lands and Poland was exploited by the Nazi state as a pretext for destroying the Versailles settlement and expanding the German Reich eastwards. The first attempt to reconcile republican citizenship and equality of minority rights thus ended in world war.

Yalta initiated the second episode in nation-building: the era of the so-called people's democracies. Thanks to the communist take-over of Eastern Europe, some societies – such as Yugoslavia – effectively passed from Austro-Hungarian rule, through monarchical dictatorship in the inter-war period, to

Stalinist autocracy, without gaining any historical experience of republican democracy. Communist power had legitimacy, therefore, to the degree that these societies were without historical memory of citizenship. In other societies, however, there was a memory of republican legitimacy. Czechoslovakia had the memory of Masaryk; the Baltic states had the memory of republican independence, admittedly in authoritarian conditions. Both memories made it impossible for the communist take-over to acquire solid popular support. In Poland, the Catholic Church continued to challenge the party monopoly of ideas, power, privilege and legitimacy. In all these places, therefore, the legitimacy of state-building was in doubt from the beginning.

By 1945, Hitler and Stalin had completed their work of extermination and forced population transfer. As a result, the people's democracies had been purged of their ethnic minorities. The Jews of Eastern Europe – a population with a particular political commitment to republican democracy and multiethnic citizenship – had been destroyed. In the Baltic states, the defenders of republican independence and Baltic nationality had been deported and murdered. In Czechoslovakia, the Sudeten Germans were driven from their homes. In Tito's Yugoslavia, the Partisans exiled, arrested and murdered their political competitors, the Serbian Chetnik movement and the Croatian Ustashe.

In this second wave of nation creation, in other words, two fatal legacies for the future were sown. Republican citizenship was uprooted and destroyed where it existed, creating a deficit of legitimacy which was bound eventually to undermine communist rule. Second, state formation was fatally associated with ethnic cleansing, population transfer and extermination. Where ethnic minorities did survive, they were explicitly forced to surrender all political manifestations of their distinctiveness – leaving only the folkloric shell – and required, on pain of punishment as 'nationalists' – to build a socialist nationhood. The suppression of ethnic difference proved fatal to the long-term stability of these popular democracies. Beneath the rhetoric of socialist internationalism, these regimes were often ethnic autocracies, and with every passing year, the contradiction between a 'classless' and 'internationalist' rhetoric and the reality of ethnic favouritism and class privilege became more flagrant and more infuriating. In the process, the very legitimacy of the state was compromised.

The same association of state formation and ethnic cleansing was evident in Africa and Asia. In the decade following 1945, the French, Dutch, British and Belgian land empires were shaken by nationalist revolts and uprisings which led to the creation of dozens of new members of the United Nations. In the Indian subcontinent, nation-building, as in Eastern Europe, was accompanied by extermination and ethnic cleansing, the mutual killings of Hindus and Muslims, the vast population transfers on partition. Another result of the British retreat from empire – the state of Israel, ceded to the Jews by the departing British mandatory authority in 1948 – was accompanied by massacre and displacement of nearly a million Palestinians. Thus, even where the state created was democratic and republican in form – as both India and Israel turned out to be – the conditions of its birth were attended by determined efforts to drive out ethnic minority populations. Much of the ongoing instability of these regions since 1945 has to be explained in terms of the fatal confluence of state-building with ethnic persecution and the related failure to combine equality with republican citizenship.

Now, in the late 1990s, we are living through the third great moment of nation-building. Just as the settlement of 1945 sought to undo the mistakes of Versailles, so we are now seeking to undo the consequences of 1945. With the coming down of the Berlin Wall in 1989, and the collapse of the Soviet empire two years later, the collapse of the people's democracies became inevitable. They were undermined by the chronic failure of the command economy, but also succumbed to the contagion of liberty: the beckoning example of republican citizenship in Western Europe and North America. Freedom – understood both as self-rule and as freedom from arbitrary power – was the great cry which animated the Eastern European nation-building after 1991.

This idea of freedom was eminently republican, but it carried an implication which West Europeans did not notice at first. The ideological burial of socialism also buried the one available language of multiethnic fraternity: class solidarity and socialist nationhood. Multiethnic citizenship was socialist, and as such disgraced. Thus when freedom came to Eastern Europe, it meant the freedom to assert and affirm ethnic identity once more. This might have been entirely harmless in societies with a civil society experienced in the art of citizenship and interest group compromise. But in these societies, democracy had always meant ethnic majority rule, backed up, where necessary, by ethnic cleansing.

In post-Titoist Yugoslavia, republican democracy and multiethnic co-operation proved incompatible. Croatia has expelled most of its Serbian minority; Serbia is tyrannizing and forcibly displacing its Albanian minority; Bosnia-Herzegovina has seen most of its Serbian minority flee, or driven out to the dubious protection of Republika Srpska. Only Slovenia has made a peaceful transition from single-party to multi-party rule, because it was the most prosperous of the former republics of Yugoslavia and the most ethnically homogeneous.

Elsewhere, Czechs and Slovaks have divorced rather than share a single state. The Baltic states would have denied republican citizenship to their sizeable Russian minorities had it not been for the continued pressure of the European Community and the Americans, and the threat of Russian intervention. In the fifteen newly emerging states of the Commonwealth of Independent States, Russian minorities have experienced similar difficulties in attaining full civic belonging in the new democracies of Russia's former Asian empire. In the central African region, no state has been able to combine representative democracy with multiethnic accommodation. All have been unstable ethnic majoritarian tyrannies, which since 1960 have attempted to solve their problems of internal cohesion by eliminating or expelling their minorities altogether. Genocide remains an instrument of state formation throughout the central African region.

In failing to create republican citizenship, these societies do not merely sacrifice multiethnic tolerance; they also sacrifice democracy itself. Under Franco Tudjman, Croatia was an authoritatian state, where dictatorship and oligarchy were ratified by elections. Under Milošević, Serbia has been the same. All over the post-communist world, former communist élites use the democratic process to legitimize the perpetuation of oligarchy and to siphon off the profits of the transition to capitalism. Democracy, in other words, did not lead to citizenship, but to authoritarian populism.

To use Isaiah Berlin's terminology, these societies have got 'negative liberty' in the worst possible conditions: that is, market freedoms without the institutional safeguards – rule of law, separation of powers, checks and balances – which provide republican freedom. The Russian transition is a frightening example of what can happen when market freedoms and republican freedoms are not created together: capitalist accumulation proceeds without law and the political system itself has become a plaything of market monopolists.

In such conditions, to use the terminology of my colleague Maurizio Viroli, patriotism is impossible. The nation exists, but not the *patria*, the republican state. Since impartial civic institutions guaranteeing the liberty of all citizens do not exist, there is no properly patriotic object of loyalty. The only available poles of loyalty are clan, family or nation.

Where communism has laid waste the very idea of republican liberty, where multi-party elections have been suppressed for fifty years, it becomes impossible to mobilize people politically except by invoking nationality or ethnicity. It is not that the idea of multiethnic political mobilization is unavailable: in former Yugoslavia members of the liberal professions understood the republican ideal of civic mobilization perfectly well and tried to organize parties along such lines. But the republican ideal is individualistic: it presupposes individuals secure enough in their possessions and identities to risk political association with strangers who may be different from them. In former communist societies, few people had experience of this kind of political individualism, and this kind of trust. Their political memory was filled instead with memories of ethnic treachery – with the ethnic cleansing – which had accompanied earlier attempts at nation creation. These memories gave a Hobbesian edge of terror to the experience of state formation after communism. With centralized state authority bleeding away in the years after Tito's death, it became a matter of life and death for individuals to find security in a post-communist world. They had too little experience of multi-ethnic political mobilization to put any trust in it – despite the fact that multiethnic parties offered the only alternative to civil war. In a frantic search for security, the populations of the Balkans flew into the arms of strong-men who promised that they would deliver the security of ethnic majority rule in the new and frightening conditions of democracy. Once again majority rule and stability in the ethnic patchwork of the Balkans were attainable only through massacre, deportation and ethnic cleansing. Republicanism has worked only where the state is ethnically homogeneous: in Poland, the Czech Republic and Slovenia. In the first case, ethnic homogeneity is a consequence of genocide; in the second, a consequence of political divorce; and in the third, a legacy of ethnic settlement in the Austro-Hungarian past.

It follows that it is both presumptuous and historically misleading to speak of republicanism as a 'shared European heritage'. We have piously lectured the nations of Eastern Europe on the republican virtues, without fully understanding the nature of their historical experience of nation-building in the twentieth century, and without understanding why republican forms of civic mobilization are impossible in societies which have been ruled by terror, force, violence and fraud.

A shared heritage implies a usable heritage, one adapted to modern conditions. But is this so? I have asked whether it is usable in Eastern Europe. Now we need to turn the question upon ourselves, and ask whether it is usable here at home. The European republican heritage was crafted in pre-modern times for a citizenship radically different from our own. It was never *intended* to apply to populations with heterogeneous religious, social, ethnic and racial origins. The tradition simply took for granted a homogeneous citizenship. From the very birth of the republican ideal, citizenship was restricted to adult males. Later on, in Renaissance Europe, citizenship was restricted to property-holders, members of the Mother Church, persons born in the commune or republic in question, and so on. Females, the propertyless, Jews, foreigners and native persons born outside the commune often – though not always – found themselves denied the vote.

Today we assume that toleration is an essential virtue of republican citizenship. In our republican tradition, however, it was sharply restricted. Locke did say, 'neither pagan, nor Mahometan nor Jew ought to be excluded from the civil rights of the Commonwealth because of his religion'. But he excluded atheists. 'Promises, covenants, and oaths, which are the bonds of human society, can have no hold upon an atheist. The taking away of God, even in thought, dissolves all.'[2] All of this highlights the challenge of making a tradition usable to a *pluralist* world: one where belief and unbelief meet on equal grounds, and where republican liberty provides nothing like a stable consensus, but only the site of an ongoing and often bitterly conflictual argument over rights.

It must be conceded, of course, that republican citizenship has been responding to the challenge of demands for inclusion at least since the French Revolution. Once the language of citizenship was premised on a metaphysics of ultimate human equality, it became impossible logically – though still

261

possible politically – to deny its rights to anyone. To assert that all men are created equal is to provide those excluded from citizenship with unassailable arguments in favour of their eventual inclusion. The first to take advantage of these arguments were religious Nonconformists, then women, then the working classes. In the process, however, Philip Pettit argues, republican citizenship itself changed:

> with citizenship extended beyond the realm of propertied males, it was no longer possible to think of making all citizens free in the old sense: in particular it was not feasible, under received ideas, to think of conferring freedom as non-domination on women and servants.

As dependent groups struggled for inclusion, freedom made its transit from ancient to modern, from active citizenship (freedom from domination), to 'negative liberty' (freedom from interference).[3] Those who struggled for civic inclusion after 1789 were fighting not just for 'negative liberty' but for civic participation. Republican aspirations were not supplanted by a demand for market freedom. The demand for market freedoms and republican citizenship – liberty ancient and modern – went hand in hand. The political history of Europe since 1750 can be largely interpreted in terms of the struggle of excluded groups – those denied full civic equality on grounds first of class, then of gender, and finally of race – for full incorporation within republican citizenship. This battle has ended only within the lifetimes of many readers of this book. It was not until the American Voting Rights Act of 1965, which fully enfranchised southern black citizens, that the American republican tradition applied, for the first time, to all persons.[4] Ours is the first historical generation actually seeking to realize the ideal of republican citizenship in conditions of total inclusion and in conditions of radical moral pluralism – that is, in conditions of acute and ongoing disagreement about the nature, extent and boundary of conflicting rights claims. Small wonder that in established republican democracies such as the United States, the question of whether you can sustain a civic republican and national identity within a multicultural society of astonishing diversity and heterogeneity of origins has become a salient cultural and political anxiety. If this is proving arduous at home, we should not be so surprised that it is proving exceptionally difficult to reconcile citizenship and multiethnicity in newly emerging states.

Ever since Benjamin Constant's famous essay,[5] the distinction between ancient and modern definitions of liberty has been salient; even more so has been the question of whether ancient liberty is applicable in modern conditions. The modern problem of virtue, liberty and order begins with the fact that modern citizens are heterogeneous. In a market society, their interests sometimes converge in market transactions; sometimes, however, their fundamental economic interests conflict. Freedom for the pike means death for the minnows. Reconciling market inequalities with civic equality has proven exceptionally difficult. And then, because labour is now free to migrate, modern polities are composed of people who do not always share the same history, religion, culture, tradition or values. This should not be overstated: the United States, for example, thinks of itself as multiethnic and multicultural, but it is also overwhelmingly white. The same is true of Britain, France and Germany. Ethnic minorities in these societies do not think of themselves as integrating into a fracturing multiethnic dispersion, but into societies which still retain strong degrees of ethnic homogeneity. Nevertheless race has been delegitimized as a basis for social cohesion. Despite the fact that the United States, for example, retains a white majority, Americans now feel that as a matter of principle they should not define themselves as a community of origins. They feel this for republican reasons: that membership of community ought to depend on civic rather than ethnic grounds. And then finally, because modern cultures change at frantic speed, there is always a strong degree of intergenerational tension about the meaning of such values, traditions and cultures which all say they share. This heterogeneity is paradoxical, of course, because modernity imposes a strong degree of homogeneity in consumption, lifestyle and commonly circulated ideas, crazes, fetishes and fashions. Yet we sense that common conditions of life, generated by the market, are not sufficient to generate commonality of political purpose.

The academic revival of the republican language of civic virtue seeks to acknowledge all these facts: seeking to turn the actual heterogeneity of interests and values in late capitalist society to its advantage by arguing, in effect, that it is precisely because we no longer – if we ever did – share common origins, traditions and interests that we can attach ourselves to a common love of republican liberty. If we do not share common myths of origin, language, tradition, religion or race, we can at least share an ethical attachment to certain rules of the road: mutual respect, tolerance, formal and substantive equality among individuals, commitment to the rule of law and democracy. Of course, playing by the rules need not mean loving the rules or loving the country which makes the rules. Some wish merely for common civic attachment – playing by the rules; others want this to be imbued with patriotic feeling, loving the rules and the traditions which sustain them.

If I can take issue with Maurizio Viroli, or at least with his fine book,[6] it seems to me that republican liberty is not the lodestar of shared attachment and moral unanimity which he supposes it to be. Liberty is a site of contention not unanimity: the word itself can be parsed in at least three conflicting ways: to mean active republican citizenship; market freedom to accumulate and acquire; and third, non-interference, liberty to think and act as one pleases. These three meanings mark the demarcation points between liberalism, social democracy and conservatism – in other words, between competing political and moral philosophies. To the degree that liberty is a unifying value, it is attachment to the procedures of liberty, not to any particular content of the value itself. What we praise about our liberty is the procedural fact that we are capable of conducting political discussion without killing each other, that we have managed to banish violence from the adjudication of political claims; in other words, that we trust each other just enough to sustain an argument about what the republic should stand for and do, in this or that practical circumstance. Trust here means that we share a faith in the capacity of our institutions to represent our interests and resolve our differences. This trust is conditional, begrudging, constantly tested, and not especially warm. Professor Viroli wants us to imbue these procedural commitments with patriotic warmth. He would insist that we are proud of republican procedures not because they work, but because they keep us free. And it is this common pride that we call patriotism. So far so good. What I have difficulty with is the idea that there is a consensual attachment to the content of liberty itself. On the contrary, it is what we argue about most: what is freedom to you is licence to me; what is power and oppression to you is the exercise of my liberty. And so on. Almost all our serious disagreements take this form. Professor Viroli would say, 'but in all our arguments, we at least accept that the liberty of the individual must be respected'. The question is how, in each particular circumstance, and to what degree. Yet the detail here is almost everything: political conflict is rarely about general principle; it is about the application of principle to concrete cases. Believing in liberty takes us only a very few paces into the wood; the rest of the way, we are on our own. The most we can say, therefore, is that republican liberty constitutes the common ground of our argument, but it cannot provide the content for its resolution. Here I conclude on a Berlinian note: our values divide us: our values themselves conflict; our moral situation is irremediably plural.[7]

Viroli's attempt to revive republicanism as an antidote to ethnic nationalism is laudable. It is worth trying to find a language of patriotic appeal, disinfested of chauvinist, ethnic, racial impulses, not just in Eastern Europe, but in those parts of Western Europe – Italy, France and Germany – where republican parties must compete for electoral survival against fascist or semi-fascist parties that are trying to hijack a properly patriotic language and turn it into a narrowly ethnic nationalism. The problem, however, is that there are difficulties in principle in distinguishing between the civic and the ethnic, and disinfesting the former of the latter. Professor Viroli not only acknowledges this, but seeks in fact to associate the civic with particularistic traditions: so that when people say they are attached or devoted to the liberty of a country, it is not abstract, cosmopolitan liberty, but the liberty characteristic of Italy or Germany or the United States or Britain. Although all belong in the same family of republican virtues and with the same origins in the Roman republic, they have all taken on different institutional colorations. In other words, there is something 'ethnic' in all 'civic' attachments. In the case of Britain, for example, there are traditions going back to Henry VIII which contrast the freeborn, Protestant English with the Catholic slaves of Europe. English ethnic bellicosity and aggression towards Europe – a feature of its character for centuries – reflects an ethnicized mythology of its own civic identity as a free people.[8] But some uncomfortable conclusions follow from Viroli's attempt to ground republicanism in particularism. If we have been urging Eastern European societies to pursue a civic course towards nation-building, rather than an ethnic one, we have been preaching a very deceptive message, because our own civic republicanism has some strongly ethnic contents to it. It may be that no nation can be created without a myth of republican particularism. But it is not as evident to me as it is to Professor Viroli that republican particularism must be associated with tolerance. Innocent victims of persecution can be plausibly turned away from our borders in the name of the republic in danger. Republican particularity can speak in the language of Mazzini, but also in the language of Saint-Just. A particularism that is not self-limited by an explicit allegiance to certain cosmopolitan, internationalist values – human rights, for instance – is bound to degenerate into a high-minded form of chauvinism. I do not think we want patriotism simply because we feel it offers us a morally acceptable way of beating the nationalists at their own game. To be committed to liberty as a value is to conceive of the nation in ways fundamentally antithetical to the ways it is conceived by a nationalist. It is to think of it as a community united in a common argument about the meaning, extent and scope of liberty; not to imagine it as a community of fate, origin or value. It is also to accept that the particularism of one country has no privileges, no monopoly on the right; that 'our' liberty must explain itself to 'other' liberties, in Europe and beyond; and that 'our' liberty must even give way when it infringes the standards and ethical principles of a larger world.

Notes

* This chapter was originally a paper delivered at Siena on 26 September 1998 to the Convegno of the European Science Foundation on 'Republicanism: A Shared European Heritage'.

1. Mark Mazower (1998) *Dark Continent: Europe's Twentieth Century*, London: Penguin, chapter 2; see also André Liebich (1998) *Les minorités nationales en Europe centrale et orientale*, Geneva: Georg, pp. 20–4.
2. John Locke (1990) *A Letter Concerning Toleration*, New York: Prometheus Books, pp. 64–70.
3. Philip Pettit (1997) *Republicanism: A Theory of Freedom and Government*, Oxford: Clarendon Press, p. viii.
4. I have outlined this argument in greater detail in my (1998) *The Warrior's Honour: Ethnic War and the Modern Conscience*, New York: Metropolitan Books, pp. 64–71.
5. Benjamin Constant (1988) 'Of the Liberty of the Ancients Compared with That of the Moderns', in Biancamaria Fontana (ed.) *Political Writings*, Cambridge: Cambridge University Press.

6. Maurizio Viroli (1995) *For Love of Country: An Essay on Patriotism and Nationalism*, Oxford: Clarendon Press, p. 14.
7. Isaiah Berlin (1997) 'Two Concepts of Liberty', in *The Proper Study of Mankind*, London: Chatto & Windus, p. 241: 'human goals are many, not all of them commensurable, and in perpetual rivalry with one another.'
8. Linda Colley (1992) *Britons: Forging the Nation, 1707–1837*, New Haven, CT: Yale University Press, pp. 8–9.

CHAPTER THIRTEEN

Republican Patriotism

MAURIZIO VIROLI

One of the aspects of current debates on patriotism, nationalism and cosmopolitanism that I find rather odd is that no one takes the trouble to find out what philosophers, historians, poets, agitators and prophets belonging to the republican family have meant to say, over the past two thousand years, when they have spoken of love of country.[1]

General Features of Republican Patriotism

For classical republican theorists, and most notably for the Romans, love of *patria* is a passion. More precisely, it is a charitable, compassionate love of the republic (*caritas reipublicae*) and of its citizens (*caritas civium*). As a Scholastic thinker, Ptolemy of Lucca, later put it, 'Amor patriae in radice charitatis fundatur ...': 'Love for the fatherland is founded in the root of charity which puts, not the private things before those common, but the common things before the private.'[2]

Even when love of country respects the principles of justice and reason, and is therefore also called a rational love (*amor rationalis*, as Remigio de Girolami put it), it is an affection for a particular republic and particular citizens who are dear to us because we share with them important things: the laws, liberty, the forum, the senate, the public squares, friends, enemies, memories of victories and memories of defeats, hopes, fears. It is a passion that grows among equal citizens, not the result of rational consent to the political principles of republics in general. Because it is a passion, it translates into action, and more precisely into acts of service to the common good (*officium*) and care (*cultus*).[3]

Last, it must be taken into account that for republican theorists, *caritas reipublicae* is an empowering passion that impels citizens to perform duties of citizenship and gives rulers the strength to accomplish the hard tasks necessary for the defence, or the institution, of liberty. As Livy explains in book II, section 2 of his *History*, where he narrates the earliest phases of the consolidation of Roman liberty after the expulsion of Tarquinius Superbus, it was charity towards the republic (*caritas reipublicae*) that gave Brutus the moral strength to overcome his reluctance and accomplish the unpleasant but necessary task of speaking against Lucius Tarquinius before the people of Rome.

As the passage I have quoted from Ptolemy of Lucca's *De Regimine Principum* shows, important components of the Roman republican language of patriotism passed into the tracts on government of Scholastic political writers and, more importantly still, into the sermons that they delivered in the churches of Florence and other Italian free republics. This marriage between the Roman republican language of patriotism and Christian patriotism, made possible by the central word *caritas*, illuminates the roots of Florentine patriotism of the *Trecento* and of the *Quattrocento*. This patriotism was fiercely anticlerical, as the the saying 'to love one's country more than one's soul' indicates, but also deeply Christian. This intellectual context permits us to understand the meaning of Machiavelli's words in *Discorsi* II.2, when, after having mounted the most devastating critique of Christian religion and Christian education, he notes that Machiavelli too had heard of a language of patriotism which combined Roman and Christian *caritas*, even if the works of Scholastic thinkers were not his favourite readings and churches were not his favourite places.

A similar use of the language of patriotism understood as *caritas* is in John Milton's *Defence of the People of England* of 1651, where he writes[4] that the execution of Charles I was an act inspired not by factiousness, or a desire to usurp the rights of others, or mere quarrelsomeness, or perverse desires, or fury or madness, but by love of country – '*patriae caritas*', as the Latin version reads.

For republican theorists, the republic is a political ordering and a way of life – that is, a culture. To describe people's love of their republican institutions and of the way of life based upon them, Machiavelli speaks, for instance, of love of the '*vivere libero*' (free way of life). Other republicans of his time defined the republic as 'a particular way of life of the city' (*una certa vita della città*).[5]

Republican patriotism surely has a cultural dimension, but it is *primarily* a political passion based upon the experience of citizenship, not on common pre-political elements derived from being born in the same territory, belonging to the same race, speaking the same language, worshipping the same gods, having the same customs. This means that the argument that republican patriotism is not a valid intellectual response for contemporary issues of democratic citizenship because 'a purely political creed is insufficient'[6] misses the point, because republican patriotism does not rely on a purely political creed.

Latin authors made a clear distinction between the political and cultural values of the republic and the non-political values of nationhood; in fact, they used two different words: *patria* and *natio*.[7] Which of the two was considered to be more important is rather obvious. The bonds of citizenship, as Cicero put it in *De Officiis* (I.17.53), are closer and more dignified than the bonds of the *natio*.

This distinction and this ranking were reiterated by later theorists. In the eighteenth-century French *Encyclopédie*,[8] for instance, we read that *patrie* does not mean the place in which we are born, as the vulgar conception believes. It means instead 'free state' (*état libre*) of which we are members and whose laws protect our liberty and our happiness (*nos libertés et notre bonheur*).

For the author of the entry, the term *patrie* is synonymous with republic and liberty, as it was for Machiavelli and the republican political writers. Under the yoke of despotism there is no *patrie*, for the obvious reason that under a despotic government subjects go unprotected and excluded, precisely like strangers. Following in Montesquieu's footsteps, the author remarked that

> those who live under the Oriental despotism, where no other law is known than the whims of the sovereign, no other maxim than the adoration of his caprices, no other principles of government than terror, where no fortune and no one are safe: those do not have a *patrie* and do not even know its name, which is the true expression of happiness.[9]

This means that the commonplace that the Enlightenment was anti-patriotic is a gross mistake. The *philosophes* were not nationalists, but they were surely patriots in the sense of republican patriotism. And to be patriots meant for them to feel the *caritas reipublicae*. As a distinguished member of the republican family, Jean-Jacques Rousseau, put it:

> It is not the walls, nor its habitants which constitute the *patrie*, but the laws, the mores, the customs, the government, the constitution, and the way of life which results from them. The *patrie* consists in the relationship between the state and its members; when these relations change or dissolve, the *patrie* disappears.[10]

It is the political experience of republican liberty, or the memory, or the hope thereof, that makes a city meaningful. Republican theorists were perfectly aware that the kind of commonness generated by the fact of inhabiting the same city, or the same nation, of speaking the same language, and worshipping the same gods is not at all sufficient to generate *republican* patriotism in the hearts of the citizens: a true *patrie*, they claimed, can only be a free republic.

They also claimed that love of country is not at all a natural feeling, but a passion that needs to be stimulated through legislation, or more precisely through good government and participation of the citizens in public life. Rousseau eloquently expressed this point in the *Économie politique*:

> Let the *partria*, therefore, show itself the common mother of the citizens, let the advantages which they enjoy in their land render it dear to them, let the

government allow them enough participation in the administration of the public that they feel themselves to be at home, and let the laws be nothing in their eyes but guarantees of the common liberty.[11]

A few years later, Gaetano Filangieri refined Rousseau's thought in *La Scienza della Legislazione*:

Let us not abuse the sacred name of patriotism (*amore della patria*) by assimilating it to the affection one has for one's place of birth, which is an appendix to the very ills of civil union, and which can be found in the most corrupt as in the most perfect society.[12]

true *amore della patria*, he claims, is an artificial passion:

it can be dominant or unknown; it may not affect one people and be all powerful with another. The wisdom of laws and government establish such a passion, firm it up, expand and invigorate it; their vices weaken, exclude and proscribe it.[13]

Another eminent jurist, Gian Domenico Romagnosi, was able to put the whole argument that true patriotism is the consequence of good government and political participation in a nutshell:

True patriotism is municipal. The real, firm, active and permanent spring of true patriotism lies in the City; and, I dare say, cannot but be there. I may even add that only the City offers secure foundation and the basis for political order in a civil state.[14]

Carlo Cattaneo, however, was even clearer, and defined the *comune* as being the nation in the society: 'The communes', he wrote, 'are the nation in the innermost asylum of its liberty.'[15]

Republican Patriotism and Nationalism

It should by now be rather easy to identify the difference between republican patriotism and nationalism. If by nationalism we mean what the founders of the language of nationalism meant, it seems to me clear that republican patriots and nationalists disagreed on the central issue of what a true *patria* is. In fact, late eighteenth-century theorists of nationalism began their efforts to build the new language of nationalism precisely by attacking the republican principle that only a self-governing republic is a true *patria*.

As early as 1761, Thomas Abbt issued a successful pamphlet entitled *Death for the Fatherland*, to challenge the idea that love of fatherland can flourish only in republics. A monarchy can be a fatherland if all, including the monarch, are subject to laws that sustain the common good. There is no difference between a subject of a monarchy and a citizen of the freest conceivable republic: they are both equally subject to the laws: none is free, but everyone is free according to the spirit of the constitution of the state.[16] In a good monarchy, all are 'citizens' (*Bürger*), regardless of their different social rank, and their good is at one with the good of the fatherland.[17] A monarchy, concludes Abbt, can also be a fatherland that we can love; and if we *can* love it, we *must* love it.[18]

This argument was forcefully restated and amplified by Johann Gottfried Herder. As he remarked in one of his earliest writings, *Do We Still Have the Public and Fatherland of Yore?*, fatherland still means freedom, but no longer the freedom of the ancients. Modern patriotism does not require the spiritual strength that the ancients deemed necessary to repel the enemies of liberty. It is a more ordinary sense of duty and attachment to a more 'modest freedom' that a just emperor can ensure better than a republic:

> In our day, all states have settled into a system of balance; whoever cannot protect himself needs a patron, a father; our people no longer are characterized by the *brazen audacity* of the ancients; there prevails, instead, a finer, more modest *freedom*, the freedom of *conscience*, to be an honest man and a Christian, the *freedom* to enjoy in the shadow of the throne one's dwelling and vineyard in peace and quiet and to possess the fruit of one's labour; the *freedom* to be the shaper of one's happiness and comfort, the friend of one's intimates and the father and guardian of one's children.[19]

Herder points to Tsar Peter the Great as a 'true patriot', who became 'the father of his old, and the creator of a new fatherland'.[20] Patriotism gave him the inspiration to emancipate his subjects, against their will, from serfdom, and the determination to stand against adverse fortune. Without citizens, the fatherland can count on a father: the grand patriotism of the Emperor and the common patriotism of the subject are sufficient to preserve the 'modest liberty' that modern men and women are longing for.

Although people of Herder's time did not possess the intense political patriotism of the ancients, a patriotic monarch could command from them the same degree of self-sacrifice that republics were said to be capable of exciting in their citizens, he believed. The words 'fatherland', 'monarch', 'empress', Herder writes, will sound for any man who is not a lifeless mercenary as 'the sound of victory impassioning his veins, stirring his heart, steadying his hands, and protecting his chest with iron armour'.[21] To die for the fatherland is sweet and honourable, no matter if the fatherland is one where 'the law and hundreds rule' or one where 'the law and only one rule', as long as the ruler is the father or the mother of a happy people.

Republican patriots and nationalists also disagreed on what true love of country is, or should be. The former considered love of country an artificial passion to be instilled and constantly reproduced by political means; the latter as a natural feeling to be protected from cultural contamination and cultural assimilation. Their different interpretations of love of country arose from their different conceptions of the *patria* and the nation respectively: the fatherland of republicans was a moral and political institution, whereas Herder's nation is a natural creation. He regarded nationalities not as the product of human beings, but as the work of a living, organic force that animates the universe. Republics originated from the outstanding virtue and wisdom of legendary founders; nations from God himself, just as the living force that fashions national organic units out of the chaos of homogeneous matter reflects God's eternal plans and will.

When Herder stresses that nature has created nationalities but not states, he means that the former is of a higher order than the latter. The loss of the republic was for republicans the greatest tragedy, but for Herder the loss of one's own nation was more tragic: deprive people of their country (in the sense of nationality), he wrote, 'and you deprive them of everything'.[22]

All this does not mean that the idea of the nation has always been used against republican patriotism or to sustain nationalist projects. The most obvious example is John Stuart Mill's definition of the principle of nationality in *A System of Logic*:

> We need scarcely say that we do not mean [by principle of nationality] a senseless antipathy to foreigners; or a cherishing of absurd peculiarities because they are national; or a refusal to adopt what has been found good by other countries. In all these senses, the nations which have had the strongest national spirit have had the least nationality. We mean a principle of sympathy, not of hostility; of union, not of separation. We mean a feeling of common interest among those who live under the same government, and are contained within the same natural or historical boundaries. We mean, that one part of the community shall not consider themselves as foreigners with regard to another part; that they shall cherish the tie which holds them together; shall feel that they are one people, that their lot is cast together, that evil to any of their fellow countrymen is evil to themselves, and that they cannot selfishly free themselves from their share of any common inconvenience by severing the connection.[23]

This conception of the nation is equivalent to what Mazzini meant by *patria*:

> A country (*patria*) is a fellowship of free and equal men bound together in a brotherly concord of labour towards a single end. ... A country is not an aggregation, it is an *association*. There is no true country without a uniform right. There is no true country where the uniformity of that right is violated by the existence of caste, privilege and uniformity.[24]

Another example of the principle of nationality being interpreted as the equivalent of the classical republican notion of *patria* is to be found in the writings of Carlo Pisacane. The principle of nationality that had excited the most generous souls in 1848, he wrote in 1860, was an ideal of liberty. Nationality means the free expression of the collective will of a people, common interest, full and absolute liberty, with no privileged classes, groups or dynasties. Love of country can grow only on the soil of liberty, and liberty alone can turn citizens into supporters of the republic. Under the yoke of

272

princes and monarchs the generous passions of patriotism are bound to degenerate.[25]

Like Mazzini, Pisacane interpreted the principle of nationality as the opposite of nationalism. In the Europe of monarchies, he wrote, the 'principle of Nationality' was corrupted into 'a mean *nationalism*'; a politics of sheer force and interest replaced a politics of free and spontaneous development of nations.[26]

Still, the difference between republican patriotism and nationalism remains rather sharp. Equally sharp is the difference between republican patriotism and civic nationalism on the one hand and between republican patriotism and ethnic nationalism nationalism on the other. Republican patriotism differs from civic nationalism in being a passion and not the result of rational consent; it is a matter not of allegiance to historically and culturally neutral universal political principles, but of attachment to the laws, the constitution and the way of life of a particular republic. Republican patriotism is also distinct from ethnic nationalism because it does not attach moral or political relevance to ethnicity; on the contrary, it recognizes moral and political relevance, and beauty, in the political values of citizenship, particularly republican equality, which are hostile to ethnocentrism.

I find the republican interpretation of patriotism more convincing than the contemporary view that, in order to hold heterogeneous peoples together, we need 'stronger fare' than the political and cultural values of the republic, as Anthony Smith recently put it. I do not know what Smith means when he speaks of 'holding together', but if he means, as I mean, holding individuals together as free and equal citizens, we need nothing more than a politics genuinely inspired by the ideals of republican liberty and republican equality, and a culture based upon those ideals. Citizenship does not grow out of the bonds of nationhood. Peoples who are culturally, religiously or ethnically homogeneous are not those who are the most civic minded; on the contrary, they tend to be intolerant, bigoted and boring. Politics, a true democratic politics, can do all the work of citizenship by itself. It does not need embarrassing helpers.

Whether or not this is a desirable and feasible political project is another matter. I have argued elsewhere that it is. Here I simply want to suggest that we are not bound at all by a choice between the myth of civic nationalism and the horror of ethnic nationalism.

Notes

1. The best examples are the articles published in Joshua Cohen (ed.) (1996) *For Love of Country*, Boston: Beacon Press.
2. Ptolemy of Lucca (1954) *De Regimine Principum*, in R. Spiazzi (ed.) *Divi Thomae Aquinatis Opuscula Philosophice*, Turin: Marietti, p. 299.

3. I provide textual references in Maurizio Viroli (1995) *For Love of Country*, Oxford: Oxford University Press.

4. John Milton (1932) *Defence of the People of England*, in *The Works of John Milton*, vol. 7, New York: Columbia University Press, p. 455.

5. Antonio Brucioli (1982) *Dialogi*, ed. A. Landi, Naples: Chicago.

6. Anthony Smith (1996) 'In Search of (One-Sided) Statues of Liberty', *The Times HIgher Education Supplement*, 9 August, p. 22.

7. See, for instance, Quintilian, *Institutio Oratoria*, V (10), 24–5.

8. Denis Diderot (ed.) (1765) *Encyclopédie*, vol. 12, Neuchâtel, p. 178.

9. 'Ceux qui vivent sous le despotisme oriental, où l'on ne connoit d'autre loi que la volunté du souverain, d'autre maximes que l'adoration de ses caprices, d'autres principes de gouvernement que la terreur, où aucune fortune, aucune tête n'est en sûreté; ceux là, n'ont point de patrie, et n'en connoissent pas même le mot, qui est la véritable expression du bonheur.' – *Ibid.*, p. 180.

10. Jean-Jacques Rosseau (1965) *Correspondance complète de Jean-Jaques Rousseau*, vol. 19, ed. R.A. Leigh, Banbury, Oxfordshire: The Voltaire Foundation, p. 190.

11. 'Que la patrie se montre donc la mère commune des citoyens, que les advantages dont ils jouissent dans leur pays le leur rend cher, que le gouvernement leur laisse assez de part à l'administration publique pour sentir qu'ils sont chez eux et que les lois ne soient à leurs yeux que les garants de la commune liberté.' – Jean-Jacques Rousseau (1964) *Économie politique*, in *Oeuvres complètes*, vol. 3, Paris: Gaillimard, p. 258.

12. 'Non abusiamo del sacro nome di amore della patria, per indicare quell'affezione pel patrio suolo ch'è una appendice de' mali istessi delle civili unioni, e che si può ritrovare cosí nella più perfetta società.' – Gaetano Filangieri (1995) *La Scienza della Legislazione*, ed. R. Bruschi, vol. 4, part 2, Naples: Procaccini, p. 42.

13. '[E]ssa può essere dominante ed ignota; essa può esser senza alcun vigore in un populo, e può esser onnipotente in un altro. La sapienza delle leggi el del governo la introducono, la staliliscono, l'espandono, l'invigoriscono, i vizii dell'uno e delle altre la indeboliscono, l'escludono, la proscrivono.' – *Ibid.*

14. Il vero patriottismo è nel municipio. La molla, solida, attiva, reale e permanente del vero e sicuro patriottismo – scriveva Romagnosi – sta nel Municipio, e oso dire che non può stare che in lui solo. Aggiungo di più: che in lui solo sta la base di sicurezza di tutto e l'ordinamento politico di uno stato civile.' – Gian Domenico Romagnosi (1841–8) *Istituzioni di civile filosofia*, in *Opere*, vol. 3, ed. Alessandro de Giorgi, Milan: Perelli e Mariani, poi Volpato, p. 1548.

15. 'I comuni sono la nazione; sono la nazione nel più intimo asilo della sua libertà.' – Carlo Cattaneo (1972) 'Sulla leggie comunale e provinciale' in *Opere Scelte*, ed. Delia Castelnuovo Frigessi, Turin: Einaudi, vol. IV, p. 406.

16. Thomas Abbt (1761) *Vom Tode für das Vaterland*, Berlin, p. 18.

17. 'Sind wir nicht verbunden unsere Wohlfahrt zu beforden sie sicher zu gründen? Und diese Wohlfahrt ist so genau mit der Wohlfahrt des Vaterlandes, das heist, mit der Ausrechthaltung der Gesetze, deren Schuss ich geniesse, verbunden!' – *Ibid.*

18. '[W]ir es lieben müssen' – *Ibid.*, p. 18.

19. Johann Gottfried Herder (1764) *Haben wir noch jetz das Publikum und Vaterland der Alten?* in *Johann Gottried Herder Frühe Schriften 1764–1772*, ed. Ulrich Gaier,

Frankfurt am Main, p. 50; English translation, *Do We Still Have the Public and Fatherland of Yore?*, p. 62.

20. 'War Petre der Grosse nicht ein wahrer Patriot, da er, als der Name und das Wunder unsers Jahrhunderts, der Vater seines Alten, und der Schöpfer eines neues Vaterlandes wurde?' – *Ibid.*; also English translation, p. 62.

21. *Ibid.*, p. 50; English translation, p. 60.

22. Johann Gottfried Herder (1880 [1785]) *Sämmtliche Werke*, ed. B. Supham, Berlin: Weidmann, vol. 13, pp. 261–2.

23. John Stuart Mill (1846) *A System of Logic*, VI.10.5, New York: Harper.

24. Giuseppe Mazzini (1972) *Dei doveri dell'uomo*, in *Scritti politici*, ed. Terenzio Grandi and Augusto Comba, Turin: UTET, p. 884.

25. 'Per esservi nazionalità bisogna che non frappongasi ostacolo di sorta alla libera manifestazione dell volontà collettiva, e che veruno interesse prevalga all'interesse universale, quindi non può scompagnarsi dallle piena e assoluta libertà, né ammettere classi privilegiate, o dinastie, o individui la cui volontà, attesi gli ordini sociali, debba assolutamente prevalare: è nazionalità quella che godesi sotto il giogo d'un assoluto sovrano?' – Carlo Pisacane (n.d.) *La Rivoluzione*, in Franco della Peruta (ed.) *Scrittori politici dell'Ottocento*, vol. 1, Milan and Naples, p. 1181; see also p. 1184: 'Col dispotismo non v'è nazionalità, qualunque lingua parli il tiranno, qualunque sia il luogo dove ebbe i natali.'

26. *Mazzini's Letters* (1979), ed. Bolton King, Westport, Conn., p. 16.

CHAPTER FOURTEEN

Patriotism is Not Enough[1]

MARGARET CANOVAN

Introduction

A national identity which is not based predominantly on republican self-understanding and constitutional patriotism necessarily collides with the universalist rules of mutual coexistence for human beings. (Jürgen Habermas)[2]

The title of this chapter alludes to the words of Edith Cavell, the British matron of a Red Cross hospital in German-occupied Belgium during the First World War. Arrested in 1915 and shot for helping to smuggle wounded British and Allied soldiers out of the country, she became a convenient symbol of British heroism and Hunnish brutality. But Nurse Cavell had also cared for wounded German soldiers, making no national distinctions in her devotion to those in need of help. Her last words, widely reported, were, 'I realize that patriotism is not enough. I must have no hatred or bitterness towards anyone.' She therefore became for many in the post-war period a symbol of revulsion *against* patriotism in the sense of an exclusive and militaristic loyalty to one part of humanity.

I begin by invoking this ambiguous figure, symbol both of heroic patriotism and of the ideal of universal humanity, because my subject is the tense and ambiguous relationship between patriotism and universalism. For most of the twentieth century, Western political philosophy was dominated by universalist principles and unsympathetic to the claims of particular, limited loyalties. But in the past decade or so there has been a novel and interesting development. An increasing number of political thinkers with internationalist sympathies have begun to defend a form of patriotism, understood as something decisively different from nationalism. This chapter will undertake a critical examination of this new form of patriotism, sometimes called 'constitutional' or 'post-national' patriotism. I shall argue that despite its attractions the notion is open to a number of objections. I shall conclude (though my point will be different from Cavell's) that patriotism is indeed not enough.

Why Do Some Universalists Defend Patriotism?

In view of patriotism's association with war and enmity, it may seem strange that any political theorist with universalist sympathies should advocate it. During the past half-century, internationalists have more often been wary of any kind of partial solidarity that might divert people from a sense of their common humanity. But although that suspicion continues to be powerfully voiced,[3] there has recently been a perceptible change of mood. Developments in theory and in practice have combined to make political theorists more aware of the attractions of particular loyalties. One reason for this is the impact of communitarianism in political philosophy. Communitarians have pointed out that the abstract and apparently rootless individuals who figure in much liberal political philosophy do not correspond to real human beings, to whom matters of communal identity, heritage and loyalty are vitally important.[4] A number of political philosophers have taken such arguments as a foundation on which to build more or less qualified defences of nationalism.[5]

Alongside those theoretical arguments, practical politics has turned the spotlight more dramatically on to matters of identity and loyalty. For one of the most striking recent political developments has been the resurgence of national claims and conflicts. That is not in itself an argument against universalist political theory: on the contrary, confronted by events in the Balkans and elsewhere, many internationalist liberals have been confirmed in their belief that nationalism is in all circumstances an evil, to be transcended by concentrating on universal human rights. But others have drawn a different and more complicated conclusion. For them, the lesson is that (at any rate for the present) the grand ideal of universal human community is too ambitious, being too distant to mobilize popular support. People may be able to extend their sympathies to take in their compatriots, but few of them are capable of consistent solidarity with the entire human race.[6] It follows that if one is appalled by nationalist conflicts and 'ethnic cleansing', if one is concerned for minority rights and multicultural harmony, then denunciations of nationalism are not enough. It is necessary also to theorize and foster an alternative form of loyalty that will be compatible with universal values but will be able to attract the people of a particular territory, perhaps as a stage on the way to world citizenship.[7]

The conceptions of patriotism currently being developed by a number of political theorists are intended to fill this gap: to describe a form of loyalty different from and superior to nationalism, but able (in the words of Maurizio Viroli) 'to fight nationalism on its own ground'.[8] This reformulated patriotism is offered (to quote Viroli again) as an 'antidote' to nationalism, sufficiently akin to it to attract popular loyalty, but sufficiently different to be compatible with respect for universal human rights and to be more tolerant of ethnic and cultural differences. Clearly, current thinking about patriotism, and particularly the attempt to establish a distinction between 'patriotism', which is desirable, and 'nationalism', which is not, is more than a matter of intellectual curiosity. It also represents a rhetorical[9] and political strategy. This in itself should prompt us to look rather carefully at what we are being offered.

Patriotism versus Nationalism

What is it, then, that is supposed to differentiate 'patriotism' (which is desirable) from 'nationalism' (which is not)? As we shall see later, the distinction is used in subtly different ways to express a range of views, but for the sake of clarity it can be stated in ideal-typical form. The central claim is that patriotism means the political loyalty of citizens to the free polity they share, whereas nationalism is a matter of ethnicity and culture.[10] Whereas nationhood is taken to be a 'pre-political' matter depending on ties of birth and blood, the bond that unites citizens in a patriotic polity is a matter of will, the free consent of citizens united by their commitment to liberal democratic principles. The distinction is among other things a contrast between art and nature.[11] Its defenders point out that republican political thought from the ancient Greeks to the French Revolution conceived of free polities as human foundations, deliberately built, whereas the post-revolutionary romantic nationalists introduced a deterministic model of national polities growing organically out of the nation's blood and soil.

According to its advocates, the distinction has particular relevance for a modern world in which matters of ethnic identity are increasingly politicized, but in which the economic and demographic realities of globalization contradict the traditional nationalist ideal that each nation should have its own state. Faced with the problems of holding multicultural societies together in harmonious tolerance, supporters claim that patriotic loyalty to the principles and practices of a free state can provide a functional substitute for nationalism, with all its advantages by way of mobilizing loyalty, but none of its disadvantages. Unlike nationalism (it is argued), patriotism is not exclusive, uncritical or bellicose, and is therefore compatible with commitments to universal humanity. Unlike nationalism, patriotism does not expect or demand ethnic and cultural homogeneity, and is therefore tolerant of diversity.[12]

This is a composite portrait of a 'new patriotism' which has not so far undergone much theoretical elaboration. It is important because it chimes in well with a prevailing intellectual mood, but there are some difficulties in coming to grips with it. Not only are we concerned with a variety of statements by writers who have their own preoccupations; more interestingly, this new discourse of 'patriotism' covers a spectrum between positions that differ a good deal. At one end of the spectrum, heavily influenced by Kantian liberalism and most closely approximated by Jürgen Habermas, lies what I

278

shall call 'cosmopolitan constitutional patriotism', the vision of a new form of loyalty to a new, supra-national polity.[13] This is balanced at the other end by what I shall call 'rooted republicanism', best represented by Maurizio Viroli's book *For Love of Country*. Drawing on the classical republican tradition of patriotism, which was displaced by nationalism from about 1800,[14] this version focuses on loyalty to one's own particular polity, but calls for this to be interpreted in terms of freedom rather than ethnicity.[15]

In practice, none of the theorists concerned can be located at any fixed point on this spectrum between Kantian universalism and classical republicanism, for there is a good deal of shifting back and forth in the middle ground. For example, although Viroli aims at a revival of patriotism in particular free polities and sets out explicitly to recover classical republican values, his reading of the republican tradition is censored by his modern liberal humanitarian and cosmopolitan conscience, and by revulsion against Italy's Fascist past. As a result, the stridently chauvinist and militaristic nature of classical patriotism drops out of view.[16] At the other end of the spectrum, too, appearances can be misleading, for Jürgen Habermas's apparently abstract and universalizable 'constitutional patriotism' is traceable to a very specific situation and a particular national history, raising questions about its wider relevance. The German term *Verfassungspatriotismus* was coined to denote attachment to the liberal democratic institutions of the post-war Federal Republic of Germany. Patriotism in those circumstances meant loyalty to a polity that was non-nationalist or even *anti*-nationalist in its structure. It was a truncated state, including only part of the nation, with a set of liberal democratic institutions imposed from without and designed to run counter to the political traditions predominant in Germany for the previous century. Furthermore, the Nazi past made the whole topic of loyalty (patriotic or nationalist) uniquely sensitive. Behind Habermas's abstract formulations, in other words, lies an attempt quite as specific as Viroli's to influence the political identity of a particular polity.[17]

One reason for the blurring between republican and liberal influences on the one hand, and cosmopolitan and local aims on the other, is that all concerned form a united front against a common enemy: ethnic nationalism. Another reason is that as well as sharing an enemy they share a model. The United States is frequently cited by new patriots as an example of a non-national polity held together by patriotism, and different aspects can be stressed according to taste: its classical republican elements or the liberal principles built into its constitution; its unique heritage or its universal significance as a gathering-place for immigrants from all ethnic groups. Later on we shall consider reasons for doubting the suitability of the United States as a model, at any rate for the more cosmopolitan versions of new patriotism. But the existence of this all-purpose example does much to bolster the plausibility of new patriotism's anti-nationalist discourse.

In order to deal with this rather amorphous discourse, I shall concentrate most critical attention on the end of the spectrum where the most ambitious claims are located, that is to say on the notion of a universalistic and universalizable 'constitutional patriotism'. Having looked at its problems, I shall turn to the other end of the spectrum, where we can find the more modest position identified here as 'rooted republicanism'. I shall argue that although this is more defensible, it cannot actually solve the problem to which it is addressed.

Cosmopolitan Constitutional Patriotism

Although the terminology of 'constitutional patriotism' arose out of the unusual circumstances of post-war West Germany, the notion has been generalized by Habermas, who suggests in his 1990 essay 'Citizenship and National Identity' that multicultural and multinational societies might be unified at the level of politics by a liberal political culture supported by a *'constitutional* patriotism'. Patriotism of this kind, he says, gives its loyalty to the universal principles and practices of democracy and human rights. He concedes that in a future Federal Republic of Europe, 'the *same* legal principles would also have to be interpreted from the perspectives of *different* national traditions and histories', but adds that

> One's own tradition must in each case be appropriated from a vantage point relativized by the perspectives of other traditions, and appropriated in such a manner that it can be brought into a transnational, Western European constitutional culture. A particularist anchoring of *this kind* would not do away with one iota of the universalist meaning of popular sovereignty and human rights. The original thesis stands: democratic citizenship need not be rooted in the national identity of a people. However, regardless of the diversity of different cultural forms of life, it does require that every citizen be socialized into a common political culture.[18]

Perhaps characteristically, Habermas's discussion is complex, qualified and somewhat opaque. Those influenced by him tend to be less cautious, and a useful expansion of these ideas has been offered by the Irish philosopher Attracta Ingram.[19] In an essay entitled 'Constitutional Patriotism', she observes:

> The idea of post-national identity is of a political identity founded on recognition of democratic values and human rights as these are contextualized in a particular constitutional tradition. Citizens are thought of as bound to each other by subscription to these shared values rather than by the more traditional pre-political ties that nation-states have drawn on as sources of unity. ...
>
> A post-national identity has to accommodate difference and plurality. So it has to be an identity in which membership is constituted by recognition of a common system of authority erected and maintained by a constitution. Unity

and legitimacy come from the constitution and the formal tie that holds people together is their continuing voluntary recognition of the constitution, their constitutional patriotism.[20]

Both Habermas and Ingram connect constitutional patriotism with hopes for the transcendence of existing nation-states. Besides looking towards supra-national citizenship and constitutional patriotism at the level of the European Union, Habermas speaks of this as a stage on the way to 'world citizenship'.[21] Ingram suggests that 'it may well be feasible and desirable to build political identities that overarch several national identities', and develops a Kantian argument according to which liberal states actually have a duty to unite with their neighbours and extend the area within which peace and political justice can be enjoyed.[22]

There is in both cases a certain lack of clarity about the relation between these universalist projects and the particular polities and specific political identities that exist. Ingram makes greater concessions to particularism, suggesting that a common set of liberal democratic values can be customized within particular traditions: 'Our particular identity is constituted by *our* effort to institutionalize principles of justice. And that effort has a different history and a different shape in different bounded communities.'[23] We shall need to return later to those tell-tale possessive pronouns ('our', along with 'we' and 'us'), for although they help to give plausibility to the project of constitutional patriotism, they also signal far-reaching confusions about the implications of collective political identity. For the moment, however, let us concentrate on the vision of a post-national polity united by this new sort of loyalty. It is not difficult to understand its attraction, for in it the conflicting demands of universal liberal principles and particularistic communities appear to be satisfied. In what follows I shall argue that this triumph is illusory, for a number of reasons:

1   The project of avoiding the illiberal effects of nationalism by basing the state upon shared liberal values is self-defeating.
2   The claim that citizens can share loyalty to the polity rather than to their nation begs vital questions about the state.
3   The cases cited to show the plausibility of this kind of patriotism do not in fact do so.
4   The notion that constitutional patriotism can provide a substitute for ties of birth and blood is incoherent.

Criticisms of Cosmopolitan Constitutional Patriotism

The Civic Faith

In their concern to replace the bond of nationhood with something less visceral and exclusive, constitutional patriots often suggest that citizens are better bound together by shared principles or values: for Habermas, a loyalty to 'abstract procedures and principles'[24] that amounts to a shared political culture into which every citizen will need to be socialized.[25] Despite the Kantian inspiration of constitutional patriotism, this acceptance of the need for deliberate political socialization echoes much older classical republican traditions. For unlike romantic nationalists (who believed that citizens of a true nation-state belong together by nature), earlier republicans always thought of polities and their citizens as creatures of artifice. Citizens were formed through patriotic education, and republicans were prepared to go to disconcerting lengths to achieve this. Adrian Oldfield, undertaking an 'exploration of what it would mean to take civic republicanism seriously in the modern world', observes that many of its aspects would be unpalatable to modern liberals, for the appropriate civic education means that 'minds have to be manipulated'.[26]

That may seem a rather highly coloured description of what constitutional patriots would see as inculcation of universal truths. But it underlines the point that if shared political principles are actually to become the unifying bond of the state, then the principles in question must be authoritatively agreed and serious efforts must be made to inculcate them into the citizens. Just as earlier generations of political theorists took for granted that states had an interest in the religious beliefs of their citizens, so the patriotic polity seems also to be envisaged as a kind of confessional state.

Constitutional patriots may object that such socialization is not only politically necessary but philosophically justifiable, since the 'common political culture' is built upon the universal principles of democracy and human rights, which Habermas evidently regards as being of a kind to which 'all who are possibly affected could assent as participants in rational discourse.'[27] But the difficulties of achieving practical consensus on such principles should not be underestimated. Although the patriotic project is hailed by its advocates as an answer to the problems of increasingly multiethnic and multicultural societies, it may be precisely in such societies that dissent from liberal democratic principles is likely to occur.[28] Religious minorities are particularly liable to find themselves in disagreement with liberal orthodoxy. Such tensions are symbolized by the French 'affair of the headscarves', the controversy caused by Muslim schoolgirls whose determination to cover their heads was taken to conflict with the republican principles of secularism expressed within that vital agency of political socialization, the state school system.[29] French experience is relevant here because the French republican version of nationalism has a good deal in common with constitutional patriotism.[30]

Loyalty to principles, then, may not necessarily be an improvement on national loyalty as a basis for a multicultural polity. But some constitutional patriots may object that this discussion of beliefs misses the point: that despite talk of 'principles' by Habermas and others, what is crucial is a more practical loyalty to the constitution itself, in other words shared allegiance to the institutions and procedures of a liberal democratic state.[31] The important thing is that citizens should share a polity without sharing a nation. Unfortunately this version of the patriotic project also has flaws, as I hope to show in the next subsection.

Whose State Is It?

Build a liberal democratic state that protects the rights of all its people and welcomes them on equal terms into a shared public arena, and national or ethnic differences can be transcended in what Habermas has called an 'abstract, legally mediated solidarity among strangers'.[32] Theoretical aspirations of this kind translate into visions of a future United States of Europe, of a non-sectarian polity of all Ireland, even of solutions to more intractable conflicts in the Balkans and further afield. Notice that this ideal goes well beyond more pragmatic schemes for coping democratically with the tensions between potentially hostile groups. In the face of communal conflicts in many parts of the world, a variety of ingenious constitutional arrangements have been devised to induce such groups to accept accommodation rather than confrontation, and some such attempts have been successful: the latest (its fate still in the balance at the time of writing) is the 1998 Good Friday Agreement in Northern Ireland. The hallmark of such arrangements is that communal divisions and mutual suspicions are not expected to go away, but the institutional mechanisms are designed to reward political bargaining rather than violence. Approaching the problems of South Africa in this spirit, Donald Horowitz speaks of 'harnessing self-interest to the cause of peace', stressing that his approach 'does not seek or need to change hearts or minds in order to succeed'.[33] Going beyond that kind of *modus vivendi*, constitutional patriots have higher hopes, aiming to lift individuals above their ascriptive identities into a shared public sphere where all are equal citizens with a shared loyalty to an impartial state.

The trouble with this appealing vision is its circularity. Supposing that a polity really does live up to Habermasian standards; then its citizens may seem to have such an obvious interest in supporting it that they may perhaps be expected to give it their loyalty regardless of national ties that pull them in a different direction.[34] But a polity needs to be strong and well integrated to be able to manifest those liberal virtues, and the states that come nearest to the ideal are in fact underpinned by something too easily taken for granted: a 'people', a trans-generational political community, members of which recognize the state as 'our' state and thereby confer upon it the legitimacy and power it needs.[35] The history of Northern Ireland illustrates the difficulties where this cannot be taken for granted. For Catholics, the state has historically not been 'ours' but 'theirs', and its corresponding lack of legitimacy has gravely weakened its authority and power, hampering attempts at impartiality in recent decades. The vicious circle is that a state is unlikely to be powerful enough to demonstrate the liberal democratic virtues that can attract constitutional patriotism unless it is very widely regarded by its population as 'our' state rather than someone else's. Those who support patriotism against nationalism as a unifying bond dodge such questions of power and legitimacy, tending to assume that 'the modern state' *per se* will deserve the loyalty of its subjects, even if they are not bound to it by ties of nationhood.[36] But many actually existing states are feeble or unworthy of loyalty, while those that are powerful and most like the Habermasian model are overwhelmingly nation-states, the possession of a specific historic people. The institutions of the European Union are notoriously weak precisely because they lack that tie to a 'people'.[37] The claim that an impartial state can form a benign umbrella soaring above rival national or ethnic identities and attracting patriotic loyalty ignores the most crucial political question, namely where is the state to draw its power from? What holds up the umbrella?[38]

Misleading Examples

Constitutional patriots may respond by pointing to a small number of effective states which (they claim) prove their point that nationalism can be replaced by constitutional patriotism. The implication is that if this can be done successfully in one place, it should also be possible in others. Post-war West Germany, where the language of *Verfassungspatriotismus* was coined, is held by Attracta Ingram to show 'that a further uncoupling of state and nation is empirically feasible'.[39] But there is room for scepticism here. A more plausible conclusion to be drawn from German experience would be that this apparent 'uncoupling' was misleading, and that behind the handful of constitutional patriots who talked about the nature of their loyalty were a great many German nationalists who did not.[40] When the opportunity for unification arrived, the political significance of that tacit identity became apparent. West Germans took for granted that they had a collective responsibility for the people of the German Democratic Republic (and not, of course, for Poles, Czechs, Hungarians and so on). Whatever the subsequent disillusionment in both parts of Germany, the power generated in 1989 by the sense of being '*Ein Volk*' was enough to transform the map of Europe.[41] The German example therefore tends to undermine rather than to support the new patriots' case. But what of the two prize exhibits always cited in this connection, Switzerland and the United States of America?[42] Do not they support the case for constitutional patriotism, demonstrating that loyalties that are political and universalistic can be constructed to hold together a multinational or multicultural society? I will try to suggest briefly why these examples should be treated with caution.

Within the Swiss Confederation, German, French, Italian and Romansch-speaking segments have long shared a political system and managed their disputes remarkably harmoniously. Indeed, the Swiss political scientist Wolf Linder claims that his country 'provides a model for finding political institutions and patterns of behaviour that enable peaceful conflict resolution in a multicultural society'. It turns out, however, that the Swiss experience is not as encouraging as it might seem. For, as Linder goes on to point out, success in this field requires a lot more than a set of well-designed institutions, let alone a set of universal principles. 'Democracy and peaceful conflict-resolution ... need the social development of a political culture. Unlike technical innovation, this takes a long time to develop.' [43] Although Swiss political institutions owe a good deal to deliberate design, their success has had at least as much to do with special circumstances and a highly contingent series of historical events. One important point is that the component parts of Switzerland are deeply rooted communities defined by birth and blood as well as geography. These have grown together in the course of a shared history, producing a strong sense of pride in distinctive Swissness, but local autonomy and local loyalties continue to be strong. The deeply historical and contingent character of Swiss unity gives little support to the project of cosmopolitan constitutional patriotism, and this unique polity might be better considered a candidate for the category of 'rooted republicanism' we shall be considering later.

The United States is a more plausible example, in that its political identity is indeed inextricably intertwined with the Constitution, and even with the political principles this articulates. To quote Benjamin Barber, 'The American trick was to use the fierce attachments of patriotic sentiment to bond a people to high ideals.'[44] This unusually ideological understanding of what it is to be American has no doubt helped the country to cope relatively successfully with immigration from all round the globe.[45] In one of the most eloquent defences of patriotism as distinguished from nationalism, John Schaar has analysed its specifically American form, finding in the speeches of Abraham Lincoln what he calls a 'covenanted patriotism', 'actively guided by and directed toward the mission established in the founding covenant'. To adopt it is to accept one's inheritance from the Founding Fathers and one's obligation to carry on their work. According to Schaar, 'This conception of political membership ... decisively transcends the parochial and primitive fraternities of blood and race, for it calls kin all who accept the authority of the covenant.'[46]

It is easy to see why cosmopolitan liberals reacting against European experiences of nationalism might wish to emulate this kind of patriotism. But we should think twice before accepting the claim that it amounts to a non-national form of loyalty. For it does not really mean a gathering of all those across the world who are willing to commit themselves to Lincoln's principles. In the same breath as speaking of transcending those 'primitive fraternities of blood', Schaar articulates an almost Roman sense of ancestral piety towards the inherited 'mission established in the founding covenant'. The point is that the principles of the Constitution are not just liberal principles but (for Americans) 'our' principles, handed down to us by our forefathers, biological or adopted.[47] To think of the United States as a society bound together by constitutional patriotism rather than by nationhood is to overlook inheritance – inheritance not only of citizenship, but of the Constitution, the principles, the national mission, the American Way of Life. Despite immigration in each generation, most Americans are so not because they willingly accept the Constitution, but because being American is in their blood. For many, this is an inheritance of only one or two generations' depth, and if the United States were a less powerful and less prosperous country, their simultaneous inheritance of diverse ethnic ancestries might pose greater political problems. But the fact remains that, like other nations, Americans are defined and united primarily by birth and inheritance,[48] and it is to these neglected considerations that we must now turn.

Ours by Right of Birth

As we have seen, some new patriots believe that they have discovered a form of solidarity founded upon acceptance by citizens of a liberal democratic constitution. Stressing the political links between individuals, they give the impression that 'subscription to shared values' and 'voluntary recognition of the Constitution' can be disconnected from the 'pre-political ties' thought to be characteristic of nation-states,[49] and thereby brought into harmony with 'the universalist rules of mutual coexistence for human beings'.[50] But this appealing vision owes its plausibility to a tacit reservation that undermines universalist aspirations. For despite the liberal language of individual commitments and abstract legal status, constitutional patriots (like everyone else) take for granted the existence of historic political communities, and therefore that the populations whom they seek to bind with political loyalties already owe their common citizenship to the most fundamental of 'pre-political' ties: familial inheritance. To the vast majority of citizens, even the most Habermasian polity is 'ours' because it was our parents' before us. One of the main purposes of the discourse of 'constitutional patriotism' is of course to play down this obvious point and to lay stress on the kinds of solidarity that settled populations can share with the increasing number of immigrants in their midst. But this leads Habermas and others to exaggerate the contrast between supposedly 'pre-political' ties of birth on the one hand and political relations between citizens on the other. Despite its prominence in the discourse, this dichotomy is in fact so implausible that even constitutional patriots themselves do not consistently stick to it. The confusion involved can perhaps be illustrated through a *reductio ad absurdum* on a Habermasian theme: citizenship of that purportedly post-national entity, the European Union.

European citizenship (something envied and desired by a great many people, especially in North Africa and Eastern Europe) is at present a secondary status added on to national citizenship within one of the component states. Some of these states are more generous than others in admitting immigrants to citizenship, but in all cases the vast majority of citizens simply inherit their status from their parents: it comes to them as a matter of birth, like a title to family property. Now imagine that 'pre-political ties' were really to be devalued in favour of 'voluntary recognition of the Constitution'. Why should being born into a family of European citizens – a Spanish family, say, or a British family, or a German family – give one a privileged claim on European citizenship? Would not considerations of equal human rights imply that one should take one's chance alongside applicants from Albania and Algeria, from Slovakia and Sudan, perhaps by taking a competitive examination at the age of 18 to determine which of the applicants showed greatest understanding of and devotion to the Constitution?

There may be some internationalists prepared to defend such an arrangement in principle, on the grounds that it is morally repugnant for rights to depend on the lottery of birth.[51] So far as I am aware, however, none of the theorists attracted by constitutional patriotism has advocated such an arrangement, and it is clear that despite their rejection of 'pre-political ties' they take for granted (just as nationalists do) that citizenship is part of the ancestral endowment that makes 'us' a 'people' in collective possession of a polity.[52] Since constitutional patriots know very well that fusion of 'political' and supposedly 'pre-political' ties is inseparable from the continuing existence of a democratic polity, why are they so reluctant to acknowledge this? The explanation lies, I believe, in a fear of racism that makes them gloss over the political significance of family membership and present us with a false dichotomy. We are warned that unless the polity is understood as a community of liberal patriots, constituted and bound together by the individual choice of its members, then it must be a 'nation' defined by a particular kind of supposedly pure blood. Either we insist on a non-national, patriotic polity to which birthright is irrelevant, or we open the door to a national polity understood in racist terms.

But this analysis of the alternatives is misleading. The fact is that any polity, however liberal its ethos, is and must be an inheritance passed on from generation to generation. Indeed, one of the best recipes for a stable liberal democracy is a widespread sense among the population that the polity is a collective inheritance belonging to a 'people'.[53] Whether or not that 'people' is conceived in terms of theories about genetic make-up is a separate issue, but the crucial significance of collective political inheritance is undeniable, and is implicitly conceded by the constitutional patriots themselves. As we saw earlier, Attracta Ingram falls back on collective pronouns (as in 'our political identity', 'our distinct political heritage', 'the constitution we made and continue to remake through the generations')[54] that reveal assumptions about the existence of political collectivities inherited through families. Even

Habermas, while arguing for a 'liberal immigration policy' that would pave the way for world citizenship, concedes 'the right to preserve one's own *political* culture',[55] a formulation which assumes that the liberal democratic polity to which immigrants are seeking entry belongs initially to those who inherit it by right of birth. For the new patriots, in other words, just as for nationalists, the (supposedly non-national) 'people' is constituted and bound together primarily by birth. As we observed in the US case, even if such a 'people' welcomes immigrants into citizenship, the newly naturalized citizens themselves pass on their membership of the people to their children in the traditional manner. It is misleading for new patriots to assert that their polity can dispense with 'pre-political' ties. But this raises a further question. Must 'the people' who inherit the polity form a 'nation'? Is it not possible for the inherited bonds that unite them to their political heritage and to one another to be patriotic without being national? That is the claim explicitly made by another group of new patriots, those I have referred to as 'rooted republicans'.

Rooted Republicanism

Even within the discourse of the new patriotism, the Habermasian version has come in for criticism on the grounds that it is too abstract and too ambitious.[56] Conceding the arguments advanced above, such critics might maintain that the real strength of the discourse lies with those who set themselves a more limited task, counterposing to nationalism a type of patriotism drawing on the classical tradition of love for one's own inherited polity. The most prominent spokesman for this strand in the discourse, Maurizio Viroli, advocates a 'patriotism of liberty' that is explicitly particularistic, but nevertheless free of illiberal characteristics because it is a 'patriotism without nationalism'.[57] This sort of patriotism has two particularly salient characteristics. In the first place, although it may arise out of 'ethnocultural unity', it is a 'political culture of liberty' which puts its stress squarely upon the republican tradition of active citizenship and civic virtue.[58] Second, and in consequence of this, it is a critical love of country, dedicated to making sure that one's polity lives up to its highest traditions and ideals, if necessary at the cost of unity.[59]

These are attractive sentiments: the obvious question they raise, however, is why they should be regarded as exclusively patriotic rather than national. It is interesting that Stephen Nathanson, who argues in favour of what he calls a 'moderate patriotism' that would be 'worthy of support by morally conscientious people', does not make a sharp distinction between (good) patriotism and (bad) nationalism, observing instead that each of them comes in different versions, some acceptable to modern liberals and some not.[60] It is hard to avoid the suspicion that the sharp distinction offered by new patriots has more to do with rhetorical impact than with cool analysis, and that it is convenient to call particularistic sentiments one approves of 'patriotism', while heaping all the blame on to nationalism, 'patriotism's bloody brother'.[61] In Viroli's account, for example, nationalism is taken to mean 'unconditional loyalty or an exclusive attachment', contrasted with the 'charitable and generous love' of country that is patriotism.[62] When an example of nationalism seems to show liberal characteristics, it turns out to have been patriotism all along.[63] This propensity to blacken the name of nationalism goes along with an inclination to play down the more illiberal aspects of patriotism. Either these are admitted *sotto voce*,[64] or else they are dismissed with the implication that bad patriotism is virtually equivalent to nationalism.[65]

The weakness of the 'rooted republican' version of the new patriotism is therefore that it trades on a caricature of nationalism as a bigoted and racist commitment to ethnic and cultural homogeneity. That caricature ignores the huge complexity of national loyalties, the differences between different national traditions and changes within specific traditions over time. This is not the place to explore those complexities,[66] except to point out that while there is plenty of evidence of racist versions of nationalism (as of chauvinist versions of patriotism), there is also a long-standing association between some nationalisms and liberal democracy.[67] The most distinguished recent defender of liberal nationalism, David Miller, denies that national loyalty has to imply ethnic or cultural homogeneity, and envisages an open-minded, inclusive national political culture that seems virtually indistinguishable from Viroli's conception of patriotism.[68]

It is relevant here that (to quote David Miller) 'national identities are not cast in stone'.[69] One reason for the convergence between the more liberal recent statements of nationalism and the more particularistic versions of new patriotism is that (at any rate among Western intellectuals, though not among militants elsewhere) nationalist discourse has been shifting further away from the nineteenth-century Romantic conception of nations as natural entities, towards the belief that nations are (in Benedict Anderson's indispensable phrase) 'imagined communities'.[70] A charge traditionally raised against nationalism is that it teaches the false doctrine that human beings are naturally divided into separate (and probably unequal) nations. But sophisticated nationalists have recognized for a long time that their nations are in fact contingent outcomes of historical events, and that the sense of naturalness is largely mythical, part of the way in which nations are imagined. The understanding of nations as 'imagined communities' is currently attracting attention not only because it chimes in well with the post-modern sense of the shifting, kaleidoscopic quality of 'reality', but also because if nationhood is something imagined, then (so its supporters often believe) it can be reimagined in a more palatable form. Instead of trying to replace national identities with patriotic loyalties, therefore, some political theorists moved by very similar concerns are suggesting the reinvention of existing national identities to make them more consonant with liberal concerns. The implication of this may seem to be that the new patriots are actually pushing at an open door: that their fear of nationalism is exaggerated and their concern to distinguish patriotism from it unnecessary, since nationalism can itself be reinvented in a form that all good liberals can endorse. But any such conclusion would be simplistic, for two reasons. In the first place, political identities cannot be made to order; and in the second place, even if they could be, that would still not solve the dilemmas of liberal patriots.

On the first point, some writers suppose that (as Richard Kearney says) 'nations and states are of our own making and can be *remade* according to other images'.[71] But this reasoning involves the fallacy (pointed out by Hannah Arendt) of mistaking 'action' for 'work'.[72] As Arendt showed, politics is not a matter of moulding passive material. Free politics means action engaged in by plural actors, and no one can control or predict its outcome. Encouraging citizens to debate matters of common identity[73] *may* generate more enlightened and cosmopolitan views, but it could just as well provide opportunities for populist mobilization that might reinforce entrenched conceptions of 'us' and 'them', or lead to reimagined identities of an even less palatable kind. The increasing success in Western Europe and elsewhere of political parties hostile to immigration is a reminder of these possibilities. Faced with the wilderness of contingency that is the real world of politics, liberals cannot find a short cut to universal harmony through new concepts of patriotism or nationalism.

Suppose, however (to move on to our second problem), that we really *could* remould a political identity within a given territory to conform to the best new patriotic or civic nationalist model: would that solve the problem we started from? Remember that our problem was the tension between particular loyalties and universal principles. In the uncompromisingly cosmopolitan words of Martha Nussbaum,

> To count people as moral equals is to treat nationality, ethnicity, religion, class, race, and gender as 'morally irrelevant' – as irrelevant to that equal standing.
> ... What I am saying about politics is that we should view the equal worth of all human beings as a regulative constraint on our political actions and aspirations.[74]

Traditionally it was in warfare that patriotism clashed most stridently with such commitments: the soldier could not treat his country's friends and enemies as moral equals.[75] It is highly characteristic of the new discourse of patriotism (bearing witness to changed political conditions in the West) that the military concerns that loomed so large in the past have almost dropped out of view. The first duty of patriots is no longer to lay down their life for their country; in the eyes of new patriots it may instead be to campaign actively to make that country live up to its pretensions by respecting human rights. But the demilitarization of borders in many parts of the developed world does not overcome the tension between particular and universal commitments and loyalties. Instead, a dramatic new source of conflict (still focused upon borders) has replaced the old one: immigration and the problem of its limits. Given the never-ending streams of would-be immigrants to prosperous parts of the world such as the United States and the European Union, there is an apparently irreconcilable contradiction between universalist humanitarianism on the one hand, and commitment on the other to the persistence of a polity (national or patriotic) belonging to a privileged subsection of humankind – 'our people'.[76] New patriotism does nothing to help solve this dilemma. As we saw, even the most apparently cosmopolitan constitutional patriotism does not alter the fundamental truth that citizenship is first and foremost an inherited privilege, and must be so if a democratic body politic is to be able to persist.

Conclusion

Despite the claims made for it, new patriotism does not provide a coherent solution to the problem of reconciling universal humanitarian principles with limited and particularistic political commitments, and has no advantages in this respect over nationalism of the more liberal sort.[77] The dilemmas to which it is addressed do not yield to philosophical solutions, and can be managed only by more or less messy political compromises. That said, there is no doubt that the discourse of new patriotism can on occasion aid such political compromises, and may in some circumstances make up in political effectiveness for its deficiencies in philosophical cogency. It is evident (as I suggested earlier) that variants of this discourse have been elaborated and adopted at least in part for rhetorical reasons, as political moves intended to gather support for liberal humanitarian commitments. Consciously or not, its supporters are employing the traditional tactics of the rhetorician, such as using familiar terms in altered senses, redescribing the political situation and shifting the battle lines to maximize support for their own position.[78] The German discourse of *Verfassungspatriotismus*, for example, should be seen as a way of managing tensions between traditional understandings of national loyalty and the post-war constitutional arrangements of the Federal Republic. As a rhetorical response to that situation it seems to have been quite successful, partly no doubt because its local resonances were decently clothed in the language of unpolitical generality. Habermasian abstraction can make it possible to talk about highly specific problems while apparently not talking about them.

There is nothing particularly unusual about this situation, for it is in the nature of political thinking to be on the one hand the elaboration of a general theoretical position and on the other a move in a political game.[79] Furthermore, it sometimes happens that arguments that are intellectually weak are rhetorically effective and politically constructive. The large issues raised by the overlaps and tensions between political rhetoric and philosophical argument cannot be discussed here. Faced with the discourse of new patriotism, however, it is possible to sympathize with the intentions it embodies (and even to commend its use as a political strategy in some circumstances) while still concluding that as a coherent theoretical solution to the problems its adherents claim to confront, patriotism is not enough.

Notes

1. This chapter previously appeared in 1999 in the *British Journal of Political Science* 29, 699–718, published by Cambridge University Press. Earlier versions were presented at the Universities of Keele and Exeter, and at the Universidad Autónoma de Madrid. I am particularly indebted for the comments of John Horton, David Miller, Albert Weale and the referees of the *BJPS*.

2. Jürgen Habermas, 'D-Mark Nationalism', *Die Zeit*, 30 March 1990, reprinted in R.T. Gray and S. Wilke (eds) *German Unification and Its Discontents: Documents from the Peaceful Revolution*, Seattle: University of Washington Press, 1996, pp. 186–205 at p. 198.

3. See, for example, Martha Nussbaum (1996) 'Patriotism and Cosmopolitanism', printed with sixteen responses in Martha C. Nussbaum and Joshua Cohen, *For Love of Country: Debating the Limits of Patriotism*, Boston: Beacon Press, pp. 2–17.

4. Charles Taylor (1989) 'Cross-Purposes: The Liberal Communitarian Debate', in Nancy L. Rosenblum (ed.) *Liberalism and the Moral Life*, Cambridge, MA: Harvard University Press; Alasdair MacIntyre (1984) 'Is Patriotism a Virtue?', The E.H. Lindley Memorial Lecture, Lawrence: University of Kansas.

5. David Miller (1995) *On Nationality*, Oxford: Oxford University Press; Yael Tamir (1993) *Liberal Nationalism*, Princeton, NJ: Princeton University Press; Neil MacCormick (1991) 'Is Nationalism Philosophically Credible?', in William Twining (ed.) *Issues of Self-Determination*, Aberdeen: Aberdeen University Press; Avishai Margalit and Joseph Raz (1990) 'National Self-Determination', *Journal of Philosophy* 87 (9), 439–61.

6. This point is made in many of the replies in Nussbaum *et al.*, *For Love of Country*.

7. Jürgen Habermas (1996) 'Citizenship and National Identity', incorporated as appendix II in Jürgen Habermas, *Between Facts and Norms: Contributions to a Discourse Theory of Law and Democracy*, Cambridge, MA: MIT Press, p. 514. Cf. Benjamin R. Barber (1996) 'Constitutional Faith', p. 36, and Charles Taylor (1996) 'Why Democracy Needs Patriotism', p. 121, both in Nussbaum *et al.*, *For Love of Country*.

8. Maurizio Viroli (1995) *For Love of Country: An Essay on Patriotism and Nationalism*, Oxford: Clarendon Press, p. 15. Cf. Attracta Ingram (1996) 'Constitutional Patriotism', *Philosophy and Social Criticism* 22, 1–18; Stephen Nathanson (1993) *Patriotism, Morality, and Peace*, Lanham, MD: Rowman & Littlefield; Mary G.

Dietz (1989) 'Patriotism', in Terence Ball, James Farr and Russell L. Hanson (eds) *Political Innovation and Conceptual Change*, Cambridge: Cambridge University Press. One of the earliest examples was John H. Schaar (1981) 'The Case for Patriotism', in John H. Schaar, *Legitimacy in the Modern State*, New Brunswick: Transaction Books.

9. A sharp contrast between 'patriotism' and 'nationalism' has more rhetorical impact than the more defensible claim (made, for example, by Stephen Nathanson) that there are liberal and illiberal versions of both (Nathanson, *Patriotism, Morality, and Peace*, pp. 185–6).

10. Habermas, 'Citizenship and National Identity', pp. 500, 507.

11. According to Attracta Ingram, 'constitutional patriotism ... is part of the idea that the creation of political community is a morally transformative act in which human beings develop relationships as citizens that tie them together independently of their prior associational ties to family, religion and the like' (Ingram, 'Constitutional Patriotism', p. 2. Cf. Viroli, *For Love of Country*, p. 121; Schaar, 'The Case for Patriotism', pp. 290–1; Dietz, 'Patriotism', p. 189).

12. Viroli, *For Love of Country*, pp. 1–2, 13–17, 183–5; Schaar, 'The Case for Patriotism', p. 293.

13. Habermas, 'Citizenship and National Identity', pp. 500, 514; Ingram, 'Constitutional Patriotism', p. 14.

14. Viroli and Dietz place themselves within this tradition. On the European transition (about 1800) from republican to nationalist discourses, see Martin Thom (1995) *Republics, Nations and Tribes*, London: Verso.

15. Viroli, *For Love of Country*, pp. 16, 183–4.

16. On this aspect of ancient republicanism, see Paul A. Rahe (1992) *Republics Ancient and Modern: Classical Republicanism and the American Revolution*, Chapel Hill: University of North Carolina Press. For Viroli the key feature of ancient Roman patriotism was 'compassion' (*For Love of Country*, p. 20).

17. This comes out clearly in Habermas's essay 'D-Mark Nationalism'.

18. Habermas, 'Citizenship and National Identity': all quotations in this paragraph are from p. 500, emphasis in the original. See also Jürgen Habermas (1989) *The New Conservatism: Cultural Criticism and the Historians' Debate*, Cambridge: Polity, pp. 256–61.

19. Like Habermas, Ingram comes from a national tradition that has been heavily contested.

20. Ingram, 'Constitutional Patriotism', p. 2.

21. Habermas, 'Citizenship and National Identity', pp. 507, 514. Cf. interviews with M. Haller in Jürgen Habermas (1994) *The Past as Future*, Lincoln: University of Nebraska Press, pp. 163–5.

22. Ingram, 'Constitutional Patriotism', pp. 11, 12–15.

23. *Ibid.*, p. 14.

24. Habermas, *The New Conservatism*, p. 261.

25. Habermas, *Between Facts and Norms*, pp. 500, 514. Writing more recently about 'the transition of the European Community to a democratically-constituted, federal state', Habermas has stressed again the need to deliberately forge a new kind of 'abstract, legally mediated solidarity among strangers' through the development of EU-wide political communication. His answer to the linguistic

barriers that at present stand in the way of any such shared public sphere is the promotion of English 'as a second first language'. Given Europe's existing level of integration, he maintains that, 'Given the political will, there is no *a priori* reason why it cannot subsequently create the politically necessary communicative context as soon as it is constitutionally *prepared* to do so.' (Habermas (1995) 'Comment on the Paper by Dieter Grimm: "Does Europe Need a Constitution?"', *European Law Journal* 1, 303–7, pp. 305–7, emphasis in the original).

26. Adrian Oldfield (1990) *Citizenship and Community: Civic Republicanism and the Modern World*, London: Routledge, pp. ix, 6, 146, 153, 164.

27. Habermas, *Between Facts and Norms*, p. 458.

28. The controversy generated by John Rawls's parallel attempt to articulate a strictly 'political' liberalism illustrates the difficulty of settling even on an 'overlapping consensus' that can in practice be shared by the denizens of plural societies (Rawls (1993) *Political Liberalism*, New York: Columbia University Press).

29. See Norma C. Moruzzi, (1994) 'A Problem with Headscarves: Contemporary Complexities of Political and Social Identity', *Political Theory* 22, 653–72. Precisely because the dominant French version of nationhood is strongly imbued with elements of constitutional patriotism, it may be in some respects less tolerant of multicultural difference than less principled and more untidy versions.

30. The tradition has been lucidly restated by Dominique Schnapper, who maintains that Habermasian constitutional patriotism (in so far as it is feasible at all) amounts to a belated German discovery of the true (French) idea of nationhood (Schnapper (1994) *La Communauté des citoyens: sur l'idée moderne de nation*, Paris: Gallimard, p. 182). Habermas himself evidently believes that socialization into citizenship does not imply French-style assimilation, contrasting this with US experience (Habermas, 'Comment on Grimm', p. 306). It may be objected, however, that unlike France, the United States has not yet had to face the challenge of deep ideological diversity presented by Islam.

31. Ingram, 'Constitutional Patriotism', p. 2.

32. Habermas, 'Comment on Grimm', p. 305.

33. Donald L. Horowitz, (1991) *A Democratic South Africa? Constitutional Engineering in a Divided Society*, Berkeley: University of California Press, p. 155. The large literature on constitutional engineering in divided societies contains some sharp disagreements, notably between supporters on the one hand of 'consociational' solutions that institutionalize group differences, and on the other side advocates of forms of majoritarian democracy that give politicians incentives to recruit voters across ethnic divides. For classic treatments, see Arend Lijphart (1977) *Democracy in Plural Societies: A Comparative Exploration*, New Haven, CT: Yale University Press, and Donald L. Horowitz (1985) *Ethnic Groups in Conflict*, Berkeley: University of California Press. Levels of optimism also vary, with Horowitz in particular stressing the very great difficulty of achieving stable democracy in the face of differences between ascriptive communities (Horowitz, *A Democratic South Africa?*, pp. 162, 241).

34. Even this apparently modest assumption is cast into doubt by the strength of nationalist sentiment in Scotland and Quebec, despite the relatively civilized political structures of the United Kingdom and Canada.

35. For arguments that liberal democratic political theory has regularly taken for granted the existence of that collective power without acknowledging that its basis was nationhood, see Margaret Canovan (1996) *Nationhood and Political Theory*, Cheltenham: Edward Elgar.

36. Cf. Bhikhu Parekh (1995) 'Politics of Nationhood', in Keebet von Benda-Beckmann and Maykel Verkuyten (eds) *Nationalism, Ethnicity and Cultural Identity in Europe*, Comparative Studies in Migration and Ethnic Relations I, Utrecht: European Research Centre on Migration and Ethnic Relations, pp. 139–40.

37. On the 'democratic deficit', see Jack Hayward (ed.) (1995) *The Crisis of Representation in Europe*, London: Frank Cass.

38. Failure to confront this question is a serious flaw in Yael Tamir's attempt to marry cultural nationalism with something like constitutional patriotism (Tamir, *Liberal Nationalism*, pp. 165–6).

39. Ingram, 'Constitutional Patriotism', p. 7. Surprisingly, this was written after unification.

40. For evidence of the topic's sensitivity, see the documents collected in (1993) *Forever in the Shadow of Hitler?*, translated by J. Knowlton and T. Cates, New Jersey: Humanities Press, especially Habermas's contributions.

41. David Miller makes the point in a private communication that while East German enthusiasm for unification could at a pinch be read as commitment to liberal democratic principles and squeezed into the model of *Verfassungspatriotismus*, the actions and motivations of West German politicians and people cannot be understood in terms of that model.

42. Habermas, 'Citizenship and National Identity', p. 500.

43. Wolf Linder (1994) *Swiss Democracy: Possible Solutions to Conflict in Multicultural Societies*, New York: St Martin's Press. Both quotations are from p. xviii.

44. Barber, 'Constitutional Faith', p. 32.

45. Note, however, that a strong commitment to the United States on the part of many immigrants may have more to do with what Harles calls 'the politics of the lifeboat' – relief and gratitude at finding sanctuary – than with understanding of or belief in the actual principles of the Constitution, as in the case of the Laotian immigrants Harles studied (John C. Harles (1993) *Politics in the Lifeboat: Immigrants and the American Democratic Order*, Boulder, CO: Westview Press, pp. 144–98).

46. Schaar, 'The Case for Patriotism', p. 293.

47. Michael W. McConnell (1996) 'Don't Neglect the Little Platoons', in Nussbaum and Cohen, *For Love of Country*, p. 82; Taylor, 'Cross-Purposes', pp. 166, 280.

48. Schaar, 'The Case for Patriotism', pp. 291–3.

49. Ingram, 'Constitutional Patriotism', p. 2; Habermas, 'Comment on Grimm', p. 306.

50. Habermas, 'D-Mark Nationalism', p. 198.

51. Cf. Brian Barry and Robert E. Goodin (eds) (1992) *Free Movement: Ethical Issues in the Transnational Migration of People and of Money*, New York: Harvester Wheatsheaf.

52. On Burke's articulation in *Reflections on the Revolution in France* of this fusion of the political with the familial, see Canovan, *Nationhood and Political Theory*, pp. 69–70.

53. Other kinds of polities have been less dependent on family inheritance among the

subject population. Monarchies could preserve dynastic continuity even though territories and subjects were lost and gained, while organizations such as the Catholic Church and the Communist Party survived wide-ranging recruitment of personnel. It is democratic polities that need lasting collective identity on the part of their citizens.

54. Ingram, 'Constitutional Patriotism', pp. 14–15.
55. Habermas, 'Citizenship and National Identity', p. 514; emphasis in original. Cf. Bernard Yack (1996) 'The Myth of the Civic Nation', *Critical Review* 10, 193–211, p. 200.
56. Viroli, *For Love of Country*, pp. 172–5.
57. *Ibid.*, pp. 17, 161. 'Patriotism without Nationalism' is the title of his epilogue.
58. *Ibid.*, pp. 175–6, 184.
59. *Ibid.*, pp. 178, 183–4. Cf. Dietz, 'Patriotism', pp. 187–9.
60. Nathanson, *Patriotism, Morality, and Peace*, pp. 185–6, 197.
61. Schaar, 'The Case for Patriotism', p. 285.
62. Viroli, *For Love of Country*, p. 2.
63. *Ibid.*, p. 7.
64. Schaar, 'The Case for Patriotism', p. 296.
65. Viroli, *For Love of Country*, pp. 184–5.
66. See, for example, Benedict Anderson (1983) *Imagined Communities: Reflections on the Origin and Spread of Nationalism*, London: Verso; Canovan, *Nationhood and Political Theory*; Liah Greenfeld (1992) *Nationalism: Five Roads to Modernity*, Cambridge, MA: Harvard University Press; Miller, *On Nationality*; Anthony D. Smith (1991) *National Identity*, Harmondsworth: Penguin.
67. As Habermas admits in 'Citizenship and National Identity', p. 493. It may be argued that without nationhood (which can incorporate a population into a single 'people'), liberal democracy would never have come about (Greenfeld, *Nationalism*, e.g. p. 10). Cf. Canovan, *Nationhood and Political Theory, passim.*
68. E.g. Miller, *On Nationality*, p. 127. Cf. Schnapper, *La communauté des citoyens, passim.*
69. Miller, *On Nationality*, p. 127.
70. Anderson, *Imagined Communities*. This does not imply that they are imaginary.
71. Richard Kearney (1997) *Postnationalist Ireland: Politics, Culture, Philosophy*, London: Routledge, p. 69.
72. Hannah Arendt (1958) *The Human Condition*, Chicago: University of Chicago Press, pp. 220–30.
73. As proposed, for example, by David Miller in *On Nationality*, pp. 179, 181.
74. Martha C. Nussbaum (1996) 'Reply', in Nussbaum and Cohen, *For Love of Country*, p. 133.
75. Alasdair MacIntyre has written provocatively that because of the particularistic demands of patriotism, 'good soldiers may not be liberals' (MacIntyre, 'Is Patriotism a Virtue?', p. 17).
76. Cf. Barry and Goodin, *Free Movement*; W. Rogers Brubaker (ed.) (1989) *Immigration and the Politics of Citizenship in Europe and North America*, London: University Press of America; Thomas Hammar (1990) *Democracy and the Nation State: Aliens, Denizens and Citizens in a World of International Migration*, Aldershot: Avebury.
77. The critique of new patriotism offered here does not imply an endorsement of

nationalism, which has problems of its own that cannot be addressed here. Cf. Canovan, *Nationhood and Political Theory*, chapters 9 and 10.

78. For an exhaustive survey of the traditional rhetorical techniques, see Quentin Skinner (1996) *Reason and Rhetoric in the Philosophy of Hobbes*, part I, Cambridge: Cambridge University Press.

79. Cf. Margaret Canovan (1987) 'The Eloquence of John Stuart Mill', *History of Political Thought* 8, 505–20.

Select Bibliography

Andrews, G. (ed.) (1991) *Citizenship*, London: Lawrence and Wishart.

Bauböck, R. (1994) *Transnational Citizenship: Membership and Rights in International Migration*, Aldershot: Edward Elgar.

Beiner, R. (ed.) (1995) *Theorizing Citizenship*, Albany: State University of New York Press.

Berlin, I. (1969) 'Two Concepts of Liberty', *Four Essays on Liberty*, Oxford: Oxford University Press.

Bock, G. and James, S. (eds) (1992) *Beyond Equality and Difference: Citizenship, Feminist Politics and Female Subjectivity*, London: Routledge.

Bock, G., Skinner, Q. and Viroli, M. (eds) (1990) *Machiavelli and Republicanism*, Cambridge: Cambridge University Press.

Bouwsma, W.J. (1968) *Venice and the Defence of Republican Liberty*, Berkeley: University of California Press.

Constant, B. (1820) 'Of the Liberty of the Ancients Compared with that of the Moderns', *Political Writings*, ed. Biancamaria Fontana, Cambridge: Cambridge University Press, 1988.

Dagger, R. (1997) *Civic Virtues: Rights, Citizenship and Republican Liberalism*, Oxford: Oxford University Press.

Dworkin, R. (1989) 'Liberal Community', *California Law Review* 77.

Ferguson, A.B. (1965) *The Articulate Citizen and the English Renaissance*, Durham, NC: Duke University Press.

Fink, Z. (1945) *Classical Republicanism: An Essay in the Recovery of a Pattern of Thought in Seventeenth Century England*, Evanston: University of Illinois Press.

Galston, W. (1991) *Liberal Purposes: Goods, Virtues and Duties in the Liberal State*, Cambridge, Cambridge University Press.

Gellner, E. (1994) *Conditions of Liberty: Civil Society and Its Rivals*, London: Hamish Hamilton.

Gutmann, A. (ed.) (1994) *Multiculturalism*, Princeton, NJ: Princeton University Press.

Habermas, J. (1996) 'Citizenship and National Identity', *Between Facts and Norms: Contributions to a Discourse Theory of Law and Democracy* (Appendix II), Cambridge, MA: MIT Press.

Heater, D. (1990) *Citizenship: The Civic Ideal in World History, Politics and Education*, London: Longman.

Hirschman, A.O. (1982) *Shifting Involvements: Private Interest and Public Action*, Oxford: Martin Robertson.

Ingram, A. (1996) 'Constitutional Patriotism', *Philosophy and Social Criticism* 22, 1–18.

Jordan, B. (1989) *The Common Good: Citizenship, Morality and Self-Interest*, Oxford: Blackwell.

Jordan, B. (1996) *A Theory of Poverty and Social Exclusion*, Cambridge: Polity.

King, D. and Waldron, J. (1988) 'Citizenship, Social Citizenship and the Defence of Welfare Provision', *British Journal of Political Science* 18.

Kymlicka W. (1995) *Multicultural Citizenship: A Liberal Theory of Minority Rights*, Oxford: Oxford University Press.

Kymlicka, W. and Norman, W. (1994) 'Return of the Citizen: A Survey of Recent Work on Citizenship Theory', *Ethics* 102 (4), 353–81.

Lister, R. (1997) *Citizenship: Feminist Perspectives*, Basingstoke: Macmillan.

Macedo, S. (1990) *Liberal Virtues*, New York: Oxford University Press.

MacIntyre, A. (1984) 'Is Patriotism a Virtue?', in M. Rosen and J. Wolff (eds) *Political Thought*, Oxford: Oxford University Press.

Manville, P.B. (1990) *The Origins of Citizenship in Ancient Athens*, Princeton, NJ: Princeton University Press.

Marshall, T.H. (1965) *Class, Citizenship and Social Development*, New York; Anchor.

Mason, A. (1999) 'Political Community, Liberal-Nationalism and the Ethics of Assimilation', *Ethics* 109 (2), 261–87.

Mead, L. (1986) *Beyond Entitlement: The Social Obligations of Citizenship*, New York: Free Press.

Miller, D. (1995) *On Nationality*, Oxford: Oxford University Press.

Miller, D. (1995) 'Citizenship and Pluralism', *Political Studies* 43 (3).

Modood, T. (1992) *Not Easy Being British: Colour, Culture and Citizenship*, Stoke-on-Trent: Trentham.

Mouffe, C. (1992) *Dimensions of Radical Democracy: Pluralism, Citizenship and Community*, London: Routledge.

Nussbaum, M.C. and Cohen, J. (1996) *For Love of Country: Debating the Limits of Patriotism*, Boston: Beacon Press.

Oldfield, A. (1990) *Citizenship and Community: Civic Republicanism and the Modern World*, London: Routledge.

Peltonen, M. (1995) *Classical Humanism and Republicanism in English Political Thought 1570–1640*, Cambridge: Cambridge University Press.

Phillips, A. (1995) *The Politics of Presence*, Oxford: Clarendon Press.

Pocock, J.G.A. (1975) *The Machiavellian Moment*, Princeton, NJ: Princeton University Press.

Pocock, J.G.A. (1992) 'The Ideal of Citizenship since Classical Times', *Queen's Quarterly* 9.

Pool, J. (1991) 'The Official Language Problem', *American Political Science Review* 85 (2), 495–514.

Rahe, P. (1992) *Republics, Ancient and Modern: Classical Republicanism and the American Revolution*, Chicago: University of Chicago Press.

Rawls, J. (1993) *Political Liberalism*, New York: Columbia University Press.

Riesenberg, (1992) *Citizenship in the Western Tradition*, Chapel Hill: University of North Carolina Press.

Sherwin-White, (1973) *The Roman Citizenship*, 2nd edition, Oxford: Clarendon Press.

Shklar, J. (1991) *American Citizenship: The Quest for Inclusion*, The Tanner Lectures on Human Values, vol. 10, Cambridge, MA: Havard University Press.

Sinopoli, R.C. (19995) 'Thick-Skinned Liberalism: Redefining Civility', *American Political Science Review* 89 (3), 612–20.

Skinner, Q. (1998) *Liberty before Liberalism*, Cambridge: Cambridge University Press.

Skinner, Q. and van Gelderen, M. (forthcoming) *Republicanism: A Shared European Heritage*, 2 vols, Cambridge: Cambridge University Press.

Steenbergen, B. van (ed.) (1994) *The Condition of Citizenship*, London: Sage.

Tamir, Y. (1993) *Liberal Nationalism*, Princeton, NJ: Princeton University Press.

Tully, J. (1995) *Strange Multiplicity: Constitutionalism in an Age of Diversity*, Cambridge: Cambridge University Press.

Turner, S. (1993) *Citizenship and Social Theory*, London: Sage.

Vincent, A. and Plant, R. (1984) *Philosophy, Politics and Citizenship: The Life and Thought of the British Idealists*, Oxford: Blackwell.

Viroli, M. (1995) *For Love of Country: An Essay on Patriotism and Nationalism*, Oxford: Clarendon Press.

Vogel, U. and Moran, M. (1991) *The Frontiers of Citizenship*, New York: St Martin's Press.

Walzer, M. (1982) *Obligations: Essays on Disobedience, War, Citizenship*, Cambridge, MA: Havard University Press.

Wootton, D. (1994) *Republicanism, Liberty and Commercial Society 1649–1776*, Stanford, CA: Stanford University Press.

Young, I.M. (1989) 'Polity and Group Difference: A Critique of the Ideal of Universal Citizenship', *Ethics* 99, 000–000.

Zurkert, M. (1994) *Natural Rights and the New Republicanism*, Princeton, NJ: Princeton University Press.

Index